James A. Ford

and the Growth of
Americanist Archaeology

James A. Ford

and the Growth of
Americanist Archaeology

Michael J. O'Brien and R. Lee Lyman

University of Missouri Press

Columbia and London

Copyright © 1998 by
The Curators of the University of Missouri
University of Missouri Press, Columbia, Missouri 65201
Printed and bound in the United States of America
All rights reserved
5   4   3   2   1   02   01   00   99   98

Library of Congress Cataloging-in-Publication Data

O'Brien, Michael J. (Michael John), 1950–
    James A. Ford and the growth of Americanist archaeology / Michael
J. O'Brien and R. Lee Lyman.
       p.   cm.
    Includes bibliographical references and index.
    ISBN 0-8262-1184-4 (alk. paper)
      1. Ford, James Alfred. 1911–1968.   2. Indianists—United States—
Biography.   3. Archaeologists—United States—Biography.
4. Indians of North America—Mississippi River Valley—Antiquities.
5. Social archaeology—Mississippi River Valley.   6. Mississippi
River Valley—Antiquities.   I. Lyman, R. Lee.   II. Title.

E76.45.F67O37   1998
973'.07202—dc21
    [b]   98-29781
                                                                  CIP

⊗ ™ This paper meets the requirements of the
American National Standard for Permanence of Paper
for Printed Library Materials, Z39.48, 1984.

Text design: Elizabeth K. Young
Jacket design: Stephanie Foley
Typesetter: BookComp, Inc.
Printer and binder: Thomson-Shore, Inc.
Typefaces: Minion and Minion Condensed

To Beverly and Barbara

Contents

Figures

Tables

Preface

For much of the twentieth century, culture history was the major paradigm of Americanist archaeology. It finally fell from favor—at least in name—in the face of increasing challenges that it was theoretically vacuous and concerned solely with the chronological ordering of artifacts. Minimally, culture history and its attendant methods were viewed as incapable of producing information relevant to understanding human behaviors that underlay the items in the archaeological record. Maximally, it was viewed as having little or nothing to say about the development of culture. This assessment was correct, though it is clear that most culture historians decidedly had the explication of cultural development as their ultimate goal. They ultimately failed on methodological grounds, not for want of purpose.

Through their development of chronological methods, culture historians provided archaeology with a sound footing in science, but because of their interest in artifacts as cultural phenomena, they were faced with a paradox: how could the units formulated to measure time be used simultaneously to monitor culture change? Nowhere is the constant tug between the two interests—time versus culture change—more apparent than in the work of James A. Ford, whose methodological achievements were hailed in most quarters but whose attempts to understand culture change were assailed in many. Ford's work demonstrates that the root of the paradox lay in the fundamental differences between two competing ontological perspectives—essentialism and materialism. No amount of tinkering could enjoin the differences; ultimately, this led to culture history's fall from grace and to its replacement by cultural processualism.

Our purpose in writing this book is to use Ford's work as a vehicle to examine the rise, development, and fall of culture history in Americanist archaeology, with specific emphasis on the lower Mississippi River valley. It was there that Ford concentrated his professional efforts for the better part of two decades, and, not coincidentally, it was there that many of the important methodological and substantive advances made under the banner of culture history were developed.

One would be hard-pressed to find another region of the United States, unless it is the Southwest, that has attracted such long-standing interest from antiquarians and archaeologists. This is not surprising, given the high visibility of the Mississippi Valley's archaeological record, especially its mounds and elaborately decorated pottery. And, unless again it is the Southwest, no area of the United States has been witness to as much development and use of culture-historical methods as has the Mississippi Valley. More specifically, no area, *including* the Southwest, has seen a fuller discussion of the issues and problems connected with actually *doing* culture history. Many of the issues that were central to Americanist archaeology after 1930 were brought to the table as a direct result of fieldwork conducted in the valley. And no one contributed more than Ford, who from the early 1930s through the early 1950s was personally responsible for or oversaw much of the fieldwork conducted in the lower valley, especially in Louisiana.

The beginning of Ford's archaeological career can be traced to his high school days in Mississippi, when he and classmate Moreau B. Chambers conducted a site survey around Jackson, Mississippi, for the Mississippi Department of Archives and History in 1927. They eventually met up with Henry B. Collins, assistant curator in the Bureau of American Ethnology, who had been invited by the MDAH to undertake archaeological work in the Choctaw region of western Mississippi. Collins later introduced Ford to Alaskan archaeology—a specialty that held his interest for several years—but it was the greater Mississippi River valley, especially Louisiana, that held a special, lifelong lure for Ford. He carried out or helped carry out survey-and-excavation projects in Colombia and Peru in the 1940s and 1950s and in Mexico in the 1960s, but his forays into Latin America were but brief interruptions in a long career. It was in the lower Mississippi River valley that Ford first worked out and later refined his methods for imposing chronological control over the archaeological record, and it was there that he laid the foundation for assigning ceramic sherds to categories useful in archaeological analysis. His fieldwork in Louisiana and western Mississippi, in conjunction with his formal exposure to anthropology, first at Louisiana State University and then at the University of Michigan and Columbia University, nurtured Ford's ideas on culture and the proper role of archaeology in understanding cultural development.

Curiously, in the three decades following Ford's death, there has been no biography written about him, and what one is able to learn about his personality, nonarchaeological interests, and the like comes from obituaries, short biographical statements, and interviews with those who worked with him. This book is not by nature a strict biography; rather, it uses Ford's published work as a vehicle to examine the underpinnings of the culture-history approach that characterized Americanist archaeology from about 1910 to around 1960. This fifty-year span is not absolute in any real sense, but merely serves to isolate a period of time during which a particular suite of methods and perspectives came to dominate the discipline.

Although we are interested primarily in Ford's role in developing the culture-history paradigm, it would be impossible to write anything approaching an authoritative account without discussing the individuals with whom Ford interacted. Culture history was not a monolithic construct to which all archaeologists faithfully adhered; there was more than one way of writing the history of culture. Unquestionably, Ford was at the center of some of the most important, and interesting, debates that arose in Americanist archaeology at midcentury. Because he was as interested, or at some points in his life *more* interested, in the fact that humans had culture as he was in artifacts, Ford also was drawn into conflicts with anthropologists. He thus becomes an excellent vehicle for examining an uneasiness that archaeologists were beginning to feel during the 1940s—one brought on by a growing suspicion that archaeology had somehow forgotten that humans were first and foremost cultural animals. Where, their anthropologist colleagues began asking, was culture amid all the discussion of time and space?

Ford, like most of his contemporaries in archaeology, received his graduate degrees in anthropology; few if any of them had extensive training in what Leslie White, one of Ford's instructors at Michigan, termed "culturology"—training that would have allowed them to write persuasively on the subject of culture. They were ill-prepared for the effort, and several of them paid the price at the hands of anthropologists. Perhaps none fared as badly as Ford. His failure to respond adequately to the charges by several cultural anthropologists that archaeologists really didn't understand culture was symptomatic of where Americanist archaeology was in the early 1960s, on the eve of the processualist revolution. Ford died in 1968 and never participated in this new archaeology—a movement spearheaded by archaeologists a generation removed from him. Although the processualists decried many of the tenets of culture history, much of what was proposed in their place really was not all that new. Ford had been thinking along similar lines for decades, as had many of his colleagues.

It is difficult to discuss Ford and not get caught up in aspects of the archaeological record that he and his contemporaries were researching. As archaeologists, we are as fascinated with the archaeological record as the next person, especially when it is the record of the lower Mississippi Valley. Here, however, what was found takes a back seat to the actual work carried out during examination of the record. Since we assume many of our readers will have a general interest in the history of archaeological research in the region, we provide a fairly comprehensive list of references to various pieces of work undertaken during the heyday of culture history—work undertaken both in and outside the Mississippi Valley—though it is by no means a complete list.

In short, our focus is decidedly on Ford and the major role he played in creating, carrying out, and ultimately contributing to the decline of the culture-history paradigm, but we do not neglect the opportunity to expand the discussion and thus place Ford's work in a broader perspective. What emerges is a fascinating glimpse into how archaeologists began using a variety of methods and units to impose spatial and temporal control on an exceedingly diverse and complex archaeological record. Perhaps even more interesting is how one person, who knew much of the record better than anyone else, wrestled with how best to impose that order while simultaneously trying to keep the people behind the artifacts squarely in his sights. In hindsight, no one at the time could have done what Ford himself tried so long to accomplish. But his failure ultimately says more about the internal inconsistencies of the culture-history paradigm than it does about the particular abilities of James Ford.

Acknowledgments

Many people contributed to any success this book might enjoy. In particular, we thank Dan Glover, who produced all the figures, tracked down innumerable references, and proofread various drafts of the manuscript. Various individuals knowledgeable about Jim Ford provided references, letters, and advice on what to include and not to include. We thank Ed Lyon for first identifying several key pieces of correspondence that later were included; Jon Gibson, for supplying much-needed information and for reading the manuscript in its entirety; the late James Griffin for his remembrances of key areas in his long relationship with Ford; Gordon Willey for his numerous helpful suggestions and for commenting on the final manuscript; Bob Dunnell for several conversations about Ford's work; Becky Saunders for allowing us unlimited access to the Museum of Natural Science archives at Louisiana State University; Keith Vaca and Sam Brooks for searching their files at the Mississippi Department of Archives and History for information on Moreau Chambers; Bob Neuman and Dick Forbis for their recollections; Ann Ramenofsky for providing us with a copy of a videotaped interview with George Quimby and Bill Haag; Steve Williams for review comments; and Ian Brown and Judy Knight for supplying unpublished manuscripts by Ford.

Carl Kuttruff and Bill Haag provided the real keys to our ability to tell the story of Ford and his involvement with southeastern archaeology. When we mentioned to Kuttruff that we were working on a project on Ford, he said that we should talk with Haag to see what he had in the way of correspondence that might not be in state or national archives. What Haag, a longtime friend of Ford's, actually had were letters, photographs, maps, and a host of other material that Ethel Ford turned over to him shortly after her husband's death in 1968. In short, he had a gold mine of information—much of it professionally related but much of it personal—and one that he generously shared with us. Kuttruff subsequently did considerably more digging in various archives and came up with Ford's manuscript on his early work at the Marksville site—a critical manuscript that many of us doubted ever existed.

As in the past, the staff of the University of Missouri Press was extremely encouraging throughout the writing and production phases, which made the entire process a most pleasant experience. We thank Beverly Jarrett for her interest in the project from the beginning and Clair Willcox, Jane Lago, Karen Caplinger, Dwight Browne, and Linda Frech for their advice on various aspects of production. We also thank John Brenner, our editor at the University of Missouri Press and the person responsible not only for keeping our style consistent but also for correcting several mistakes. Finally, we thank E. J. O'Brien, who not only read the manuscript in its entirety, checked all references, compared all the material in figures against the text, and made numerous suggestions for changes, but also rewrote several sections so that they made sense to a nonspecialist. This is the seventh book he has edited for the senior author and the third one he has done for the two of us jointly. Hence, he now must forfeit his amateur standing as an archaeological editor.

James A. Ford

and the Growth of
Americanist Archaeology

1

Culture History in Americanist Archaeology

The archaeologist is not a student of "man." The physical anthropologist studies the human animal; the archaeologist studies the culture of this species of animal. It is frequently stated as a profound truth that culture does not exist without man, so the two must be considered together. This is faulty reductionism. The numerous attempts to reduce culture to strictly human terms have been fruitless. Culture can no more be explained in terms of biological man than the form of man can be accounted for by the physical environment.

The ethnologist is also a student of culture rather than of "man," and the two approaches are complementary. Ethnology, in its concern with living cultures, concentrates on aspects of form and function. The archaeologist has to deal with the stripped bones of old cultures, but he has the unique responsibility and privilege of viewing the phenomenon as it evolved through time. Without chronology the archaeologist is helpless; with chronology he can proceed to re-create as much of the form and function of the ancient cultural stream as evidence permits. (James A. Ford 1962:5)

When James A. Ford wrote the preceding paragraphs as part of a student training manual, he did not know that he had just provided succeeding generations of scholars with his most concise and insightful statement not only on the appropriate subject matter of archaeology—culture—but also on the need to control time in order to study culture. For more than three decades, Ford was one of the most visible archaeologists working in the Americas—a visibility due in part to his entrance into the field of Americanist archaeology at a critical time, in part by his publication record, and in part by his personality. Ford, a young, energetic worker from the South, came into his own in the mid-1930s, at a time when southeastern archaeology was wide open (Figure 1.1). His unswerving desire to bring chronological order to the archaeological record of the Southeast, coupled with his aggressiveness and commanding presence, ensured that he would leave an indelible mark. When he died in 1968, he was hailed by his friend and colleague Clifford Evans (1968:1161) as "an innovator, a pioneer, a creator of new techniques and methodologies, a synthesizer, [and] a builder of solid foundations of knowledge upon which numerous other scholars have built their research for years and will continue to build for many decades to come." Gordon Willey (1988:51), who had known Ford since the mid-1930s, labeled him "one of America's most remarkable archaeologists, one of the very few, in my opinion, to whom that controversial term 'genius' might be applied." With his broad knowledge of archaeology in the Western Hemisphere and his strong personality, Ford tended to command the respect of most of his colleagues. They might not always have agreed with him, or even have liked him at times, but they respected him. As Evans (1968:1161) put it, Ford was impatient with both ignorance and failure to change one's opinion in the face of contrary evidence, but "to anyone willing to work hard, apply himself by independent work, and show evidence of thinking, Ford was outstandingly cooperative and generous of his time and advice."

Given Ford's standing in the field and the controversial nature of his work and his personality, it is unfortunate that no comprehensive biography has chronicled his life and the importance of his work in the development of Americanist archaeology. Several short biographical accounts (e.g., Brown 1978; Willey 1988) and obituaries (Evans 1968; Haag 1968; Webb 1968b; Willey 1969) highlight some of his many achievements. Yet the lack of a critical examination of Ford's work, particularly of his methods, has led to a false impression of his contributions to archaeology. Ford's career coincided with the height of the culture-historical period, when the study of space, form, and especially time was at the center of what archaeologists did—literally, the writing of culture histories.

Two methods—percentage stratigraphy and seriation—were of particular importance in culture history, and both figured prominently in Ford's work. Despite received wisdom, neither was invented by Ford, nor did he make major methodological improvements to them. Seriation (measuring time through the use of form) and percentage stratigraphy (measuring time through the use of fluctuating percentages of artifact types in a column of sediment) had been around for decades before Ford used them, but it was through his work that these methods, especially seriation, received broad notice in both the Southeast and Latin America. As a result, seriation has become inextricably linked with Ford's name, though it is more the visible technique of presenting seriation and percentage-stratigraphy data—a technique derived directly from his view of time—rather than the method itself that should be linked to him. When one examines all of Ford's work instead of only a selection, it almost seems as if Ford independently invented seriation and

Figure 1.1. Photograph of James A. Ford in Louisiana, ca. 1933 (photograph courtesy W. G. Haag).

percentage stratigraphy because he rarely cited any literature that would indicate he was aware of previous efforts. We do not, however, think this was the case. It also is clear, especially in Ford's earlier publications, that he was grappling with things he only partially understood. The false starts, the experimentation, and the preliminary statements he made regarding the archaeological record of the lower Mississippi Valley are hallmarks of someone attempting to wend his way through a maze of difficult problems, not signs of someone who is applying a set of methods with which he is intimately familiar.

What, then, *was* Jim Ford's major contribution to American archaeology? In our opinion it was his overwhelming commitment to the study of time in a region that in the 1930s was a frontier in terms of what was known about the archaeological record. From 1938 through the first half of the 1950s, no one working in the lower Mississippi Valley came close to matching Ford's commitment to the region or his knowledge of its prehistory. For example, in 1938 Ford assumed the directorship of the Works Progress Administration program in Louisiana, which generated an enormous amount of information about the prehistory of the state. Ford not only dictated which sites would be excavated but also how the information would be reported. Although he was ably assisted in this massive effort, it fell to Ford to organize the fieldwork, see that the excavations and analyses stayed on schedule, and ensure that the reports were prepared in a timely fashion. That most of the reports carry Ford's name is no guarantee he had anything more than a casual hand in the analysis and writing, since most of the reports are coauthored. After perusing them, however, one cannot mistake the Fordian stamp. In reading historical accounts of the WPA project in Louisiana (e.g., Lyon 1996; Quimby 1979; Willey 1969, 1988), one begins to appreciate not only Ford's organizational abilities but also how much of the prehistory of the lower Mississippi Valley was worked out under his direction.

When the WPA program drew to a close, Ford turned his attention to several major sites in Louisiana and Mississippi, taking time out for several stints of fieldwork in South America, one in connection with his doctoral research. He also found time to participate in a large-scale survey of a portion of the northern half of the lower Mississippi Valley, which led to what arguably is one of the most important monographs ever produced in American archaeology. The explicit airing of the differences of opinion among Ford and coauthors Philip Phillips and James B. Griffin in *Archaeological Survey in the Lower Mississippi Alluvial Valley, 1940–1947* makes it clear that there was in the 1940s and 1950s no single, universally accepted method for approaching the archaeological record, even when there was agreement that the goal of archaeology was the writing of culture history.

At a deeper level, the differences of opinion also make it clear that there was no single epistemological basis for viewing the passage of time. The overwhelming majority of archaeologists in Ford's generation viewed time as a series of individual, bounded segments that took on the characteristics of empirical (real) units. An important consideration under this view was where to draw boundaries between temporal units so that they coincided with breaks between cultural units. Refinement was seen as bringing cultural-unit boundaries and temporal-unit boundaries closer together. Ford, however, was the chief proponent of a minority view among culture historians—that time was a continuum and as such could be sliced into any number of units that the analyst saw fit. Hence, boundaries between temporal units were strictly arbitrary. Refinement to Ford meant moving beyond chronology to the exploration of culture. The differences between the two views of time and the role they played in shaping culture history forms the basis of much of our discussion throughout this book.

Examining Ford's work in the Mississippi Valley provides an interesting glimpse into his thought processes. Ford's contributions to culture history and influence over a generation of scholars who adhered to it were central to the paradigm, replete though it was with internal inconsistencies. Ford became ensnared in some of culture history's inconsistencies, though in this respect he was no different from any of his contemporaries.

Several inconsistencies in the culture-history paradigm became noticeable in the 1950s, and perhaps because of his standing in the field, Ford and his work were singled out for criticism from other archaeologists, though none of them recognized the more fundamental problems facing culture history. With two major exceptions, most of the polemic was directed toward the inadequacy of one method or another for solving a particular problem. The exceptions, first the celebrated series of debates between Ford and Albert Spaulding in the early 1950s (e.g., Ford 1954a, 1954b; Spaulding 1953a, 1953b, 1954b) on the meaning of types, and the second a series of exchanges with Morris Opler that resulted from Ford's views on culture, were directed at much deeper issues, but they too overlooked the more basic flaws in the culture-history approach.

By the 1950s, numerous archaeologists were beginning to question the relevancy of culture history and several of its tenets, but there is little evidence they realized that what they wanted culture history to become—an integrated set of approaches aimed at understanding culture change—was an impossibility. Behind those approaches was supposed to be a coherent and organized conception of what culture was, and it was taken for granted that culture could be extracted from the archaeological record, if appropriate methods were used. That this was an impossible task would have surprised most culture historians, including Ford, who probably would have pinned the blame simply on the use of inappropriate methods. The problem did not revolve around methods, though there was a methodological issue involved—the same analytical units constructed to measure the passage of time were then used to measure culture change. Ford himself, despite his insistence that archaeological types were arbitrary units used to monitor the passage of time, succumbed to the ease with which one can slip from time-related issues to those of a cultural nature.

Culture history came under intensive fire in the early 1960s from a group of archaeologists who viewed the paradigm as anachronistic and certainly not the direction in which they thought their field should head. However, it would be nothing short of revisionist history to claim that archaeologists abandoned culture history because they realized the inherent weaknesses in it. The plain truth of the matter is that no one at the time understood the fundamental problems with culture history and with the way Americanist archaeology in general, regardless of the label that was placed on it, had come to view the archaeological record. Culture history fell from favor primarily because archaeologists became dissatisfied with the continual emphasis on time and space at the expense of culture. At first, the number of archaeologists expressing disfavor was small, but by the mid-1940s there was growing concern that culture was being short-changed and that the only way to remedy the situation was to somehow make archaeology more anthropological. Thus archaeologists might not have liked what Walter Taylor (1948) had to say in his *A Study of Archeology*, but their dissatisfaction had much more to do with how he said it than with what he said. Lewis Binford came along in the early 1960s and offered a "new" archaeology—one that on the surface appeared to be a chance to move beyond the simple chronological ordering of cultures.

Ford may or may not have paid much attention to the clamor of the 1950s and 1960s; in his mind, he had been studying culture since his entrance into the field. His reaction to Taylor's (1948) monograph (Ford 1952a:317–18) shows this clearly. Regardless, by the time the new archaeology was beginning to take hold, Ford had become preoccupied with the notion that much of the prehistoric record of the Americas could be explained in terms of diffusion and migration. This preoccupation led to the last project he ever worked on, published with the appropriately descriptive title "A Comparison of Formative Cultures in the Americas: Diffusion or the Psychic Unity of Man" (Ford 1969). In our opinion this monograph, which was published the year following Ford's untimely death at the age of fifty-seven, was the worst of his career and an unfitting testament to the breadth and depth of his understanding of archaeology and the archaeological record. It also was an unfitting end to the great era known as the culture-historical period. To those "new" archaeologists who had abandoned time and space in their pursuit of cultural processes, the monograph must have symbolized all that was bad about the paradigm they were trying to replace—boring trait lists, an emphasis on radiocarbon dating, and a heavy dose of speculation. Surely this was not the way to approach the study of culture. But lost amid Ford's flights of fancy and his outright mishandling of radiocarbon-dated pottery sequences—all in an effort to derive the answer he saw as patently obvious—was the man's desire to gain *exactly* the same thing archaeologists of the newer generation wanted to gain: an understanding of culture.

BASIC ELEMENTS OF CULTURE HISTORY

We have long been interested in the history of Americanist archaeology, and in the waxing and waning of its various paradigms—those views one has about how the world operates, or as Thomas Kuhn (1977) put it, the intellectual grounds upon which one meets experience. Labeling paradigms and trying to pinpoint when they appeared and disappeared often is difficult to do, though the task is simplified somewhat in archaeology because there has been no shortage of labels that have been assigned to various sets of perspectives and methods. For example, archaeologists whose work we would label as "culture history" used the term themselves (e.g., Caldwell 1959; Kidder 1932; Willey and Phillips 1958) to refer to what they did—literally, attempting to document and interpret the historical development of cultures in various regions of North America. Likewise, there appears to be enough consensus in the literature to talk about another paradigm, *cultural reconstructionism,* that was always in the background of culture history but which made an ascendancy as a separate entity in the late 1930s and early 1940s as archaeologists began trying to reconstruct primitive cultures as opposed to simply chronicling them.

Jim Ford played a prominent role in both culture history and cultural reconstructionism, and in fact it would be difficult to find another archaeologist whose work better symbolized both paradigms. Ford was an innovator in terms of cultural-historical method, and he was a true believer when it came to using the archaeological record to track the development of prehistoric cultures. His work points out that there were no clear, sharp edges between culture history and cultural reconstructionism. Although understanding time and space was prefatory to reconstructing culture, there generally was a working back and forth between history and reconstruction, with the result that the historical framework never moved too far ahead of the cultural framework. Therefore, when we contrast the two paradigms, it is primarily to illustrate how culture historians went beyond the study of time and began to bring into their purview issues that previously had resided in the domain of anthropologists. The incorporation of these issues was problematic for culture historians–turned–reconstructionists and created a situation in the early 1960s where the discipline quickly turned its back on culture history and struck out in what it thought was a new direction, the study of culture process.

That we label culture history a "paradigm" is slightly misleading because it makes it sound as if there were a unified perspective among archaeologists as to how best to study culture and a concise set of methods used to explore both its history and development. In fact, lack of agreement led to some of the more interesting, and at times downright nasty, confrontations among Americanist archaeologists. Not surprisingly, Ford was right in the middle of several of them.

All of this said, we would quickly add that "culture history" is still not a bad term to use with respect to what was going on in Americanist archaeology between roughly 1910 and 1960. We suspect that one reason for the broad use of the term in the literature lies in its convenience as a means of separating what came before 1960 from what came after that date. Because of the growing dissatisfaction with culture history (and with reconstructionism), the term took on a pejorative meaning in the sixties as a growing cadre of "new" archaeologists attempted to distance themselves from the kind of archaeology that had occupied their predecessors. Hence we see continued use of the term "culture history" well into the 1960s and 1970s (e.g., Binford 1965, 1968a; Deetz 1970; Dunnell 1978; Flannery 1967) as a foil against which to contrast the new, or processual, archaeology, which had as its goal identifying the mechanisms involved in cultural evolution rather than simply documenting that some kind of change had taken place.

Culture-Historical Methods

In examining the roots of the methods commonly associated with culture history, the most appropriate place to start is the American Southwest, which by the second decade of the twentieth century had begun to attract the attention of some of the more important archaeologists and ethnologists of the day. Personnel connected with the American Museum of Natural History in New York and with Phillips Academy in Andover, Massachusetts, made the methodological advances that set the course for the growth of culture history (Lyman et al. 1997a, 1997b; Willey and Sabloff 1993). In the following pages we focus on three methods—stratigraphy, seriation, and typology—that enjoyed fairly wide usage throughout the culture-historical period, and which Ford introduced into the lower Mississippi Valley. The methods were first worked out and later refined in the Southwest. In subsequent chapters we expand the discussion to the role the methods played in the Midwest and Southeast as well as the introduction of new methods incorporated into the archaeology of the lower Mississippi Valley.

Stratigraphy

Most accounts of the birth and development of culture history single out the so-called stratigraphic revolution (Willey 1968:40) in the Southwest between 1910 and 1920 as a high-water mark (e.g., Browman and Givens 1996; Schuyler 1971; Willey and Sabloff 1993). Trying to figure out who was the first archaeologist to excavate stratigraphically is akin to figuring out when and where the first baseball game was played, though credit usually is given to Manuel Gamio (1913), who in 1911 took his mentor Franz Boas's advice and excavated a site in the Valley of Mexico in arbitrary levels. However, the lion's share of attention is paid to southwestern archaeologists Nels C. Nelson (1916) of the American Museum and A. V. Kidder (1916, 1917) of Phillips Academy (Figure 1.2), both of whom are portrayed in the literature as having led Americanist archaeology out of the Dark Ages and into a period where chronological control could be established by making simple observations of which objects lay above or below others in a stratigraphic column (e.g., Willey 1968:40).

It is clear from the literature that neither Kidder nor Nelson considered what they were doing revolutionary. Neither of them ever claimed credit (Willey and Sabloff 1974:94)—they did not think they were doing anything particularly new or innovative. By the time they began working in New Mexico—Nelson in 1912 and Kidder in 1915—archaeologists across the United States were routinely recording where artifacts happened to lie in a vertical column, and had been doing so for several decades. But chronological issues were seldom addressed because of the perception that no significant cultural change had occurred, given the then-perceived short chronology of human occupation of the Americas (Meltzer 1985). That Nelson and Kidder excavated deep cuts at San Cristóbal (Nelson) and Pecos Pueblo (Kidder), both located near Santa Fe, New Mexico, and kept sherds separate by excavation level was old news by the middle of the second decade of the twentieth century (Lyman and O'Brien 1998).

Nelson and Kidder were quite direct in explaining why they bothered to excavate stratigraphically in the first place: they saw it as a way to solve very *particular*

Figure 1.2. Photograph of A. V. Kidder (center) with Alfred M. Tozzer (left) and Carl E. Guthe, Kidder's assistant, at Pecos Pueblo, New Mexico, 1916 (from Woodbury 1973 [photo courtesy Columbia University Press]).

and very *local* chronological problems. Nelson (1916:162) stated explicitly that when he went back to San Cristóbal in 1914, he sought to test a suspected *local* sequence of four pottery types. He knew or suspected the relative chronological positions of pottery types, but only by excavating at San Cristóbal was he able to establish their relative chronological positions (Nelson 1916:163–66); all previous superpositional indications of chronology were "incomplete and fragmentary, each showing *merely* the time relations of two successive pottery types at some place or other in the total series of four or five types" (Nelson 1916:163; emphasis added). Nelson's use of the word "merely" demonstrates that as early as 1916 archaeologists viewed the temporal implications of superposed pottery types as nothing out of the ordinary.

Kidder also had a particular and local problem in mind when he turned his attention to Pecos Pueblo. The historically documented occupation of Pecos was impressive: "So long an occupation does not seem to have occurred at any other place in New Mexico available for excavation and it was hoped that remains would there be found so stratified as to make clear the development of the various Pueblo arts and to enable students to place in their proper chronological order numerous New Mexican ruins" (Kidder 1916:120). Establishing this chronology was the "chief reason for the choice of Pecos" (Kidder 1916:120). Hence it is difficult to make the case that Kidder was seeking to "revolutionize" his profession; rather, he was only trying to solve a regional chronological problem.

What *was* revolutionary, and what scholars of the discipline up to this point have missed, is that Nelson, Kidder, and their colleagues actually *counted* various kinds of artifacts that lay in various levels of excavated cuts and then used those counts—in some cases raw frequencies and in others relative frequencies—to make chronological observations. This technique, referred to variously as *percentage stratigraphy* (Willey 1939:142) and *ceramic stratigraphy* (Nelson 1919a:133), was worked out late in 1914 or early in 1915 by Leslie Spier of the American Museum during his analysis of materials from near Trenton, New Jersey (Spier 1916, 1918b; see Lyman and O'Brien 1998). The method was immediately applied to pottery from a stratigraphic cut made by Nelson at San Cristóbal. The importance of Nelson's analysis resided in his demonstration that pottery types changed in absolute frequency through time in a pattern that he characterized as "very nearly normal frequency curves [that reflected the fact that] a style of pottery . . . came slowly into vogue, attained a maximum and began a gradual decline" (Nelson 1916:167). Clark Wissler, who was Spier's and Nelson's supervisor at the American Museum, remarked that it was likely Nelson's frequency distributions of types "represent in the main the rise and decline of a culture trait" (Wissler 1916a:194), or *stylistic pulsations* (Wissler 1916a:196)—what A. L. Kroeber (1909:5) had earlier characterized as "nothing more than a passing change of fashion." We elsewhere have referred to these statements as components of the "popularity principle" (Lyman et al. 1997a:43).

Seriation

As important as stratigraphic excavation was in the development of culture-historical methods, especially when coupled with percentage stratigraphy, its importance was superseded by seriation. Seriation is the use of form, specifically *changes* in the presence or absence of artifact forms or of their frequencies, to measure time. In the early stages of the culture-historical period, stratigraphic excavation was more of a *confirmational* rather than a *creational* method relative to chronological construction (Lyman and O'Brien 1998), meaning that it was used to check or test chronological orderings derived using other methods, including seriation. By the 1930s, stratigraphic excavation assumed primacy as a *creational* method. It was the major chronological tool used by Ford throughout his career, though for some reason he is remembered more for seriation (e.g., Quimby 1979; Teltser 1995b; Trigger 1989:202–4; Willey and Sabloff 1993:114–15).

We credit A. L. Kroeber with introducing frequency seriation into Americanist archaeology. Kroeber (and later Spier) used the method to bring chronological order to Puebloan sites. Before describing Kroeber's contribution, it is critical to note two things. First, failing to distinguish among different techniques of seriation—as well as failing to distinguish seriation of whatever stripe from percentage stratigraphy—has resulted in considerable confusion in the literature dealing with the history of Americanist archaeology (e.g., Browman and Givens 1996; Willey and Sabloff 1993). And it certainly has contributed to a misunderstanding of Ford and his work. What most chroniclers of Ford mean by seriation is in reality percentage stratigraphy. Completely overlooked is Ford's use of what John Rowe (1961) called similiary seriation and what we call phyletic seriation.

Rowe (1961:326) distinguished between

> evolutionary seriation and similiary seriation, the latter term meaning "seriation by resemblance." Evolutionary seriation is done by assuming a universal rule of cultural or stylistic development, such as, for example, that development is always from simple to complex, or that artistic style always develops from realism to conventionalization. . . . Similiary seriation is quite a different matter. It is based on the assumption that, within a given cultural tradition, change in culture in general and change in style in particular are both usually gradual processes. . . . No assumptions are made about the nature or direction of the changes taking place.

Similiary seriation can be implemented in one of three ways: "ordering by type frequency and ordering by continuity of features and variation of themes" (Rowe 1961:327). Seriating by type frequency is done by ordering the relative frequencies of various types so that each makes an entrance, reaches a peak, and then dies out. Practically speaking, a frequency seriation charts the life histories of types at a locale. Seriating by continuity of features involves the assumption that "the occurrence of features of style in time is not random, but that most features have a continuous span of existence" (Rowe 1961:328). It later was termed "occurrence seriation" (Dunnell 1970; Rouse 1967). Seriating by variation in themes involves the selection of some "complex feature or theme which is found in several variations [and making] an arrangement of the variations in order of similarity [such as] variations in the proportions of bottle spouts" (Rowe 1961:328). Here, resemblance or similarity literally means likeness of form. Although he did not use the term, Rowe implied that materials seriated on the basis of variation of themes produces a phyletic ordering—one form is ancestral to another—hence our term "phyletic seriation."

Irving Rouse (1967:188) used the term "development seriation" rather than "evolutionary seriation" to underscore that not all temporal orderings followed the same rule of simple to complex or realism to conventionalism, yet "within any [cultural] tradition, the constituent modes, types, or phases have an inherent order." Development(al) seriation is geared toward producing an order "which provides the most gradual transition from one to another" mode, type, or phase (Rouse 1967:191). Although he was not explicit, Rouse implied that the resulting arrangement is basically phyletic, though the order is not necessarily progressive in the sense of Rowe's evolutionary seriation.

In the following discussion, we use "frequency seriation" in the sense of Rowe and Rouse, and we use "phyletic seriation" to denote Rouse's developmental seriation and a nonrule-laden version of Rowe's similiary seriation by variation in themes (see also Lyman et al. 1998). To help clarify our distinction among the various kinds of seriation, as well as to identify who used which kind, we offer Figure 1.3. Reference to this figure should assist in understanding the next several pages and our discussion in later chapters of Ford's contributions. We emphasize that seriation, at least as we conceive of it, does not involve any use of stratigraphic evidence to help sort and order collections. Rather, it simply uses formal attributes of artifacts, whether those attributes are size, shape, or decoration.

The second point concerns Kroeber's vision of culture change. As Rowe (1962:399) indicated, between 1897 and 1902 German prehistorian Max Uhle spent his time "sorting out chronological differences in the archaeology of the Peruvian coast, and he had learned to see cultural change in his archaeological data at a time when no one else working in New World archaeology was able to do so." Uhle's (1907) inferences concerning culture change at the Emeryville Shellmound on San Francisco Bay were summarily discounted by Kroeber (1909:15–16), who admitted that although some change was apparent, it "was a change of degree only, and one in no way to be compared even for a moment with a transition as fundamental as that from palaeolithic to neolithic." Thus Rowe (1962:400) noted that "Kroeber at this time visualized cultural change in terms of major shifts in technology and subsistence; any changes of less moment were insignificant. He could not comprehend Uhle's interest in all changes, however minute."

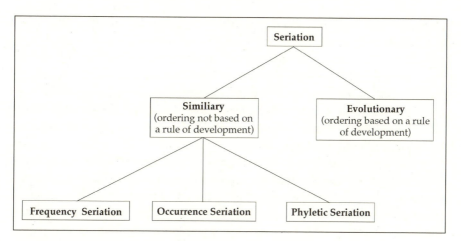

Figure 1.3. A taxonomy of seriation techniques.

In Kroeber's view, at least the one he held until roughly 1915, culture change was possible and even likely, but only *epochal* change was significant to anthropological concerns. Thus, Kroeber, like his mentor Boas (e.g., 1896), never truly discarded outright all notions of cultural evolution that had originated with Edward B. Tylor, Lewis Henry Morgan, and others. Rather, Kroeber sought to determine the *history* of cultural development (hence his later debates with Leslie White [e.g., Kroeber 1946; White 1945]; see Lyman and O'Brien 1997). For Kroeber (e.g., 1916c, 1917), culture was like a stream—it had a flow—and it was heritable, certainly not in any genetic sense but rather in the sense that it was learned.

Kroeber, as another of his students, Julian Steward (1962:203), wrote, "added time depth to the essentially synchronic ethnology of Boas" and believed that cultural evolution involved a braided stream created by historical processes such as diffusion, trade, migration, and the like. Kroeber "constantly saw changes in styles as flows and continua, pulses, culminations and diminutions, convergences and divergences, divisions, blends and cross-currents by which cultures develop and mutually influence one another" (Steward 1962:206), but he did not attempt to determine causes of culture change, much to Steward's (1962:206) chagrin (see also Manners 1973:889). Nelson (1932:122) wrote, "Final explanations of [culture change], as well as of the driving force and the ultimate goal of culture, may be left to the philosophers." Or, as we will see, to Jim Ford.

Kroeber (1916b), in his remarkable paper "Zuñi Potsherds," presented a lengthy account of how he came up with the idea of frequency seriation. His discussion makes it clear that earlier explorations of phyletic seriation (e.g., Evans 1850, 1875; Petrie 1899) played no role in the development of the method in Americanist archaeology, as is often claimed or implied (Browman and Givens 1996; Willey and Sabloff 1993).

While walking across the countryside around Zuñi Pueblo, New Mexico, in 1915, Kroeber (1916a, 1916b) began collecting sherds from the surfaces of more than a dozen prehistoric sites. Some collections tended to be dominated by "red, black, and patterned potsherds," whereas others were dominated by white sherds (Kroeber 1916b:8). He concluded that there "could be no doubt that here, within a half hour's radius of the largest inhabited pueblo [Zuñi], were prehistoric remains of two types and two periods, as distinct as oil and water. The condition of the sites indicated the black and red ware ruins as the more recent" (Kroeber 1916b:9). Based on historical information and on the condition of structures on the sites (dilapidated as opposed to nondilapidated—conditions he assumed were equated with age), Kroeber (1916b:9–10) concluded that concerning "the type and period of white ware and the type and period of black and of red ware, the latter is the more recent [belonging] in part to the time of early American history; the former is wholly prehistoric."

Kroeber (1916b:8) "attempted to pick up all sherds visible in certain spots [of each site], rather than range over the whole site and stoop only for the attractive ones." He did not excavate, noting that "I have not turned a spadeful of earth in the Zuñi country. But the outlines of a thousand years' civilizational changes which the surface reveals are so clear, that there is no question of the wealth of knowledge that the ground holds for the critical but not over timid excavator" (Kroeber 1916b:14). But he was cautious. Kroeber (1916b:20, 21) believed that for his proposed chronological classification, the "final proof is in the spade," and he lamented that "in the present chaos of knowledge who can say which of these differences [in frequencies of sherd types] are due to age and which to locality and environment?" Ford would have more to say on such matters two decades later.

Kroeber (1916a, 1916b) arranged his surface collections to derive not just a two-period sequence but a five-period (actually six, if one includes modern Zuñi pottery) cultural sequence—what he referred to as "shorter epochs" (Kroeber 1916a:44). Kroeber's frequency seriation began with corrugated ware as the oldest and most frequent type. Collections of pottery from individual sites were arranged so that the relative abundance of that type consistently decreased. His short epochs "shade[d] into one another," and there was "no gap or marked break between periods A and B" (Kroeber 1916a:44), his two main periods. In other words, Puebloan culture change was a flowing stream (a metaphor that will crop up continually throughout this volume). The two major periods might originally have been "as distinct as oil and water" (Kroeber 1916b:9), but they were originally distinguished on the basis of criteria (e.g., degree of deterioration of associated ruins) *other* than those used in the seriation. Kroeber (1916b:15) believed that the two major periods "can normally be distinguished without the least uncertainty, and the separateness of the two is fundamental, [but] nevertheless they do not represent two different migrations, nationalities, or waves of culture, but rather a steady and continuous development on the soil."

In his paper "An Outline for a Chronology of Zuñi Ruins," Leslie Spier (1917:253) expressed concern that Kroeber's surface samples might not be random but rather selective. Wedding Kroeber's proportional frequencies to Nelson's superposed levels was, Spier (1917:253) suggested, a method that "is strikingly direct and entirely eliminates the error of selection, but it is only applicable to refuse heaps of considerable depth" (Ford later would demonstrate that the latter was not universally true). Most of Spier's sites contained shallow deposits, but the few that contained deeper deposits provided checks on his seriations of sherd collections made from site surfaces. Based on Nelson's, Kroeber's, and some of his own stratigraphic work, Spier knew the basic sequence: "It seems reasonable to believe that we are dealing with no other phenomenon than the several phases of a single pottery art" (Spier 1917:281). But how was he to deal with the surface collections? Citing his own superpositional data and Kroeber's (implied popularity) principle of ordering corrugated ware from having a high relative abundance early and being absent late in the temporal sequence, Spier (1917:281) used "fluctuations in this type for a first grouping, a preliminary seriation of the data from superficial [i.e., surface] samples," arguing that "It might prove fertile then to arrange these data according to their percentages of corrugated ware in sequence from lowest to highest" (Spier 1917:281–82). He never questioned the theoretical basis of this (popularity) "principle for the seriation of the data," indicating the principle was "to be subjected to the method of proof of concurrent variations" (Spier 1917:281). The latter statement, however, referred only to the correctness of the resulting arrangement rather than to the notion that the arrangement represented the passage of time.

After noting that the seriation based on the frequency of corrugated ware resulted in the recognition that painted wares apparently preceded glazed wares in time—all inferential and implicitly founded on the popularity principle—Spier elaborated on his method of proof: "The test of such a seriation as an historical series will lie in the observed seriation of the accompanying wares; for, when a group of three or more distinct, but mutually dependent, values are ranked according to some postulated sequence for one, and the other values are found to present serially concurrent variations, it may be concluded that the result is not fortuitous" (Spier 1917:282). The conciseness of that statement is unparalleled in the literature. By demanding that at least three types be used, Spier revealed his awareness of the problem of closed arrays—if only two types are used, and one decreases in relative abundance, then the other must increase in relative abundance because the sum of the two must always equal 100 percent. Not so if three types are used, because although their abundances must sum to 100 percent, a monotonic increase in one type demands only that (a) one of the other two types decrease monotonically, or (b) one of the other two types first decrease and then the third type decrease, or (c) both of the other two types decrease. Smooth—in the sense of consistent increase or consistent decrease—nonfluctuating frequencies of all three types would suggest all three were measuring the same thing, which, for Kroeber and Spier, was inferred to be the passage of time. The implicit rationale for the inference was the popularity principle.

After arranging his collections on the basis of consistent frequency change in one type, Spier then determined if the other types included in his seriation consistently increased or decreased in the arrangement of assemblages. He used a form of simple least-squares regression to determine if the other types included in his seriation displayed approximately monotonic frequency distributions (Spier 1917:283, 285). He then noted the direction—not the degree—of the slopes of the lines defined by the regression analysis and finally indicated that what we would today term residuals "are as often positive as negative" and thus "the variations [between observed values and values predicted by the regression] appear to be accidental and that the [regression line] curves represent the [frequency] distributions rather well" (Spier 1917:283, 285). He considered this to be "the usual test for fit" (Spier 1917:285)—which it was, and is, in statistics—despite its seminal character in archaeology, and indicated that it suggested the seriation was valid "but not certain." That is, the arrangement was good, but whether it represented the passage of time was unclear.

Spier (1917:293) found some of his seriations to be corroborated by Kidder's (e.g., 1916) stratified sequences of type frequencies. He also noted that "parallel development" might invalidate his sequence (Spier 1917:305)—a problem that Ford later confronted in Louisiana. In his summary, Spier (1917:326) suggested that there was "no reason to doubt that samples of potsherds collected from successive levels of the ash heaps present us with valid chronological indices," and he argued that he had demonstrated "that it is possible to collect surface samples approximating in [chronological representativeness] those from refuse heaps." Of course, he knew which way time was going in his frequency seriation of surface collections based on superposition of the stratified sequences and on the general nature of the frequency distribution of particular kinds of pottery that resulted from the work of Nelson, Kidder, and others. His test of concomitant variation in types used in the seriation was innovative, as were his regression analysis and analysis of residuals.

It is critical to note here that the techniques developed by Kroeber and Spier involved what we are calling frequency seriation and percentage stratigraphy. Historians of Americanist archaeology have suggested that Kidder performed "seriations" in his work at Pecos Pueblo (Browman and Givens 1996; Willey and Sabloff 1993). They are correct, but they fail to note that what Kidder did was not frequency seriation. Rather, Kidder's seriations were of what we would call the phyletic sort and focused on variations on a theme, particularly design motifs (e.g., Kidder 1915, 1917). This distinction, as we pointed out earlier, is key to understanding what Ford later did. Further, only once did Kidder use percentage stratigraphy, and that was during the early phase of his work at Pecos (e.g., Kidder and Kidder 1917), though one of his coworkers used it again later (Amsden 1931). Thus, there were two intellectual traditions early in the development of culture history—one focusing on shifting frequencies of variant types and another focusing on the suspected development, or evolution, of particular design motifs. The chronological implications of the orders resulting from both of these techniques, however, had to be tested with superposed collections. Frequency seriation thus was tested with percentage stratigraphy and phyletic seriation, with index fossils plotted against their position in a stratigraphic column. Both frequency seriation and phyletic seriation would be used by Ford in his later work, though typically it is frequency seriation for which he is remembered. Ironically, in virtually *all* cases Ford used *stratigraphy* as the basis of his chronologies and only supplemented them with seriations.

Typology

The subject matter of stratigraphic and seriational studies is artifacts and the categories into which they are placed. Throughout the history of archaeology, as more artifacts and more variant forms have become known, it has become increasingly difficult to keep track of where particular kinds of things came from and for individual investigators to communicate with one another about the particular forms in their respective collections. The history of artifact classification is, therefore, critically important to the foundation of modern Americanist archaeology (see Dunnell 1986b). We can only touch on that history here (see Lyman et al. [1997a] for more details), but this brief summary will serve to place later discussion of Ford and typology in perspective.

The development of archaeological classification in the second half of the nineteenth century marked the emergence of archaeology as a distinct area of inquiry. Classification serves two functions: to structure observations so that they can be explained, and to provide a set of terminological conventions that allows communication. In the United States, early classification systems (e.g., Rau 1876; Wilson 1899) were developed solely as a way to enhance communication between researchers who had multiple specimens they wanted to describe.

Piles of more or less similar-looking specimens that early twentieth-century classifiers were forever creating lacked any archaeological meaning: "In an effort to make categorization more systematic and scientific, these early workers had arbitrarily focused on formal criteria that lacked any archaeological or ethnographic rationale" (Dunnell 1986b:159). Variation in artifact form within each pile—and to some extent between piles—of specimens often had no perceived explanatory value and was simply conceived as noise resulting from variation in skill in manufacturing and in raw-material quality. Even ethnic, or spatially based, classifications were disparaged because particular forms were found in widely separated areas (e.g., Fowke 1896). The problem was that common sense dictated the choice of attributes; thus groups of artifacts were largely ad hoc and only accidentally had chronological or ethnic meaning (Dunnell 1986b:159).

In the late nineteenth century, classification systems for pottery lagged behind those developed for stone artifacts because most classifications used shape, and ceramic specimens more often than not were represented by sherds rather than by intact vessels. During the last half of the nineteenth century, Bureau of American Ethnology prehistorian William Henry Holmes worried about how to explain variation in vessel form. He was, as David Meltzer and Robert Dunnell (1992:xxviii) point out, "embued with anthropological evolutionism, particularly the cultural evolutionism of Lewis Henry Morgan, [and] like many of his colleagues, employed the Morgan stages of humanity (i.e., savagery, barbarism, etc.) as if they were matters of fact." But he also was "ambivalent about [the] precise direction and form" of such progressive evolution (Meltzer and Dunnell 1992:xxxvi). Time was not of paramount interest for Holmes, and his chronological controls were stratigraphic. Thus he "frequently found it difficult to see the evident change [in artifact forms] as progressive. Consequently, he was forced to seek other (e.g., racial, environmental, and diffusionist) explanations for the differences" (Meltzer and Dunnell 1992:xxxvii). Holmes's seminal papers on pottery classification (e.g., Holmes 1886a, 1886b, 1886c, 1903) were focused on establishing ceramic groups that were internally consistent and actually may have served as a reinforcement or justification for emerging notions of culture areas (e.g., Mason 1896).

From the discussion thus far, it should be clear that archaeological emphasis, at least in the Southwest, shifted to the creation of types that were *chronologically* significant. How those types, or units of measurement, were to be created is an issue that has never been settled and one on which Jim Ford had plenty to say. Typically termed "styles," in part because of the analytical importance placed on stylistic (decorative) aspects of pottery, the ability of such styles (types) to measure time could be tested empirically, given that stratigraphic excavation techniques were part of the archaeologist's tool kit. As a result, chronological inquiry came to dominate archaeological research during the first half of the twentieth century. Classification efforts focused on only one kind of unit—the historical type. Functional variation in artifact form, still speculative in terms of methodological consideration, was effectively eliminated from discussion, despite occasional calls for its examination (e.g., Bennett 1943; Steward and Setzler 1938). As Brew (1946:230) noted, such calls were merely ignored—not derogated—because of the singular focus on chronology.

As time went on, more and more kinds of pottery were found and described and more types were created—some not very well—which led to further problems in communication among archaeologists. A number of monographs on southwestern archaeology in the 1920s and 1930s attempted to standardize descriptions of various pottery forms and surface treatments (e.g., Gladwin and Gladwin 1928, 1930b, 1931, 1933; Haury 1936) and to funnel those descriptions into pottery types that integrated the dimensions of time, space, and form. In naming a type, a binomial nomenclature was used, with color or surface treatment constituting the first (genus) part of the type name and geographic locale the second (species) part (Gladwin and Gladwin 1930a; see also Gladwin 1936:256). First suggested at the original Pecos Conference in 1927 (Kidder 1927:490), the binomial pottery classification procedure grew out of a consensus reached at the first Gila Pueblo Conference in 1930 (Brew 1946:58; Gladwin 1936:256). Procedures and rules for naming new types were produced (e.g., Colton and Hargrave 1937), and these often were repeated in following decades (e.g., Colton 1965). This binomial system eventually became the basis for creating most pottery types used in Americanist archaeology, with its transfer into the Southeast being completed by 1938, largely through the efforts of Ford and James B. Griffin (Ford and Griffin 1937, 1938).

BEYOND HISTORY: CULTURAL RECONSTRUCTIONISM

Elsewhere we chronicle the rise and eventual fall from favor of culture history as the leading paradigm in Americanist archaeology (Lyman et al. 1997a; O'Brien 1996a) and present some of the benchmark papers that characterize the paradigm (Lyman et al. 1997b). What became obvious to us during the preparation of those volumes was the lack of a detailed examination of why, after it had dominated the discipline for half a century, culture history fell from favor during the second half of the twentieth century. By the early 1960s a clear split had developed between those who referred to themselves as "culture historians" and those who called themselves "processualists." Something was going on in archaeology long before the sixties that eventually opened the door for the processualists to walk through uncontested. The major contribution culture historians made to the discipline was the study of time through superpositioning, percentage stratigraphy, and seriation, all of which came to depend on the recognition of specific artifact types. Surely time is an important dimension of *any* archaeological study. Without control over when certain variants appeared and when they were replaced, how can we ever hope to understand culture change? The term "change" literally forces us to control for time. Why, given its importance, did the study of time begin to take a back seat to other considerations?

The answer is found in the ways in which archaeologists view change. Because the artifacts contained in the archaeological record were manufactured, used, and discarded by humans, any change evident is of the *cultural* sort. Artifacts are *material culture.* In a very real sense, all of the methods of fieldwork and analysis that were developed and used by culture historians were geared toward understanding change in the archaeological record that was identified clearly as *cultural change.* That the concepts of cultures and culture change were intertwined is exemplified by Kroeber's work in the 1920s with the Peruvian pottery collected by Uhle. Kroeber and two of his students—Anna Gayton and William Duncan Strong—seriated those collections using both a phyletic technique and frequency seriation as well as the little evidence of superposition available to them in Uhle's notes (Gayton 1927; Gayton and Kroeber 1927; Kroeber 1925a, 1925b; Kroeber and Strong 1924a, 1924b; Strong 1925). Importantly, Kroeber (1925a:229–31) noted that "distinguishable," or "well-marked," styles of pottery did *not necessarily* represent different temporal periods. Rather, Kroeber held "a working belief in the sanctity of types," and "he would classify a collection by grouping together the pieces which shared the most obvious formal similarities, believing that in this way he was securing units which represented in some sense 'natural' units, like species in biology" (Rowe 1962:402). Thus, for Kroeber (1925a:230–31), several temporally associated styles "represent different groups or strata of the population." To Kroeber styles were *ethnically* distinctive. This view epitomizes the equation of artifacts—material culture—with culture construed as shared ideas. Artifacts change, therefore, as culture changes. It was precisely this equation that Ford maintained throughout his career.

Just when culture history appeared to stabilize as a paradigm, archaeologists in some quarters were becoming dissatisfied with the approach—a dissatisfaction that apparently no amount of fieldwork or additional analysis could ease. Dunnell (1978:194) traced the roots of this dissatisfaction to the nineteenth century, though as he points out it did not show up clearly until the late 1930s or early 1940s. We would place it slightly later in the Southeast, probably because culture-historical methods were so much later in arriving there than in the Southwest. Some of the dissatisfaction was promoted by anthropologists (e.g., Kluckhohn 1939a, 1939b, 1940), who increasingly argued that archaeologists spent too much time worrying about such things as artifact types and where they fit in time and space and not enough time worrying about the people who made the artifacts, but some of it clearly came from archaeologists (e.g., Bennett 1943; Childe 1946; Dixon 1913; Steward and Setzler 1938). Without doubt, the most vocal of these was Walter W. Taylor, whose Harvard doctoral dissertation was published as *A Study of Archeology* (Taylor 1948). Archaeology, according to Taylor, was supposed to be the study of past *cultures* and cultural *lifeways,* but in his view archaeologists—and here he singled out some of the leading culture historians of the day (e.g., Kidder and Griffin)—had tended to concentrate instead on constructing chronological frameworks and making comparisons between site assemblages. Where, Taylor asked, were the studies of human behavior, especially studies of function?

The product that emerged from this growing body of criticism was *cultural reconstructionism,* which Dunnell (1978:194) described as "a reaction to culture history that has its roots in the association of archaeology and anthropology in North America and in the observation that culture history is not very anthropological." This may be true, but not all anthropologists, or even archaeologists for that matter, felt that culture history was an end in itself. Kroeber (e.g., 1931a:155) argued that "historical reconstruction" was the major goal of archaeology, though determining which cultural "processes" were involved "could never be traced with the same fullness in excavated as in historic or living cultures." He suggested that while culture history—his historical reconstruction—was, for some archaeologists, "to remain a descriptive prolegomena," others viewed culture reconstruction "as a waste of effort or dangerous delusion" (Kroeber 1931a:156). Julian Steward and Frank Setzler (1938:5) took these notions a step further: "We believe that treatment of archaeological objects would be more meaningful if they were regarded not simply as museum specimens but as tools employed by human beings in some pattern of behavior. This requires a deliberate effort to understand their functional place in the total configuration of activity" (Steward and Setzler 1938:8).

As archaeologist John Bennett (1943:219) remarked, "a new set of premises must be accepted if the archaeologist is to adopt a functional outlook. . . . Archaeological data must be considered as essentially similar to that gathered by any social scientist. The difference is one of degree, not kind." Thus, what followed were discussions of the kinds of cultural or anthropological inferences that could be drawn from the archaeological record and the confidence one might have in them (e.g., Hawkes 1954; MacWhite 1956; Osgood 1951). For culture reconstructionists, the method of choice was ethnographic analogy (e.g., Ascher 1961)—the result, essentially, of the wedding of archaeology to anthropology. Culture history had an interest in culture, but the union between archaeology and anthropology under that paradigm was more of an engagement than a marriage. By the early 1940s, the marriage had been consummated.

The apparent ease with which many culture historians, including James Ford, slipped into cultural reconstructionism is not too surprising, since Americanist archaeologists were (and still are) trained in departments of anthropology. Thus they had to take the requisite courses in kinship, social organization, and the like— certainly not to the extent that an ethnologist studied such things, but at least so that they had a basic grounding in the broad field of culture. Ford apparently had no trouble incorporating cultural reconstructionism into his outlook:

> In a recent monograph, Walter Taylor has clearly defined the difference between the
> interests of history and cultural anthropology, stating that archaeological activity,
> if successful, is, at best, historiography [Taylor 1948:25–44]. . . . I have no quarrel with

either Taylor's definition or his conclusion. . . . If an archaeologist becomes a cultural anthropologist when he begins to inquire into the uniformities of his data, the change in classification has no great significance. (Ford 1952a:317)

If most archaeologists were comfortable with a foot in either camp, it is logical to think that one natural extension of culture history to cultural reconstructionism would be the application of various archaeological units to anthropological problems. As we demonstrate throughout the book, it was this singular practice of turning units constructed to measure time, and to a lesser extent space—both pursuits of culture history—into behavioral correlates—the pursuit of reconstructionism—that was a major weakness of the broader culture-history program in general and of Ford's views in particular. Perhaps such a weakness was to be expected in the absence of theory, where common sense becomes the warrant for such a transfer. Regardless, this weakness for the most part went unnoticed.

The use of ethnologically documented mechanisms of culture change by Ford and his contemporaries in the 1950s and 1960s would lead ultimately to the downfall of culture history. If anthropological theory constructed around anthropologically meaningful units is to account for, interpret, or somehow explain the archaeological record, the units for measuring and documenting that record had damn well better be anthropologically meaningful. The units culture historians used had no such unequivocal meaning, despite their ascription of this sort of meaning to the units in their efforts at reconstruction.

BEYOND CULTURAL RECONSTRUCTION: PROCESSUAL ARCHAEOLOGY

By the early 1960s, Americanist archaeology was deeply involved with cultural reconstructionism, but there was a movement afoot that would transcend the comparatively modest efforts of the reconstructionists and bring archaeology closer to the study of culture than it ever had been. This time, the emphasis was squarely on the mechanisms that in effect cause culture to evolve rather than on the small-scale changes in culture that the historians and reconstructionists studied. The name for this replacement paradigm was *cultural processualism,* or what some archaeologists called the "new archaeology."

The reorientation that Americanist archaeology went through during the 1960s, at least in purpose, was to draw a sharp contrast between the study of process on the one hand and what was considered passé on the other. Outdated subjects included culture history, characterized basically as an intellectually sterile exercise, and cultural reconstruction, which, though viewed as a preliminary means of getting at the "Indian behind the artifact" (Braidwood 1959:79), was considered to be too restricted in perspective. Whereas cultural reconstructionism had taken the tack of understanding how various parts of a culture operated in a functional sense, processualism was designed to do much more than that. Understanding how things functioned was one thing; understanding what led them to work in the first place was something else entirely. Further, if you could wrap yourself in the mantle of science while analyzing culture process, that would take archaeology into an entirely new dimension, seating it at the table with the likes of physics and chemistry. Of course, for a discipline to be scientific meant that it had to have laws. Not surprisingly, much of the new archaeology was concerned with a search for laws that governed human behavior—something that cultural anthropologists of the mid–twentieth century had grappled with in their search for cultural universals.

Some of the polemic of the 1960s and 1970s had been anticipated by the classic culture historians/reconstructionists (e.g., Ford 1952a; Taylor 1948; Willey and Phillips 1958), but Lewis Binford (e.g., 1962, 1964, 1965, 1968a, 1968b), Kent Flannery (e.g., 1967, 1968), and others carried the discussion to new heights. For those entering the profession during the halcyon years of processual archaeology, it was a heady experience, somewhat along the lines of attending a revival meeting. Looking back on those days, one can draw a loose parallel to China's Cultural Revolution. The "classics" were no longer read in archaeology courses, for the simple reason that they no longer were classics. More to the point, they were considered completely irrelevant to the loftier goal of studying culture process. Topics such as stratigraphic excavation, percentage stratigraphy, and seriation might be introduced in lower-level courses, but they were not discussed from a historical perspective, nor was their utility as time-measuring devices discussed at length, that role having been usurped by radiometric dating. Given that the new goal of archaeology was to become increasingly anthropological, which meant that culture had to assume center stage, such things as chronology and type construction—the mainstays of culture history—were either relegated to the wings or thrown out entirely.

Conversion to the paradigm was widespread, though there were scattered pockets of resistance (e.g., Bayard 1969). There also were those who seemed unconcerned that a revolution supposedly was taking place. Archaeologists working in the lower Mississippi Valley, like most of their counterparts in areas to the south and east, did not take part in the great debates of the 1960s and 1970s over how to reorient Americanist archaeology (Dunnell 1990). Many factors undoubtedly played a role in this conservatism, but one stands out (O'Brien and Dunnell 1998): the Mississippi Valley had been an important and early donor to the culture-history paradigm; thus, archaeologists working in the region either had played a direct role in creating the paradigm or were students of those who had. Many students of the original creators continued to work in the valley after receiving their degrees, and they continued in the same vein as their predecessors, adding new data to the growing pile of information rather than reinterpreting old facts. Most of them dabbled in cultural reconstructionism to one degree or another, but almost no one did processual studies in the post-1960 sense.

The reorientation in aim that Americanist archaeology went through was widely heralded as a revolution (e.g., Leone 1972; Martin 1971), though several scholars with a sense of the discipline's past (e.g., Meltzer 1979) have questioned this bold assertion. Regardless of whether it was a revolution, processualism did not escape the paradox that was born in culture history and nurtured to adulthood in cultural reconstructionism. Binford (1964:440) argued that "as archaeologists we are faced with the methodological task of isolating extinct socio-cultural systems as the most appropriate unit for the study of evolutionary processes which result in cultural similarities and differences." Hence, cultural reconstruction was seen as the necessary precursor to the study of cultural processes, and thus it received considerable attention from archaeologists during the 1960s and 1970s. Reconstruction was founded on one basic assumption: "The formal structure of artifact assemblages together with the between element contextual relationship should and do present a systematic and understandable picture of *the total extinct* cultural system" (Binford 1962:219).

For processualists, "the dynamic relationships (causes and effects) operative among sociocultural systems, [the] processes responsible for changes observed in the organization and/or content of the systems, or . . . the integration of new formal components into the system. . . . [In short, the] dynamic relationships operative among cultural systems," formed the appropriate focus of study (Binford 1968a:14). Further, "Explanation . . . within a scientific frame of reference is simply the *demonstration* of constant articulation of [functional] variables within a system and the measurement of concomitant variability among the variables within the [cultural] system. Processual change in one variable can then be shown to relate to changes in other variables, the latter changing in turn relative to changes in the structure of the system as a whole" (Binford 1962:217). The possible catalysts for such change were to be sought "in systemic terms for classes of historical events such as migrations, establishment of 'contact' between areas previously isolated, etc." (Binford 1962:218). Thus, the historical *processes* of cultural change were largely those of the culture historians and were derived from ethnology and anthropological theory.

Being largely unrecognized at the time—Albert Spaulding was an important exception—the paradox of using archaeological units to do anthropology became even more ingrained in Americanist archaeology because the new archaeology of the 1960s and 1970s shifted focus away from an emphasis on homologous similarity—the essential cornerstone of culture history—and toward analogous similarity—the use of ethnoarchaeological and behavioral inference (e.g., Binford 1967; Gould 1978; Kramer 1979; Schiffer 1976) to create a new cornerstone (Lyman et al. 1997a). This shift was geared toward making archaeology more scientific through the discovery of behavioral regularities that could be called laws, though the kind of science that its advocates had in mind—physical science, founded in an essentialist metaphysic—was of the completely wrong sort. This doomed the efforts of the processualists (Dunnell 1980, 1982, 1985b, 1989; O'Brien 1996b, 1996c; O'Brien and Holland 1990, 1992, 1995a, 1995b), who were vitally interested in how culture, as well as specific cultures, evolve. No amount of recourse to the scientific method could make up for the fact that archaeology had based its future totally on the science of inanimate objects, not on the science of organic evolution. In the former, analogs give us the key to understanding the past; in the latter, they do not—a point still not appreciated in archaeology.

THE ROLE OF EVOLUTION IN ARCHAEOLOGY

The shift in emphasis from homologs to analogs has long been of interest to us because of our views on what archaeology should be and where it can profitably spend its time. Those views can be subsumed under the broad heading of evolutionary archaeology, though the kind of evolution in which we are interested has little to do with the evolutionary perspective the processualists of the 1960s and 1970s adopted. The kind of evolution we are talking about is grounded in Darwinian theory and has as its main focus explaining the archaeological record in terms of differential selection of variants—artifacts—that were part of prehistoric phenotypes. Importantly, much of what we view as essential to a Darwinian evolutionary archaeology (Dunnell 1980; O'Brien 1996b; O'Brien and Holland 1990) derives directly from culture history, especially its concern with time. In effect, any study of evolution is a study in time, principally the careful tracking of variation, often minute variation, through time. In such an analysis the vital question is, "When was one variant *replaced* by another?" rather than, "When was one variant *transformed* into another?" The difference between these two questions is anything but semantic or trivial. Suffice it to say that the difference is of critical importance in forever separating Darwinian evolution from cultural evolution as understood by most culture historians and processualists.

The relevancy of the question, "When was one variant replaced by another?" is, of course, predicated on the assumption that we have the means to identify and measure variation that might happen to be present in a sample. Equally important is having a theory that guides not only the *way* we measure variation but also how we *explain* it. Culture history, though it was built around interpretation rather than explanation (Lyman et al. 1997a; O'Brien 1996a) and often dealt with transformation of variants rather than replacement of one by another, contained various methods and techniques that, given certain conditions, could be used to track variation temporally as well as spatially. It was precisely because of their interest in cultural evolution (synonymous in most culture-historical usage with *change*) that culture historians put so much energy into constructing units that allowed them to keep things in chronological and spatial order. Otherwise, how could one tell what was changing, and when? Culture historians, because of their interests in time, tended to focus on what turned out to be homologous traits— traits that are similar in structure because of a common origin. Things commonly referred to in archaeology as stylistic features—pottery designs, for example— are treated as homologs based on the assumption that styles are so complex that the probability of duplication by chance is astronomically low (Dunnell 1978; Gould 1986; O'Brien and Holland 1990). Conversely, analogs are ahistorical in that they arise not from phyletic relatedness but rather as similar solutions to similar problems. The term "solution" is in keeping with the definition of analogs as features similar in function but different in structure and origin (O'Brien and Holland 1990:51).

Putting Culture in Culture History

Although culture historians might not have taken a Darwinian outlook on evolution, they were not altogether ignorant of the topic. However, much of what they knew came not from biology but from the work of nineteenth-century cultural evolutionists such as Tylor (1871) and Morgan (1877), with a heavy dose of the twentieth-century work of Kroeber (e.g., 1915, 1917, 1931a, 1946) thrown in (see Willey and Phillips 1955). Because Kroeber himself was as much an archaeologist as an ethnologist, his archaeologist colleagues paid attention to his views on culture and culture change. Ford apparently was not *directly* influenced by Kroeber (though there was a strong *indirect* influence [Chapter 3]), and certainly was not by Tylor and Morgan, but early in his career he reflected Kroeber's deeply held notion that cultural development was like a flowing, braided stream. Even a cursory glance at Ford's early publications makes it clear that he was always interested in culture and how cultures changed. Whether, as some of his colleagues suggested (Evans 1968; Willey 1969:63; but see Willey 1988:58), Ford's notions on culture began to crystallize after he began graduate work at Michigan in 1937 and became acquainted with Leslie White, or whether his views were self-developed, his embracement of cultural-evolutionary "doctrine . . . seemed to go beyond intellectual appreciation, to something akin to an emotional response" (Willey 1988:58).

From his entrance into the field, Ford had been concerned with how to make archaeology more relevant to the study of culture. He apparently had little influence on the processualists and in fact was derogated by them (e.g., Binford 1965:203), but it is clear that he directly influenced many of those culture historians/reconstructionists whose writings contained the seeds of the coming reorientation in direction—for example, Philip Phillips (1955:246–47), who published that oft-repeated phrase "New World archaeology is anthropology or it is nothing" (see also Willey and Phillips 1958:2). Ford's preoccupation with culture and all of its sociological aspects was perhaps not atypical of the period, but he was one of the more vocal proponents of approaches that allowed the archaeologist to monitor the behaviors of prehistoric humans. The trouble was, Ford, as well as numerous other culture historians, monitored the flow of populations and/or ideas with the same units that they had devised to keep track of time.

Underlying this conflation of different kinds of units—those that are useful for telling time versus those that *might* be useful for other purposes—was confusion over exactly what culture was and specifically over how culture change could best be measured. Competing positions were held throughout the long tenure of culture history. One view was that culture and its development was a series of stops and starts—periods of stasis interrupted by sudden spurts of change; the other view was that culture and its development was a placid stream that ever so slowly changed its composition over time.

Nels Nelson's work is an excellent example of the two ways of looking at culture change. Nelson had found superposed remains before the critical 1914 field season in the Southwest, but he noted that in such cases "there is often no appreciable [chronological] differentiation of remains" (Nelson 1916:163). When he found evidence of chronological differentiation, it was between the ends of a continuum of several pottery types, and thus he lamented that such instances were "merely clean-cut superpositions showing *nothing but time relations*" (Nelson 1916:163; emphasis added). But when two types in the continuum were found stratigraphically mixed together, "one *gradually replacing* the other [this] was the evidence wanted, because it accounted for the otherwise unknown time that separated the merely superposed occurrences of types and from the point of view of the merely physical relationships of contiguity, *connected them*" (Nelson 1916:163; emphasis added; see also Nelson 1919a, 1919b, 1932). Plotting relative frequencies of sherds of various types against time, which is rendered as geologically vertical space, would illustrate the gradual cultural evolution Nelson sought and eventually would allow one to document the relative ages of the cultural stages (e.g., Nelson 1937).

Some culture historians adhered to one or the other framework throughout their lives; others fluctuated between the two positions in what appears to be random fashion; but most adopted elements of each and interwove them into what might best be referred to as a schizophrenic interpretation of cultural development. This same problem continued to plague the discipline after 1960, despite a decided deemphasis on homologous similarity and an increased emphasis on analogical reasoning. This continuity demonstrates forcefully that the dichotomy in how culture and culture change are viewed transcends confusion over kinds of units and strikes at the core of how archaeologists come to know what they think they know about the past. And what we think we know is conditioned to a large degree on how we view reality.

THE ESSENTIALIST VS. MATERIALIST METAPHYSIC

There are perhaps as many views of reality, formally termed *ontological positions,* as there are viewers, all of which revolve around how one perceives the nature of being and the process of becoming. For our purposes, we focus on two of them—essentialism and materialism—both of which play as important a role in archaeology (e.g., Dunnell 1982, 1987; Leonard and Jones 1987; Lyman et al. 1997a; O'Brien 1996a, 1996b; O'Brien and Holland 1990, 1992; O'Brien et al. 1994; Teltser 1995a) as they do in biology (e.g., Mayr 1977, 1982, 1987; Sober 1980, 1984), though explicit recognition of the distinction is of more recent origin in archaeology than in biology (Dunnell 1982). We adopt this dichotomy not because we seek to legitimize one position at the expense of the other but rather because of the nature of what we are evaluating, namely evolution and change. It appears to us irrelevant what the subject matter of that change is, whether it be organisms or culture; if the issue is evolution, the dichotomy between the contrasting positions is relevant. What makes Ford's work such an interesting example of the culture-history paradigm is that he at various times had one or both feet in either the essentialist or materialist camp.

Under essentialism, the essential properties of a set of things define an ideal (archetype), "to which actual objects [are] imperfect approximations" (Lewontin 1974b:5). Thus variation between and among objects placed in the set, because it contributes nothing to the "essentialness" of the objects, is viewed as "annoying distraction" (Lewontin 1974b:5). Under this perspective, variation between and among *sets,* or *types,* of entities—not between and among the *individual objects* themselves—is of explanatory significance. Single sets, or kinds, of entities ("things") are presumed to be real; thus relations between units—each comprising specimens—can be formulated without reference to time or space and thus are redundant, universally true statements (meaning they are true for all times and all places). Change is seen strictly in terms of conditionally reversible transformations between kinds. Because things grouped within a set share a definitive *essence,* the essentialist view focuses on replacement of one set by another or on the transformation of one set into another (Hull 1965).

In contrast, the materialist view does not assume that reality is a unified system. Phenomena—things—are always in a state of flux—that is, they are in a state of becoming something else. Hence, relations between phenomena are not timeless, nor can universal statements be made about the relations because no static set of phenomena exists. Time and space are kept separate, and relations between phenomena are time- and space-bound. "Kinds" (types) are nonempirical con-figurations that are changing constantly, though at any given moment in time and space we can create kinds based on observations. As Dunnell (1988:16) points out, "Since neither boundaries nor central tendencies exist apart from the effects of the observer[,] variation is rendered as *change*. Difference may arise only in the epistemological context. Observations may *differ* because they are *samples,* but reality only changes."

A key point in differentiating essentialism from materialism is not that the former treats difference and the latter change, but that essentialism treats *only* difference while materialism treats difference *and* change. Under a materialist view, explanation is tied intricately to observed variation. Inferences are made about the nature of change *only* after variation has been identified and measured; hence, variation becomes the cornerstone of the materialist metaphysic. Scales— grams or inches, for example—must be designed by the analyst to document and measure the variation across real things. Theoretically informed unit construction involves the selection of properties or attributes of phenomena that are relevant to the questions being asked. Specimens are considered to be of the same kind or type *only* because of the analyst's choice of properties, not because they have some inherent property that automatically causes them to be placed in a certain kind or type. For any given problem, several or many specimens may exhibit *properties in common,* which in no sense is the same as saying that it is the existence of a common "essence" that permits multiple specimens to be grouped together. This point was made forcefully by Mayr (1987:155) with respect to organisms: "To be sure every essence is characterized by properties in common, but a group sharing properties in common does not need to have an essence. The outstanding characteristic of an essence is its unchanging permanence. By contrast, properties in common of a biological group may be variable and have the propensity for evolutionary change. What is typical for a taxon may change through evolution at any time and then no longer be typical." In short, differences in kind are the arbitrary results of analytical choices, and change is rendered as variation in frequencies of kinds over time.

Archaeology's Long Participation in Essentialism

Much of the evolutionary biology carried out today, with its focus on tracking variation through time and its specific emphasis on historical connectedness rather than historical differences, clearly falls under materialism (Lewontin 1974a). Conversely, archaeology has maintained an essentialist position throughout most of its existence—in many ways, by default (Dunnell 1980, 1982, 1986b; O'Brien 1996c; O'Brien and Holland 1990, 1992, 1995b; Lyman et al. 1997a). Objects are lumped or split into categories (types) according to perceived ("real") similarities, and change typically is viewed as transformation of one artifact type into another. Archetypes are not limited to the discrete objects we call artifacts but also include culture areas, a host of temporal and spatial units, and sociopolitical units. The use of such archetypes shows up clearly in the reliance archaeologists placed on units created by anthropologists to categorize social and political phenomena.

Early use of evolutionary terms in Americanist archaeology (e.g., Colton 1939; Colton and Hargrave 1937; Gladwin and Gladwin 1934; Kidder 1915; Kidder and Kidder 1917), in those rare cases where it wasn't tied strictly to unilinear cultural evolution, was founded on a commonsense understanding of biological evolution. Some of this understanding—actually *mis*understanding—spilled over into unit formation. The lack of development of a scientific theory of cultural evolution that could be applied archaeologically resulted in the largely trial-and-error construction of units employed to establish temporal control over assemblages of artifacts (Lyman et al. 1997a). Such units, once tested for their temporal sensitivity, might or might not also reflect ancestral-descendant relationships (e.g., one "evolved" from another)—Ford wavered on this point—but no one really knew how to construct units that clearly would reflect such relationships, though Kroeber (1931a) explained how biologists did it. It was not until the mid-1940s that the door was finally slammed shut on the potential analogy between biological and cultural evolution (see Kroeber [1931a] for an early explicit statement on the parallels). This happened when J. O. Brew (1946:53) declared that "phylogenetic relationships do not exist between inanimate objects"—a view reiterated, if implicitly, by Phillips and Willey (1953; see also Willey and Phillips 1958) a few years later, near the end of the heyday of culture history.

The Problem with Units

There is nothing inherent in the units we use that makes them real. Artifacts might share certain properties in common, which allows us to place them in categories, but there is no reason to think that the categories themselves are real. Similarly, we might use units such as grams or inches to categorize artifacts, but no one would seriously suggest that a gram or an inch is real. Dunnell (1971) distinguished between what he termed *phenomenological* units and *ideational* units, later referring to them as *empirical* and *theoretical* units, respectively (Dunnell 1986b; see also Dunnell 1995). The formal distinction between the two, at least to our way of thinking, is one of the major advancements in modern Americanist archaeology because in that distinction lies the means of escaping the essentialist-materialist paradox (Dunnell 1986b, 1995).

No one would make the claim that the objects assigned to archaeological types or to biological categories (e.g., species) are not empirical, that is, real; what is arguable, depending on one's view of reality, is whether the *units* to which objects are assigned are real. Are there essential properties that objects exhibit that make their assignment obvious, or do certain objects have properties in common that cause an analyst to group them together for a particular purpose? An essentialist would argue the former, hence creating a redundancy in terms of reality between object and category, while a materialist would argue the latter, keeping distinct the reality of the object and the nonreality of the category. In one of the clearest statements regarding the creation of pottery types that exists in the culture-historical literature, Phillips et al. (1951:221) noted that

> Exigencies of language require us to think and talk about pottery types as though they had some sort of independent existence. "This sherd *is* Baytown Plain." Upon sufficient repetition of this statement, the concept Baytown Plain takes on a massive solidity. The time comes when we are ready to fight for dear old Baytown. What we have to try to remember is that the statement really means something like this: "This sherd sufficiently resembles material which *for the time being* we have elected to call Baytown Plain." Frequent repetition of this and similar exorcisms we have found to be extremely salutary during the classificatory activities.

Here Phillips et al. made the important distinction between ideational and empirical units without using the terms. To them, pottery types were first and foremost units for telling time. The types could be created by using combinations of any number of traits, with the usefulness of the type being determined solely on its reliability to mark the passage of time. In this sense, there was nothing "real" about them. Such clear separation between objects and types, unfortunately, was not an integral part of most culture-historical work, ensuring that the paradigm remained mired in the paradox.

Two decades after working at Pecos, A. V. Kidder wrote:

> The division of the Glaze ware of Pecos into six chronologically sequent types is a very convenient and, superficially, satisfactory arrangement. For some time I was very proud of it, so much so, in fact, that I came to think and write about the types as if they were definite and describable entities. They are, of course, nothing of the sort, being merely useful cross-sections of a constantly changing cultural trait. Most types, in reality, grew one from the other by stages well-nigh imperceptible. My groupings therefore amount to a selection of six recognizable nodes of individuality; and a forcing into association with the most strongly marked or "peak" material of many actually older and younger transitional specimens. . . . This pottery did not stand still; through some three centuries it underwent a slow, usually subtle, but never ceasing metamorphosis. (Kidder 1936b:xx)

Kidder's discussion reveals a fundamental paradox in the early foundations of the culture-history paradigm. The conceived materialistic "slow, usually subtle, but never ceasing metamorphosis" of forms through time is to be perceived or monitored with the typological, essentialist, *"recognizable* nodes of individuality." By "recognizable," Kidder of course meant "recognizable to the archaeologist." The problem of "transitional specimens"—an issue that will crop up continually throughout this book—is a predictable result of using the concept of "nodes of individuality." Southwestern archaeologists Lyndon Hargrave and Harold Colton also confused empirical and theoretical units, suggesting that "there are sherds that are intermediate between types" (Colton and Hargrave 1937:31) and that the members of a type "will not [always] fit the [type] description perfectly" (Colton and Hargrave 1937:30). Their types could never be theoretical units, the empirical representations of which should display certain distributional properties if properly structured (like Kidder's). Rather, they were simply shorthand notations of what a "typical" (Colton and Hargrave 1937:31) specimen looked like.

Kidder's types, and perhaps to a lesser degree Kroeber's, Nelson's, and Spier's, were units that they hoped reflected the passage of time *as well as* cultural-evolutionary relationships. Kidder (Kidder and Kidder 1917:349) stated, "One's general impression is that [the types] are all successive phases of [particular pottery traits], and that each one of them developed from its predecessor." Hence, variation in pottery was temporally continuous. To measure time, Kidder erected types that were both "more or less arbitrarily delimited chronological subdivisions of material" (Kidder 1936b:xxix) and "chronologically seriable" (Kidder 1936a:625). Types had to undergo a test of "chronological significance [via] stratigraphic tests" (Kidder 1936b:xx). Kidder's types thus were theoretical units constructed to measure time: (a) variation is continuous—things are in the continuous process of becoming, and thus kinds or types are artifacts of observation (of the etic sort); and (b) change in variants reflects the passage of time. This is the materialist metaphysic.

This position is in stark contrast to the essentialist underpinnings of common sense and ethnology, both of which came to play increasingly greater roles in archaeology, first in the Southwest and then in the Midwest and Southeast. This created a fundamental contradiction (Dunnell 1980, 1982). As Julian Steward (1941:367) remarked, "the purpose [of archaeology] is to represent the development, interaction, and blending of diverse cultural streams." Thus, on the one hand, human history was a stream of attributes, ever-changing, flowing from past to future; on the other hand, experience suggested that humanity was divisible into more or less discrete groups or cultures, and it was these groups that required explanation. The implications for classification were enormous. In the materialist view, types, cultures, and all other units were artifacts of observation; they were *tools* used to measure variation that constituted the past and of which the present was just a terminal snapshot. In the essentialist view, types, cultures, and other units were empirical and real; they were the things to *be* explained, not the means *of* explanation.

Thus, Kidder's (1936b:xx) "recognizable nodes of individuality" represented "ceramic periods" (Kidder 1936b:xxi) as well as distinct cultures (Kidder 1936a: 623, 1936b:xxviii). This clearly essentialist view is what made the assignment of "older and younger transitional specimens" (Kidder 1936b:xx) a predictable problem (Dunnell 1980). Kidder's goal was the formulation of "ceramic periods" (Kidder 1936b:xxi) and the identification of "nuclear cultures" (Kidder 1936a:623) that would allow him to write culture history. He believed that one could trace "the descent of types and [establish] collateral relationships" between types and cultures (Kidder 1936b:xxviii). The influence of cultural anthropology's essentialist viewpoint is clear. Real cultures were the subject of anthropological and archaeological study. Culture traits—shared ideas (after Tylor's [1871] definition)—expressed as archaeological types could be used to tell time, and they could *also* be used to discuss population movements and the cultural relations of sites from which artifact assemblages were collected. But by structuring change as discontinuous nodes, explanations had to be of the transformational sort, in which differences between the discretely variable nodes (essentialist artifact types) are noted rather than the materialist measurement of change as the differential persistence of variants.

Ideational, or theoretical, units—those units created by the analyst to assist in solving a problem—offer a way out of the paradox "because, and just because, they are not empirical" (Dunnell 1995:35). They accommodate continuity as a change in frequency of theoretical units, which in archaeology usually are, but need not be, artifact types. Having said this, we need to note that simply distinguishing between theoretical and empirical units does not guarantee that any particular units, even if they are treated as theoretical units, will necessarily prove helpful. As Ford and other culture historians found out, type formulation was—in the absence of theory—an inexact science, containing considerable trial and error. The test of a type's usefulness resided strictly in how well it performed during analysis. Did it, for example, have limited distribution in time so that it could be used in chronological ordering, or, alternatively, did it appear to have an extensive temporal distribution, thus making it less useful? If the latter, could the criteria used to create the type be modified so as to be less inclusive, thus creating a new type that might pass the historical-significance test (Krieger 1944)? Ford and others did this consistently, always searching for more and more useful types. This worked fine when it was chronological control they were after, but things began to unravel when they used historical types—those created for the express purpose of telling time—for numerous other purposes.

Types as Groups or as Classes?

Equal in importance to the distinction between empirical and theoretical units is the distinction between groups and classes. The distinction has been made before in archaeology (e.g., Dunnell 1971, 1986b; O'Brien 1996a), though clearly the discipline has often ignored it. Types, regardless of whether they are treated as empirical or theoretical units, can be further subdivided into two kinds—groups and classes. A group consists of members that are more similar to one another than any one is to a member of another group. A class is made up of members that *must* share one or more *unique* traits that *by definition* distinguish them from members of other units. In short, a group comprises a description whereas a class comprises a definition. The difference between types as groups and types as classes is sometimes difficult to detect. Were the pottery types developed by Kidder and others in the Southwest and by Ford and others in the Mississippi Valley classes or groups? Were sherds and vessels assigned to a particular type simply more similar to one another than any one of them was to a sherd or vessel in another type, or, conversely, were there explicitly stated necessary and sufficient characteristics that a sherd or vessel had to possess before it could be included in a type? If the former, then the type was a group; if the latter, then it was a class. In reality, most of the pottery types used in the Southwest and the Mississippi Valley—the majority of which are still in use today—conform more closely to groups than to classes, though some types have such precise criteria for membership—criteria that define the class—that they in essence become classes.

The distinction between classes and groups will become important when we discuss Ford's early work in Louisiana. In fact, to our way of thinking it would be difficult to find a better illustration of the different methods of creating pottery types than Ford's work during the early 1930s, when he was casting about for a way to categorize surface-collected and excavated pottery from Louisiana and Mississippi. Ford started out using a sophisticated classification system—it was *so* sophisticated that he was unable to produce what he viewed as usable types. Thus, despite the brilliance of the system for tracking change, it was too cumbersome, at least in Ford's mind, to be useful. He then experimented with different ways of creating types, finally adopting the binomial system that had been used in the Southwest.

In the binomial system the first (genus) part of the type name contained a reference to color or surface treatment and the second (species) part to geographic locale (Gladwin and Gladwin 1930a; see also Gladwin 1936:256). The addition of (genus) and (species) in the preceding sentence is not something we are reading into the types; some southwestern archaeologists actually thought of the type name in biological terms. This transference, plus the casual language archaeologists used in referring to types, created an intellectual problem in southwestern archaeology. Kidder, for example, discussed different kinds of pottery—referred to by him (e.g., Kidder 1915:453, 1916:122), Kroeber (1916b:36), Nelson (e.g., 1916:162), Spier (e.g., 1917:277), and Wissler (1916a:195) as "styles"—in terms of ancestral-descendant relationships. One pottery type might, for example, "father" another (Kidder 1915:453), and a pottery type might also become "extinct" (Kidder and Kidder 1917:348).

Brew (1946:58) later suggested it was precisely this pottery-nomenclature system that resulted in the " 'family tree' concept of culture classification designed to describe all Southwestern prehistory." The notion of a family tree implies genealogical connectedness, which might sound like a strange notion to apply to inanimate objects, but this is how several southwestern archaeologists chose to view pottery typology. The two chief proponents of this perspective were Hargrave

(1932) and Colton (e.g., 1932). Actually, theirs was not such a strange notion, though what must be remembered is that the ancestral-descendant relationship was between potters and not pots. One of the basic tenets of a scientific, evolutionary archaeology is that artifacts—pots, projectile points, and the like—were once part of human phenotypes in the same way that bird nests and beaver dams are phenotypic (Leonard and Jones 1987; O'Brien and Holland 1995a, 1995b). Culture historians actually came close to making this connection, but the general lack of scientific theory explaining culture change precluded taking the concept in a fruitful direction.

Colton and Hargrave's study of the pottery of northern Arizona, published as *Handbook of Northern Arizona Pottery Wares* (Colton and Hargrave 1937), although ostensibly an attempt to integrate form, space, and time, was a complete break with the tradition of Kroeber, Kidder, Spier, and others. Colton and Hargrave (1937:2–3) defined a pottery *type* as "a group of pottery vessels which are alike in every important characteristic except (possibly) form"; a pottery *ware* as "a group of pottery types which has a majority of [the important] characteristics in common but that differ in others"; and a pottery *series* as "a group of pottery types within a single ware in which each type bears a genetic relation to each other." The problems with such a scheme are immediately apparent and resulted from Colton and Hargrave's conflation of the necessary and sufficient conditions of membership in a class (type, ware, series)—the definition of a class—with interpretations of classes. Thus the difference between type and ware appears to reside in the number of attributes held in common (though *which* attributes is not specified), but the differences between series and type and/or ware resides in the interpretations given them. In addition, there was, of course, no warrant for the genetic interpretation of series. This did not stop Colton and Hargrave from differentiating among derived, collateral, and ancestral types, nor from graphing the relations among the types (Colton and Hargrave 1937:4), similar to what biologists do in cladistic analysis. Their unabashedly biological model of pottery classification is today seen as non-Darwinian in structure (e.g., Neff 1992, 1993).

Colton and Hargrave's contemporaries were not fooled. Their model met considerable resistance and was a short-lived phenomenon. In his review of their handbook, Ford (1940:264) lamented that Colton and Hargrave did not consider "the utility of the types for discovering cultural history." Ford noted that Colton and Hargrave ignored the problem of selecting "a class of features [attributes] which will best reflect cultural influences [transmission via contact; homologous similarity], and which in their various forms will be mutually exclusive, to serve as guides in the process" of determining ancestral-descendant relationships (Ford 1940:265; see also Ford 1938a). These words came easily to Ford because he had recently completed a study (Ford 1936a) in which he had done exactly that: pick a feature, in his case pottery designs, and examine how they changed through time. He decidedly regarded his sequence of designs as evolutionary (see also Reiter 1938).

It is hardly surprising that Colton and Hargrave provided no examples of the genetic relations of their types, because those types were empirical units rather than theoretical ones. They did not develop Kidder's evolutionary speculations into a robust account of the behavior of historical types. To hypothesize that two sets of things are related in an ancestral-descendant fashion demands specification of how that relationship is generated. Lacking archaeological theory, Colton and Hargrave provided no such specification. Thus they were forced to suggest that (a) indigenous pottery will be made of local materials, (b) changes in technology represent changes in "people," and (c) styles of design diffuse (Colton and Hargrave 1937:xii). These suggestions were derived from limited observations of the behaviors of living Puebloan people and reflect the typical, commonsensical approach to culture history.

If groups are made up of members that look more like each other than like things in other groups, then description is an adequate means of characterizing the group. Such description tends to be *extensional,* meaning that things are put in piles based on perceived similarities and dissimilarities, and then an average, or "typical," specimen in each pile is described. The descriptions are extensions of the piles; a description cannot exist for a nonexistent pile. When new specimens come along, they are placed in one pile or another based on the descriptions of the piles, or, if the new specimens are sufficiently different from all known specimens—*sufficiently* being the operative, and highly subjective, word here— a new pile (group) can be created. It follows, then, that groups are extensions of actual specimens, and descriptions are extensions of the groups. In short, no specimens, no groups; conversely, no groups, no descriptions.

Classes, since they are definitional, are not mere extensions of specimens; rather, they are units that are *imposed* on an assemblage of artifacts. Because they are impositional—what Dunnell (1971) termed *intensional*—rather than extensional units, it would be difficult to imagine a situation in which classes were not also theoretical units. The construction of classes derives directly from how an analyst perceives a problem and its solution. Different problems require different solutions; classes used to solve one problem probably will not be applicable to solving another.

The principal reason one might select classification over grouping is because classes are easily manipulable in terms of measuring change. Ford throughout his career was interested in not only measuring change but also interpreting it in terms of cultural effects. He was more successful at some times than at others, especially when he used a system that measured continuous change rather than one that treated change as a discontinuous set of empirical (real) categories. Any system that views change as continuous falls comfortably into the materialist camp, while systems that view change as a series of plateaus separated by natural disjunctions are essentialist. Note that we are not talking about the *tempo* of change, which can be brief and rapid, long and gradual, or anything in between, but rather the *kind* of change. If change is viewed as continuous, it is illogical to employ units that can only deal with disjunctive change. Ford at one point examined minute changes in what he termed pottery "decoration complexes" to develop a chronology for the lower Mississippi Valley—obviously a materialist strategy. He did not refer to his methods as such, though his archaeological procedures, especially when viewed in light of his constant reference to culture as a flowing stream, clearly identify him, at least in this instance, as a materialist. Ironically, though fully understandable when viewed in historical perspective, Ford then turned around and used his units (types), some of which approached being classes because of the rigorous boundaries set for them, to talk about cultures, human groups, and the like. This was not an uncommon occurrence in culture history.

The same criteria used to distinguish groups from classes relative to artifact types applies to other kinds of units such as phases. If phases are truly classes, then the members of a phase (typically called components, assemblages, occupations, etc.) must share one or more unique and definitive traits. If, on the other hand, phases are groups, then the members of a phase are construed as being more similar to one another than to a member of another phase (e.g., Fox 1998). In practice, traits used to create phases are usually some set of in-use historical types shared by phase members. The procedure typically is intuitive, resulting in definitive traits being conflated with traits—other artifact types—that happen to be associated with the diagnostic ones and the entire suite of materials being included within a phase. This results in phases often having both classlike and grouplike properties (e.g., Fox 1998).

In our view, such results have prompted little remark from culture historians largely because of the so-called stratigraphic revolution. Virtually from the birth of the culture-history paradigm, each stratum containing artifacts in a site was perceived as a single occupation (e.g., Wissler 1917a:275; see also Fowke 1922:37). Thus, a component (Colton 1939; McKern 1939; Phillips and Willey 1953) or an assemblage (Spaulding 1955) was not only a manifestation of a phase at a site but also an *occupation*—another conflation of the materialist and essentialist metaphysics. A component consists of "a layer of refuse [read *a stratum*], [an] analysis unit [read *arbitrary level*] [that] comprises all the remains encountered within this division. Hence, it is objective and has *physical reality*" (Rouse 1955:713; emphasis added). The boundaries between strata are geologically real, but their reality in terms of the history of cultural evolution is inferential, though this was not recognized by culture historians. This equation of the geological jointedness of the depositional record and the jointedness of cultural history led Americanist archaeologists to become strongly rooted in the essentialist camp and made phases—like many artifact types—appear to be real and to have properties of both groups and classes. That the phases were nothing more than loosely conceived accidents of depositional history went unrecognized—except by Jim Ford. Not surprisingly, most phases formulated over the past fifty years to compartmentalize the archaeological record of the Mississippi Valley are just such accidents (Fox 1992, 1998; O'Brien 1995; O'Brien and Fox 1994a).

FORD AND THE MATERIALIST-ESSENTIALIST PARADOX

Using the collected works of an individual or a group of individuals to demonstrate a particular point or to illustrate a general history of a discipline is a risky practice, if for no other reason than the facility with which straw men can be constructed. We could, for example, through selective choice, use Charles Darwin's work to show that he was as much of a Lamarckian in outlook as J. B. Lamarck himself, the paramount supporter of the importance of directed variation in biological evolution. Darwin's major contribution—pointing out the central role played in biological evolution by *nondirected* variation, the antithesis of Lamarck's position—could easily be lost or buried. So it is with Jim Ford, whose ideas on such topics seemingly as diverse as cultural evolution and pottery typology—indeed on the proper role of archaeology generally—evolved over time into views that at first glance appear quite different from his original points of departure. Thus for any particular time period we could make Ford look very different than he would appear at another time.

But in a real sense, Ford is the perfect vehicle for examining the rise and fall of culture history. In no one else's work does one find all of the complexities of trying to do culture history laid out so well and in such uncomplicated language. And certainly nowhere else is there clearer representation of what we term the great paradox in Americanist archaeology—the desire to study a materialist subject but to do it using an essentialist strategy. Ironically, the very units that were correctly formulated to deal with time in a materialistic manner were then coopted for use under the essentialist strategy. The paradox ensnared not only culture historians but also those who set out in the 1960s to completely revamp Americanist archaeology from the ground up—a worthwhile endeavor to be sure, but one that was built on ground shakier in some respects than that which supported culture history. This also was ironic, because the proponents of the new movement wanted to be explicitly scientific. As it turned out, they picked the wrong kind of science after which to model the new archaeology, and as a result the paradox remained as strong as ever. Because of culture history's deep interest in time as a focus of study, it at least offered a way out of the great paradox. That culture historians failed to see this—or even to more than occasionally recognize that the paradox existed (Kidder recognized it, as did Brew slightly later)—tells us something important about the minor role that appropriate theory has played in the discipline.

2

Bringing Chronological Order to the Archaeological Record

The Pre-1937 Years

James Alfred Ford, the son of an Illinois Central engineer and a schoolteacher, was born in Water Valley, Mississippi, on February 12, 1911.[1] His father, James Alfred, Sr., died in a railroad accident in 1914, and five years later he and his younger brother, David, and their mother, Janie Johnson Ford, moved to Clinton, Mississippi. He graduated from high school there in 1927. The beginning of Jim Ford's archaeological career can be traced to his high school days in Mississippi, when in 1927 he and fellow classmate Moreau B. Chambers conducted a site survey around Jackson for the Mississippi Department of Archives and History. They continued their work for the department during the summers of 1928 and 1929, eventually meeting Henry B. Collins (Figure 2.1), assistant curator of ethnology in the U.S. National Museum, Smithsonian Institution, who had been invited by the MDAH director, Dunbar Rowland, to undertake archaeological work in the Choctaw region of western Mississippi. It was Collins who solidified Ford's and Chambers's interest in archaeology and taught them the basics of fieldwork—something both sorely needed since they had received no training in archaeology. What Ford and Chambers had been doing for MDAH amounted to what Gordon Willey (1969:62) referred to as "officially sponsored 'pothunting,' traveling from site to site by team and wagon."

1. Various pieces of strictly biographical information on Ford in this and other chapters were extracted from interviews, obituaries (Evans 1968; Haag 1968; Webb 1968b; and Willey 1969), and short biographical sketches (Brown 1978; Willey 1988), including one compiled by Ethel Ford after her husband's death (LSU Museum of Natural Science archives). The obituaries all contain essentially the same information, though the various authors tended to highlight different aspects of Ford's career. Brown (1978) obtained additional information from friends and colleagues of Ford's, and Willey (1988) added recollections based on a long-standing and personal friendship.

Figure 2.1. Photograph of Henry B. Collins, assistant curator of ethnology, U.S. National Museum, Smithsonian Institution, ca. 1930 (negative no. 11,033-A; photograph courtesy National Anthropological Archives, Smithsonian Institution).

Collins, himself a Mississippian, had conducted extensive fieldwork in the Arctic and was fast establishing himself as one of the leading authorities in the prehistory of that region. By the time he began his Mississippi Valley fieldwork in 1925, Louisiana and Mississippi had witnessed decades of investigation by prehistorians and antiquarians such as Cyrus Thomas (1894), Charles Peabody (1904), Clarence B. Moore (1905, 1908, 1911, 1912, 1913), David I. Bushnell, Jr. (1919), and Gerard B. Fowke (1927, 1928). Despite all of this work, much of which we would also label as "officially sponsored pothunting," Collins was forced to admit that certain sections of the lower Mississippi Valley, including coastal Louisiana, were virtually unknown archaeologically:

> This section of Louisiana is but slightly above sea level and consists for the most part of great stretches of marsh, habitable only along the narrow ridges of comparatively high land that border the many lakes and bayous. It is not a region which might be expected to have supported either a large or a very highly developed aboriginal population, and yet unmistakable evidence was found that in pre-Columbian times

Indians had lived here in considerable numbers, and that some of them possessed a culture closely allied or identical in general to that found throughout the widespread mound area to the east and north. (Collins 1927b:78)

The primary reason for the unknown nature of the archaeological record of southern Louisiana, and in fact of most of the Gulf Coast, was that no one with much knowledge of archaeology had ever been particularly interested in the region. This was not atypical of vast portions of the South in the late 1920s, including the lower Mississippi Valley. Despite the long-standing interest in that region on the part of prehistorians, there had been little in the way of sustained activity. Scattered surveys and excavations had been undertaken by northern institutions—the Smithsonian Institution (Thomas 1894) and Phillips Academy (Peabody 1904), for example. Field parties had massive amounts of ground to cover and usually relied on the opinions of local informants for the best places to search for artifacts. Coverage thus was spotty and unsystematic. Given what these early investigators found in select areas—northeastern Arkansas, for example—it is no wonder areas such as the Gulf Coast, which is not exactly the most inviting place to work, were left untouched. To really understand the work that Collins, and, a few years later, Ford, carried out, requires a basic understanding of what came before it.

EARLY ARCHAEOLOGICAL EXPLORATION IN THE MISSISSIPPI VALLEY

When Collins began his fieldwork in Mississippi, barely three decades had passed since Cyrus Thomas (1894) had published the final report of his massive effort to record mounds and other earthworks across the eastern United States. That effort in many respects drove the final nail in the coffin of the pseudo-scientific belief that the American Indian had succeeded in vanquishing a race of people responsible for constructing the tens of thousands of mounds and other earthen monuments that dotted the eastern states. After 1880, massive evidence started pouring in that demonstrated the Indians and the mound builders were one and the same.

In 1879 the Bureau of Ethnology (the name was changed to the Bureau of American Ethnology in 1894) was founded within the Smithsonian Institution, and John Wesley Powell was selected as director. The Division of Mound Exploration was formed within the bureau in 1881, and the following year Cyrus Thomas was appointed as its head. From the start, Powell's mandate from Congress was to solve the problem of who built the mounds. By the time Thomas was appointed to head the division, he, like Powell, was convinced that the mound builders were American Indians. In 1884 he wrote, " 'Who were the mound-builders?' We answer unhesitatingly, Indians—the ancestors of some, perhaps of several of the tribes of modern or historic times" (Thomas 1884:90). Thomas published the "Report on the Mound Explorations of the Bureau of Ethnology" in the *Twelfth Annual Report of the Bureau of Ethnology, 1890–1891* (Thomas 1894), and in it he discussed in great detail the mound explorations carried out by his crews as they worked their way over two dozen Eastern states, including Louisiana and Mississippi.

Thomas's report has been called the birth of modern American archaeology (e.g., Jennings 1974:39), though this may be an overstatement. Prior to the Division of Mound Exploration's founding, archaeology was primarily an antiquarian activity—interest was placed on artifacts and earthen monuments themselves rather than on using such things as a means to other ends. The work summarized by Thomas (1894) had been done to solve a particular problem and demanded rigor in how materials and information were gathered. Most site discussions in the final report were accompanied by plan views of the earthworks and surrounding archaeological and physiographic features. Despite the detail shown, many of the maps are problematic. Thomas's field party in Louisiana had little impact on the archaeology of the state, mapping and excavating at only two sites, the most prominent of which was Troyville, in Catahoula Parish (Figure 2.2).

In contrast to Thomas's limited work in the lower Mississippi Valley, another easterner, Clarence B. Moore, spent four field seasons between 1908 and 1917 in the central Mississippi Valley exploring mounds along the Mississippi and also along the Yazoo and Sunflower Rivers in western Mississippi, the St. Francis, White, and Black Rivers in eastern Arkansas, and several drainages in Louisiana. Moore, independently wealthy and a tireless researcher, carried with him on his sternwheeler a complete excavation team and a physician to analyze the skeletal material recovered. For a quarter century or so—a period stretching from the 1890s to the second decade of the twentieth century—Moore explored southern rivers and bayous in search of burial mounds, in the process excavating several thousand skeletons and recovering countless ceramic vessels and other artifacts. He sponsored his own fieldwork and underwrote the production costs of twenty reports dealing with the excavations, which appeared in the *Journal of the Academy of Natural Sciences of Philadelphia*. The reports are rather sketchy, but the accompanying field photographs and artifact illustrations are excellent.

Robert Neuman (1984:38) went through Moore's reports and tallied 104 sites in Louisiana that were visited by his team between 1908 and 1917. Drainages examined included the Red, Ouachita, Tensas, and Atchafalaya Rivers, Bayou Bartholomew, and Bayou Maçon. Moore did not excavate at every site he visited, adopting the tack of opening pits only where he thought there was a good chance of finding artifacts and burials. Perhaps more important than his excavations were the site descriptions—the number of mounds present, for example—many of which have subsequently been damaged or destroyed through agricultural and other land-modifying activities.

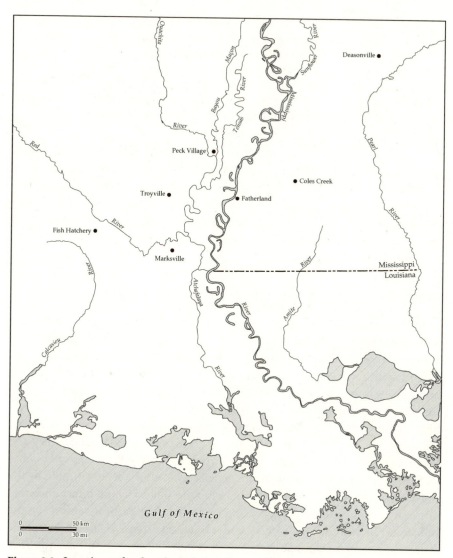

Figure 2.2. Locations of archaeological sites discussed in the text.

Even in Moore's day, pot hunting was taking a tremendous toll on archaeological resources. In 1910 Moore wrote the following comment about commercially motivated looting along the St. Francis River in northeastern Arkansas:

As the St. Francis (with the possible exception of the Mississippi, a river very many times the length of the St. Francis) long has had the reputation of being richer in aboriginal earthenware than is any other river in the United States, the territory through which the river passes has been for years the headquarters for collectors and for persons wishing to make a livelihood or to increase their means by the sale of Indian pottery, and these individuals have worked for long periods and with indefatigable zeal. Moreover, vast numbers of vessels have been destroyed along the St. Francis in the process of cultivation of cemeteries in which they lay, while others have been dug out or have been shattered in the digging by unskilled local endeavor. Consequently the limitations of the scientific worker along St. Francis river at the present time are apparent. (Moore 1910:259)

At the Parkin site, a large, Late Mississippian–period village in Cross County, Arkansas, Moore (1910:303) noted that "The Lumber Company, which later had acquired the property on which the cemetery is, and erected a sawmill nearby, in dull times when the mill was closed, permitted its employees to eke out a livelihood by digging for pots, and this became the avocation of many. Men were actually seen by us at Parkin walking around with sounding-rods in their hands, as elsewhere they might carry canes."

HENRY B. COLLINS AND THE DIRECT HISTORICAL APPROACH

It is clear from his brief reports on work conducted in Mississippi and Louisiana in 1925–1926 (Collins 1926, 1927a, 1927b) that Collins not only was interested in temporal differences among artifacts from various sites in the lower Mississippi Valley but also was very familiar with a practice that had become commonplace in the Southwest: anchoring chronological sequences in the near past and then working backward in time. This method later became known as the direct-historical approach, popularized in the writings of William Duncan Strong (e.g., 1935) and Waldo Wedel (e.g., 1938) in the 1930s, though as Gordon Willey and Jeremy Sabloff (1993:126) note, "the basic principle behind it is almost as old as archaeology." It certainly underlay the nineteenth-century demonstration by the Bureau of American Ethnology that the mound builders were direct ancestors of the American Indians, not an extinct race that had been driven out *by* the Indians (O'Brien and Lyman 1997), and it was used extensively in the Southwest as a starting point for chronological constructions. The direct-historical approach was, of course, applicable only in those areas with sufficient historical detail to allow one to relate excavated prehistoric materials to known ethnic groups.

In Mississippi, Collins relied on pottery for his analysis:

Archaeological research in the southeastern states can probably never reach the point of exactness that it has in the Southwest. There are no stone ruins, and barring a few exceptional kitchen middens along the coasts, no extensive refuse heaps showing successive culture layers. The climate, furthermore, is not such as to preserve textiles, basketry, wood-work or other perishable objects so that about all that is now left of the once high material culture of the Southern tribes is the pottery and the ornaments and implements of stone, shell, and bone. It is very desirable, therefore, to seize upon every available source of tribal identification of the cultures represented, and to accomplish this end there is probably no safer beginning than to locate the historic Indian village sites and to study their type of cultural remains for comparison with other sites of unknown age. (Collins 1927a:259–60).

Collins (1927a) identified what he referred to as "types" of Choctaw pottery, though his reference was casual in the sense that *type* was used as a synonym for *kind*, with no definitive indication of what a particular type might include. The most noticeable attribute of sherds from the two sites he collected—Chickachae in Clarke County and Ponta in Lauderdale County—was the presence of multiple 5- to 10-mm-wide trailed lines that had been made by a comblike instrument dragged across the surface of a vessel prior to firing. Collins (1927a:262) noticed that the mean width of the lines was larger on sherds from Chickachae than on Ponta sherds, but he did not comment further, noting instead that except for "these slight variations, however, the ware from the two sites is identical." He found similarly decorated pottery at known Choctaw sites in three other Mississippi counties, leading him to note that

> The presence of this single type of pottery of decorated ware from such widely separated Choctaw settlements, covering the entire area known to have been occupied by that tribe, suggests very strongly that it was the prevailing type of pottery in use at some period of their history. It may safely be regarded as historic, in the sense that it is found thus far only at Choctaw sites known to have been occupied as late as the 19th century, but further than this its age cannot at present be determined. (Collins 1927a:263)

Collins's comment implies (a) a pottery type designates an ethnic group such as a tribe, (b) ethnic groups have histories, and (c) a pottery type designates a specific period in the history of an ethnic group. If pottery types can be equated with ethnic groups, then such types are emic units and probably essentialist units as well. Keep these implications in mind in the following discussion.

Deasonville

Collins was interested in the origin of the pottery, as Ford was several years later: had it "developed locally" (Collins 1927a:263), or did it have its origins to the west? Was there even an earlier occupancy of Choctaw territory by some other tribe? To answer these questions, Collins (1927a:263) noted that it "would be very desirable . . . to have additional collections of pottery from other known Choctaw village sites and from the little known mounds and unidentified sites of central and western Mississippi." One site that provided additional collections was Deasonville, which Ford and Chambers had found during their survey (Figure 2.2). Collins, Ford, and Chambers spent a week in December 1929 and three days the following December excavating a small part of the site and, despite the short excavation period, were able to uncover the outlines of three round structures. If one were forced to pick a particular piece of work as the point at which culture history in the lower Mississippi Valley was born, Collins's (1932a) analysis of Deasonville could arguably serve that purpose. What Collins had to say heavily influenced Ford's thinking. Ford not only participated in the fieldwork at Deasonville, but between the two brief excavation periods he served as Collins's archaeological assistant in Alaska. Thus Ford undoubtedly knew what Collins would put in the report long before it appeared.

Deasonville probably looked very similar to dozens of other sites that Collins, Ford, and Chambers had seen in western Mississippi, and unfortunately Collins didn't explain why it was chosen for excavation. He made it clear, however, that he was not particularly interested in excavating yet another mound, noting that "there are other remains—Indian village sites—which promise to yield data that will be of considerable value when Southeastern archeology comes finally to be synthesized and interpreted" (Collins 1932a:1). Collins found what he was looking for. Using a combination of hand shoveling and mule-drawn scraping, he uncovered three wall-trench structures—apparently the first such structures found in the Southeast (Collins 1932a:8). Collins was attempting to interpret and explain the archaeological phenomena he found, and he used ethnographic analogy—an important tool of cultural reconstructionists/processualists three decades later—in his attempt. He dedicated considerable space in his report to a survey of ethnographic accounts of aboriginal house structures of the Cherokee, Choctaw, Creek, Chickasaw, Tunica, and Natchez to determine whether there was a match with the Deasonville structures. Although he found some similarities, he stated that "on the basis of the present evidence no definite conclusion seems to be warranted" (Collins 1932a:12).

It was the pottery from Deasonville, however, that received the lion's share of Collins's attention. The excavation, limited though it was, produced a large sample of sherds, but in order to gauge the "relative proportions of the various types of ware represented," Collins (1932a:12) had his crew pick up "every sherd on and between three cotton rows for a distance of about 100 feet" (Collins 1932a:12). This surely was the first attempt at systematic surface sampling ever employed in the region. Sherds in both the excavated and surface-collected samples were described in the report, but Collins, perhaps realizing that numerous sherds had been missed during the hurried excavation, reported frequencies of only the surface-collected sherds. He recognized seven pottery types, or what he referred to as "kinds of wares" (Table 2.1). The classification system Collins employed was largely extensional, meaning it was created out of the sherds he had available from the site, though the terms he used to create the categories were well established. It seems probable that Collins took many of the terms from Carl E. Guthe's widely circulated "A Method of Ceramic Description" (Guthe 1928). Unlike Collins, Guthe defined such terms as *ware*—a group of pots or sherds that exhibit "fundamental similarity"—*style*—pots or sherds that exhibit "superficial similarity"—and *type*—"a large generic group." Unfortunately, Guthe did not elaborate on those definitions, though one gets the feeling that he had in mind some of what Kidder, Nelson, and others were suggesting with respect to southwestern pottery.

The seven "kinds of ware"—undecorated, cordmarked, painted, incised on the rim, incised on the body, punctated, and rouletted/stamped—were further subdivided by vessel shape (bowl or jar), paste (texture, color, and temper), surface treatment (finish and color), decoration, and rim treatment (shape and decoration). In many respects, Collins's matrix (Table 2.1) approached a paradigmatic structure (Dunnell 1971). Although he was not entirely clear in the report, it is obvious that his categories "paste color" and "surface color" were separate entities—the first referring to the color of a sherd's interior and the latter to the color of a sherd's surface—as was his inclusion of painting as decoration.

In 1932 the binomial system of pottery categorization was still several years away from being introduced into the Southeast, but one can easily translate between several of Collins's kinds of wares and later-named types. This shouldn't be too surprising since Collins was using the same technological and decorative features to create his units that Ford and others would eventually use to create types. For example, Collins (1932a:16) described a variety of incised ware having

> one to four—usually two—parallel incised lines encircling the vessel immediately below the rim. Some of the sherds have also a line incised along the top of the rim. Most of the lines below the rim are somewhat deep and were made by trailing a sharp stick held straight against the side of the vessel. . . . In some cases, however, the implement had been held with the point toward the rim, resulting in a somewhat wider and beveled line, deeper at the top and having an "overhanging" appearance.

Even without looking at the illustrated sherds, one would quickly realize this description applies to the decoration Ford (1935c, 1936a) used as the basis of his Coles Creek complex and which he (Ford 1951a; Ford et al. 1955) and others (e.g., Phillips 1970; Phillips et al. 1951) subsequently referred to as Coles Creek Incised.

Collins recognized that the incised design was restricted to the rim of vessels, and thus he commented that "it may be regarded as certain that a number of the undecorated sherds, which are identical in color, surface finish, paste, and tempering, were from vessels having this simple incised decoration restricted to the region of the rim" (Collins 1932a:16). This point would be raised in subsequent discussions of pottery categorization in the Mississippi Valley (e.g., Phillips et al. 1951), but Collins, like archaeologists who followed him, had as his primary purpose the creation of categories that would help measure the passage of time. Decorated sherds were the focus of analysis because decoration was seen to have changed over time; undecorated sherds were usually counted and then shunted aside.

Table 2.1. Pottery-Classification System Used by Henry B. Collins for Sherds from the Deasonville Site, Yazoo County, Mississippi

Kinds of Wares	Shape of Vessels	Paste			Surface		Decoration	Rims	
		Texture	Color	Temper	Finish	Color		Shape	Decoration
Undecorated	Bowls and jars	Coarse	Gray, black, or reddish	Pulverized potsherds	Usually smooth	Drab gray or light brown		Straight or slightly incurved	Occasionally a line on top
Cordmarked	Jars	ditto	Buff, gray, or black	ditto	Cordmarked	Light brown to dark gray	Cord impressions	Straight or slightly incurved (seldom everted)	
Painted	Conical and rounded bowls	Fine	Blue-gray	Pulverized mussel shells	Smooth	Red, white, and gray	Alternating red and white bands and scallops	Enlarged; slightly overhanging on both sides	Usually painted red
Incised (rim only)	Bowls and jars	Coarse	Gray, black, or reddish	Pulverized potsherds	Usually smooth	Gray or brown	Band of lines below rim	Straight or slightly incurving	Occasionally a line on top
Incised (body of vessel)		Usually fine; some porous	Light brown or gray	Pulverized mussel shells (some vegetable fiber)	Somewhat rough	Buff or cream	Straight and curved lines over body of vessel	Straight, incurved, and everted	Looped handles
Punctated		ditto	ditto	ditto	ditto	ditto	Punctations, usually in bands	Usually everted	ditto
Roulette or stamped		Fine	Gray	Pulverized mussel shells			Rouletted or finely stamped area inclosed deep lines		

Data from Collins (1932a).

In beginning the section of his Deasonville report entitled "Distribution of the Pottery Types," Collins echoed a point he had made earlier (Collins 1927a):

> The most important immediate problem of Southeastern archaeology is to establish a basis for a chronology of prehistoric sites. From the fragmentary nature of the evidence this will have to be for the most part a disjointed and patchwork chronology, far less perfect and comprehensive than that which has been worked out in other areas. . . . The most valuable material for this purpose is pottery; and broken fragments, if sufficiently numerous, are very nearly as useful as whole vessels, or even more so if the latter should not happen to include the entire range of types present. (Collins 1932a:17–18)

Ford would use virtually identical wording in his writings—chronological control was paramount, and pottery provided the requisite data.

The way in which Collins went about using the pottery from Deasonville to create a chronological ordering was innovative. He had already identified what he considered to be Choctaw pottery (Collins 1927a), characterized by multiple 5- to 10-mm-wide trailed lines made by a comblike instrument. The pottery he identified as Choctaw might also extend back before the nineteenth century— Collins as yet had no way of knowing this—but there was little doubt in his mind that it could be identified with that ethnic group. By the time Collins was writing the Deasonville report, Ford and Chambers had succeeded in locating what appeared to be Natchez and Tunica sites in western Mississippi, including what became known as the Fatherland site, or the Grand Village of the Natchez, in Adams County, Mississippi (Neitzel 1965) (Figure 2.2). Collins (1932a:18) thus was able to use these additional data as "comparative references" in the Deasonville report—data that figured prominently in his chronological positioning of the site.

Collins began his discussion of chronological ordering by noting, "Red and white painted ware was the most characteristic single type of decorated pottery found at the Deasonville site" (Collins 1932a:18). He noted that Moore (1911) had found similarly decorated pottery in Warren, Bolivar, and Tunica Counties in western Mississippi, though it was more common in eastern Arkansas and north- eastern Louisiana (Moore 1910). Collins also observed, "European material was found by Moore at several of the sites from which came the red and white painted pottery" (Collins 1932a:18). Collins's assessment of the spatial distribution of red-and-white vessels was essentially correct: they occur more frequently north of the mouth of the Arkansas River (southeastern Arkansas) than in areas to the south, and there is a geographic division of vessel shapes. North of the Arkansas River, bowls and bottles are common, but to the south vessel shape is restricted almost entirely to everted-rim bowls identical to those Collins described from Deasonville.

Collins then turned his attention to the incised sherds from Deasonville, noting, "This is a style of decoration which Ford and Chambers have found to be characteristic of certain prehistoric sites in western Mississippi *as distinguished from near-by historic sites of the Natchez and Tunica*" (Collins 1932a:19; emphasis added). This is where Ford and Chambers's data became so important: the data demonstrated that sherds containing the overhanging incised lines did not occur on sites known from ethnographic sources to have been inhabited by the Tunica or Natchez, the latter group's pottery exhibiting a "usually polished surface and scroll or meander design" (Collins 1932a:19). Nor were there at Deasonville any sherds of Choctaw ware, "which is characterized by straight or curving bands of very fine lines applied with a comblike implement [Collins 1927a], or of Tunica ware, in which the decoration consists of somewhat enlarged rims bearing indentations or scallops together with a single encircling line along the top" (Collins 1932a:19).

Given (a) the absence of pottery that had been found associated with known groups, (b) the absence of European items, and (c) "the presence of another type [the one with horizontal, overhanging incised lines] which at other Mississippi sites appears just as definitely prehistoric," Collins (1932a:19) made the obvious conclusion: Deasonville was a prehistoric site. But he wasn't sure how old the site was: "Study of the potsherds from Deasonville fails to reveal any clues which might be of value as showing the chronological position of the site beyond the mere fact that it is prehistoric" (Collins 1932a:19). He commented further, "We must know . . . much more about the geographical range of the various types of Southeastern pottery and the relative position occupied by each, and especially we must know which types are found associated with European material and which types are never found in such association" (Collins 1932a:20). For some reason it never occurred to Collins—or if it did, he abandoned the thought—that he had evidence right in front of him that would have given him a clue to the antiquity of the site.

Given that he knew his painted pottery from Deasonville was similar to that which Moore had found, and given that he had already pointed out that Moore had recovered European items from some of the same sites, why didn't Collins take the next obvious step and remark that perhaps his painted-pottery type was a fairly late occurrence, though not as late as the pottery of the historic Natchez, Tunica, and Choctaw? We'll never know, though part of the answer might lie in how Collins— and he certainly wasn't alone—viewed chronology and site occupation. It is clear that to Collins, prehistoric peoples inhabited sites for fairly short periods of time and then abandoned them. He never came right out and said it, but nonetheless it is apparent that he dichotomized between prehistoric and historical-period sites, with little or nothing in between. In this all-or-nothing game, a site either had sherds left by the Natchez, Choctaw, or Tunica, or it had sherds left by prehistoric groups. This rings of essentialist thinking. Perhaps it never occurred to Collins that sites could span both periods—such as some of Moore's Arkansas sites that contained painted pottery and European trade goods—or perhaps he completely dismissed it. We suspect he was so firmly grounded in essentialism that sherds were either early or late; there was no intermediate position.

Later, when we begin to examine some of Ford's notions on how long sites were occupied and whether sites were ever "reoccupied," keep in mind that much of what he knew he learned from his early mentor. Ford took chronological construction in the Southeast to new heights, but he carried with him several biases picked up from Collins. The notion of multi-occupation wasn't in the vocabulary of southeastern archaeologists. For the most part, time was viewed as a continuum against which little discontinuous blips—occupations—could be placed. Unlike their colleagues working in the Southwest, archaeologists in the Southeast had not yet begun to carve up time into ceramic periods or other, similar units. This situation, however, would soon change, and the chief architect would be Jim Ford.

BACK FROM ALASKA

By the time Collins's Deasonville report appeared in 1932, Ford was set to return from an eighteen-month stint in Alaska, his second trip north. Not much is known of this period in Ford's life, but based on the letters he wrote back to Collins at the Smithsonian and to Chambers and his mother in Mississippi, he enjoyed the rigors of a harsh life where existence depended on getting along with the local inhabitants and making friends with ship captains, whom you hoped would see you safely from one remote stop to the next. Still, Ford was only twenty years old, and Collins and the Smithsonian administration stayed in fairly constant contact not only with him but also with his mother, even to the point of seeking her permission for her son to remain in Alaska.[2]

When the weather precluded excavation, Ford turned to collecting natural-history specimens for the Smithsonian, one of which is shown in Figure 2.3. Ford wrote in a letter to Collins:

> My only notable achievement since the last letter has been to go whaling and catch a whale. As the natives could bring the carcass very near the beach to cut it up, I was able to drag the skull and lower jaws ashore and so save them to science and future generations. He was a big fellow, larger than average. Would like to bring it out on the cutter so perhaps you had best begin pulling strings. I'm afraid there is going to be some objection because that skull is really big—twenty feet long at least. It will have to be carried on the quarter deck and you know how these Coast Guard captains are about their quarter decks.[3]

Ford returned to Mississippi late in 1932. He had attended Mississippi College on an intermittent basis since graduating from high school in 1927, but in 1933 he

2. Letter from Wetmore to Janie Ford, August 26, 1931 (LSU Museum of Natural Science archives).

3. Letter from Ford to Collins, October 22, 1931 (LSU Museum of Natural Science archives).

Figure 2.3. Photograph of James A. Ford in the West Court of the National Museum of Natural History, Smithsonian Institution, examining the whale skull he brought back from Alaska in 1932. Parenthetically, Henry Collins, in 1963, provided some interesting information on the man looking out the window at Ford, which was added to the back of the photograph. His name was Riley Moore, "an osteopath who worked for awhile in Physical Anthropology in 1912 circa and then in later years (30's) came to Museum each Wednesday to tell everyone what a terrible [g]uy Hrdlicka was." Aleš Hrdlička dominated the field of skeletal biology during the first several decades of the twentieth century (negative no. 72–8412; photograph courtesy National Anthropological Archives, Smithsonian Institution).

dropped out, opting to apply for and receive (with the support of Collins and others in the Bureau of American Ethnology) a grant-in-aid from the National Research Council to continue the survey he and Chambers had started six years earlier, this time concentrating on sites in Louisiana. In his letter to A. T. Poffenberger, chairman of the Division of Anthropology and Psychology at the NRC, Neil Judd of the Division of Archeology in the U.S. National Museum noted that "Mr. Ford is peculiarly fitted to pursue serious investigations. Indeed, he is one of a very limited number, resident in the South, prepared to carry on researches helpful to students of prehistory; his approach is from the historical side, a fact of supreme importance."[4]

4. Letter of March 24, 1933, from Judd to Poffenberger (National Anthropological Archives).

In Ford's one-page proposal to the NRC, he stated his intention of locating sites in five parishes in north-central Louisiana and four counties in western Mississippi. Surface collections were to be made at the sites, and several were to receive excavation. His research design was short and to the point: "The determination of an archaeological chronology in this area would outline the prehistory of the Lower Mississippi Valley area and doubtless, through intrusive culture elements, would throw some light on neighboring Southeastern areas. The position of the 'Hopewell' pottery in such a chronology would tie the Upper and Lower Mississippi Valley cultural sequences together and might indicate the origin of the 'Hopewell' people who seem to have been intrusive in Ohio."[5] Ford figured $750 would see him through the project, but he wound up with only $500—still, not a bad sum for those days and enough to complete the work.

In the end, Ford conducted site surveys in more than the nine parishes and counties indicated, and he concentrated his excavation efforts on Peck Village, in Catahoula Parish (Figure 2.2)—a site that figured importantly in Ford's views of how pottery could be used as time markers. Since Ford did not begin publishing his reports until 1935—about a year and a half after he completed the fieldwork—we will delay discussion of that work and focus in the meantime on another project with which he was involved and another person who undoubtedly had a significant influence on his thinking.

FRANK M. SETZLER AND THE MARKSVILLE SITE

That person was Frank M. Setzler (Figure 2.4), assistant curator of archaeology at the National Museum and a scholar on Ohio Hopewell. He had studied archaeology first at Ohio State University and then at the University of Chicago, where he received an undergraduate degree in 1928 (Herskovits 1950). The lack of an advanced degree apparently was little or no hindrance to his professional standing. He advanced through several levels at the National Museum, becoming curator in 1937. He was secretary of the American Anthropological Association from 1937 to 1940, president of the Anthropological Society of Washington from 1940 to 1942, and anthropology representative to the National Research Council from 1940 to 1942. Setzler was intimately familiar with the work of prehistorians such as Warren Moorehead and Henry Shetrone and had viewed firsthand the artifacts that had come out of the southern Ohio mounds.

Given Setzler's knowledge of and interest in Hopewell, it was natural for the museum to dispatch him to Louisiana in early 1933 when Shreveport architect Edward F. Neild reported that sites in the northern part of the state had produced

---

5. Application of Ford to the National Research Council (undated but written in early March 1933) (National Anthropological Archives).

Figure 2.4. Photograph of Frank M. Setzler, assistant curator of archaeology at the U.S. National Museum, excavating at the Marksville site, Avoyelles Parish, Louisiana, 1933 (photograph courtesy Louisiana State University Museum of Natural Science).

sherds with elaborate designs similar to those on pots from the Ohio Valley. One site was Marksville, in Avoyelles Parish (Figure 2.2). Even in 1933, after decades of excavation and pillaging (it sometimes was difficult to separate the two), Marksville was an impressive site. It contained at least twenty mounds and three linear earthworks spread out in the bottomland and on the bluff along Old River, a former channel of the Red River. In 1926, as part of his Smithsonian-sponsored survey of the Red River valley, Gerard Fowke had spent three months excavating mounds in the Marksville vicinity and constructing a map of the earthworks. His detailed description of the area is informative in light of subsequent modifications made to it:

> The largest and most complicated group of ancient remains in the State is located from a mile to 2 miles eastwardly from Marksville. . . . They reach for more than a mile along Old River. . . . The inclosures or embankments, the lodge sites, and some of the mounds are on the bluff; other mounds are on ground subject to floods. . . .
>
> The most conspicuous feature of the group is the large inclosure. . . . It forms an irregular curve, the ends resting on the bayou bluff. . . . Its total length is almost 3,300 feet; the height ranges from less than 3 to nearly 7 feet for most of its length. . . .
>
> An outside moat . . . borders the outside of the wall for its entire extent. (Fowke 1928:411–12)

Fowke knew what he was looking for at Marksville. He bypassed the flat-topped mounds, which, aside from the enclosures, were the most prominent features at the site, and concentrated on what he assumed were conical burial mounds. The mounds he excavated contained a number of what appeared to be wood-lined burial pits, though few of the pits in one mound actually contained much in the way of skeletal material. Of much more importance than human remains were the pottery vessels that came from mounds 4 and 8 because they bore designs strikingly similar to those on vessels from the Scioto, Muskingam, and neighboring drainages of southern Ohio—a region that by 1933 was widely regarded as the heartland of "Hopewell culture." Named for earthworks on the M. C. Hopewell farm near Chillicothe, Ohio, excavated by Warren K. Moorehead (1922) and Henry C. Shetrone (1927), Hopewell sites by the late 1920s had produced artifact inventories that rivaled any in North America—copper axes and celts, copper-covered wooden tubes and earspools, drilled grizzly-bear canines, pearls, large obsidian blades, sheets of mica cut into figures, and the like. Above all, sites assigned to the Hopewell culture contained pottery jars and bowls with intricate stamped and/or incised designs on the exteriors, often in the shape of raptorial birds or spoonbills. When similar pottery turned up in northern Louisiana, there was reason to look into the matter further.

Setzler and others were well aware of what Fowke had uncovered at Marksville, though ironically, Fowke never mentioned any similarity between the pottery from Marksville and that from southern Ohio. Surely, as Neuman (1984:140) and others have speculated, Fowke, who had spent considerable time working in Ohio, recognized the similarities, but if he did, they went unmentioned. Setzler, after his return from Louisiana and perhaps spurred on in part by John Swanton, his National Museum colleague who in 1930 had found more Hopewell-like pottery at Marksville while examining the open trenches left by Fowke (Setzler 1933b), published two articles on the pottery from Marksville—a short one entitled "Hopewell Type Pottery from Louisiana" (Setzler 1933a) and a longer piece entitled "Pottery of the Hopewell Type from Louisiana" (Setzler 1933b). The articles focused on Fowke's vessels, which were housed at the National Museum, with lesser attention paid to other artifacts from the site.

Setzler's (1933b) longer paper is of considerable interest because it obviously had an influence on Ford. In the first paragraph, Setzler noted that his paper, "which includes a detailed description and a comparative study of the pottery from Marksville, may offer a clue regarding the *migration* and development of the northern Hopewell culture" (emphasis added). Setzler, in the fashion of the time (e.g., Steward 1929), believed that the *only* way vessels from the Ohio Valley could contain virtually the same decorations as vessels from the Red River valley of Louisiana was by direct contact: "Independent invention of so complicated a technique of decoration where there is such striking similarity would seem improbable" (Setzler 1933b:6). But which way did the contact run—north to south, or south to north? This is the way Setzler posed the question:

> Either the pottery was carried into the South by the northern Hopewell Indians themselves or else it reached the region through trade. Definite evidence of contact between the North and South is found in the northern Hopewell mounds. This consists of tortoise shells, barracuda jaws, and other articles from the Gulf. On the other hand, the Hopewell Indians and their characteristic culture could have originated in the South and spread or migrated to the northern Mississippi States. The former would imply a northern origin for the decorative technique; the latter, a southern. If the latter hypothesis were true, we should expect to find a relationship between this technique and other southern pottery decorations. . . . Also, presuming the Hopewellians used pottery before the southern or Marksville type spread to the North, we might expect to find in the northern mounds a type of ware, different from the typical Hopewell vessels, that had been used before the intrusion of a southern type. Up to the present time there is no such evidence, so far as the writer is aware. Future investigations may prove that the Hopewell culture in the North is an amalgamation of certain characteristics—mound building, pottery, barracuda jaws, tortoise shells—derived both by trade and contact from the South and a definite group of characteristics—realistically carved stone pipes, copper, and obsidian—which originated with and were developed by the Hopewell people themselves. (Setzler 1933b:6)

Setzler's discussion revealed an essentialist leaning typical of the time—cultures migrate, pottery styles are ethnically distinctive, and so on. To this point, he was ambiguous about whether the influence ran north to south or south to north. But then he delivered the punch line:

> Although there is not so much evidence of trade from North to South as *vice versa,* these vessels, nevertheless, might have been traded into the South. Yet this would hardly account for the variations from typical Hopewell decorations at Marksville, which have been reported from the North. Even though the direction of spread is not entirely clear, there seems to be an adequate basis for some correlation based on pottery alone. The study made later in this paper would seem to show that in comparison with other ceramic ornamentation in the Southeast the Hopewell style of decoration is not so outstanding nor so highly developed as it is when contrasted with the pottery from other cultures in the upper Mississippi Valley. (Setzler 1933b:6–7)

What Setzler was getting at is this: the contrast between Ohio Hopewell pottery and pottery from the upper Mississippi Valley was more impressive than the contrast between the decorated pottery from Marksville and that from other areas of the greater Southeast. The implication was clear: the fairly widespread distribution of elaborately decorated pottery in the Southeast and its concentration in only a few areas of the upper Mississippi Valley signaled that the Southeast was the center that produced the pottery. Southern peoples then contributed either the vessels or the ideas for making and decorating the vessels to their northern neighbors.

The notion of a south-to-north spread of Hopewellian pottery designs along with a few other "basic Hopewellian elements" (Setzler 1940) had an impact on Ford, who by the early 1940s (e.g., Ford and Willey 1941) regularly referred to the northern movement of a people carrying such elements with them. Later, this notion became even more firmly fixed in Ford's mind, so much so that by the 1950s (e.g., Ford et al. 1955; Ford and Webb 1956) he visualized a reverse flow of the same people back down the Mississippi Valley. In 1933 the movement of peoples up or down the valley perhaps had not yet become much of an issue to Ford, who was busy looking for sites in Louisiana as part of his work sponsored by the National Research Council. It was also during the summer of that year that he undertook his brief though extremely important excavation of Peck Village.

In the spring of 1933 it appeared that the archaeological potential of the Marksville site would be lost to the enthusiasm of local residents for its potential as a park and recreation center. The town had by then put up money toward purchasing the area and had secured funds from the Federal Emergency Relief Administration (FERA) to assist in the project. The United States was in the midst of the Great Depression, and no place was hit harder than the Deep South. People were out of work, businesses were closing, and anything that could be done to spur the local economy was seen as a godsend. As Lyon (1996:1–4) relates, the Smithsonian became alarmed at the townspeople's growing interest in "restoring" the mounds to their original grandeur. In an apparent moment of calm, both the Marksville city council and the local FERA office asked the Smithsonian to send a representative to oversee the restoration and to conduct excavations. Neil Judd dispatched Setzler to Marksville, where he arrived on August 22, 1933 (Setzler 1934:38). Upon the recommendation of Henry Collins, Setzler hired Ford as his field assistant (Figure 2.5), and in November Ford became excavations supervisor after Setzler returned to Washington (Setzler 1934:38).

The details of the excavation have no particular bearing on our story, and we would urge the interested reader to consult Toth (1974) for a discussion of the work conducted by Setzler and Ford. It might seem strange to consult a secondary source for details of an excavation conducted three decades earlier, but the truth is that until recently, it was doubtful that a report was ever written on the work. Setzler started to prepare one—Ford (1936b:279) referenced a manuscript by Setzler entitled "Marksville: A Louisiana Variant of the Hopewell Culture"—but he never finished it. Ford, however, borrowed the unfinished manuscript—a compilation of notes is a better term—from Setzler in 1961, hoping to turn to that project at a later date. He never finished it before his death, but he did provide detailed information about one of the mounds that was excavated (Kuttruff et al. 1997). A year after fieldwork was completed, Setzler (1934) published a two-page synopsis in *Explorations and Field-Work of the Smithsonian Institution,* and in that same year a one-paragraph note in *El Palacio,* "Mound Builders Were Pit Dwellers," stated,

Figure 2.5. Photograph of James A. Ford excavating at the Marksville site, Avoyelles Parish, Louisiana, 1933 (photograph courtesy Louisiana State University Museum of Natural Science).

"The home of a Hopewell Mound Builder has been discovered. James A. Ford, who is excavating at Marksville, Louisiana, under auspices of the Smithsonian Institution, has reported the discovery" (Ford 1934:74).

The structure was not a house pit, but more important is that Ford's name was inextricably linked to a site that would continue to exert an influence in southeastern archaeological circles. Relevant to our discussion is Ford's opinion in the southern Hopewell argument: in closing his brief communiqué, Ford (1934:75) stated, "Recent discoveries in Louisiana have shown that a southern variation of the Hopewell culture existed contemporaneously with it *and was closely allied*" (emphasis added). Thus to Ford, as to Setzler and a growing number of archaeologists, the elaborately decorated pottery from Marksville not only resembled Ohio Hopewell pottery but had been made by a culture closely allied to the one that had occupied the Ohio Valley. And, if we can read between the lines of what Ford wrote, it wasn't pottery from Marksville only that resembled Hopewellian pottery. He used the word "discoveries," which, we assume, referred to the results of his reconnaissance in Louisiana and Chambers's contemporary survey in western Mississippi for the Mississippi Department of Archives and

History.[6] Those surveys resulted in the discovery of numerous sites that contained sherds similar to those from Marksville, but because the sites were smaller and were not excavated, they never produced the quantity of sherds recovered from Marksville. Thus it was only natural that Marksville became the type site and that the name would be assigned to the decorated pottery.

FROM LOUISIANA TO GEORGIA AND BACK

The year 1934 was a busy one for Ford. After completing the work at Marksville late in 1933, he was hired by Arthur R. Kelly to assist in managing a federally funded project at Macon, Georgia. The project, one of the largest of the time, was funded through the short-lived Civil Works Administration (CWA). As Lyon (1996) details in his excellent overview of New Deal archaeology in the South, CWA-sponsored archaeology was in large part a Smithsonian-run program devised by Matthew W. Stirling, William Duncan Strong, and Setzler. In the words of Setzler (1943:207), "previous experience at Marksville had convinced the Smithsonian officials that under proper supervision, and with a sufficient number of trained men, worthwhile scientific results on a large scale could be obtained." Setzler's use of the term "men" was an accurate assessment of most of the federally funded archaeology of the 1930s, where the emphasis was on employing males. However, this was not always the case. For example, the excavation crew used at Irene Mound near Savannah, Georgia, was made up of eighty African American women (see McIntyre [1939]).

In January 1934, Ford was approached by Fred Kniffen, a geographer at Louisiana State University, to join him in applying for funding to initiate a CWA project in Louisiana. Ford apparently would rather have worked in Louisiana than remain in Georgia, but Setzler insisted that the large-scale excavation project Kelly was trying to get off the ground was more important than anything Ford and Kniffen might undertake, so Ford stayed (Lyon 1996:78). Kelly undoubtedly was relieved to retain Ford's services, given that by mid-January 1933 his excavation crew had reached an astounding size of 243 men. The two men seem to have had a pleasant relationship. Ford, in a letter to Collins in late December 1933, noted, "I like Kelly fine" (cited in Lyon 1996:31), and Kelly, in separate letters to Roland B. Dixon and Stirling in December 1933 and January 1934, noted that Ford's "technique in exploring house sites is one of the finest examples of workmanship I have seen" (cited in Lyon 1996:32).

After the CWA was absorbed back into the FERA, Ford left Kelly's employment and went to work for the Georgia Park Service. He also married Ethel Campbell (Figure 2.6), a lovely young woman from Eastabutchie, Mississippi, who had been

---

6. Chambers's survey notes are housed at the Mississippi Department of Archives and History.

secretary to Dunbar Rowland, director of the Mississippi Department of Archives and History. When he told Collins in November 1933 of their plans, Collins warned Ford of the effect marriage might have on his future:

> Instead of a conventional congratulations, I am going to be perfectly frank and say that I think you are making a mistake. . . . How can you think of taking on the responsibility of a wife when you have no regular salary? . . . This chance you have at L.S.U. is something which may never come again. I had hoped very much that you would start in there with the determination not only to impress them with you[r] ability but to get the groundwork you so badly need. And I honestly believe that you will be severely handicapped if you should get married at just about the same time and have other cares thrust upon you. Of course, I don't expect you to pay any attention to this, but I cannot help but tell you that I greatly fear that the move will not be for your good.[7]

Ford didn't follow Collins's advice, and he and Ethel were married on March 3, 1934.

Ford's work for the park service and his subsequent brief stint with the Southeastern Fair Association in Atlanta in late 1934 are of no particular interest to our story line except for what they tell us about Ford as a person. He was hired by the park service association to excavate what supposedly was an old Spanish mission on the Georgia coast near Brunswick. As Willey (1969:63) later put it, "Instead, much to local dismay, he demonstrated with embarrassing convincingness, that the ruins in question were those of an early 19th-century sugar mill. Jim's 'direct historical approach' in this instance gave evidence of the directness with which he was to handle other archaeological problems. He was never one to pull his punches or to suffer fools gladly." This aspect of Ford's personality, which comes up time and again in talking to his old colleagues, cost him his job with the park service. Brunswick was proud of its mission—Santo Domingo de Talaje—and so was Mary Ross, who had identified the ruins as the location of the mission and who, along with Herbert E. Bolton, the leading expert on Spanish colonialism in the United States, had written the introduction to "Arredondo's Historical Proof of Spain's Title to Georgia" (Bolton 1925).

In a letter to her mother-in-law dated June 3, 1934, Ethel Ford wrote, "James is not at all sure this was the site of the Santo Domingo mission." A month or so later, she again wrote her mother-in-law:

> Mary Ross spent quite a long time in Brunswick in July. She knew before her departure Jim had discovered that his dig was a sugar mill and not Santo Domingo de Talaje. I wrote her on July 11, 1934, and the bomb burst in Brunswick. . . . The entire town was enraged. Savannah, the long-time rival of Brunswick, laughed and enjoyed the entire affair. . . . The men at the camp got mad because as a result of James' report, they may all lose their jobs. . . . The night after you left, Mrs. Ford, James and I sat up all night

7. Letter from Collins to Ford, November 16, 1933 (LSU Museum of Natural Science archives).

Figure 2.6. Photograph of Ethel Campbell Ford, ca. 1934 (photograph courtesy W. G. Haag).

and finished his report, and got it off. We had to do it, so the camp superintendent said, because of the political situation.[8]

As if the experience at Brunswick were an omen, Ford's work for the fair association went even worse. Ford was hired to plan and supervise the construction of buildings in conjunction with the American Indian Exposition, but as Evans (1968:1162) later wrote, he also "managed the exposition, fed, housed, nursed, and bailed out of jail the forty Cherokees, thirty Seminoles, and thirty assorted southeastern Indians provided by the Bureau of Indian Affairs. This one venture alienated him from 'action anthropology' for the rest of his life."

8. Letter from Ethel Ford to Janie Ford, July 1934 (exact date unknown) (LSU Museum of Natural Science archives).

Disgusted with his short stay in Georgia, Ford returned to Louisiana in the fall of 1934 and accepted a fellowship to attend Louisiana State University. Given Ford's later achievements in American archaeology, one can overlook the fact that he was, on a good day, a mediocre student at best. His transcripts make it apparent that he did well in classes he liked, chiefly those in anthropology, and fared much worse in those he probably was forced to take. Religion courses, for example, seem to have held no special appeal—he had failed Christian history while at Mississippi College (his transcript says, however, that it was a "conditional failure," which must have taken the edge off the pain) and made Ds in his other Bible courses. He had also failed drama and geometry and barely passed Spanish, literature, and mathematics courses. He showed some proclivity for physics, and in a remarkable turnaround went from a D to an A in mechanical drawing (noteworthy because he later became well known for his drafting ability).

Clearly, Kniffen had a lot to do not only in getting Ford a fellowship to LSU but in getting him admitted to the university in the first place. Ford had further problems with grades while at LSU, making Ds in German and geology and Fs in psychology and, surprisingly, cartography. Much of his required coursework was in sociology, and there Ford's grades were all over the map. His mind simply was focused on sites and sherds, not on the classroom, and without Ethel's help, he never would have graduated. In what today would be viewed as cheating (maybe it was then, too), Ethel became her husband's surrogate in the educational process. In letters to Jim's mother, Ethel detailed her involvement:

> There will be a steady stream to the library at night. James works and I go to the library at night and read his sociology for him. Sociology is his major and there are so very many reading assignments in books that are on reserve that James would have to spend too much time in the library if he read them. He did not make good grades on his six weeks test so I am going to write his term papers and keep up his assignments for him the rest of the year. I take notes on the readings, and read them to him on his way to school and at breakfast. He just hates this sociology.[9]

> Last week we finished two term papers that were due this morning as we did not finish the last of the typing until late last night. One was a study of sociological groups, and the second was on domestic groups. The first James wrote and the second I did. There remains only one more term paper. We have to read about ten books in social psychology and report on each book separately. I suppose it will take about all this week to finish that one.[10]

Ford undoubtedly had been thinking about what to include in the report on the Peck Village excavation and in the one on surface collections from sites in

9. Letter from Ethel Ford to Janie Ford, October 28, 1935 (LSU Museum of Natural Science archives).

10. Letter from Ethel Ford to Janie Ford, 1936 (exact date unknown) (LSU Museum of Natural Science archives).

western Mississippi and northern Louisiana. In the first few months of his tenure at LSU, he kicked the analysis and report preparation into high gear, apparently at the expense of his grades. By the end of February 1935, he was, as Ethel wrote her mother-in-law, "about to complete [the] article on Sicily Island [Peck Village] which has occupied most of his time up to 12 o'clock at night these last 2 or 3 weeks."[11] Ford was also feverishly working on several other papers of a more general nature, and in January 1935 he produced what we consider to be his first real publication on archaeology (the *El Palacio* piece on the "house" at Marksville was more of a communiqué than an article). The article, "An Introduction to Louisiana Archeology" (Ford 1935a), was published in the *Louisiana Conservation Review*, a magazine aimed at a general audience. Ford summarized what was known of the archaeological record of the state, paying particular attention to remains from the historical period as well as to the pottery from Marksville. The article has escaped critical attention over the years, but contained within it are the elements of a position that is recognizable throughout Ford's career. He laid out not only his basic ideas on culture but also, and more importantly, his ideas on how culture changes and how archaeologists read that change. The article is a beautiful exposition of the materialist position, which is why we devote considerable attention to it.

HOW TO CREATE A CHRONOLOGICAL SEQUENCE

In a few paragraphs, Ford set out the archaeological problem he was trying to solve—the chronological ordering of archaeological remains (though he often phrased it in terms of such things as "recovering lost history")—established his position on what culture is, and then tied that position directly to the archaeological methods that would be used to examine culture change:

> The first step in recovering this lost history is to locate by means of the early descriptions and maps the sites inhabited at the time of first contact with the Europeans. From this point the story may be followed back into the unknown past by the aid of *one of the dominant axioms of culture: it is always changing.* It should be understood that by "culture" is meant the component of the customs and styles of languages, handicrafts, arts and ceremonials practiced by any particular group of people at any one time. *Culture is in reality a set of ideas* as to how things should be done and made. It is in a continuous state of evolutionary change since it is constantly influenced both by inventions from within and the introduction of new ideas from without the group. . . .
>
> This principle of the gradual change of culture with the passage of time applies quite directly to the lives of the ancient Indians of Louisiana, and clear indications of

11. Letter from Ethel Ford to Janie Ford, February 27, 1935 (LSU Museum of Natural Science archives).

it may be noted by a study of the articles they have left behind them. . . . All of these man-made things were subject to the principle of constant change, hence those on any one site are *more or less* peculiar to the time that produced them.

It is apparent that if the different forms of the various implements, houses, mounds, etc., used during time covered by one of these ancient cultures can be arranged in the sequence in which they occurred, it is possible to determine the relative ages of the various old towns, not in the accurate terms of years but in relation to one another. The origins, migrations, developments and final disposition of the different groups of people by this means are made apparent. Thus the prehistory of the area is outlined. Such an arrangement of cultural elements, called a chronology, is one of the primary purposes of archaeological research. The simplest means of arranging such a chronology is to select some one element of culture which appears commonly on the ancient sites and which was subject to rapid change in form. After the chronology of this one element is discovered, it serves as a "yardstick" for the remaining elements of the culture history. (Ford 1935a:8–9; emphasis added)

The obvious artifacts to use in uncovering the past were the millions of pottery sherds littering the Louisiana landscape, and the obvious place to look for change was in designs on the pottery:

On prehistoric villages in Louisiana and neighboring southern states, the most common of the remaining elements of the old cultures, and fortunately one which appears to have been subject to fairly rapid change, is the pottery found in graves and in the village garbage heaps. As the chronology of this key culture element is easier to discover by working from the known back into the unknown past, the first task becomes that of discovering the types of pottery and pottery decorations used by the tribes that came in contact with the whites. (Ford 1935a:10)

It is not difficult to "discover" the types of designs on prehistoric and historical-period ceramic vessels—you can do that by looking at a vessel of known age—but how does one "discover" the types of *pottery* used? What *is* a type? Ford did not address this issue directly, but it is clear that decoration was the basis for his pottery types. For example, he noted that

Several of the historic tribal pottery types have already been discovered. That of the Caddo Indians occupying the northwestern part of the state was definitely determined at the "Fish Hatchery" site near Natchitoches [Figure 2.2] by Mr. Winslow Walker, of the Bureau of American Ethnology, in 1931 [Walker 1934]. This ware is characterized by incised lines which form elaborate scroll and meander designs and by a profuse use of spurs and delicate cross-hatching. . . . This pottery is identified as historic by implements found accompanying it which were traded to the Indians by the Europeans.

Pottery characteristic of the Natchez tribe was discovered at a village near Natchez, Mississippi [the Fatherland site; Figure 2.2], by Mr. M. B. Chambers, of the Mississippi Department of Archives and History, in 1929. This ware was similar to, but not identical with, the Caddo. It is ornamented with graceful scrolls and meanders formed by bands of three lines. . . . A definite date of 1720 is indicated for this pottery not only by the early descriptions of the Natchez villages, but by the quantity of French trade objects accompanying the finds.

Thus by identification of the historic pottery a basis is established for a chronology. (Ford 1935a:10)

By the early 1930s archaeologists in Louisiana and Mississippi had tied specific kinds of pottery decoration to four major ethnic groups of the historical period: the Caddo, located primarily in northern Louisiana; the Choctaw, in central Mississippi along and east of the Pearl River; the Natchez, in western Mississippi from about Vicksburg on the north to roughly Natchez on the south; and the Tunica, in extreme northeastern Louisiana and in western Mississippi from Vicksburg north to about Yazoo City. Each, of course, had been preceded in various areas by prehistoric peoples, but it was still unclear how far back in time individual pottery types or sets of types could be pushed.

In his article, Ford focused only on Caddo and Natchez pottery, noting that "Comparative studies show . . . that although the Caddo had occupied the territory where they were first described longer than had the Natchez, both cultures at comparatively recent times had displaced others which had entirely different pottery designs and which very likely represented an entirely different people" (Ford 1935a:10). Here, Ford seems to have equated what he later termed a "ceramic complex" (Ford 1935b), or a "decoration complex" (Ford 1935c), with a culture; he would, in a few short years, abandon this equivalency (Ford 1938b).

The notion that the Caddo had occupied their territory longer than the Natchez had occupied theirs was a recurring theme in Ford's later publications on materials from his surface collections and his excavations at Peck Village. We can only guess that the sources of his so-called comparative studies were Harry J. Lemley and S. D. Dickinson, who were analyzing pottery from the Crenshaw site in Miller County, Arkansas, and who corresponded with Ford. Clarence Moore had earlier excavated a number of vessels at Crenshaw (Moore 1912:620–27), all of which, according to Lemley (1936:26), were "unquestionably Caddoan." In 1933 and 1934, several local people uncovered a number of vessels from the mounds that "did not appear to be Caddoan and indicated the existence of another culture on the place" (Lemley 1936:26). Subsequent excavation uncovered more of what Lemley (1936) and Dickinson (1936) referred to as "pre-Caddoan" pottery. Importantly, the basis for this designation was not simply that the pottery looked different from what had become known as Caddoan pottery but also that it lay below Caddoan pottery: "In the body of Mound 'D' and in four burial pits under Mound 'B' which had been dug before the erection of the mound we found burials and artifacts of a culture differing radically from that of the Caddo, whereas, in two intrusive pits cut down from the surface of Mound 'D' and in eight similar intrusive pits and three upper burials in Mound 'B' we found Caddo burials, furnished with pottery and other artifacts typical of that culture" (Lemley 1936:29). Dickinson (1936:68) stated, "The discovery of the pre-Caddo culture at the Crenshaw Place is the most important step so far made in the study of Arkansas archaeology. It affords the student of Arkansas aboriginal antiquities material for the study of various aspects of a purely prehistoric culture antedating the Caddo. A tentative chronology, which may be elaborated later, can now be established."

It can be assumed that Ford referred to the as-yet-unpublished work of Lemley and Dickinson when he declared that comparative studies had demonstrated a deeper time depth for Caddoan peoples than for the Natchez. Several lines of evidence, all circumstantial, support this assumption. For example, Lemley and Dickinson themselves were convinced that there was considerable time depth to Caddoan–pre-Caddoan occupation of Crenshaw and that there was a basic *continuity* in pottery design—a phenomenon that to them was "natural, for succeeding potters would certainly have either retained or borrowed a few cultural elements from their predecessors" (Dickinson 1936:57–58). This sounds a lot like Ford. Dickinson noted that much of the pre-Caddoan pottery from Crenshaw resembled what Ford (1935a:10) had recently referred to as Coles Creek, named for a site northeast of Natchez (Figure 2.2).

In his article, Ford (1935a:10) stated that the "people of this pre-Natchesan and [pre-]Caddo pottery that disappeared before the historic period merely for convenience are called 'Coles Creek' people. They appear to be descended, culturally at least, from a still older group of people known as 'Hopewell.'" This "cultural descendancy"—a relatively smooth transition from Marksville to Coles Creek (pre-Caddoan) to Caddo-Natchez—was a natural outgrowth of Ford's view of culture as something that "is in a continuous state of evolutionary change," subject to "inventions from within and the introduction of new ideas from without" (Ford 1935a:9). The equation of form with time was obviously strong in Ford's thinking as well. Why else would he implicitly equate the temporal position of "pre-Natchesan" and "[pre-] Caddoan" pottery by subsuming them under Coles Creek? In short, we see here an implicit axiom of culture history—similar forms in more or less the same locality denote similar age.

Ford's 1935 Chronological Ordering

Ford presented his notion of chronological ordering in another popular article in the *Louisiana Conservation Review* a few months later (Ford 1935b), this time in graphical fashion (Figures 2.7 and 2.8). He was finishing his report on Peck Village, and was analyzing the surface-collected sherds from sites in Louisiana and Mississippi. In a change from the earlier article, Ford split the chronology into two geographically distinct pieces, one representing what he called the Yazoo City, Mississippi, area and the other representing what he called the Natchez, Mississippi, area. He stated that the "sites within the areas, as shown on the map [Figure 2.7], divide themselves according to the pottery decorations found on them into seven broad groups called 'complexes.' Some of these complexes were contemporaneous in different areas, hence they all fall into three main time divisions" (Ford 1935b:33; he labeled them "horizons" in Figure 2.8). The youngest of the three divisions (labeled "III" on Figure 2.8), which began sometime in the prehistoric past and continued past A.D. 1700, contained pottery made by the four historical tribes, the Caddo, Tunica, Natchez, and Choctaw. Ford's "intermediate" period ("II" on Figure 2.8) consisted of pottery he placed in the Deasonville and Coles Creek complexes, and his oldest division ("I" on Figure 2.8) contained pottery he placed in the Marksville complex.

Ford defined a "ceramic complex" as "a small group of unrelated [formally dissimilar?] pottery-design types that were fashionable in the same region at the same time" (Ford 1935b:34). Thus, following his notion of a culture comprising a set of shared ideas, the warrant for his ceramic-complex units was the popularity

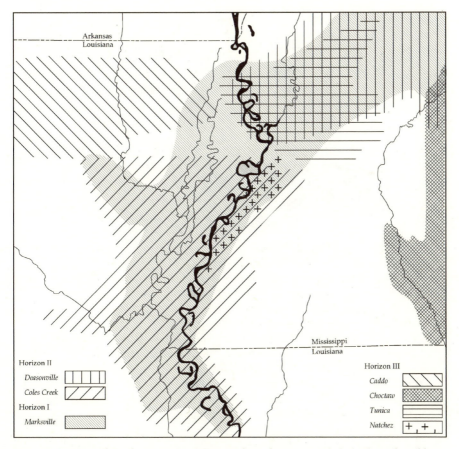

Figure 2.7. Map of northeastern Louisiana and southwestern Mississippi produced by James A. Ford showing his proposed distribution of seven pottery complexes (from Ford 1935b).

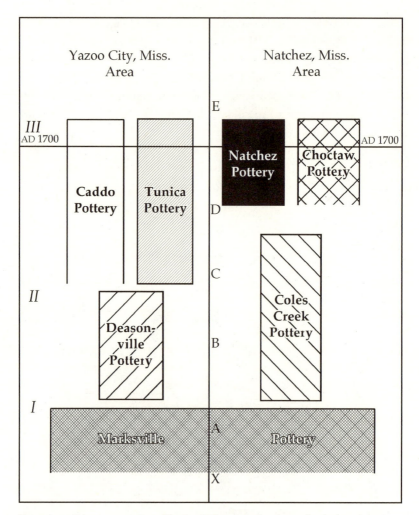

Figure 2.8. Diagram produced by Ford showing the chronological positioning of seven ceramic complexes from northeastern Louisiana and southwestern Mississippi. Here Ford took the seven complexes shown in Figure 2.7 and arranged them into two sets—those in the southern half of the area (labeled "Yazoo City" on the figure) and those in the northern half (labeled "Natchez"). The labels actually are misnomers because the complexes extend well beyond the areas immediately around those Mississippi towns. Points X–E are arbitrary points along the vertical time line. The open bottoms of three of the complexes meant that they might have extended further back in time than Ford suspected at the time he constructed the diagram. Note that both evolutionary trajectories sprang from a common Marksville base (from Ford 1935b).

principle. Each type within a complex constituted a "style" that would change over time (Ford 1935b:37). *Why* a style changed was left unspecified, but the implication was that as culture—ideas—changed, so too would the styles of artifacts, just as they did in modern society (e.g., Ford 1935b:34).

Marksville was viewed as what might be termed the "basement" complex of pottery designs—a complex that at some unknown point in the past was replaced by the Coles Creek complex in the Natchez area and by the Deasonville complex in the Yazoo City area. Then, at some unknown point in the prehistoric past, the Coles Creek pottery-design complex was replaced by the Natchez and Choctaw complexes in the Natchez area, and the Deasonville complex was replaced by the Caddo and Tunica complexes in the Yazoo City area. Evolutionary biologists would quickly recognize that what Ford proposed was a phylogenetic reconstruction of decoration complexes showing speciation events. In Figure 2.8, the species *Marksville* gives rise to two species, *Coles Creek* and *Deasonville,* each of which divides into two more species. The type of speciation—allopatric, sympatric, or parapatric—would depend on the reason for the divergence (speciation)—for example, the development of physical or cultural barriers between, say, different groups using Marksville decorations on their vessels. In very simplified terms, allopatric speciation occurs because individuals in two geographically separated groups no longer have the opportunity to interbreed with members of the other group; sympatric speciation occurs because individuals in two groups living in the same area can but do not breed outside their group; and parapatric speciation occurs among groups that have contiguous but nonoverlapping geographic distributions and which do not crossbreed.

The Caddo and Choctaw complexes are open-ended in terms of when they began, as opposed to the Tunica and Natchez complexes. Also, the Coles Creek complex was posited to have lasted longer than the Deasonville complex—in large part a result of Ford's belief that "the Caddo had occupied the territory where they were first described longer than had the Natchez" (Ford 1935a:10). Simply put, if the Caddo had occupied their territory longer than the Natchez had occupied theirs, then one could conveniently shift the relative ending dates of the prehistoric decoration complexes upward or downward to allow for the difference. Ford illustrated various pottery decorations that allowed time and space to be carved up into the neat units, and he subdivided the sherds carrying various designs into types, based on similarity in design. Descriptions of the various types appeared in the Peck Village report (see below) but were not reproduced in the popular article.

Spatial Overlap in Decoration Complexes

Ford did, however, address one very important issue in the article, and we examine it here briefly as background to his later discussions in the Peck Village report (Ford 1935c) and the surface-collection monograph (Ford 1936a). Recall that in his Deasonville report, Collins (1932a:19) had lamented that analysis "of the potsherds from Deasonville fails to reveal any clues which might be of value as showing the chronological position of the site beyond the mere fact that it is pre-historic." Subsequent work at Marksville and other sites (especially Peck Village) was beginning to demonstrate there was some time depth to the prehistoric period, which Ford was already conceiving of as being divisible into two units—Marksville and either Deasonville or Coles Creek, depending on where in the Mississippi Valley a site was located. In writing for a general audience, Ford certainly could have left things at that, but he didn't. Despite the neatness of the scenario, it oversimplified matters considerably because it did not account for sites that might contain sherds of more than one contemporaneous complex. Ford knew that the Deasonville site contained sherds of both the Deasonville and Coles Creek complexes, as did Peck Village. Similarly, for the historical period, the Fatherland site contained sherds of the Natchez, Tunica, and Caddo complexes (Ford 1936a).

What we see here is an essentialist-like epistemology. Recall Ford's (1935a) apparent equation of a decoration complex with a particular culture. Such typo-logical thinking precludes ready placement of hybrid units such as the Fatherland site into a scheme such as Ford's. That Ford was thinking in such terms is clear from his statements that he was seeking not only to build a chronology of "ancient cultures" but also to clarify "the origins, migrations, developments and final [geo-graphic] disposition of the different groups of people" (Ford 1935a:9) by plotting ceramic complexes in time and space. Similarly, his analytical procedure would allow "movements of people and of culture [to] be detected" (Ford 1935b:33).

Ford must have realized his map (Figure 2.7) was too clean, meaning that it misrepresented the true areal extent of individual pottery complexes, and thus he inserted two columns of letters in what we reproduce as Table 2.2. The letters in the left two columns refer to the time periods shown in Figure 2.8, ranging from time X in the prehistoric past up through time E. What Ford was showing were the major and minor ceramic complexes that theoretically could (and in reality did) appear on a site depending on its location in the valley. For example, a village in northern Louisiana or west-central Mississippi—Ford's Yazoo City area—that was settled at time B and not abandoned until time D might contain large percentages of sherds of both the prehistoric Deasonville complex and the historical-period Tunica complex, and it might also contain a lesser percentage of Coles Creek–complex sherds. He subsequently used this discussion as a springboard for an extended treatment of the temporal span and areal extent of decoration complexes in his monograph on the surface collections.

Henry Collins's Influence and the 1935 Chronology

The chronological-ordering paper (Ford 1935b) in many respects is a mature piece of work, but much of its finished look was a result of Henry Collins's

Table 2. 2. Ford's Depiction of the Overlapping Nature of Ceramic Complexes on Sites in the Yazoo City and Natchez Areas

Village Settled at Time	Village Abandoned at Time	Area of N. La.-W. Central Miss.		Area of S. La.-S. W. Miss.	
		Major Proportion	Minor Proportion	Major Proportion	Minor Proportion
D	E	Tunica	Natchez Caddo Choctaw	Natchez	Tunica Caddo Choctaw
C	D	Tunica	Coles Creek	Coles Creek	Tunica
B	D	Tunica Deasonville	Coles Creek	Coles Creek	Tunica Deasonville
B	C	Deasonville	Coles Creek	Coles Creek	Deasonville
A	B	Deasonville Marksville	Coles Creek	Coles Creek Marksville	Deasonville
X	A	Marksville		Marksville	

Data from Ford (1935b).

influence on Ford. In one of those serendipitous happenstances that comes along once in a blue moon, we found in the LSU Museum of Natural Science archives the typescript of the original article that Ford wrote—an article that, with the exception of the maps and sherd illustrations, bears almost no resemblance to the published version. Ford sent Collins a copy of the initial manuscript, and in his reply,[12] Collins asked Ford why, "when mimeographing is so easy, did you confine yourself to a single page of terse text. It seems to me that the relationships could have been brought out much more clearly if you had offered some explanations." Collins then asked if Ford "could not work up a short but adequate summary of your potsherd chronology so that the essential features could be known to those interested in the SE. It would be well to get such a paper out now that the field is coming into its own. I could get it published in the Journal of the Washington Academy of Sciences; the main problem would be illustrations for the limit is two pages of illustrations, beyond that each page is $5."

Ford avoided the extra charges by publishing the article in the April 1935 edition of the *Louisiana Conservation Review*. But he clearly took Collins's comments to heart in revising the original paper, which was little more than a telegraphed summary of pottery designs—twelve pages of rough sherd illustrations (the same ones that were included in the published paper, albeit professionally drawn), one page of figures, and one page of text, which also contained two tables. In short, the paper explained almost nothing—hence Collins's gentle criticism.

12. Letter from Collins to Ford, February 17, 1935 (LSU Museum of Natural Science archives).

Collins also had a few other things to say about the paper:

> On p. 7 you say that the cord marked ware from Deasonville is "rough, friable, fibre temp." Those which I examined and reported on had no fibre tempering, but small particles of fire-burned clay which I interpreted and listed as "potsherd tempering". . . . Next, on p. 8 you speak of Coles Creek being grit tempered. What does that word mean? The only definition of grit that I know of is sand or gravel, but you didn't mean that did you? At any rate, the Deasonville "overhanging type" had ground up potsherds for tempering just as the cord marked ware.

When the article appeared, there was no mention of fiber tempering in Deasonville sherds, and "crushed potsherds," along with grit, appeared under the heading of temper for Coles Creek sherds. Perhaps Ford kept grit tempering as an attribute because of the way in which he was using the term "Coles Creek"—as a catchall category for all sherds with incised horizontal lines. Collins, however, was more restrictive, and in the same letter to Ford warned against using his types over too large an area:

> I notice that Coles Creek is overflowing its banks and spreading to the Florida Keys. Now don't you think it would be wiser to restrict the name to the type of pottery found at those key sites in Mississippi. In that way you will be proceeding step by step and the word will have a clear and definite meaning. If you include in it another type of pottery typical of the Gulf Coast you will have the somewhat paradoxical situation where some Gulf Coast site is purer Coles Creek than Coles Creek itself because it contains all the elements while the type site in Mississippi only has the "overhanging lines" etc. Good methodology would have the type site stand out in clear relief. Step by step you would carry it back (or up, rather) showing its relationship with other pottery types of Mississippi and Louisiana. Your discovery that it was contemporaneous with the dominant Gulf Coast pottery would [then] assume its proper significance; to my mind it is a backward step, one opposed to clarification, to suddenly diffuse Coles Creek until the word becomes a catch-all for a whole pottery complex stretching from the Texas border to the tip of Florida.

Collins's remarks demonstrate the conflict over what to call pottery from widely separated areas that carries similar designs. As early as May 1933, Collins had cautioned Ford "not to use the word Hopewell; that has been accepted as meaning a certain combination of design elements (with regard to pottery) and we would be no more warranted in calling our sherds with smooth and widely incised lines and bands of rouletting Hopewell than in calling all scrolls Natchez as you so clearly pointed out to me. Give it a name of some sort and then with its position and affiliations known the real Hopewell will fit into the scheme easily enough."[13] The "real" Hopewell? Here is a classic case of dichotomous thinking about types: Ford was interested in using designs simply to mark the passage of time; to Collins and other archaeologists, types were real units, and by spreading a type too widely,

---

13. Letter from Collins to Ford, May 5, 1933 (LSU Museum of Natural Science archives).

one destroyed its utility as a meaningful (essentialist) category. In his letter of February 27, 1935, Collins admitted to Ford, "I have not read your article in the Conservation magazine [Ford 1935a], only saw it in [Setzler's] office, but it looks nice." If he *had* read it, he might have realized the extreme difference in positions between himself and Ford.

In his February 1935 letter, Collins questioned Ford on a number of other points, including the evolution and spread of various design motifs. Lest Ford take his criticisms too personally, Collins tried to bolster his confidence:

> Well, anyway you keep at the problem and sooner or later it will begin to clear up. I don't think it an exaggeration to compare the work you have in mind with that done by Nelson and Kidder; the only thing is that it is much more difficult, for all they had to do was dig trenches in refuse heaps and note the different types of pottery. The work loomed up as highly significant mainly because a generation or more of rather slow witted specimen gatherers had up to that time occupied the field alone.

Comparing Ford to two giants of the field was high praise to heap on a young archaeologist who was barely twenty-four years old. Within a few months, Ford would demonstrate that trenches through refuse heaps in the Southeast could yield results as good as those in the Southwest.

Peck Village

Ford's first monograph, "Ceramic Decoration Sequence at an Old Indian Village Site near Sicily Island, Louisiana" (Ford 1935c), initiated the *Anthropological Studies* series published by the Louisiana Department of Conservation through the Louisiana Geological Survey. As state geologist Cyril K. Moresi noted in his preface to the monograph, the series was begun in part because of favorable responses to the articles by Ford and Fred Kniffen in the *Louisiana Conservation Review*. In the forty-one-page monograph, written in February 1935,[14] Ford detailed the results of his excavation of Peck Village, a small site in Catahoula Parish (Figure 2.2) that he discovered during his site survey in 1933 and excavated later that year. In the first paragraph, Ford stated his reason for excavating the site: "the possibility of vertical stratigraphy." In Ford's words,

> In the bottom of small washes, cutting through a twenty-inch accumulation of midden debris, were found potsherds characteristic of three decoration complexes that *theoretically* had been used in the region in two distinct prehistoric time periods. The uniqueness of the situation did not lie in the particular combination of decoration complexes, since that had been observed at a number of other sites, but rat[h]er in the unusual depth of midden deposits, *which indicated a possibility of vertical division of the two time periods.* (emphasis added)

14. Letter from Ethel Ford to Janie Ford, February 27, 1935 (LSU Museum of Natural Science archives).

Thus, Peck Village held the promise that no other site up to that time had: vertical— hence, implied chronological—separation of distinct "decoration complexes." Ford later remarked that vertical stratigraphy "constitutes the best basis for the relating of time changes," a position he held to strongly throughout his career. He also indicated that "sites may be related to changes in the natural feature of the landscape in order to determine their relative ages"—changes such as coastal subsidence and "shifting stream meanders" (Ford 1936b:103–4), both notions he undoubtedly learned from Fred Kniffen and/or Richard Russell while at Louisiana State University. Ford clearly recognized that the archaeological record had a geological mode of occurrence.

In a footnote, Ford (1935c:1) defined a decoration complex as a "group of pottery decorations characteristic of an area at a definite period of time"—a definition that was a bit more open-ended than what he had presented a few months previously, in the second of his popular articles (Ford 1935b), for the term "ceramic complex." Note the absence here of the qualifications "*small* group of *unrelated* pottery design types" found in the popular article and the presence of the perhaps more formal and explicit wording "decoration" rather than the earlier "design." As we will see, Ford's *decoration* complexes were analytical, or ideational, units, the empirical manifestations of which indicated the distributions of the units in time and space. This critical fact is obscured in Ford's early writings because the historically anchored decoration complexes were established by extracting definitive marker types from ethnographically documented ethnic or tribal units. All decoration or ceramic complexes—regardless of their source—thus had an essentialist feel; they seemed to be real, a perception exacerbated by how the units were discussed and explained within the context of Ford's model of culture change.

We have never seen any comment regarding the manner in which Ford excavated Peck Village, though it had a direct bearing on his interpretations of stratigraphic ordering of the various decoration complexes. Four separate "cuts" were placed in the site, each measuring 10 feet square. Then, each unit "was carefully dug by trowelling. A level floor was maintained until an appreciable amount of material was found. The depth of the cut was then measured and designated as section '1' of that cut. The second lowering of the cut floor was known as section '2', etc." (Ford 1935c:6). Depths of cuts ranged from 15 inches to approximately 22 inches, with the thickness of sections varying between 3 and 6 inches (Figure 2.9).

It is important to note that Ford was using the technique known as "ceramic stratigraphy" or "percentage stratigraphy." The technique was used by Nelson (1916) in his work at Pueblo San Cristóbal and later at Pueblo Bonito (Nelson 1920), and was mimicked by Kidder and Kidder (1917) and Amsden (1931) at Pecos Pueblo, by Spier (1917) near Zuñi Pueblo, by Schmidt (1928) in Arizona, and by Vaillant (1930, 1931) in the Valley of Mexico. Ford referred to none of these

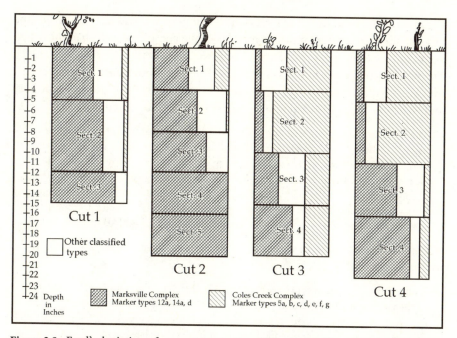

Figure 2.9. Ford's depiction of percentage stratigraphy at Peck Village, Catahoula Parish, Louisiana, using pottery marker types (after Ford 1935c).

works, leading us to suspect that he either invented the technique independently or, more likely (for reasons we discuss later), learned it from Kniffen. If Collins or Setzler told Ford about it, we wonder why they did not use it. Certainly Ford's graph is unique. Most users of percentage stratigraphy published tables of numbers (e.g., Nelson 1916; Spier 1917) or used broken-stick graphs (e.g., Amsden 1931; Kidder and Kidder 1917) (see Lyman et al. 1998).

In the Peck Village report, Ford (1935c) presented his spatial-temporal ordering of decoration complexes and then demonstrated how he arrived at the ordering. Because of its location, Peck Village exhibited very little pottery carrying the decorations evident on pottery from Deasonville and other sites in the Yazoo City area. However, the site, like Deasonville, contained a large number of incised "Marksville complex" sherds. What made the presence of those sherds at Peck Village so important was their stratigraphic position: the separation was not perfect, but there was clear indication that coming up through the levels of the site, "marker type" sherds of the Marksville complex were being replaced in terms of relative abundance by sherds of what Ford was calling the Coles Creek complex.

The scenario was obvious to Ford: the Marksville complex was the basement of the Louisiana-Mississippi pottery sequence. At Peck Village, sherds of that complex were replaced by sherds of the Coles Creek complex, whereas at Deasonville, the Deasonville complex had replaced the Marksville complex—as he had presented graphically in the second article in the *Louisiana Conservation Review* (Figure 2.7). The pottery complexes of the four historical-period groups had in turn replaced the Deasonville and Coles Creek complexes in each of the two regions (Yazoo City and Natchez), though at different times. Ford (1935c:23) noted that

> The most important implication of the Peck Village situation is that with the passage of time, while deposition of the midden was in progress, the ceramic art of the inhabitants was *slowly* changing from decorations consisting of wide, deep, closely-spaced lines forming curvilinear and angular designs . . . and curving bands of rouletting enclosed by wide deep lines . . . to decorations formed with overhanging lines which usually encircled the vessels parallel to the rim . . . and curvilinear lines with which triangular punctates were employed. (emphasis added)

Note Ford's use of the word "slowly"—a term on which he elaborated in the following passage:

> As there is no apparent typological connection between the dominant decorations of the two complexes, the change in ceramic art probably is not the result of local evolution of Coles Creek out of Marksville, but rather a *replacement*. The Coles Creek decorations appear fully developed although in all cases they are not as specialized or as neatly executed as at many sites of the pure complex. Some of the types which form a minor proportion of the Coles Creek Complex do seem to be typologically related to Marksville. They probably resulted from the *gradual replacement of complexes,* indicated by the *smooth changes in proportion in the graphs.* This may have allowed a certain amount of Marksville to be absorbed into the Coles Creek. (Ford 1935c:24; emphasis added)

Here, Ford was attempting to explain the change from one decoration complex to another, and although he didn't specify a particular mechanism for the change, we can look ahead at his slightly later surface-collection monograph and see that he viewed replacement as occurring "either through gradual infiltration or conquest" (Ford 1936a:5). Ford stated that there was little "typological connection" between the "dominant" decorative types—his "marker types"—making up the complexes, which suggested to him that Coles Creek "replaced" Marksville. By this we believe he meant that the lack of "typological connection" between the dominant types of the two sequent complexes suggested the absence of a direct *phyletic* connection between the types. Then, he indicated that some of the Coles Creek decoration types, which made only minor contributions to the assemblage, "do seem to be typologically related to Marksville." By this we suspect he meant that he perceived a direct phyletic connection or relation between the less dominant types. Finally, Ford believed that the decorations executed on the Coles Creek pottery from Peck Village were not as "fully developed" as those on pottery from sites that contained only Coles Creek–complex pottery. This suggested that some of the Marksville designs had slowly been "absorbed" into Coles Creek. We take this to mean that the replacement of Marksville decoration by Coles Creek decoration was not complete because some vestiges of the former—probably at the scale of attribute rather than of type—remained in what he recognized as the later Coles Creek complex, but in muted or modified form. The Coles Creek material at Peck Village was a blend, then, of pure Coles Creek and pure Marksville. This notion flowed directly from the way in which Ford viewed culture—as something that was, as we quoted before, "constantly influenced both by inventions from within and the introduction of new ideas from without" (Ford 1935b:9).

Ford, like virtually all of his contemporaries, wanted to discuss the history of "ancient cultures" and "different groups of people" (Ford 1935a), both of which are ethnographic units of the essentialist sort. Thus, his archaeological units were warranted by the commonsense notion that they represented ancient and distinct ethnic units, just as the historic ethnic units variously termed Choctaw, Tunica, and the like could be distinguished by their ceramic-decoration complexes. For Ford to argue that his archaeological units represented ethnographic units of a particular sort represented not only an interpretation but also his first encounter with the essentialist-materialist dichotomy. He ignored it in 1935 because he did not recognize either it or its significance. In all fairness to Ford, the problem was not his alone, as individuals who had been doing culture history from the start made similar interpretations. Although by the middle of the 1930s at least Kidder (1936b:xx) had identified the dichotomy, he too brushed it aside because of his failure to recognize its significance (Lyman et al. 1997a).

Ford's (1935c:24) discussion of pottery-design complexes was derived from his materialist view of culture as constantly in a state of change. But he stumbled, like his contemporaries, because his complexes measured that change as discontinuous chunks, and those chunks—manifest as decoration complexes—were thought to represent, potentially at least, distinct cultures or peoples—a patently essentialist notion. Correlating pottery with ethnic groups provided a commonsense warrant for the chunks. In his three 1935 publications, Ford failed to explicitly acknowledge that the chunks were merely arbitrary units of measurement. Thus the *kind* of culture change he studied at Peck Village was one tied to the mechanisms of replacement or absorption—ethnologically documented mechanisms of culture change thought to be visible archaeologically. *Replacement* denoted the gradual cessation of one complex and the initiation of another, and *absorption* denoted the continuation of a type across sequent complexes—a direct phyletic continuity of a decorative theme—but with modifications from outside. Again, these were interpretations much like those made by many of Ford's predecessors (e.g., Kidder 1917; Kidder and Kidder 1917; Schmidt 1928).

Pottery Types from Peck Village

To this point we have focused almost exclusively on Ford's development and use of decoration complexes, but this overlooks the important point that the complexes were made up of individual pottery types, which subsequently were lumped under one complex or another based on a combination of two things: similarity in decoration and perceived or inferred contemporaneity. As Jon Gibson (1982:264) aptly put it, to Ford, "the goal of pottery classification virtually became one with deriving cultural chronology; there is no really logical way to separate them." Certainly, given an interest in culture history, one *had* to measure time. And, in the absence of superposed collections, one had to resort to typology (despite Walker's [1932:45] claims to the contrary). Ford (1935b:102), like many of his contemporaries (e.g., Kidder 1915, 1917; Kidder and Kidder 1917), believed that "pottery is the most plastic remaining element of the old cultures and probably changed most with the passage of time." Thus, pottery constituted the " 'key fossils' of culture" (Ford 1936b:104).

Ford's earliest published categorization of pottery centered on sherds from his 1933 excavation of Peck Village. He noted that all "pottery decorations found at the Peck site were classified according to an index," developed to study the large collections of sherds from the surfaces of sites in Louisiana and Mississippi (Ford 1935c:8). He obviously did not anticipate that his index system would later be scrapped and a new system implemented to deal with the surface collections (Ford 1936a). Ford (1935c) noted that even prior to implementing that index system of classification, he had considered and abandoned other methods:

> Noteworthy among the discarded methods is a morphological, biological-like arrangement of decorations into orders, suborders, families, etc. This proved unsatisfactory because of the extreme flexibility of pottery types, as well as doubt as to their generic [in the sense of a biological genus; thus phylogenetic] relationships. The frequent migration of decoration elements from what seemed to be their native types was of significance, and could not be indicated by the method. Zoological classification is not embarrassed by such anomalies as would result from the frequent crossing of different species. (Ford 1936a:17–18).

It is now abundantly clear that biological species *do* often interbreed—a fact over which biologists are not embarrassed at all.

As he was analyzing the excavated sherds from Peck Village and the surface-collected sherds from Louisiana and Mississippi, Ford also tried a system that "attempted to record specific decoration features, combinations of these features, execution, temper, paste, texture, thickness, hardness, vessel shape, and vessel appendages. The impracticability of this plan developed in attempts to detect significant correlations" (Ford 1936a:18). The system was doomed from the start, however, because it hopelessly mixed functional attributes such as vessel shape, techno-functional attributes such as paste, and stylistic attributes such as decoration. Only the last would provide an unambiguous measure of time unconflated with variation in adaptation or space. The system probably was unwieldy as well, making it difficult to keep straight all the variant combinations of attribute states.

Ford's statement about categorization touches upon important points concerning a biological-like system of classification. His comment that types contain "flexibility" suggests he was not imposing order on the sherds by using previously defined ideational units. Rather, he was apparently extracting type descriptions from the sherds themselves, perhaps by placing all similar sherds into a pile and then deriving from that pile what an average or typical specimen looked like. This accounts for how Ford and his early mentors such as Collins and Setzler were able to determine which "types" were diagnostic of particular historical-period tribes. Thus, his types *were* flexible; their definitive criteria could change as specimens were added to or subtracted from a pile (see below). As analytical constructs for measuring chronology, they were trial-and-error formulations. However, although the types perhaps were constructs of the archaeologist, they also were something real that could "migrate" and "cross-breed." Clearly, Ford had met head-on the essentialist-materialist paradox. The problem was exacerbated by his failure to clearly distinguish among the sherds—the stuff—he sought to classify, the units—types—into which he sorted the sherds, and the interpretations he rendered from the types.

Ford (1935c:8) referred to his index system—the one employed in the Peck Village report—as "merely a list of decoration types," noting that as "distinct decorations were encountered in the collections *in sufficient numerical quantity and areal distribution to permit their acceptance as a type,* they were illustrated on an index card" (Ford 1935c:8; emphasis added). In other words, the actual types he used were decoration-based, but Ford recognized types only *if* they were represented by enough sherds and *if* they occurred across enough space to preclude them from being idiosyncrasies. Thus his types were analytical—materialist—units useful for measuring space and time if they occurred in superposed sequences and/or their frequencies fluctuated monotonically through time.

Evidence that Ford's types may have been somewhat schizophrenic units is apparent in other remarks:

> Typologically [read *phylogenetically*] related decorations found together in the same collections, thus indicating the probability that they represented variations of one major idea of decoration, were filed as "a", "b", "c", etc., under a common numerical heading. If no such grouping already existed for a newly-encountered decoration type, it was filed as "a" of a new numerical heading. These groups were used only for the most apparent relations and were intended to have no cultural or absolute typological significance; they served mostly to facilitate filing and reference to the index. (Ford 1935c:8)

Such a conception implies that to Ford, there was some reality to his types—that is, they reflected ideas in the heads of the prehistoric ceramicists. This, of course, was derived from Ford's notions of culture and culture change, which in turn served as a commonsense warrant for the variation he perceived. Such rationales for types were typical of the time (e.g., Rouse 1939). But Ford's varieties had no "cultural or typological significance" and instead were merely reference units. That is, his varieties were analytical constructs only; they had no necessarily inherent reality, though such reality might be present. Ford's "one major idea of decoration," with "variations" on that theme, was the basis of Phillips's (1970) later type-variety system, which characterizes most typological efforts in the Mississippi Valley today. It also is similar to the type-variety system of Wheat et al. (1958), though the similarity is superficial. Ford's varieties had no analytical significance; the varieties of the type-variety system were meant to measure chunks of the time-space continuum that were smaller than those measured by types.

Ford (1935c:10) made a very perceptive statement when he claimed, "The limitations and crudity of this means of classifying potsherd decoration are obvious. Increasing understanding of the chronology will doubtless demonstrate the stages of southeastern ceramic evolution and make possible a more analytical classification, which at present promises to be the *result of rather than the means to* prehistoric chronology" (emphasis added). This point—that the analytical classi-fication was the result of chronology rather than a means to measure or document it—underscores that Ford constructed types by enumerating the characteristics of a set of objects rather than by identifying objects as belonging to a particular ideational unit. It also suggests Ford sought to discover types that were not only useful measures of time and space but also measures of cultural variation. This gave the units an essentialist quality. What else *could* they be, given that they were derived from chronology? Not unexpectedly, then, how type boundaries were originally established is somewhat murky, but we suspect it was in part based on geography, as exemplified by the identification of the various historical-period design complexes (e.g., Ford 1936b).

The murkiness of Ford's procedure for constructing units at the scale of an artifact type is not apparent in his construction of his larger-scale aggregates of types, the decoration complexes. Regarding the sherds from Peck Village, for example, he stated, "The sherds from this site fall into four divisions: 1. Decorations, because of their consistent occurrence on typical Marksville sites, can be recognized as belonging to the Marksville Complex. 2. Sherds typical of the Deasonville Complex. 3. Sherds belonging to the Coles Creek Complex. 4. Unusual decorations which cannot with certainty be assigned to any of the above complexes" (Ford 1935c:10–11). In other words, on the one hand, new types were thought to represent a particular complex because they were associated with already established types that were thought to represent a complex. On the other hand, Ford assigned types to one of the three prehistoric complexes based on the occurrence of sherds of those types on sites that he had already placed into one of the three complexes. How the original definitive types of a prehistoric complex were determined is obscure, though we suspect they were extracted from collections that came from sites that did not contain sherds associated with one or more of the historical tribes (e.g., Ford 1936b).

Marker Types

Key to Ford's analysis of chronological change at Peck Village was the vertical distribution of what he termed "complex markers":

> From observations made on a number of village site collections in the lower Mississippi Valley, it has been noted that although each of the several decoration complexes of the area include a number of different and often unrelated types which appear at the various villages typifying any one complex, there are one or two small groups of closely related types peculiar to each complex that statistically dominate to a marked degree. *These decorations must be considered as the most typical of their complex*, and from the role they play serve as "complex markers." (Ford 1935c:21; emphasis added)

In short, complex markers—"marker types"—were pottery types that could be employed as index fossils. Lyon (1996:229) notes that George I. Quimby, a longtime colleague of Ford's, "many years later mentioned the importance [Ford placed on] the concept of index fossils." Hence, for Ford a multicomplex site—a site, for example, that he mapped as containing sherds of both the Marksville and Coles Creek complexes (Ford 1936a:31)—was identified as such only if it exhibited *marker* types representing more than one complex. Ford (1935c:21) stated that prior to the work at Peck Village there were only a handful of marker types for the lower Mississippi Valley—two for the Marksville complex, six for the Coles Creek complex, and three for the Deasonville complex. By the time he reported the analysis of the surface-collected sherd assemblages, Ford (1936a) had expanded the number of Marksville-complex types to three, and had reduced the number of Coles Creek–complex marker types to five and the number of Deasonville-complex marker types to two. The extra Marksville-complex type apparently was derived from the excavation of Peck Village. Ford used the marker types—and *only* the marker types—to demonstrate the replacement of Marksville sherds by Coles Creek sherds at Peck Village.

Although sherds of other complexes were recovered from the site, Ford (1935c: 22–23) noted that, particularly relative to Deasonville-complex types, sherds

> are not present in sufficient numbers in the collections to show definitely the relation in which they stand to this indicated superposition of complexes. As shown by [Figure 2.7], the Peck Village site lies well within the area covered by the Coles Creek Complex, and is a hundred miles south of the Yazoo River Basin where *typical* Deasonville sites

are found. Sherds of this complex occurring at Peck site probably are the result of either trade or influence from the Deasonville area. (emphasis added)

In Ford's graphs of proportions of pottery types (marker types as well as non-marker types) in each of the four stratigraphic cuts, one of which appears in Figure 2.10, Deasonville-complex sherds were shown as present in varying amounts throughout the sequence. Comparison of his graph of marker types in the four cuts (Figure 2.9) with the graphs of the proportion of all types (marker or otherwise) (e.g., Figure 2.10) shows that sherds of other, unmentioned complexes were present. Ford ignored those in his discussion, since he was interested in the overall waxing and waning of marker types, not small fluctuations between excavation sections. Here, then, was his "one element of culture [pottery] subject to rapid change in form" (Ford 1935a) that allowed him to build a chronology.

The Louisiana-Mississippi Surface Collections

Ford extended that chronology out from Peck Village when he published the results of his and Chambers's survey of sites in Louisiana and Mississippi. The report, published as the second monograph in the *Anthropological Studies* series, carries the imprint date of November 1936, though it was not released until June 1937. Ford began the report during the winter of 1935–1936 and finished it in May 1936, the night before he left on yet a third archaeological trip to Alaska on behalf of Collins. Ethel apparently was to send the manuscript on to the printers, but in June he wrote her from the Aleutians telling her to hold it back because it lacked both polish and information. Ford delivered it to the printers in New Orleans in November 1936.[15]

In the report (Ford 1936a), Ford summarized sherd collections from 103 sites (Figure 2.11). He had abandoned the index system of type construction, noting that it "is highly subjective; much is left to the judgment of the classifier" (Ford 1936a:18). Because it was so dependent on the "classifier's acquaintance with the material"—a strong reflection of the extracted nature of his type definitions—Ford (1936a:18) decided it was "not suitable for presentation." He also claimed that it "was only semi-systematic, was non-analytical, was meaningless unless memorized in detail, and was not capable of logical expansion" (Ford 1936a:18). Ford wanted something more manageable, replicable, and useful for measuring chronological variation.

His replacement system, which Gibson (1982:265) referred to as Ford's "analytical formula plan," was based strictly on decoration, which Ford viewed as comprising two "components"—*motif,* the "plan of the decoration" (e.g., herringbone pattern), and *elements,* the "means to express the motif" (e.g., incised lines) (Ford

---

15. Letters from Ethel Ford to Janie Ford, June 19(?), 1937; October 11, 1935; and May 6, June 27, and November 10, 1936 (LSU Museum of Natural Science archives).

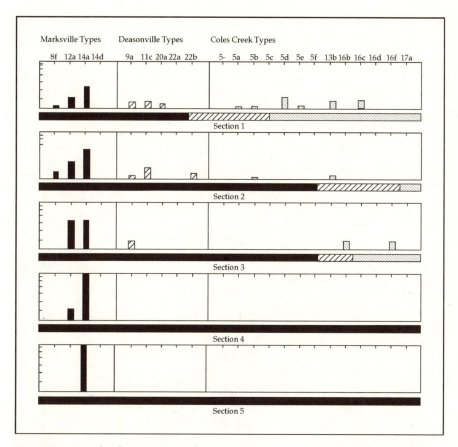

Figure 2.10. Graph of proportions of pottery types in cut 2 at Peck Village. Compare proportions with those shown in Figure 2.9, in which Ford illustrated only the proportions of marker types (from Ford 1935c).

1936a:19). Ford's choice of the word "component" was unfortunate because it was coming to have a rather different meaning in Americanist archaeology (e.g., Gladwin 1936; McKern 1934, 1937) than the "constituent part or feature" Ford meant to denote. Such word choice suggests that Ford had little knowledge of some of the programmatic discussions taking place in the discipline (Lyman et al. 1997a). The two components became the cornerstone of the new system. To these Ford added a third, though it was less relevant to the system than were the other two. The third component accounted for the "specific and peculiar manner of using the elements to form the motif" (Ford 1936a:19)—what Ford (1936a:22) formally referred to as "adaptation and arrangement of features." In cases where

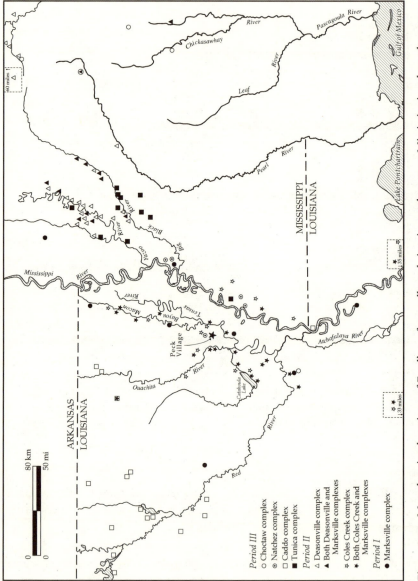

Figure 2.11. Map showing locations of Ford's surface-collected sites in southwestern Mississippi and northeastern Louisiana (after Ford 1936a).

he assumed that decoration was, for example, "very carelessly applied" (Ford 1936a:103), he ignored the component altogether.

Ford's units were ideational—that is, the necessary and sufficient conditions for membership were stated explicitly—and they were not extracted from the sherds but rather were used to *identify* the set of attributes the sherds displayed (Dunnell 1971; Lyman et al. 1997a). Types were particular combinations of attributes that were immutable, atemporal, and aspatial—that is, type 21;21;7 exists for all time and all space (just like an inch or a gram) as opposed to being time- and space-bound (the basis of Phillips's [1958, 1970] type-variety system). Ford's system allowed him to sum the frequency of occurrence of any attribute—whether a particular motif, an element, or an application—as well as the frequency of any class—that is, the frequency of the actual representatives of a particular class. What kept Ford's system from being a paradigmatic classification in the sense that Dunnell (1971) uses the term was that some of the attributes were not mutually exclusive, either within or between components—Dunnell's "dimensions." In addition, some types contained the designation "or" relative to motif and/or element.

The reason for this is that when he changed from the index system to the analytical-formula plan, Ford did not have at hand all of the collections from all the surface-collected sites. Instead, he transferred *data* on the sherds between systems by examining original type descriptions, then transferring the counts from his tally sheets resulting from use of the index system into the new types. There were bound to be a few problems in not having the actual sherds: "In some cases the old classification included two sets of elements or modes of application, either of which was allowed in the same type. To transfer these it is necessary to show that either one or the other comprises the type. This is effected by listing both feature designations and separating them by a slanting line to signify 'or'" (Ford 1936a:23).

Ford's analytical-formula system was, as Gibson (1982:265) suggested, "the most sensitive and rigorous classification scheme to be used in the Lower Mississippi Valley." Despite minor inconsistencies in how Ford handled variation, the system was based on objective criteria—an objectivity derived from direct definition of attributes and attribute combinations that were unbiased by a priori assumptions regarding the spatial and temporal distributions of those attributes. In other words, "it was uncontaminated by notions, suspected or stratigraphically demonstrated, of chronological order or cultural relationships" (Gibson 1982:266). Given that Ford (1936a) chose to examine only motifs, elements, and arrangements thereof, he did select attributes that he no doubt believed, based on previous experience, would allow the measurement of time and space. The system was *imposed on* rather than *extracted from* the sherds. The system was also infinitely expandable. If, for example, new attributes were discovered, they could be accommodated simply by adding them under the appropriate component or dimension.

Despite the rigorous nature of the analytical-formula system, Ford abandoned it shortly after publication of the surface-collection monograph (Ford 1936a). Our guess is that the system was far too intricate for other researchers, who would have had to not only learn how the system worked but also memorize the list of attributes for each dimension. In the end, Ford probably came to the conclusion that the system was far too detailed even for his own purpose. The original decoration-complex marker types he had devised (Ford 1935c) measured chronological order a lot more simply. Ford would, in a few years, become one of the major champions of a new system of type nomenclature for the Southeast—one that had, for several years, been gathering steam in the Southwest. This new system would completely supplant any vestiges of the older Fordian schemes.

Ford's work in 1935–1936 produced a system of categorization of sherds that resulted in the creation of classes, the distributions of which could be plotted in time and space. The classes were ad hoc units, built by trial and error rather than theoretical constructs, but they were ideational units nonetheless. Ford stated the necessary and sufficient conditions for unit membership and held to the system faithfully during the classification. His analytical-formula system certainly was a materialist's construct, but what really is at issue is how he himself *viewed* the units he had created.

In none of his writing prior to 1936 did Ford ever state explicitly that types were "real" in the sense that they were somehow inherent in the data. His occasional comments such as " 'ceramic complexes' are so called from the fact that they consist of a small group of often unrelated pottery design types which were fashionable in the same region at the same time" (Ford 1935b:34) lead us to suspect that although he originally thought types were somehow real, he never was truly wedded to this position. Thus early on he wavered. It is one thing to speak colloquially of pottery types occurring on a site—which conflates the material itself and the categories containing the material—and quite another to view types as real. The Ford of the 1940s and 1950s, as is well documented (e.g., Ford 1949, 1951a, 1952a, 1954a, 1954b, 1954c), went out of his way to demonstrate that types were the creation of the analyst—that is, there was no inherently "correct" way to construct a type. The important thing was to create types—using whatever means possible—and then to test their historical significance.

It has generally been overlooked (Gibson [1982] is a rare exception) that Ford did not start his professional life with this perspective, nor did he come to it quickly. Careful reading of Ford's pre-1938 publications indicates that he could not make up his mind *what* pottery types were, though he appears to have leaned more strongly in 1935 toward thinking that both they and the decoration complexes that housed them were somehow real. One clue to his thinking is contained in his definition of "type," which appears in the glossary to the surface-collection report (Ford 1936a). Instead of defining just the word "type," he appended the modifier "cultural" to it, defining a "type, cultural" as a "standard about which a cultural expression clusters" (Ford 1936a:276). This definition came as much from his views on culture and how it changes and is transmitted as it did from anything else. Ford's activities prior to 1936 were, however, geared less toward discovering what those standards were than toward measuring culture change and documenting culture history. While conflation of the essentialist and materialist metaphysics is apparent in his pre-1938 publications, the former is used more in the role of a commonsense warrant and interpretive algorithm for his units. By 1938, Ford's use of the two metaphysics would shift a bit.

The Complex-Linking Approach

Several of the sites, especially those occupied during the historical period, contained sherds of only one decoration complex, but many sites west and south of Natchez contained sherds of both the Marksville and Coles Creek complexes, and many of those around Vicksburg contained sherds of both the Marksville and Deasonville complexes. A few sites that were known locations of the historical-period Caddo and Tunica contained scattered Coles Creek– complex sherds, but they were not found on Choctaw or Natchez sites, nor did any historical-period sites contain Deasonville-complex sherds (Ford 1936a). This pattern led Ford to suspect that the Coles Creek complex might have been in part contemporaneous with the Caddo and Tunica complexes and that it certainly outlasted the Deasonville complex:

> In searching for connections between the historic and prehistoric horizons, it will be noted that the sites of the Tunica and Caddo have a conspicuous amount of types that are characteristic of the Coles Creek complex. Also several of the Coles Creek sites show small amounts of Caddo and Tunica marker types. As typical Coles Creek sites are not found in the region of either of the two historic complexes, it is easily possible that at one time Coles Creek may have existed in its geographical area alongside the Caddo and Tunica. The evidence of interinfluence points to this condition. Neither the Choctaw nor the Natchez complexes shows any relation to the Coles Creek or any other of the prehistoric complexes. Evidently the Tunica and Caddo were established in their regions before the Choctaw or the Natchez appeared in the area.
>
> None of the historic complexes show any direct relation to Deasonville. Although at one time it was contemporaneous with Coles Creek, it seems to have disappeared before the advent of either of the two earlier historic complexes, Caddo and Tunica. Tunica took over part of the area that Deasonville had occupied.
>
> If it is true that the Coles Creek–Deasonville time horizon interlocks in this way with the historic horizon, then the time horizon of Marksville complex must have been the earliest of all. (Ford 1936a:254)

Ford (1936a:254) referred to this method of chronologically arranging sites as "'complex linking'—connecting time horizons by the overlapping of complexes occupying neighboring areas." This is remarkably similar to the concepts of *horizon* and *horizon style* discussed a decade later by Kroeber (1944) and Willey (1945) with reference to South American prehistory.

Ford also realized that "mixing" of sherds of different decoration complexes could result from several factors. Earlier, he had commented that there is "system to this mixing of complexes. It can usually be attributed to one or two causes. Mixture often results from trade or borrowing of ideas having occurred between neighboring, contemporaneous complex areas [e.g., the presence of Deasonville sherds on sites containing primarily Coles Creek sherds], so that foreign designs become incorporated in the village refuse dumps" (Ford 1935b:34–35). Ford assumed both conditions—trade and diffusion—had created the mixture of complexes seen in the 103 sherd assemblages he analyzed. He also was well aware that reoccupation of a site could result in the mixing of decoration complexes, but he discounted such a possibility as largely improbable: "The village dump or midden deposit was accumulated during the years of occupancy, and if [it] had reached any appreciable depth would show by changes in types of artifacts from the bottom to the top the transitions in style which had occurred when the town was alive. However, the great majority of Louisiana sites never had any great accumulation so that younger and older types are helplessly intermingled" (Ford 1935b:37).

Ford's Notion of Continuous Change

A year later, Ford clarified what he meant. Reoccupation was possible, but "it would be unlikely that a succeeding people should select the exact [previously occupied] habitation spot for their use. If the old locality had been intentionally reoccupied, the odds are that the dumps of the succeeding group would be located near but not precisely on those of the original inhabitants" (Ford 1936a:255). In short, mixing of complexes *resulting from reoccupation* was unlikely. Ford believed it was more likely the result of *continuous occupation:* "It seems more reasonable to suppose that sites on which apparently subsequent complexes are mixed were either settled in the time of the older and were occupied on into the time of the following complex; or that the villages were inhabited during a period of transition from one complex to the other. . . . If the art styles changed without disturbance of the population, it is reasonable to expect that there should be such a period" (Ford 1936a:255–56).

Apparently, Ford thought even long-term continuous occupation was rare, because most sites did not contain thick accumulations of artifacts. The few that did have such accumulations contained, according to Ford, "transitional-period" assemblages. To demonstrate that there indeed were such transitional periods,

Ford (1936a:262–68) discussed "certain decoration *types* which suggest that they are the results of an evolutionary trend which runs through two or more of the subsequent complexes" (emphasis added), being careful to point out that such continuation "does not imply that this evolutionary process occurred in the local geographical area. In most cases it is more likely that the evidence is a reflection of the process taking place in some nearby territory." If we read Ford correctly, he was suggesting that particular attribute states of decoration types originated in and diffused from one area to another, where they subsequently became part of the local decoration complex by replacing or modifying an attribute state of a vessel. He noted, for example, how one *type* was found throughout the sequence of complexes, but it "also took on, in each complex, the features [read *attributes*] peculiar to that complex" (Ford 1936a:263). Such "lines of development" (Ford 1936a:263) provided historical links between complexes.

Thus, Ford's lines of development suggested evolutionary trends through two or more sequent complexes and involved the notion of phyletic evolution of one form into another via gradual alteration. In the cases he cited, alteration was at the scale of one or more attributes of a type. The evolutionary continuum is marked, in Rowe's (1961:327) words, "by the continuity of features and variation in themes." This is precisely the form of seriation mentioned by Wissler (1916a) and used twenty years earlier by Kidder (e.g., 1915, 1917; see also Kidder and Kidder 1917) and earlier still by Petrie (e.g., 1899) and Evans (1850) in Europe. It is unclear if Ford invented phyletic seriation independently, though he probably didn't. He did not cite Wissler, Kidder, Petrie, or Evans in his early publications. He had worked with Collins, who perceived different artifact-bearing strata as representing different occupations and distinctive pottery styles as representing different cultures (Collins 1927a, 1927b)—a point with which Ford (e.g., 1936b:103) at least initially agreed. Ford was also aware of some of the methods used by others, such as Matthew Stirling, who at the landmark Birmingham Conference of 1932 spoke of working "from the known [historic] to the unknown [prehistoric]," or what was known as the direct historic approach, and using "both vertical and horizontal stratigraphy" to form a chronology (Stirling 1932:21). The latter involved the identification of pottery types that were diagnostic of historic tribes; the former "constitutes the best basis for the relating of time changes" (Ford 1936b:103).

The Birmingham Conference, officially known as the Conference on Southern Prehistory, was "called for the purposes of reviewing the available information on the pre-history of the southeastern states, discussing the best methods of approach to archaeology in this region, and to its general problems, and the developing of closer cooperation through the personal contacts of the members of the conference" (National Research Council 1932:1). The meeting was, as Gibson (1982:258) pointed out, "without doubt one of the most influential professional meetings ever held on Southeastern archaeology" (see O'Brien and

Lyman 1997). Presenters at the conference, sponsored by the National Research Council's Committee on State Archaeological Surveys, included a host of well-known archaeologists and anthropologists of the time—William Duncan Strong, Ralph Linton, Carl Guthe, Warren Moorehead, John Swanton, Winslow Walker, William Webb, Matthew Stirling, Clark Wissler, and Henry Collins, for example—as well as lesser-known individuals, including Moreau Chambers, Fred Kniffen, and James Ford. Gibson (1982:259) argued that what Walker in particular had to say about the promise of Louisiana's archaeological record and the future directions that should be taken to understand it must have had a profound effect on Ford and Kniffen, both of whom oriented some of their early work in the directions in which Walker was pointing. In his paper on historical-period sites in Mississippi, Collins (1932b:39) promised that an upcoming paper by Ford would describe the "potsherds from these historic sites, as well as those from neighboring sites of unknown age."

Given Ford's "dominant axiom of culture: it is always changing," we have to ask why, within his framework, evolution could not happen in situ, that is, at the site producing the sherds. Recall Ford's (1935a:9) statement, "Culture is in reality a set of ideas [that] is in a continuous state of evolutionary change since it is constantly influenced both by inventions from within and the introduction of new ideas from without the group." First, it was clear that to understand phylogenetic evolution required the control of time, and time was surely visible given superposition. As Walker (1932:45) had noted at the Birmingham Conference, "It is not permissible to assume that all [artifacts] are the products of the same makers, merely because they happen to be found in the same mound or village site. Unless the method of excavation employed is such that the exact vertical as well as horizontal position of all the artifacts can be determined, it is useless to attempt further classification based on typology alone." Ford had superposed artifacts from Peck Village. Second, the general approach to archaeology in the Southeast (and elsewhere) involved plotting artifacts in space and correlating them with historic tribes. This focus on space, as Stirling's remarks at the Birmingham Conference make clear, helps us understand what Ford was thinking:

> The difficulty of defining a general culture area is obvious. A culture area after all is an arbitrary and artificial device whereby a certain region characterized by distinctive traits is set apart for purposes of consideration. We should not let this spoil our perspective on the inter-relationship of cultures as a *flow* rather than as a series of static jumps. It is only to be expected that certain traits characterizing any region are likely to merge into marginal areas until the problem arises as to where we must stop and at which point we are to draw the limits of the area which we have under consideration. It is quite possible, however, to recognize in the Southeast a general area which may be definitely contrasted with other areas of similar extent, as, for example, the Southwest. (Stirling 1932:22; emphasis added)

A culture was a flowing stream of ideas, but because cultures are not autonomous —they interact—the appropriate model for culture change was a *braided* stream— each intersection of two trickles representing "cultural influences" (Stirling 1932: 22). Such influences were the result of ethnographically visible processes such as diffusion, trade, or even immigration, but regardless of which mechanism operated in a particular time-space context, they all provided a new source of variation for the local pottery tradition, just as in situ invention did.

But Ford's decoration *types* evolved as a result of influences from outside— an idea perfectly in concert with, and probably derived from, the then-prevalent notion that it was unlikely that a "complicated technique of decoration" could be independently invented in two distinct areas at approximately the same time (Setzler 1933a:153). This proposition was one with which culture historians would contend on a continual basis (see Steward [1929] for a review). New decoration complexes—aggregates of types—evident in an area thus represented the replacement of one culture by another. In both cases—the former at the scale of what we would call a discrete object, the latter at the scale of a set of multiple types—in situ evolution via invention was largely precluded because of Ford's view of culture change. Within a given culture, change was continuous, *and* it usually was gradual. For Ford, this meant phyletic evolution was perceivable at the scale of *attribute,* as we have seen. Change in *types* was at the scale of discrete object and thus involved a combination of attributes.

The lack of apparent phyletic ties between types construed as *sets* of attributes and representing different time periods simply did not fit Ford's model of gradual and continuous change within a culture. There was no obvious cause for an internal innovation or invention at such a scale, and this strengthened the notion that the source of innovation must be external. Apparent phyletic ties between one or two attributes suggested only a minor internal source of change that Ford's model could accommodate. At the scale of decoration complex, the major source of innovation must be external. Thus Ford (1936a:270) ended his monograph on the surface collections by noting, "Even with this modest beginning there is quite a temptation to see a story of ancient movements of people and cultural forces in the local region with ramifications spread over much of the eastern United States." The inability of Ford's model of culture to accommodate significant internal innovation or invention explains perfectly why in the 1960s Ford could become a leading champion of large-scale migration and diffusion of ideas throughout the Americas.

TEMPO AND MODE IN EVOLUTION

Evolutionary biologists have long been interested in these kinds of problems, summarized beautifully in George Gaylord Simpson's classic *Tempo and Mode in Evolution* (Simpson 1944). Simpson (1944:xxix–xxx) defined *tempo* as having to do with "evolutionary rates under natural conditions, the measurement and interpretation of rates, their acceleration and deceleration, the conditions of exceptionally slow or rapid evolutions, and phenomena suggestive of inertia and momentum," and *mode* as the "way, manner, or pattern of evolution. . . . [that is,] how populations became genetically and morphologically differentiated." Isn't this pretty much what Ford was interested in? To him, a culture consisted of a set of shared ideas held in common by a group of interacting people (a population). Ideas within any particular set change as a result of invention or diffusion from elsewhere (mode), and the rate (tempo) at which they change is for the most part gradual and continuous. For Ford, determination of the tempo and mode of change required an intimate knowledge of the time-space distribution of decoration types, which allowed one to track the time-space origins of ideas and their movements. Determination of the source of change—internal or external to a culture—required intimate familiarity with the attributes, types, and complexes of pottery available for study. Similarity between pottery phenomena at whatever scale allowed one to track homologous—common ancestry—relationships.

By the time he published the surface-collection monograph (1936a), Ford had decided that he saw enough difference in tempo between the Yazoo City area and the Natchez area to postulate an earlier terminal date for the Marksville complex near Yazoo City than for the one near Natchez (Figure 2.12). The ordering of complexes was unchanged from that presented in his second *Louisiana Conservation Review* article (Ford 1935b) (Figure 2.8); only the timing was different. Ford made no comment on the difference in thinking, but it must have grown out of his analysis of overlapping complexes. Regardless, Figure 2.12 also makes it clear that late in 1936, Ford, who as we will see became the champion of creating arbitrary periods, was still thinking in terms of design complexes, not periods.

Ford had, by 1936, demonstrated that chronological order could be brought to the archaeological record of the lower Mississippi Valley, as it had been brought to the Southwest. The archaeological literature since the 1930s, while crediting Ford as the primary author of southeastern chronology, has completely missed the subtlety and cleverness of how he accomplished what he did. Received wisdom seems to be that Ford started in the historical period and worked his way through time, piggybacking one decoration complex on another until he had the complete sequence, at which point he used Peck Village as a check. In a manner of speaking he did, but this obscures the important point that Peck Village contained no pottery from the historical period. What Ford had was a prehistoric sequence that was represented stratigraphically—Marksville to Coles Creek, with a minor representation of Deasonville alongside Coles Creek—but it all apparently dated to the prehistoric period. This gave him stratigraphic control for one end of the

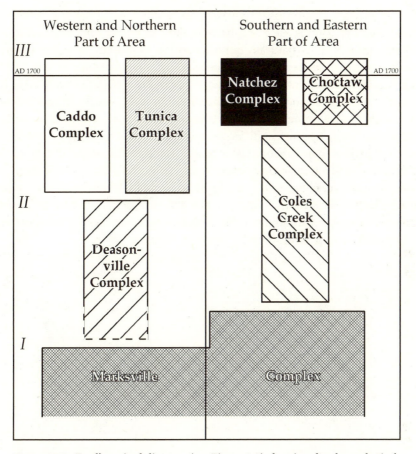

Figure 2.12. Ford's revised diagram (see Figure 2.8) showing the chronological positioning of seven ceramic complexes from northeastern Louisiana and southwestern Mississippi. The major difference between this arrangement and the one he produced a year earlier (Figure 2.8) is in the ending date for the Marksville complex. Here, he extended the complex later in the Natchez area (labeled "Southern and Eastern Part of Area") than in the Yazoo City area. As in the earlier rendition, the Roman numerals stand for points in time (after Ford 1936a).

sequence—he already had the other end anchored—but the two ends did not join. Rarely did a "late prehistoric" site—one containing an overwhelming preponderance of either Coles Creek or Deasonville pottery—contain any historical-period sherds, and even in the cases where one did, Ford could not be sure there was not an occupational hiatus. He suspected, however, that geographically overlapping decoration complexes demonstrated contemporaneity, especially in the northeastern portion of the survey area, where sherds of the Coles Creek complex occurred alongside a few sherds of the Caddo and Tunica complexes.

Ford's thinking grew naturally out of a perspective that culture was a peaceful, braided stream of ideas, each channel containing a more or less unique set of ideas, which, upon intersection, exchanged varying amounts of what they were carrying. Cultures might occasionally "invent" new ideas, but this was a commonsensical process observable in the ethnographic record, just as were the more important mechanisms of change such as diffusion, migration, trade, and the like. There was no robust archaeological theory cast in terms of culture change and development, so Ford and his contemporaries borrowed heavily, and often uncritically, from anthropology, occasionally throwing in a term from biological evolution to help express the notion of cultural development. The net result, unfortunately, would ultimately lead to the undoing of the culture-history paradigm, though in 1936 no one could have predicted this.

3

LSU and Federal Archaeology
1937–1941

By the time his "Analysis of Indian Village Site Collections from Louisiana and Mississippi" was published in November 1936, Ford had graduated with a bachelor's degree from the School of Geology at Louisiana State University and had begun graduate studies there. To this point we haven't said much about Ford's formal education, but to understand where some of his ideas came from—and probably some of his analytical methods as well—we need to discuss people around Ford and examine the roles they played both in his education and in archaeology. The LSU faculty provided some very interesting links, some less direct than others, between Ford's work and what had transpired in southwestern archaeology between roughly 1914 and 1930. In particular there was Fred Kniffen, who came to the university in 1929. Kniffen's work undertaken in the mid-1930s as part of two geomorphological studies of coastal Louisiana provided important keys to Ford's thinking relative to chronological ordering—keys that are missing or only vaguely detailed in Ford's own publications.

The role played by LSU in southeastern archaeology has been ably chronicled by Lyon (1996), and our goal here is not to repeat in detail the information he provides. Several tributes and obituaries of faculty members in the various departments in which archaeology was taught at LSU over the years also exist (e.g., Haag 1994; Howe and Moresi 1933; Kniffen 1973; Moresi 1939; Neitzel 1991; Richardson 1994; Walker and Richardson 1994), and interested readers should consult them for details.

THE LOUISIANA STATE UNIVERSITY PROGRAM

At the time of his enrollment at LSU, Ford's educational background consisted of one part formal junior-college coursework and several parts on-the-job training. It is fair to say that by the time Ford enrolled at LSU in 1934, Kniffen knew enough about him to realize that although Ford didn't lack for native intelligence, he was a little short in terms of formal education. For his part, Ford must have realized that to have any chance at leaving a mark in Americanist archaeology, he had to have a college degree. Given his growing attachment to southeastern archaeology, and to the prehistory of Louisiana in particular, LSU was the obvious place to pursue a degree.

The LSU from which Ford graduated in 1936 was a far cry from what it had been in the mid-1920s, when the university offered no courses in anthropology. However, several faculty members in the department of geology had some interests in it, including Henry V. Howe, a University of California–Berkeley graduate who was hired in 1922, and Richard J. Russell, another Berkeley Ph.D. who was hired in 1928 (Howe and Moresi 1933; Moresi 1939). Howe remained a geologist throughout his career, but Russell, through his early exposure to geography at Berkeley, wavered between the two fields. His undergraduate mentor was the highly respected vertebrate paleontologist John C. Merriam, but for some reason Russell switched to structural geology in graduate school (Kniffen 1973). Although he had no training in geography, he received a teaching assistantship in the geography department, and in 1923 (Walker and Richardson [1994:734], however, state it was 1924), when Carl Sauer arrived at Berkeley from the University of Michigan, Russell fell under the influence of one of the most prolific geographers of the first half of the twentieth century. Russell's hybrid interest served him well after he graduated in 1925, first landing him a position at Texas Technological College in Lubbock and then at LSU, where he was assigned to develop a program in geography. That program soon took on a decided anthropological slant with the addition of Kniffen, yet another Berkeley graduate, in 1929.

Fred B. Kniffen: A Geography-Anthropology Hybrid

The man responsible for bringing anthropology to LSU was a Michigan native who received his bachelor's degree in geology from the University of Michigan in 1922. However, it was geography, not earth science, that interested him most during his time in Ann Arbor. Although Kniffen never took a formal course in geography while a student at Michigan, he accompanied Sauer on an extended field trip to Kentucky and Tennessee, after which he realized that the study of people and places was his first love (McKee 1976:6). Kniffen knocked around for several years after graduation, working in Minnesota, Washington, and Alaska. He then wrote to Sauer, who had since moved to Berkeley, and asked him what the chances were of pursuing an advanced degree with him. Sauer accepted Kniffen as a graduate student in 1925.

Kniffen had long been interested in anthropology, and it was natural that Sauer would introduce him to A. L. Kroeber, the most prominent West Coast anthropologist around (not that there were too many of them at the time).

Kniffen and Kroeber must have hit it off, because even though he was a grad-uate student in a different (though somewhat allied) field, Kniffen worked on several projects under Kroeber. In fact, Kniffen's first publication—"Achomawi Geography" (Kniffen 1928), published in Kroeber's series, *University of California Publications in American Archaeology and Ethnology*—was a direct outgrowth of his work on a Kroeber-supervised project. Two other publications, on the Walapai (Kniffen 1935) and the Pomo (Kniffen 1939), also were outgrowths of Kniffen's work with Kroeber.

It wasn't, however, Kniffen's documented ethnographic work that is important here but rather something that is undocumented (and probably undocumentable) and thus strongly inferential. We think that Ford, through his association with Kniffen, learned about percentage stratigraphy and seriation, which had been perfected in the Southwest. Ford never cited the work of any southwestern archaeologists in any of his early publications, but it is unlikely that he arrived at these methods independently. Ford's views on culture and how it changed over time were compatible with both methods—a better way of putting it is that those methods allowed him to measure change as a gradual occurrence—so it may be that he *did* come up with them on his own, but the better bet, at least in our view, is that Kniffen related to Ford some of the things he had seen Kroeber and his students doing in the Berkeley laboratories. And what he must have seen them doing was seriating collections of pottery.

In the 1920s Kroeber and two of his students, William Duncan Strong and Anna Gayton, established a temporal sequence for Peru using the large collections of ceramic vessels assembled by Max Uhle that were housed at Berkeley (Gayton 1927; Gayton and Kroeber 1927; Kroeber 1925a, 1925b; Kroeber and Strong 1924a, 1924b; Strong 1925). To create a chronology, they used both phyletic seriation and frequency seriation, as well as whatever evidence of superposition was available to them in Uhle's notes. It is reasonable to assume that Kniffen, though he was more interested in human geography and ethnology, was at least aware of the methodological underpinnings of what Kroeber, Strong, and Gayton were doing as well as *why* they were doing it. It also is reasonable to assume that when he saw Ford's surface collections from Louisiana and Mississippi, he realized that here was an opportunity to put his Berkeley experience to good use. In his Peck Village report, Ford didn't acknowledge the assistance of anyone other than the National Research Council, the landowner, and his field assistant, but in the surface-collection monograph he noted that Kniffen's "constant encouragement, advice, and frank and penetrating criticism have been invaluable" (Ford 1936a:3). Does this short note indicate that Ford learned his analytical methods from Kniffen? No, not really. We suspect Ford learned about at least some of the critical literature from Kniffen because sometime in 1937 he wrote a paper (Ford 1938b) in which he mentioned work in the Southwest by Kroeber, Kidder, Nelson, and Spier. Ford did not actually cite specific pieces of work in the text but instead simply listed four articles in a section entitled "bibliography." Some of that literature represents the earliest uses of percentage stratigraphy and seriation and the first enunciation of the popularity principle. Although circumstantial, the evidence suggests that Ford might have learned of these techniques from Kniffen.

Kniffen's Chronological Work in Southeastern Louisiana

Kniffen did more than simply pass out advice on archaeology to younger colleagues; among his numerous investigations were two important chronological studies. Their main value today lies in what they tell us about what culture histori-ans, particularly Ford, were thinking at that time. In the first study (Kniffen 1936), undertaken as part of Russell's (1936) larger geomorphological examination of Plaquemines and St. Bernard Parishes east and south of New Orleans, Kniffen dated surface collections at a number of archaeological sites. He did not employ seriation to order the collections, nor did he ever (to our knowledge) excavate a site to check his ordering, though he was aware of the value of superposed collections and, apparently, of percentage stratigraphy. His method for ordering sites was based on the simple assumption that prehistoric peoples lived along waterways and that as those waterways changed course, the inhabitants moved their settlements accordingly. Ford (1936b:104) also mentioned this dating tool in a paper published in March 1936. He undoubtedly learned it from Kniffen and/or Russell. If the sites could be dated, then not only could terminal dates be established for the landforms on which they were located—for example, levees—but the latest period of occupation, as demonstrated by pottery types, should date to the abandonment of the nearby river course. The real beauty of what Kniffen proposed, however, was not in the proposition itself but in how he went about dating the sites.

Russell and Howe had long been interested in the development of the Missis-sippi Delta and the submergence of land in southern Louisiana caused by the sheer weight of the sediment continuously deposited by the Mississippi River and its distributaries. What was missing was a way to date the various events connected with subsidence and the development of deltaic lobes. In addition to dumping an astronomical amount of sediment onto the Louisiana coastal plain, both the Mississippi and its distributaries had, throughout the Pleistocene and Holocene, changed course any number of times in response to changes in such things as water volume and sediment load. Many of the physiographic features that marked the dynamic history of the lower Mississippi Valley were evident, but again, could they be dated in relative fashion?

Kniffen worked out a method of relative-dating southern Louisiana physio-graphic features, which Bill Haag (1994:28) summarized beautifully:

In 1936 [Kniffen] set forth in simple terms understandable and useful to archaeologists and to geomorphologists that aboriginal peoples lived on the natural levees of different courses of the [Mississippi River] and different lobes of the delta at different time periods. This was an entirely new concept that drew upon neither California experience directly nor contributions from the American archaeological experience in the Southwest. Kniffen recognized that the assemblage of potsherds in some areas was quite different from that in other areas. Further, he noted that some kinds of pottery were totally absent from other middens and mounds occurring along the natural levees. From these data he and his colleagues developed working hypotheses that enabled mapping the courses of the river and chronologically relating the prehistoric remains. These hypotheses largely evolved from the fact that Kniffen and his co-workers moved in an intellectual atmosphere of awareness of the relationships between stratigraphy and chronology, whether it be Mesozoic, Pleistocene or Protohistoric times.

Kniffen recognized four kinds of sites—man-made mounds of either earth or shell, shell middens, and redeposited accumulations of artifacts on beaches. He also recognized two distinctive pottery complexes—an earlier Bayou Cutler complex and a later Bayou Petre complex—and argued that they were intermediate in age between what he called the Earthen Mound period (earliest) and the Late Prehistoric period (latest). As Gibson (1982:267) pointed out, Kniffen assigned the earthen mounds to the earliest period in part because the mounds contained very little pottery of either the Bayou Cutler or Bayou Petre complexes, and in part because of a difference in shellfish remains found in the earthen mounds and in shell middens:

> Immediately adjacent to the most southerly earth mounds are small shell middens, lying on the marsh deposits and showing no appreciable subsidence. It is significant that these superficial middens are composed dominantly of salt-water oysters [*Crassostrea* sp.], while the occasional shells appearing in cuts in the adjacent earth mounds are invariably brackish-water [*Rangia* sp.]. Here is good evidence of two distinct periods of occupation, the older represented by the earth mounds, the younger by the shell middens. There is also the implication of an increasing salinity since the [building] of the earth mounds. (Kniffen 1936:415)

The last line is the key to why Kniffen believed the earthen mounds were at the early end of the sequence: as the land subsided under the weight of increased sediment load, the Gulf of Mexico began to flood previously fresh-to-brackish-water bayous and basins, thus turning the water more saline. Since the earthen mounds contained brackish-water *Rangia* shells and the middens saline-water *Crassostrea* shells, *Rangia* had to date to when the local waters were fresh to brackish. Hence the mounds were older than the middens.

Kniffen indicated there were notable differences between his two newly named ceramic complexes. What he called Bayou Cutler sherds were often check-stamped and not tempered with shell (they were clay-tempered, though he did not point this out). Rim lugs and nodes were plentiful, but handles were not. Bayou Petre sherds were shell-tempered and noncheck-stamped. Rim lugs and nodes were absent, but handles were abundant. Kniffen immediately recognized formal similarities between the Bayou Cutler complex and Ford's Coles Creek complex, the main differences being "the absence in the Bayou Cutler complex of the overhanging-line decoration *motif*, so characteristic of the Coles Creek of central Louisiana; and the infrequent appearance in the Coles Creek complex of the check-stamp ware found abundantly in the Bayou Cutler complex" (Kniffen 1936:413). Of course, central Louisiana is a long way from southeastern Louisiana, but, based on his observations of formal similarities, Kniffen felt comfortable in drawing comparisons between what he saw as contemporary pottery complexes. But what about two complexes from roughly the same area? Could they be contemporary, or were they from two distinct time periods? Kniffen came down decidedly in favor of the latter:

> The definite distinction between the Bayou Cutler and Bayou Petre complexes seems certain. It also seems clear that they must differ in time. It is unlikely that two [human] groups could exist side by side without showing some mixture of pottery designs. Assuming that they are different in time, it is important to know which is the older. The evidence is not conclusive. What there is favors the greater age of the Bayou Cutler complex. The check-stamp ware of the Bayou Cutler complex occasionally appears in the Bayou Petre. On the other hand, no diagnostic trait of the Bayou Petre complex, such as handles, appears in the type Bayou Cutler collections. (Kniffen 1936:143)

Kniffen's use of the word "trait" is significant. He did not say that no diagnostic *type* of the Bayou Petre complex showed up in Bayou Cutler collections. This kept his argument from being tautological, meaning he did not decide an assemblage was either Bayou Cutler or Bayou Petre on the basis of a Bayou Cutler or Bayou Petre pottery type. He used specific traits—empirical things—to make such assignments. The absence of *some* traits—handles—on *some* sites and the occasional presence of *other* traits—check-stamped sherds—on *other* sites allowed him to construct an ordering. This was simply occurrence seriation.

Kniffen's second study focused on Iberville Parish (Figure 3.1), again as part of a project headed by Russell to examine subsidence and coastal geomorphology (Russell 1938). Kniffen used the same methods he had employed in Plaquemines and St. Bernard Parishes, and he also used the same rationale for his analysis, though this time he spelled it out more explicitly:

> Great midden accumulations of [*Rangia*] must indicate close proximity to a source of supply at the time the structures were built. It seems unlikely that a primitive people, however fond they might be of these clams, could or would afford to transport them more than a few miles in an amount sufficient to build middens measurable in terms of hundreds and thousands of cubic yards. If this reasoning is valid, one must postulate environmental conditions substantially different from the present for the time when many of the shell middens shown on the map [Figure 3.1] were built. (Kniffen 1938:196)

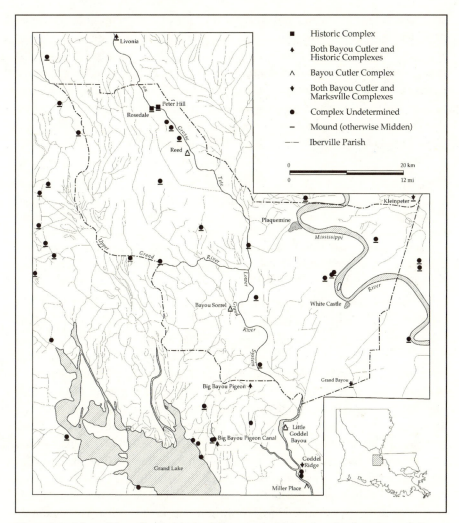

Figure 3.1. Map of Iberville Parish, Louisiana, and vicinity showing locations of sites Kniffen used in his analysis. Two types of sites—mounds and middens—are shown, as are the ceramic complexes (if known) represented at each site (after Kniffen 1938).

Kniffen's use of shellfish remains as a chronological tool might have been the same as in the earlier study, but his use of sherds as chronological indicators was vastly different. Whereas in the Plaquemines and St. Bernard report he had used traits, in the Iberville Parish report he used *types*—a result, no doubt, of Ford's influence. There was the perfunctory acknowledgment of Ford's (1936a) work: "Making particular use of [decoration], Ford has found it possible to group the sites of northern Louisiana and adjacent sections of Mississippi into a number of pottery complexes expressive of differences of either time or space or of both" (Kniffen 1938:198). Kniffen then created a table (Table 3.1) in which he listed the frequencies of sherds collected from twelve Iberville Parish sites "for which the pottery collections are considered sufficiently large to be representative" (Kniffen 1938:199). He didn't elaborate on what he meant by sufficiently large—a problem that Ford (1936a) had addressed by comparing collections made at different times from thirteen sites in his sample. Kniffen then arranged the Iberville Parish sites so that

> the youngest appear at the top, the oldest at the bottom. The analysis is based on Ford's criteria. [Table 3.1] is really a summary of the several analyses; instead of expressing the percentage representation of each design type, the individual site is summarized as to percentage of "marker" (M) and percentage of characteristic but "other than marker" (OT) types for each complex represented. The percentage representation of design types not peculiar to, or diagnostic of, any complex is shown in the column headed "unrelated." (Kniffen 1938:199)

By "Ford's criteria," Kniffen was referring to those that Ford (1936a) had established in his surface-collection monograph for placing sherds in one of the seven pottery complexes he identified. But what about sherds/collections that didn't fit nicely into one complex or the other? Kniffen had the solution: "Ford has come to the conclusion that relatively few sites are occupied for long periods of time. Few sites are 'pure,' in the sense that they contain pottery all belonging to a single complex. Based on the percentage dominance of design types the sites are assigned to a single complex or to an intermediate position between two complexes differing in time or in place" (Kniffen 1938:198–99). This method of carving up time is evident in the right-hand column in Table 3.1. Kniffen created four periods—Historic, Historic–Bayou Cutler, Bayou Cutler, and Bayou Cutler–Marksville—each of which was represented by from two to four ceramic assemblages. No site contained sherds from only one period; rather, Kniffen simply decided whether there were so few sherds of another period present that he could ignore them when assigning an assemblage to one period or another.

One critical point to Kniffen's analysis is examined here in detail because of the effect it could have had on his results. We say "could have had" because it is impossible to determine the nature or magnitude of the effect. The same is true for Ford's analysis, but the point is easier to make using Kniffen's work as an example. Note that several sites listed in Table 3.1 contained significant amounts of "unrelated" types, which Kniffen (1938:199) defined in the same way Ford had:

> The types and features of pottery decoration that are classed as "unrelated" are either those which do not appear often enough to identify themselves with any of the complexes, or those which appear frequently on sites of all the complexes. In other

Table 3.1. Pottery Types Used by Fred B. Kniffen to Categorize Sherds from Sites in Iberville Parish, Louisiana

Site	Number of Sherds	Natchez M[a]	Natchez OT[b]	Tunica M	Tunica OT	Caddo M	Caddo OT	Bayou Cutler M	Bayou Cutler OT[c]	Coles Creek M	Deasonville M	Deasonville OT	Marksville M	Marksville OT	Unrelated	Periods
Peter Hill	80	5[d]	29	9	6	...	7	...	1	...	...	...	1(?)	...	46	Historic
Rosedale	205	19	14	4	13	...	10	...	8	1	2	4	...	...	28	
Livonia	35	6	11	...	...	...	3	20	...	...	...	...	...	...	61	Historic & Bayou Cutler
Big Bayou Pigeon	...	...	...	2	9	...	10	34	36	4	...	2	...	...	4	
Big Bayou Pigeon Canal	28	11	...	...	...	...	3	72	10	...	...	...	...	...	9	
Reed	114	1	...	1	...	...	1	82	5	...	...	...	...	...	12	
Little Goddel Bayou	428	...	...	...	...	...	...	84	11	3	...	...	...	...	...	Bayou Cutler
Bayou Sorrel	85	...	...	...	...	...	...	86	8	2	1	...	...	...	3	
Miller Place	124	...	...	...	...	...	...	86	8	2	...	...	...	...	5	
Grand Bayou	98	...	...	...	...	...	...	66	15	1	2	...	2	...	13	Bayou Cutler & Marksville
Kleinpeter	54	...	...	...	...	...	4	33	10	15	2	2	17	...	17	
Goddel Ridge	15	...	...	...	...	...	...	27	40	...	...	...	20	...	14	

Data from Kniffen (1938).
a "Marker" design types.
b Characteristic but "other than marker" design types.
c Common to both Bayou Cutler and Coles Creek complexes.
d Figures are percentages of total for each site.

words, these are types which are not diagnostic; they are as likely to be connected with one complex as another.

Some of the unrelated types may occur promiscuously because their description is very indefinite and may actually include a great range of different decorations. . . .

Still other types appear to be typologically related to some of the complexes, but do not occur frequently enough to prove their relationship. (Ford 1936a:242)

As Table 3.1 shows, the percentage of unrelated types was quite high at several sites, such as Peter Hill (46%) and Livonia (61%). Many of Ford's (1936a) sites also contained varying percentages of "unrelated" types. We thought at first that most sherds of unrelated types were probably what typically are referred to as "plain" sherds—those containing no decoration. However, we soon realized that this supposition was incorrect, at least as it pertained to Ford's collections. Since he not only listed the unrelated types in his table of sherd frequencies (Ford 1936a:figure 1) but also defined them, one can backtrack through the numbers to find the actual types represented. It turns out that *all* of his "unrelated" types were created on the basis of decoration. We assume the types used by Kniffen also were decoration-based. This means that most if not all plain sherds, if any were even collected, were not used in the analyses. This is what Ford (1936a:11) meant when he said, "Either while making the collection, or later in the laboratory, the sherds were sorted. Only those pieces were retained which promised to yield information concerning decoration, shape, tempering material, or appendages. All rim sherds and all pieces that showed untypical texture or thickness were saved." Our guess is that there was considerable "sorting" going on in the field. At Little Goddel Bayou, which produced by far the largest sherd collection (428 sherds), *all* of the sherds fell either into the Bayou Cutler complex or the contemporary Coles Creek complex (Table 3.1). No sherds are listed in the "unrelated type" column. Thus Kniffen could classify all of the sherds. Such precision, while remotely possible, almost defies imagination. Even Goddel Ridge, which produced the smallest collection (15 sherds), contained 2 sherds (14%) that fell into unrelated types. Perhaps not all sites were collected by the same individual. Such sherds might have been saved, but they were not included in the assemblage totals. We assume Kniffen's weren't either.

What effect this bias might have had on Kniffen's and Ford's results is, of course, unknowable. However, it would have had more of a potential effect on Kniffen's work because he actually seriated sites based on percentages of pottery types (Table 3.1 is a frequency seriation), whereas Ford presented only gross arrangements of sites in terms of design complexes. The "plainware problem"—that is, what one does with sherds that contain no decoration and hence do not appear too useful for chronological purposes—is still around today, and how it is handled can affect results dramatically (Fox 1992, 1998; O'Brien and Fox 1994b). In the end, perhaps Kniffen's seriation wasn't significantly affected—the patterns in Table 3.1

are strong—but interestingly, what is missing from the ordering are the early and late ends of the prehistoric sequence—the periods that later would be termed Tchefuncte (early) and Plaquemine (late).

There were no sites in the sample that Kniffen identified as "pure" Marksville, though a few contained Marksville-complex marker types. Gibson (1982:270) pointed out that based on the marker types Kniffen used, the Marksville assemblages he identified dated to the latest part of the Marksville period—what in a few years would be referred to as Troyville (Ford and Willey 1940). Each of those sites also contained numerous Bayou Cutler–complex sherds, so Kniffen accommodated the sites under a period he termed Bayou Cutler–Marksville—a transitional unit reflecting Ford's axiom that culture is always changing. Four sites seemed "pure" enough to warrant placing them in the Bayou Cutler period. Based on the overwhelming percentages at two sites of pottery that Collins, Ford, and others labeled as Natchez, Tunica, or Caddo, Kniffen placed these sites in the Historical period. Three others, because of the mixture of sherds from both the Bayou Cutler and historical-tribes complexes, were placed in the Historic–Bayou Cutler period—another transitional unit.

Implications of Kniffen's Work

Gibson made a number of interesting observations about Kniffen's use of pottery types and drew a conclusion with which we agree completely:

> The inclusion of Coles Creek markers along with Bayou Cutler diagnostic types in both the Historic–Bayou Cutler and Bayou Cutler periods is a very interesting admission, as is the inclusion of a column . . . showing types common to both Coles Creek and Bayou Cutler complexes. This implies that Kniffen, or perhaps Kniffen and Ford, had established some definite ideas about which pottery types "belonged" with each culture period. Unfortunately, neither Kniffen nor Ford ever published a "trait list," or similar device, detailing these marker types. (Gibson 1982:269)

We believe that Ford *had* decided which types went with which periods, just as he had earlier decided which types were "marker" types for a particular complex and which were "related" types. How he decided this is not at all clear. We suspect he variously constructed, dismantled, and reconstructed types and complexes on a trial-and-error basis until he derived some that allowed him to measure time and space. This obscure procedure would, early in the 1950s, lead to several heated debates with some of his contemporaries. It is also true that when Ford abandoned the analytical-formula method, he ended any chance of using ideational units to distinguish among the complexes. As we will see a bit later, the analytical system was replaced with the binomial type, which had been gradually developing in the Southwest. When it sprang up in the Southeast in the late 1930s, largely at the hands of Ford and Griffin, it did so full-grown. Ford and several of his southeastern colleagues were in a sense preadapted for the simpler type designations because what they had been using for years was, as Gibson (1982) pointed out, unwieldy. The new system would slice through all the dizzying array of variation, pick out a few variants, and wrap the subsets into neat little packages. Those kinds of types, at least in the Southeast, had their origins in Ford's use of marker types, which by definition were diagnostic—type fossils—of specific decoration complexes. Ford (1936a) began referring to the complexes as "periods." Kniffen (1938) followed Ford's lead when he added the right-hand column to Table 3.1. Since marker types for any one complex occurred on sites that contained marker types for other periods, Kniffen was faced with the problem of what to call the periods. Our bet is that Ford gave him the answer: create intermediate periods to reflect the occurrence at sites of marker types for more than one complex. Thus Kniffen ended up with a period labeled Bayou Cutler–Marksville and another labeled Historic–Bayou Cutler.

Why would we bet that it was Ford who suggested this to Kniffen? Think back to Ford's view of culture—that steadily flowing stream (culture's mode) that sometimes changed speed (tempo) but whose course, unless interrupted by outside influence, remained constant. This view comes through clearly in Kniffen's creation of intermediate periods. Take what he said about Goddel Ridge, the oldest site shown in Table 3.1: "[It] yields an appreciable percentage, although by no means a dominance, of potsherds referable to the Marksville complex, the oldest identified for Louisiana. The pottery is dominated by Bayou Cutler types, but not in sufficient amount to class the site as Bayou Cutler. *Rather, it belongs to a stage marked by the waning influence of Marksville types and the growing importance of Bayou Cutler types*" (Kniffen 1938:201; emphasis added). Sound familiar?

Can there be any doubt that Gibson was right about Ford and Kniffen "knowing" which types went with which time period? The nice, neat arrangement shown in Table 3.1—much nicer than Ford's (1936a) tabular summary of pottery types plotted against the surface-collected sites—is beguiling in its simplicity, which obscures all of the details that had characterized Ford's earlier work. Many of those details were difficult to deal with—this is why he abandoned the analytical-formula system—and maybe by 1937 Ford was fed up with detail when he could already see the grand patterns he was looking for. The blueprint was simple: use the existing marker types, developed in part from ethnohistorical research (the historical-period types) and in part from stratigraphic positioning, to order assemblages by means of what Ford (1936a) referred to as "complex linking." Then, turn the decoration complexes into periods to emphasize the temporal component. Where the situation warranted, create a new period and slide it into the sequence. The product was the creation of "index fossils"—marker types—to measure the slow, inexorable march of time. What may not have dawned on Ford or Kniffen was that by creating periods, which highlight only *difference*, they precluded any measurement of materialist-like *change* within the temporal continuum. Their pottery types, which began life as measurable attributes under Ford's guiding hand at Peck Village, had, by the time Kniffen wrote the Iberville Parish report, become empirical units with lives of their own. Within a few years, those types would assume almost supernatural qualities.

THE BINOMIAL SYSTEM COMES TO THE SOUTHEAST

The year 1937 was a busy one for Jim Ford. He had graduated from LSU in the spring of 1936 and had begun graduate studies there after returning in the fall from his third Alaskan trip, but the following year he decided to transfer to the University of Michigan to complete his master's degree. James B. Griffin (Figure 3.2), a 1936 doctoral graduate of Michigan's anthropology department who was attached to the university's anthropology museum, was developing a reputation as the premier pottery analyst in the eastern United States. Ford and Griffin had corresponded, but they didn't meet until June 1937 at a professional meeting in Columbus, Georgia. Griffin urged Ford to come north to graduate school.[1] Given Griffin's interest in pottery and his growing stature in the field, there probably was no better person around under whom to apprentice. It would have been difficult to predict, but the linkage between Ford and Griffin in 1937 would forever change the course of southeastern archaeology. Both were bright, energetic young men, but together they were much more than the sum of the parts.

The immediate productivity of that union was, we think, in part predicated on what Ford learned during the summer of 1937 somewhere between Macon, Georgia, and northwestern New Mexico. The summer would be pivotal for Ford and his emerging ideas on culture history, especially his approach to pottery classification.

Ford's first important move was his return to Georgia in June 1937 to oversee the restoration of the ceremonial earth lodge at Macon Plateau, which the National Park Service had renamed Ocmulgee National Monument. While there, he met Gordon R. Willey (Figure 3.3), a young archaeologist who attended the University of Arizona for both his undergraduate and master's degrees. Willey had spent parts of 1936 and 1937 as an assistant to A. R. Kelly, who was directing several federally funded excavations around Macon (Willey 1988). The second important move for Ford occurred later in the summer, when he spent six weeks in Chaco Canyon, New Mexico, as part of the University of New Mexico field school. Up to that point, Ford, to our knowledge, had never set foot in the Southwest. He must have heard or read of the work of Kroeber, Kidder, and their colleagues, but until 1938 he never cited the work of any southwestern archaeologist.

1. Letter from Ethel Ford to Janie Ford, June 1937 (LSU Museum of Natural Science archives).

Figure 3.2. Photograph of attendees at an impromptu meeting at Serpent Mound, Adams County, Ohio, April 1938. Left to right: George K. Neuman, John L. Cotter, James B. Griffin, George I. Quimby, John Buckner, James A. Ford, Ethel Ford, Richard G. Morgan, and William G. Haag (photograph courtesy the Museum of Anthropology, University of Michigan).

In a letter to Henry Collins dated September 5, 1937,[2] Ford wrote, "Ethel and I have just returned from a month with [Donald] Brand in Chaco Canyon, where we lived in the shadow of Pueblo Bonito." The report of that work appeared in Brand et al. (1937; see also Senter 1937). Ford apparently enjoyed his brief foray to the Southwest, making specific mention to Collins of the wildlife encountered: "I have no objection to the [southwestern] flora except the cactus, and the fauna meets both Ethel's and my approval except for a few examples of the Harvard attitude." The date of the letter, September 5, makes us think that the Fords stayed at Chaco after the field school to participate in the Pecos Conference, which was held there that year. If so, one can only wonder if he was referring to A. V. Kidder, whom he surely would have met at the meeting.

By the time Ford returned to Baton Rouge in September, he was full of ideas about expanding the scope of archaeology in Louisiana, which, following the early project at Marksville, had grown rather quiet. Willey's recollection of the drive

2. LSU Museum of Natural Science archives.

Figure 3.3. Photograph of Gordon R. Willey, ca. 1943 (photograph courtesy National Anthropological Archives, Smithsonian Institution).

he and Ford made from Macon to Baton Rouge indicates something about Ford's vision for archaeological work in the Deep South:

> Jim told me that after a year at Michigan he would return to Louisiana and set up a big WPA program of excavation in the state. In this connection, he planned a large, central laboratory, and he wanted me to take charge of it for him. . . . I was excited

by the idea. Jim could outline and present a research program like a call to arms. No loyal archaeologist could refuse. Victory was just over the horizon. Together we would solve all kinds of problems as we envisaged them then: Hopewellian origins, the rise of Middle Mississippian, the role of the Caddoan cultures. That night . . . I fell asleep and dreamt of archaeological glories to come. (Willey 1988:57)

Big plans Ford had—big enough that, as Willey noted, any archaeologist would get excited. But before those plans could be put in operation, Ford would have to further his formal education, and that need brought him to Griffin's doorstep in the fall of 1937.

James B. Griffin and the Fort Ancient Aspect

James B. Griffin grew up in Chicago and attended the University of Chicago, from which he received his bachelor's degree in 1927 and his master's degree in 1930. In 1933 Griffin received a graduate fellowship to the University of Michigan, becoming attached to Carl E. Guthe's Ceramic Repository for the Eastern United States, which was housed in the anthropology museum. Griffin's initial instructions from Guthe were "to bring some semblance of order into the heterogeneous prehistoric pottery materials in the Midwest and in the eastern United States. This was to be done by the study of material already out of the ground in Museums and in private collections" (Griffin 1976:21). These instructions, which sounded simple enough in purpose, started Griffin down a road that spanned a long and distinguished career. In part because of his position in the ceramic repository and in even larger part because of his developing stature in the field, he was asked to undertake the analysis of pottery from various field projects in the midwestern and eastern United States, including two large programs funded by the Tennessee Valley Authority—Norris Basin in northeastern Tennessee (Griffin 1938) and Wheeler Basin in northwestern Alabama (Griffin 1939).

Griffin and Ford began corresponding in 1935. Ford didn't understand how the Midwestern Taxonomic Method worked, and Griffin patiently explained it to him, in terms that were much easier to understand than those of W. C. McKern (1934, 1937), whose name became inextricably linked to the system:

Clearly understood this classification has absolutely nothing to do with temporal or geographical conditions. The only thing which the classification attempts to do is to group sites on the basis of the materials found. A number of localized areas having sufficient differences within a more generalized group should be classified on the basis of the point by point differences or similarities existing. Whether those local variances appear in Louisiana, Florida, Tennessee or Wisconsin makes absolutely no difference in the classification if they are sufficiently alike to warrant being classed in the same group. That is done irrespective of their geographical position. For instance, the two or three foci referred to in my Ft. Ancient paper appear at the present writing to be both geographical and perhaps temporal differences. What the features are that cause the appearance of this foci from the standpoint of classification is not too pertinent to the classification. When the attempt is made, however, to correlate the various foci with other cultures from a geographical or temporal basis one is working on another problem as I see it.[3]

Our main interest here is how Griffin approached the categorization of pottery from 1933 to 1937, because this set the stage for what Griffin and Ford did together in 1938. The centerpiece of Griffin's early work while at the repository was his analysis of Fort Ancient pottery from the upper Ohio Valley. What makes the project interesting from a historical standpoint was Griffin's use of the Midwestern Taxonomic Method (McKern 1934, 1937, 1939)—a classificatory method that focused on the formal similarity of archaeological materials and relegated time to a position of secondary importance (Lyman et al. 1997a). In what he later referred to as the "second major application of the Midwest[ern] Taxonomic Method and . . . the first to recognize significant subgroupings of [the Fort Ancient] complex" (Griffin 1976:22), Griffin focused almost exclusively on pottery, noting that "it has been demonstrated that pottery is the most important single factor in the interpretation of archaeological cultural relationships" and that it "appears to be of such particular value in indicating the various cultural divisions herein established" (Griffin 1943:3). He indicated that his description and classification of pottery was based on the notion of "types, in accordance with a method of approach that has been used with marked success in the Southwest and in other areas the pottery of which has been intensively studied" (Griffin 1943:3), and then he quoted at length a statement by Charles Amsden (1931:22) on the concept of types. He noted that in describing his types, he had followed Guthe's analytical procedure as laid out in "A Method of Ceramic Description" (Guthe 1934; see also Guthe 1928).

In the Fort Ancient monograph, Griffin (1943:5) stated that "any type can be described on the basis of characters which serve to set it apart from all other types"; in short, he was trying to construct internally homogeneous–externally heterogeneous sets of pottery. Interestingly, he indicated, "The exact meaning of any particular object for the living group or individual is forever lost, and the real significance of any object in an ethnological sense has disappeared by the time it becomes a part of an archaeologist's catalogue of finds" (Griffin 1943:340). We take this to mean that in 1937–1938, Griffin, like Ford, was skeptical of whether the cultural norm behind a type could be discovered. Griffin paid considerable attention to detail in his various analyses, but in the end, all that detail got in the way of replicating the systems or of comparing variation between and among assemblages. The ability to communicate between and among archaeologists was important, and, as Griffin (1976:25) later noted, "One of the best tools

3. Letter of May 29, 1935, from Griffin to Ford (LSU Museum of Natural Science archives). For a reappraisal of the Midwestern Taxonomic Method with the benefit of hindsight, see Griffin (1959).

for communication between archaeologists in the eastern United states was the development of the system of pottery type descriptions that came into widespread use during the late 1930s to the present."

To us, the development of that "system of pottery type descriptions" was perhaps *the* critical turning point in southeastern archaeology. No longer was it necessary in a report to write paragraph upon paragraph of description; one had simply to insert a type name (and perhaps a short description) and everyone who saw the name knew automatically what a vessel or sherd looked like. At least that's the way it was supposed to work. As it turned out, things were a bit more complicated—actually, a *lot* more complicated—and as a result culture historians thereafter were forced to deal with philosophical and methodological problems that arose on a continual basis.

The Griffin-Ford Collaboration

When Ford arrived in Ann Arbor, he must have found the ceramic repository a lively place. This is what Griffin had to say about the center and Carl Guthe's vision for it:

> One of Guthe's primary interests was the study of pottery for he had worked with Kidder at Pecos for years, written an excellent monograph on the pottery of San Ildefonso [New Mexico], and a short paper on a method of pottery description (Guthe 1928, 1934). He brought in Benjamin March (1934), a specialist in Oriental ceramics, to work in the Oriental range of the Museum, and he brought F[rederick] R. Matson to Ann Arbor to develop ceramic technology. He arranged for a conference on ceramics with such people as H. S. Colton and Anna Shepard in attendance. This was the environment at the Museum when I began in 1933 to study the large Fox Farm collection from the American Museum. It rapidly became apparent that there were marked differences in the pottery within and between sites and I mentioned to Guthe that it *was possible to have pottery types in the East just as they did in the Southwest.* The different ceramic groups of the Norris and Wheeler Basin reports done in 1934 and 1935 were readily transposed into formally described types, particularly for the Wheeler Basin. (Griffin 1976:25; emphasis added)

Griffin then summarized the situation in the repository when Ford was added to the equation:

> When James A. Ford arrived in Ann Arbor to work on a Masters degree in the fall of 1937 he had just returned from a summer in the Southwest and (if I recall correctly) felt he should do his pottery classification of village site collections in terms of the Southwestern model. I had begun to work up the Fort Ancient pottery in terms of the order followed by Guthe and March but with some modifications adapted to eastern material. As the result of innumerable conversations it was agreed that we should try to have a meeting of working archaeologists to discuss a typology framework. Ford only wanted to have a small number, while I argued we should invite as many as we thought would be able to contribute pottery descriptions. It was finally agreed to hold

the meeting in Ann Arbor in the Ceramic Repository, which was then my office, May 16–17, 1938. (Griffin 1976:25–26)

One could infer that Ford's trip to Chaco Canyon was the catalyst for the meeting Griffin and Ford proposed as a first step in bringing order to pottery analysis in the East. By the mid-1930s, southwestern archaeologists were routinely using binomial pottery classification, and procedures for naming new types had become fairly standardized (see Chapter 1). If it was indeed Ford who suggested to Griffin in 1937 that the new procedure was useful, the suggestion fell on receptive ears because, as we pointed out, Griffin had made a similar suggestion to Guthe a few years earlier. Alternatively, if Griffin had made the suggestion to Ford, it likewise would have been enthusiastically received. Who first brought up the subject to whom is lost to history, but it is largely irrelevant as Ford and Griffin were thinking along similar lines. Griffin no doubt knew what was happening in the Southwest, given both his formal education and his position in the ceramics repository. How did Ford gain that knowledge?

As important as his 1937 trip to the Southwest was to Ford's intellectual development, we have long suspected that he learned much of what he knew about the Southwest, especially pottery classification, through his early friendship with Gordon Willey when they both worked in Georgia. Willey had the requisite southwestern training at the University of Arizona, studying with Byron Cummings and taking courses with astronomer A. E. Douglass, the developer of dendrochronology. Willey takes no such credit in his biographical essay on Ford, noting only that Ford "came back to Macon in September [1937], full of ideas about pottery classification, in the wake of the Southwestern experience" (Willey 1988:56). However, a few years ago, one of us asked him if perhaps it hadn't been he who initially suggested to Ford that he try the southwestern binomial system on southeastern pottery. After pausing for a few seconds, almost as if he had never thought about it before, he responded, "Yes, I believe I was."

This small, seemingly insignificant admission is important because it helps complete the bridge between late 1936, when Ford finished the surface-collection monograph, and late 1937, when he and Griffin began preparing to reorganize pottery classification in the Southeast. Given Ford's interests and intellectual position in 1937, there was no better person to be around for a summer than Gordon Willey. Willey was fresh out of the master's program at Arizona when he went to Georgia to work with A. R. Kelly, and from the time he arrived in Macon his main interest was chronology—first attempting to derive a master dendrochronological chart for the region (Willey 1937, 1938) and then concentrating on "relative chronology as this would be carried by pottery stratigraphy and seriation" (Willey 1988:42). Who better to discuss the finer points of pottery with?

Throughout late 1937 and early 1938, Ford and Willey schemed on how to get other archaeologists interested in the binomial system. Correspondence between the two regularly carried news of someone else coming around to their way of thinking. Willey wanted the meeting to be held in the South, preferably in Savannah, so that Kelly could attend,[4] though this became less of an issue after Kelly came on board. David DeJarnette, working in nearby Alabama, became a natural target, and Willey wrote Ford, saying, "Let's encourage him because this will eventually lead to the Southeast all falling under the naming system."[5] Converting both DeJarnette *and* Kelly was not an easy task because of bad blood between the two, primarily a result of Kelly's consistent snubbing of Alabama archaeologists. Willey continued: "Will you write David and tell him that Griffin is opening up shortly with our naming system in a report and is well sold on that. They (Ala.) think a lot of both you and Griffin and will listen."

Apparently Willey was not the only person with whom Ford discussed pottery typology and how to change classification procedures in the Southeast. In a letter to Henry Collins written in September 1937,[6] Ford suggests others were in on the act: "[Preston] Holder, Kelly, Willey and I had a 'brain wave' and are all enthused on the matter of naming southeastern pottery. We hope to take in [Matthew] Stirling's work in Florida and [William S.] Webb's in Tennessee as well as my own, and in the first publication encircle the Southeast with a ring of precedence which must be followed by anyone else working in the area. At the same time we are setting up a Board of Censors and types that don't pass won't be published." Graduate students being graduate students, Ford's visionary zeal is understandable. Archaeologists of the older generation had had their way, and now it was time for the next generation to point out the errors their elders had committed. In those days, there weren't too many "older-generation" archaeologists around, but Ford had identified two of them—Matthew Stirling, a prominent archaeologist with the Bureau of American Ethnology whose fieldwork had included excavations in Florida, and William S. Webb, a physicist-turned-archaeologist who not only was chairman of the anthropology department at the University of Kentucky but also in 1934 had assumed responsibility for the massive Tennessee Valley Authority archaeological program. Griffin (1974:vi) once characterized Webb as "a man of very strong opinions, both personal and professional; having once made up his mind that a given research path or idea was correct, he followed it with drive and determination. He was able to develop or accept a new notion, work on it, worry over it, and finally convince himself that it must be true. Thereafter, no amount of argument or contrary evidence was likely to sway him." If Ford and his co-conspirators were going to encircle Webb, they were not going to do it easily.

4. Letter of November 2, 1937, from Willey to Ford (LSU Museum of Natural Science archives).
5. Letter of February 15, 1938, from Willey to Ford (LSU Museum of Natural Science archives).
6. Letter of September 24, 1937, from Ford to Collins (LSU Museum of Natural Science archives).

The inclusion of Kelly in the radical group is interesting and in a way under-standable. He was closer in age to Ford and Willey than to Webb, and he had employed the two younger men over the course of several seasons. He had worked with Holder in Georgia. Kelly had received his doctorate at Harvard in 1929 and had taught at the University of Illinois from 1929 until 1933, when his position was abolished because of financial exigency brought on by the Depression. Willey began working on Kelly late in 1937 to get him to use the binomial system. In a letter to Ford, Willey stated that "I . . . have had long arguments with AR [Kelly] . . . in defense of survey and in defense of our system of nomenclature. Lost the first count . . . but he is incorporating the Bi-nomial names in the revision of his first report as well as saying that a nomenclature will probably be forthcoming."[7] It didn't hurt Willey's cause to have a prominent southwestern archaeologist in the camp: "Was glad to hear that such a man as Kidder thinks our idea feasible. This, incidentally, will help convince A. R. as I some times think he rather fears getting into the boat with such juniors as ourselves."[8]

Whether his short-lived professional experience in Illinois had soured his outlook on midwestern archaeologists, or whether his dealings with Washington bureaucracy during the early days of federal archaeology had made him wary of northerners, a letter from Kelly to Ford in January 1938 leaves no doubt that Kelly didn't want any interference from outsiders in setting up the new system of typology: "A great deal of progress will probably be made if the people most familiar with the area are enabled to work out their ideas in conjunction without interference. It is my intention that the center of gravity, as far as Southeastern archaeological problems per se are concerned, should remain in the region" (cited in Lyon 1996:192). Specifically, as Lyon (1996:192–93) points out, Kelly was worried that one center of gravity would end up being Griffin's ceramic repository in Ann Arbor. Better, he said, to invite Griffin as an individual and not as a member of the repository's staff.

The Conference on Southeastern Pottery Nomenclature

Regardless of graduate-student zeal or personal animosities, the frustration of Willey, Ford, and other southeastern archaeologists in the late 1930s with existing pottery-classification systems was exacerbated by the frenzy of federally sponsored archaeological work in the region. In the words of Ian Brown (1978:8), "the resulting collections were . . . getting out of control. Each archaeologist, unaware of the work of others, had his own typological system. Chaos was imminent. The need for a uniform nomological system was apparent." And, as Brown (1978:8) pointed out, "Griffin and Ford were the two principal agents in bringing it about."

7. Letter of October 21, 1937, from Willey to Ford (LSU Museum of Natural Science archives).
8. Letter of November 2, 1937, from Willey to Ford (LSU Museum of Natural Science archives).

Ford certainly saw himself as a principal agent. In a letter to his mother dated May 7, 1938, he noted that "we are having a meeting here at Ann Arbor to discuss Southeastern pottery types. Will be chair of that meeting as I have served as a moving factor in organizing it."[9] Late in 1937, Griffin and Ford circulated a short proposal calling for a "Conference on Pottery Nomenclature for the Southeastern United States" (Ford and Griffin 1937). The opening paragraph of the proposal is instructive for what it tells us about how Ford viewed the then-existing confusion over pottery types:

> It is felt by several of the investigators working in the southeastern states that the time has arrived for the development of a standard method of designating and comparing the different varieties of pottery in Southeastern archaeological research. Through the efforts of former and present investigators, it is probable that the major types of pottery of the region have already been excavated. A most significant problem is the ordering of this material. (Ford and Griffin 1937:5)[10]

Thus Ford and Griffin, as early as 1937, suggested that the "major" types of pottery had already been discovered. What they were calling for was a way to organize the descriptions of those types. How to apply standard terms was treated in a section entitled "Discussion of the Theoretical Basis of Classification," though the discussion was more methodological than theoretical. Ford and Griffin discussed "style" and its role in the creation of pottery types in the following terms:

> Each of these styles consisted of several characteristic elements that tended to cling together through a limited span of time and space. These styles are expressed concretely by characteristic associations of certain specific decorations, shapes, appendages, materials, firing processes, etc. *It is the most clearly recognized of these associations that we want to name at this time.*
>
> The influences of a particular style could be most freely expressed in such features as decoration, surface finish, appendages and, to a certain degree, shape. . . . The definition of pottery types should be based mainly on those features which can best reflect stylistic trends and are least affected by extraneous factors. . . .
>
> [Because sherds are used as opposed to complete vessels] it is suggested that in the selection and descriptions of types, particular attention be paid to all variations of decoration and surface finish that are to be included. Decoration, particularly, should be minutely described. (Ford and Griffin 1937:6–7; emphasis added)

The first paragraph suggests that type descriptions were extracted from specimens. That such descriptions would thus be historical accidents contingent on the specimens examined escaped notice. More importantly, the second paragraph implies that styles or types of pottery were aboriginal units—real, emic, essentialist—consisting of recurring sets of attributes. To be analytical or materialist units—

---

9. LSU Museum of Natural Science archives.

10. The original proposal was circulated in mimeographed form. We here use the pagination found in the version reprinted in the *Newsletter of the Southeastern Archaeological Conference* in 1960.

ones that reflect stylistic (read *historical*) trends—each style or type should have a limited time-space distribution. The absence of theory in the construction and use of units is apparent in the commonsense rendition of *style*, a concept that was neither discussed nor defined by Ford and Griffin. Archaeologists of the time knew what style was—that is, something that changed over time (and sometimes in predictable ways, as Kroeber [1919] had demonstrated with fashions)—so no one bothered to talk about it. Kidder (1915:453; see also Kidder and Kidder 1917:341, 348) was perhaps the first Americanist to use the term "style" specifically in reference to ideational (our term) units that displayed monotonic frequency distributions through time.

Ford and Griffin echoed a point that Ford had earlier emphasized: if pottery types were going to help untangle southeastern prehistory, then they had to have more than local significance:

> there is no excuse for setting up types on the basis of a few vessels from one site only. The specific combination of features must be repeated at different sites in order to be certain that we are dealing with a pottery style that had a significant part in the ceramic history of the area. In other words, there can be no such thing as a "type site." *One must have series of sites which present materials clustering about a norm which is to be designated as a type.* (Ford and Griffin 1937:7; emphasis added)

Clearly, by late 1937 Ford was much less interested in documenting the kinds of subtle variation in decoration than he had been earlier, when he devised his intricate classification systems. Within a short time, he had gone from teasing out minute variation to focusing on a central tendency, or norm. Variation was only important if it was informative about time or space: "Some of the types will doubtless prove to be rather variable. As demonstrated by experience in the Southwest, there is really no profit in labelling variations which can be readily recognized as related to types already set up, unless the variations can be demonstrated to have significance of either an areal or chronological nature. To do so will result only in pointless and confusing 'splitting' " (Ford and Griffin 1937:7). Splitting was acceptable *if and only if* the new type had time-space significance and could thus do analytical work.

Although Ford and Griffin leaned toward materialism in their concern with types as units of analysis, an essentialist tone ran through their discussion. It is particularly obvious in the statement, "Combinations of recognized types can be dealt with in two ways. Where they are rarely found and do not appear to have become *stable products of crossing*, they had better be regarded as what they seem to be—one type strongly influenced by another. If they are consistently repeated, they can be set up as a distinct new type" (Ford and Griffin 1937:7; emphasis added). Ford and Griffin were referring to what in other contexts were termed "hybrid types." Such a notion suggests that Ford and Griffin had at least one wheel stuck in the essentialist sand. While their "crossing" is in one sense surely metaphorical, in the essentialist sense it is very possible. A new type could be the product of such crossing of two cultures or streams of ideas, or one set of ideas might merely influence another and be manifest as a "strongly influenced type." Again, a commonsense perception of how cultures work and evolve, founded in ethnology, was being used to explain archaeological phenomena.

Thus after casting about for several years, trying one method after another to categorize his sherds and worrying about the meaning of types in a cultural sense, Ford found a way out of his predicament: create finite (bounded) units based on variation in decoration that were useful analytical tools, and slap names on them, as was done in the Southwest:

> It has been suggested by [Preston] Holder, Willey and Ford that names be applied to specific ceramic types in a manner similar to that used in the Southwest. It is felt by these men, however, that an improvement over the Southwestern system of nomenclature could be introduced by the use of a middle term in the name which would usually be a descriptive adjective modifying the last term. Then the first part of the name would be the name of the site from which the type was first adequately described or recognized. The second term would be a modifying or suggestive adjective; the last term would be a "constant" which would designate the broad class to which the type belongs. (Ford and Griffin 1937:7)

It was this last point—the constant—that bothered Willey early in 1938. Could archaeologists agree on how to define constants? Could they even *recognize* such constants on a consistent basis? He posed these concerns to Ford two months before the pottery-typology meeting:

> I know as well as you do that we'll have to take some long steps and short cuts toward comprehending pottery in the sense that it is a cultural and chronological indicator. Nevertheless we are also hooking names on types that will stick to them for some time. Why hang on "Moundville Engraved" if it can be proven that it is incised? Why call something "roulette" if we have even more reasonable proof that it is stamped. Primarily we are working with time intervals as delineated by artifactual remnants in the form of potsherds. Granted. But we have also selected for our "constants," in the nomenclature, terms which hinge directly upon execution techniques.[11]

A two-day meeting was held in Griffin's office at the ceramic repository at the University of Michigan on May 16–17, 1938. Fifteen archaeologists attended the conference—subsequently recognized as the first Southeastern Archaeological Conference (Williams 1960:2)—and were listed in the report as "members." Attendees were J. L. Buckner, J. L. Coe, D. I. DeJarnette, C. H. Fairbanks, V. J. Fewkes, J. J. Finkelstein, J. A. Ford, J. B. Griffin, W. G. Haag, C. Johnston, A. R. Kelly, T. M. N. Lewis, F. R. Matson, S. Neitzel, and C. G. Wilder. George Quimby is not listed as an attendee, though Griffin (1976:26) later stated he was there.

11. Letter of March 12, 1938, from Willey to Ford (LSU Museum of Natural Science archives).

Preston Holder and Gordon Willey did not attend, but Ford and Griffin (1938:22) noted that they "should be considered members of the Conference because of their interest in its purpose and their valuable assistance in developing the ideas presented." Attending members thought enough of Willey to appoint him, along with Griffin and Ford, to a board of review, which was "to control and unify the processes of type selection, naming, and description" (Ford and Griffin 1938:17). The idea of a review board was dropped later that year at the second Southeastern Archaeological Conference (Griffin 1976:26).

Ford had originally wanted to invite only a few participants (Griffin 1976:26)— probably Kelly, Willey, Holder, and perhaps Haag—but Griffin advised inviting as many as might contribute useful pottery descriptions. Kelly had proffered the same advice to Holder in October 1937: "the scheme must have sufficient backing to withstand the sniping of discomfited individuals who might resent the automatic and implicit judgment that they are not competent to make determinations" (cited in Lyon 1996:192).

Ford and Griffin summarized the meeting in a subsequent report (Ford and Griffin 1938) that laid down agreed-on standards for creating pottery types. The original, unpaginated copy had no author or editor listed; the 1960 reprint in the *Newsletter of the Southeastern Archaeological Conference* states that Ford and Griffin were coauthors of the report. Willey and Sabloff (1974:216) indicated that "Ford is best described as the editor of this report, [and] there can be little doubt, in view of the phraseology and idea content, that [some statements in the report] are directly from him" (see also Willey and Sabloff 1993:149). Griffin (pers. comm., 1996) told us that "Ford was the correspondent" and implied that the report was coauthored.

The authors began the report by noting, "For the purposes of discovering culture history, pottery must be viewed primarily as a reflector of cultural influence" (Ford and Griffin 1938:12, page number from 1960 reprint), but from that point to the end of the paper, the term "culture" never appeared again except as a modifier to the word "history." Given that Griffin was a coauthor, it is not too surprising that culture was relegated to a bit role. Throughout his career, Griffin never showed much interest in culture as an entity that can be studied; where he used the term, it was more in the form of a modifier—for example, cultural processes or cultural development. Ford, who in his early writings made repeated references to culture and its evolution (e.g., Ford 1935a), may have fought to get any mention of culture in the paper. As an important aside, much has been made of Ford and his exposure at Michigan to Leslie White (Brown 1978; Evans 1968; Willey 1969, 1988), who eventually became the leading cultural evolutionist in American anthropology. In his obituary on Ford, Clifford Evans wrote, "While at Michigan [Ford] found the cultural evolution theories of Leslie White unusually exciting because they permitted his mass of information gathered from extensive

fieldwork . . . to fall into some theoretical meaning beyond the mere reconstruction of cultural sequences" (Evans 1968:1163). It is clear, however, that Ford really
didn't understand the difficult subject of cultural evolution, especially White's
brand (e.g., White 1949, 1959a, 1959b).

In the report issued by Ford and Griffin on the pottery conference, once culture
had been paid its perfunctory due, it was time to get on with the creation of
pottery types that would not only organize the large amount of pottery coming
out of the Southeast but also help bring chronological and spatial order to it. The
authors were clear on the role of types: "Types should be classes of material which
promise to be useful in interpreting culture history. . . . A type is nothing more
than a tool" (Ford and Griffin 1938:12). Again, this is a clear expression of the
materialist metaphysic.

There was, in Ford and Griffin's eyes, "no predetermined system for arriving at
useful type divisions. Types must be selected after careful study of the material and
of the problems which they are designed to solve. . . . If divisions in an established
type will serve that purpose more accurately, they should be made; otherwise there
is little purpose in crowding the literature with types" (Ford and Griffin 1938:12).
Perhaps the most important passages in the report are the following remarks about
how to create a type:

> A type must be defined as the combination of all the discoverable vessel features: paste,
> temper, method of manufacture, firing, hardness, thickness, size, shape, surface finish,
> decoration, and appendages. The range of all these features, which is to be considered
> representative of the type, must be described. By [these] criteria two sets of material
> which are similar in nearly all features, but which are divided by peculiar forms of one
> feature (shell contrasted with grit tempering, for example) may be separated into two
> types *if there promises to be some historical justification for the procedure.* Otherwise,
> they should be described as variants of one type.
>
> A type should be so clearly definable that an example can be recognized entirely
> apart from its associated materials. Recognition must be possible by others who will
> use the material, as well as by the individual proposing the type. (Ford and Griffin
> 1938:12; emphasis added)

If we take Ford and Griffin literally, their criteria for types created an unworkable
system, mired down as it would be in an endless list of types created to encompass
the enormous variation in the "discoverable [read *observable*] vessel features"
they listed. Griffin (pers. comm., 1996) stated that the recommendations in the
1938 report derived from a combination of typological procedures used in the
Southwest, outlined in Guthe (1928, 1934) and used by Griffin in his Fort Ancient
analysis (Griffin 1943). The heaviest borrowing was from Guthe's suggestions
because, Griffin indicated, they were "more flexible." Ford, in both his index system
and his analytical-formula system, had already shown the unworkable nature of
such a scheme, meaning that no one wanted to take the time to understand it,

let alone to memorize it. Such a tool might have its place, but certainly not when one was faced with a mountain of potsherds to sort. Paradoxically, although Ford and Griffin listed a lengthy series of vessel features, the range of which should be considered in developing types, their take-home message was clear: keep the process short and simple; don't create new types unless they are useful for writing culture history.

The way out of this paradox, at least the one taken by southeastern archaeologists, was to make an implicit distinction between *description* and *definition* and, contrary to stated procedure, to reduce the number of vessel features used in a type definition to one—either decoration or surface treatment. In practice, types usually were defined on the basis of one of those features, while the other features became descriptive add-ons, or as Ford (1936a:15) earlier termed them, "usual accompanying characteristics." Thus, the type Lamar Complicated Stamped was *defined* on the presence of a particular kind of design; sherds and vessels were assigned to that type because they carried that design. In the accompanying type *description,* an investigator could list the range of features displayed by specimens identified as members of the type. The first type descriptions to come out of the Ann Arbor conference were published in the inaugural February 1939 issue of the *Southeastern Archaeological Conference Newsletter.* The conference report indicated that a pottery handbook was "to be issued by J. A. Ford" (Ford and Griffin, 1938:18), but such a volume never appeared. Rather, type descriptions were submitted to the newsletter, which was edited by Bill Haag (Figure 3.2) from its inception until 1960. In a letter of January 30, 1939,[12] Griffin reported to Ford that he was receiving feedback on the pottery conference held the previous May. "Unsolicited" comments included "it was too damn elemental and a lot of childish argument, and . . . it was slightly ridiculous listening to Ford lay down the law and practically no one making any objection or having a different idea." The former was insignificant in the long run, as the system was adopted by most archaeologists. The latter says a lot about Jim Ford and anticipates comments some of his collaborators would make a decade and a half later.

As the system caught on, types became so well known by archaeologists working in various areas of the Southeast that rarely was there a need to present a formal definition. Also, many types were given only a binomial designation—for example, *Fatherland Incised*—instead of the originally recommended trinomial designation, further signifying that there was general agreement on what a particular type was. This would ultimately lead to the initial formulation of various types, some with varieties that might eventually be granted type status, followed by a constant reformulation of some types, discarding of others, and the creation of new ones every time additional collections were added to the mix (e.g., Phillips

12. LSU Museum of Natural Science archives.

1970; Phillips et al. 1951). But the bottom line was that there was general agreement on the basic types. And why was there such agreement? Look at what Willey wrote to Ford in April 1938 after Willey had examined some photographs of David DeJarnette's pottery from southern Alabama:

> Best part is: DeJarnette had already worked out types for these things, A, B, C, etc. His types, as near as I can tell from the pictures, coincide with yours. It will be a mere matter of name transference for the most part. There must really be something to this if a man, isolated from us as he has been, can arrive at practically the same answer. He has also worked up the accompanying characteristics of these design types. Thought you would be interested to know this if you haven't already seen it.[13]

It is difficult to overemphasize the importance of the Ann Arbor meeting's significance for southeastern archaeology. Before we began this project and a related one (Lyman et al. 1997a, 1997b), we were under the erroneous assumption that the Southeast was merely a recipient of a pottery-typing system that had been completely worked out in the Southwest to everyone's satisfaction. Nothing could be further from the truth. Little was settled in the Southwest by 1938. In fact, the unanimity among southeasternists reached after the Ann Arbor meeting was unduplicated in the Southwest. Ford must have taken some pride during his attendance at the 1938 Pecos Conference (Woodbury 1993:134), again held at Chaco Canyon, where one of the main topics of discussion was "debating the merits of Kidder's Pecos Classification versus the Gladwin scheme" (Woodbury 1993:134–35). Donald Brand (1938:14) had this to say about the meeting:

> The Chaco conference opened Saturday evening, August 27, with a discussion of the proposed central shard laboratory for Southwestern pottery types. The plan in mind included a committee . . . for the purpose of standardizing terminology of these pottery types. Consensus of opinion on this subject pointed to the fact that such a laboratory or clearing house would be difficult to set up, because of the difficulty of getting cooperation among the various workers in the Southwest. The obvious stumbling block would be in setting up such a standard terminology to which everyone would agree.

That stumbling block might well have been overcome if Jim Ford had worked in the Southwest instead of the Southeast.

Types as Units of Evolution

In the same year that Ford and Griffin published the ceramics-conference report, Ford submitted his master's thesis, *An Examination of Some Theories and Methods of Ceramic Analysis* (Ford 1938a), and also an article to the fledgling journal *American Antiquity* entitled "A Chronological Method Applicable to the Southeast" (Ford 1938b). The thesis, "conducted under the close tutelage

---

13. Letter of April 13, 1938, from Willey to Ford (LSU Museum of Natural Science archives).

of James B. Griffin and Carl E. Guthe" (Griffin, pers. comm., cited in Brown 1978:9), was a rehash of many of the points Ford had raised in the reports on pottery from Louisiana and Mississippi (Ford 1935c, 1936a). He argued that the analyst had to be familiar with all the pottery from a region, not solely that from a single locality (to avoid the problem of idiosyncratic types discussed earlier); had to group the specimens into types on the basis of *significant* features; and had to begin forming types at the start of analysis, not at the end. Too often, Ford realized, archaeologists had gone through laborious exercises, dividing and subdividing pottery assemblages based on subtle variations, to the point that there were almost as many "types" as there were sherds. This had happened to Ford in his attempts to categorize the Louisiana-Mississippi sherds (and he well knew the same problem was occurring in the Southwest [Ford 1940]), and he wanted to avoid such confusion at all costs, just as he and Griffin had advocated in their proposal and report (Ford and Griffin 1937, 1938). If, alternatively, one immediately began sorting sherds into types based on historically significant—usually decorative— attributes, one could avoid becoming bogged down in minutiae.

Ford obviously was interested in types from the standpoint of chronology, but another current also ran through his thesis—one that had been in his earlier reports and must have been stimulated in part by some knowledge (by way of Kniffen?) of phyletic seriation. Recall that Ford (1936a) had explored the notion that pottery decoration evolved through time and that slow, gradual change in, say, a design motif could guide the chronological ordering of materials carrying that design. The obvious extension of this notion is to erect "classifications [that] approach the status of true genetic arrangements" (Ford 1938a:34). Ford (1938a:30) believed that if types were created properly, it would be possible to argue, on the basis of homologous similarity, that certain types could be grouped together because "they sprang from a common ancestor." More importantly, in Ford's (1938a:82) view, such sets of types represented "significant idea groups"— the usual commonsense, anthropologically based explanation. Groups of types could be linked together at successively higher levels of inclusivity such as series and wares. These successively higher levels of grouping had but one purpose, namely "the translation of ceramic history into the history of cultural spread and development" (Ford 1938a:86). Not surprisingly, then, Ford (1938a) noted with approval Colton and Hargrave's (1937) use of a hierarchical system of nomenclature for pottery categorization, but he took them to task for their failure to consider "that the division of the material must be controlled by the utility of types for discovering cultural history" (Ford 1940:264; see also Ford 1938a:31–32).

Brown (1978:11–12) pointed out the obvious flaws in Ford's scheme, not least of which was how the analyst knows whether he or she has discovered "significant idea groups." The last was, of course, an inference founded in common sense and the empirical generalization that different (historically documented) cultures—

sets of shared ideas—produced different types of pottery, so different types of pottery must represent different sets of ideas. Ford clearly believed it was possible, through a mix of inductive and deductive reasoning, to discover "general principles which may be expected to underlie the phenomena" (Ford 1938a:5). The basis for the general principles Ford desired had been outlined by Kroeber (1931) a few years earlier, but no one, not even Ford, took notice—as Kroeber (1943) later lamented—probably because the model of cultural evolution then being proposed (e.g., White 1943) and soon to be adopted by Americanist archaeologists and anthropologists was of a rather different sort than that originally in Ford's and Kroeber's minds (e.g., Dunnell 1980).

Decoration Complexes as Analytical Tools

"A Chronological Method Applicable to the Southeast" was an important paper because it established clearly and concisely the methodological assumptions that underlay Ford's subsequent use of pottery to establish chronological control. The paper contains many of the same elements found in his earlier monographs (Ford 1935c, 1936a) and thesis (Ford 1938a), but are presented with minimal brief excursions into side topics. Part of the reason for this might have resided in the fact that by the time he wrote the paper he was aware of the attempts of others (e.g., Kidder, Kroeber, Nelson, Spier) in the Southwest to measure time from variation in artifacts. The paper made clear, like no other he had written previously, that he was interested almost exclusively in time. Here the materialist metaphysic overshadowed the essentialist one in major and explicit fashion. Ford's pottery types were based exclusively on decoration; whether a type was "real and significant" was determined by the "repeated occurrence of a certain decoration at separate sites [to ensure the type was not] merely a local variation" (Ford 1938b:262; see also Ford 1938a:24). To be a useful analytical tool, a type must have a distribution across *big* chunks of time and/or space. As he had earlier (Ford 1936a), Ford indicated, "It probably will develop that not only one but several distinct decorations will be found associated at a number of sites. These associated decorations will be a group of styles that occur together, and form what has been termed a 'decoration complex' " (1938b:262). This passage demonstrates that when he wrote the paper, the essentialist metaphysic was all but dead in Ford's thinking; however, like the phoenix, it would rise from the ashes at a later date.

For Ford (1938b:262), regularly associated decoration types represented not only a decoration complex but "probably a distinct time horizon. [Once decoration complexes are determined, such] stylistic time horizons that have existed in [an] area may now be logically separated." Although a horizon style might loosely be construed as a synchronic slice of time (as it seems to have been for Ford two years earlier [Ford 1936a]), this clearly is not true in practice. Ford's decoration complexes, shown as boxes in Figure 3.4, were meant to represent spans of time, or "time *periods*" (Ford 1938b:262; emphasis added). Within the blocks are lines representing the spans covered by "definite style types." The combinations of these style types denote the position on the continuous time scale where boundaries should be drawn between periods. This criterion for defining period boundaries might seem to differ from that used by southwestern archaeologists, some of whom used the peaks in frequency of occurrence of types to denote "ceramic periods" (e.g., Kidder 1936b), but it really doesn't, because as Ford (1935c:21) had noted earlier, his decoration complex marker types "statistically dominate to a marked degree" an assemblage of pottery deposited during the span of one complex or "stylistic time period" (Ford 1935c:8). Ford, then, was mimicking Kidder in many ways.

The major difference from the Ford of 1936 was that he carefully pointed out that ceramic complexes were temporal units rather than cultural units: "[I]t cannot be accepted that these ceramic complexes will represent different cultures or cultural phases. It is entirely possible that two cultures may have used the same pottery, or at different times a culture may have changed its pottery types. What the method attempts to do is to use ceramic decoration, probably the most flexible of the remaining cultural features, as 'type fossils' to distinguish the passage of time" (Ford 1938b:263). Thus, some style types might extend through only a single time period, indicated by the italicized "1's" in Figure 3.4, whereas others might extend through two or more periods. Earlier, Ford (1935c, 1936a) had referred to the short-lived types as "marker types"; here, he referred to them as "type fossils," the sole purpose of which was to "distinguish the passage of time." Clearly, these were materialist units meant to do analytical work—specifically, to measure time. Such units might also be used to link sequent decoration complexes if they occurred in more than one, but this, too, was analytical work that potentially showed some sort of connection—not necessarily of the phyletic or ancestral-descendant sort— between complexes. Most importantly, Ford's insistence that types be analytical constructs useful for telling time was to become his trademark, and in remarkable anticipation of that, he ended his paper with the comment that "it is impossible to see, without chronology, how we can ever hope to discover the cultural history of the Indians of the Southeast" (Ford 1938b:263–64).

THE WORKS PROGRESS ADMINISTRATION PROJECTS

As he had promised Gordon Willey in 1937, Ford returned to Louisiana the following year to initiate a large federally sponsored project, and he hired his friend as part of his research team. It was hardly the case, however, that Ford simply returned to Louisiana and was handed a large sum of money with which to hire a crew and do some archaeology. Nothing could be further from the truth. In what had become a cumbersome process, one made application through the state

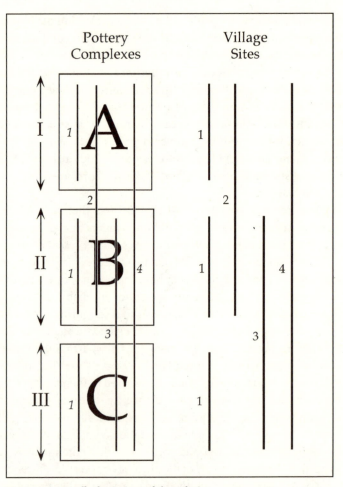

Figure 3.4. Ford's depiction of the relation among pottery types, pottery complexes, time, and village sites. The complexes are labeled A–C; time is labeled I–III; and pottery types are labeled 1–4. Although he provided little explanation in either the original figure caption or the text of the article in which the figure appeared, this visual representation of complexes, types, and time is key to understanding Ford's position. Notice that some types occur in only one complex and thus are marker types (labeled "1" [each "1" is a different type]). Other types crosscut complexes. On the right half of the diagram, Ford is showing how villages follow the same pattern: some were of short duration; others persisted longer. Notice that Ford's periods coincided with his pottery complexes. Later, Ford would confuse his contemporaries by arguing that periods were completely arbitrary constructs that had nothing to do with the beginning and ending of such things as pottery complexes. Critics found this difficult to accept when Ford himself often equated periods and pottery complexes (after Ford 1938b).

Works Progress Administration (WPA) office, which then had to decide which projects were to be funded. Unlike the earlier Civil Works Administration or the Federal Emergency Relief Administration, the WPA was much less centralized, a result of the perceived need to get federal money in the hands of the states, which could spend it most effectively. After Congress passed the Emergency Relief Appropriation Act of 1935, the states suddenly found they had $4.88 billion with which to put their unemployed citizens back to work.

As Lyon (1996) documents, from the beginning WPA-sponsored archaeology was fraught with problems, the major one being that no one knew how to administer the overall archaeology program:

> On the surface, archaeology was an ideal project for the WPA because it required large numbers of unskilled men and women as well as professional people and used relatively inexpensive equipment. But archaeology always occupied an ambiguous position within the WPA. The combination of white-collar and unskilled labor with the scientific goals of archaeology was not easy for the WPA to administer. And archaeologists not only had to adjust to the control of the WPA but the WPA itself was a constantly changing organization during its existence as a federal agency. (Lyon 1996:63)

In truth, there really wasn't a single archaeology program in the WPA; rather it was "fragmented and decentralized. The WPA sponsored its own relief projects, supported Tennessee Valley Authority salvage archaeology, and assisted National Park Service preservation archaeology. Each type of archaeology presented different problems to WPA administrators" (Lyon 1996:63). Archaeologists bristled at the interference of administrators in what they perceived to be their bailiwick, and administrators were often angered by what they saw as a lack of responsibility on the part of archaeologists.

Finally, out of sheer desperation, the WPA heeded the advice that archaeologists with the Smithsonian and the National Park Service had long been giving and hired someone to oversee the archaeological program, though the person hired, Vicenzo Petrullo, was an ethnologist by training, not an archaeologist. Petrullo managed to bring some of the bureaucratic problems under control, but despite his success, he often was severely criticized by archaeologists, who wanted no controls on what they were doing. Early in 1939, the WPA asked the National Research Council to organize a committee to examine the state of archaeology in the United States, much as its earlier Committee on State Archaeological Surveys had done. Out of this request grew the Committee on Basic Needs in American Archaeology, organized by Carl Guthe and chaired by William Duncan Strong. Through the efforts of Petrullo and the committee, standards for archaeological fieldwork and report preparation were established and mailed to archaeologists across the country. The committee early on had decided against evaluating individual WPA projects per se or enforcing compliance with the guidelines, but the stature of the committee's members helped ensure compliance. Informal, and sometimes not so informal, policing of the discipline led by mid-1939 to a significant reduction in the number of projects in operation (Lyon 1996:74).

Ford waded into this arena of uncertainty and bureaucratic red tape in the summer of 1938. Although Ford is rightfully recognized as the director of the WPA-sponsored program that began in Louisiana, he was not ultimately responsible for initiating it. Rather, as Haag (1994:29–30) points out, it was Kniffen who launched the program, though certainly at Ford's urging. Ford might eventually have been successful in obtaining the funding, though Kniffen, being a faculty member, was better positioned in the university to seek the matching money that federal law required. This "local match" could have been a sticking point in those economically tough times, even though it represented only about one-tenth of the total project cost—$112,000 in federal funds and $12,852 in LSU funds (Lyon 1996:82). Kniffen secured the funding, and Ford and Kniffen together convinced the state WPA office to fund the program.

The success of any archaeological project hinges directly on those hired to do the work. Are they competent in the field? Are they organized? Can they complete the work on time? And, most importantly, do their ethics dictate that a report of their fieldwork eventually will be written, even though they might have moved on to other positions? In some instances, the lack of publication was appalling, leading Strong, as chair of the National Research Council Committee on Basic Needs in American Archaeology, to note, "Millions are being poured into archaeological work, with very little thought given to the mechanisms for publication. It is as if a big factory were working and yet not producing anything" (cited in Lyon 1996:71–72). Without exception the men Ford selected, unlike numerous others involved in WPA archaeology, had those productive qualities. He picked Willey to run the central laboratory, which was first located in the Louisiana Department of Conservation building on Chartres Street in New Orleans (Figure 3.5) before being moved to the LSU campus in Baton Rouge. In 1939, when Willey left the project to attend graduate school at Columbia University, Ford replaced him with Preston Holder, who had graduate training at Columbia and considerable experience in Florida and Georgia. Holder in turn was succeeded by George I. Quimby, who had a master's degree from the University of Michigan and considerable experience in the Arctic.

For his field supervisors, Ford picked Robert S. Neitzel—"Stu" to his friends—who had an undergraduate degree from the University of Nebraska and graduate training at Nebraska and the University of Chicago, and William T. Mulloy, who at the time had almost completed his undergraduate degree at the University of Utah. Ford placed Neitzel in charge of work in Avoyelles Parish and hired Edwin B. Doran, Jr. (Figure 3.5), who had an undergraduate degree from LSU in geology, as his assistant. He placed Mulloy in charge of work in LaSalle Parish

Figure 3.5. Photograph of the WPA lab on Chartres Street, New Orleans. Left to right, standing: Gordon Willey, ? Beecher, Jim Ford, Andrew Albrecht; sitting: Edwin Doran (photograph courtesy Louisiana State University Museum of Natural Science).

and hired Arden King, who had an undergraduate degree from the University of Utah, as his assistant. As Lyon (1996:83) points out, Mulloy had two summers of experience working at the University of New Mexico field school, and King had spent two summers working in Utah. With the addition of Willey, Ford had a trio of supervisors with considerable experience in the greater Southwest, which probably was not coincidental. The supervisory staff was rounded out by the project ethnohistorian, Andrew C. Albrecht (Figure 3.5), who had received an undergraduate degree from Berkeley and a doctorate from the University of Vienna.

From all accounts—and here we are relying on firsthand accounts from those who worked with him (e.g., Willey 1969, 1988)—Ford was a master at organization, especially when it came to setting up a laboratory. Much of the information on the organization of Ford's lab comes from Lyon (1996), who examined documents in the WPA files in the LSU Museum of Natural Science archives. We made a cursory examination of the records but relied more heavily on Lyon's summary. Ford produced a short summary for the *Louisiana Conservation Review* (Ford

1939a). All materials from the field were immediately shipped to the central laboratory, which was divided into at least eleven divisions and sections. Artifacts were first sent to the catalog division, where they were cleaned and marked with a catalog number. If artifacts and human remains could be restored, they were then sent to the preparing division. After artifacts were cataloged and, where applicable, restored, they were sent to the analysis division for classification. Information was entered on note cards, which then were sent to the statistical section of the analysis division. At that point, the number and percentage of artifact types were calculated, and comparative charts and graphs of typological trends were constructed. The engineering division was responsible for drawing in final form all maps and excavation plans sent in from the field and for preparing artifact illustrations and line drawings that would be included in the final reports. The photography division developed negatives sent in from the field and photographed artifacts for the reports. Albrecht's archives-and-records division was in charge of gleaning information on the locations of ethnic groups in the Southeast and summarizing information that might prove useful in assigning ethnic affiliations to archaeological sites.

Ford was an excellent organizer, but according to Willey he could, at times, be difficult to please:

> Jim was a driven leader, driven by those forces within himself that saw the digging, the sorting, the classifications, the tabulations, the correlations—as the enormous job to be gotten through before we could arrive at results. We must work unstintingly, passionately, to achieve the latter. He would come into the lab with those great loping strides, his eyes burning down on me. There were never casual salutations; he would get right to the point. "Say," he would intone, in that deep voice, "why haven't those chaps in the restoration section moved along faster with those pots from the Crooks Mound? You'd better get them going. I'll be bringing in another big load of restorable vessels from there early next week."
>
> Jim then might suddenly stride over to the photographic dark room in a corner of the lab to review the work of our photographer. The photographer was a sad little man who at one time had some marginal association with Hollywood. One result of this former, and almost certainly more fascinating, employment were residual bits of slang retained in his speech, such as "douse the glims," which he used in reference to turning off his floodlights. His results were never quite up to snuff. For example, the edges of the projectile points in his photo prints might all look a little furry—the unavoidable result, he assured me, of the vibrations caused by the movement of heavy trucks in the street below just as the shutter was snapped. I was unable to advise him how to cope with this deranging factor other than, perhaps, to wait cautiously until such tremors had stilled before pushing the button. Jim made no attempt to be so understanding, and, as a consequence, the photographer lived in awe and fear of this grimmer head boss. I can see him looking up beseechingly at Jim's towering figure for the word of praise which never came. Indeed, the offending photographic prints might be tossed down with the single word "worthless," and the poor man, near tears,

could only reply, "Oh, Mr. Ford, I tried so hard!" He finally retired into his dark room one day with a bottle—not developing fluid—and, as the saying goes, was "invalided out." (Willey 1988:59)

One of the people Willey hired in the laboratory was a bookkeeper, C. H. Hopkins, who was soon given the responsibility of sorting pottery from the various excavations into types (Ford 1951a; Ford and Willey 1940). Such an assignment to a nonarchaeologist might seem odd at first, especially given the importance of ceramic material in Ford's ever-present goal of chronological ordering, but Ford (1951a:91) later noted that someone like Hopkins, who was "selected from the personnel available because of his carefulness and consistency," was ideal for the task: "The setting up of a classification system requires a grasp of the historical problem and knowledge of related materials in surrounding areas. However, once a system is established, it frequently happens that an intelligent and careful person who has had no training in archaeology will do a better and more consistent job of classifying material than will the archaeologists who have originated it" (Ford 1951a:91). Ford had a reason for this—one that reveals as much about his ideas on types as it does about his and Willey's confidence in Hopkins: "This is because such a classifier can readily learn the range of variation allowed for each group and with no knowledge of the broader implications of the work is not tempted to expand the range in one direction or another, to provide for divergent material. He has no preconceived ideas, no theories to prove, and he is less likely to let the classificatory categories 'creep'" (Ford 1951a:91). Although that statement was written in 1951, it summarized Ford's belief in 1938—a belief shared by Griffin and Willey—that types, while created from a continuum of variation, were worthless for chronological purposes if allowed to encompass too much variation. Collins had drilled this into Ford several years earlier. The problem of "creep"—a result of the extensional, or extracted, nature of type descriptions— would be addressed head-on again by Ford, this time with Griffin and Phillips, in their final report on the lower Mississippi Valley survey conducted during the 1940s (Phillips et al. 1951).

Gordon Willey (pers. corr., 1996) related to us how Hopkins got the job in the first place: "There in the New Orleans Lab the only two WPA employees with any real sense were Hopkins and [statistician B. B.] Levy. Hopkins got his job from a sherd identification test I gave the Lab employees after the first two weeks on the job, during which time they had some preliminary exposure to our pottery 'types.' As I recall, Hopkins scored about 90% on the exam while his nearest runner-up had about 40%. As a result, I made Hopkins the Chief Classifier and so promoted him right off." After being trained by Willey to recognize the various types that they, Griffin, and others had described, Hopkins "achieved an almost machine-like precision in his separation of pottery into type groups" (Ford 1951a:91). As a test, Willey or Ford would give Hopkins, without the latter's knowledge, the same batch of sherds that he had analyzed as much as three months previously to determine the reliability of the sorting. Hopkins apparently always passed the test.

Ford knew the success of his archaeological program was tied not only to the supervisors he hired but also to the speed of the workers hired to excavate the sites. In effect, the $125,000 or so that was available to the project—a large amount even by today's standards—was only as good as the amount of dirt it could be used to move. And it moved a lot of dirt. Neitzel, in one of his quarterly reports from the Avoyelles Parish unit, reported the following statistics: "The work on the present projects was begun on the 19th of September, 1938, and, at present (19th of December, 1938), is still being continued. To date the project has been in operation fifty days, an average of thirty-seven and three tenths men being present each day, and one thousand-eight hundred and sixty-six man days of work having been expended. One thousand five hundred and fourteen cubic yards of earth have been moved" (cited in Neuman 1984:45–46). That works out to slightly less than a cubic yard of earth moved per man per day—a lot of dirt.

Although there were only two officially defined units within the project—one at Avoyelles Parish and the other at LaSalle Parish—crews eventually branched out to work on sites in at least six other parishes (Figure 3.6). Excavation procedures usually consisted of trenching and, in the case of mounds, the subsequent peeling back of individual layers to expose horizontal surfaces. At several sites, including Greenhouse in Avoyelles Parish and Big Oak Island in Orleans Parish (Figure 3.6), hand augers were used to determine the depths of deposits and the relations of the deposits to underlying physiographic features.

Discussing the fieldwork and the results of the excavations is well beyond our scope here; excellent summaries are presented in Lyon (1996) and Neuman (1984). Rather, we pick and choose among the various pieces of work to get some sense of how Ford and his associates approached the culture history of eastern Louisiana. The WPA program in Louisiana was important in several respects, especially in terms of producing temporal control. By 1941, when the program ended, Ford and his team had greatly refined the known ceramic chronology by extending it back in time, shortening some periods, and sliding new ones in when needed. With a few exceptions, the ordering as it was determined in that year is the one still in use today.

It is difficult to write a coherent summary of the WPA period in Louisiana— worse yet to attempt to follow individual lines of discussion—because only a single major excavation report was published during the course of the project. Ford's report on the Greenhouse site (Figure 3.6), which was excavated in 1938–1939, was not published for a dozen years (Ford 1951a), though a short article written during excavation summarized the 1938 work (Ford 1939a). Likewise, almost a dozen years passed between the time work was completed in 1940 at the Medora site in West Baton Rouge Parish (Figure 3.6) and the time of publication (Quimby

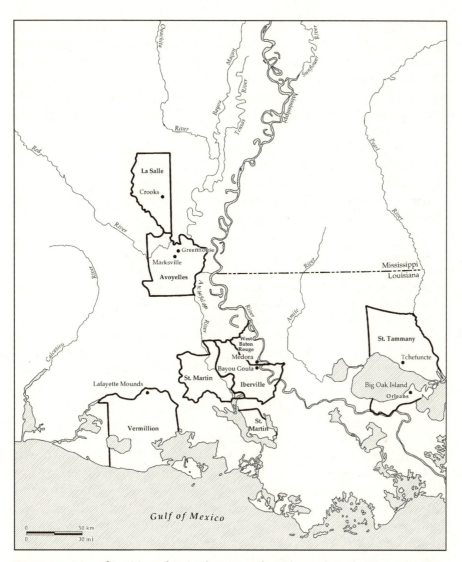

Figure 3.6. Map of Louisiana showing locations of parishes and sites mentioned in the text.

1951). Publication of investigations at the Tchefuncte site in St. Tammany Parish (Figure 3.6), together with those undertaken at other early ceramic-period sites in Vermillion, St. Martin, and Orleans Parishes, while not as delayed as Ford's Greenhouse report, did not appear until four to six years after the excavations were completed. The greatest time lag involved the report on the Bayou Goula site in Iberville Parish (Figure 3.6), which was excavated in 1940–1941 but not reported until 1957 (Quimby 1957).

In reading the later reports, it is difficult to sort out when various ideas on chronology and the like started taking shape. Did the ideas follow slowly from the excavations and subsequent analysis, or was there almost instantaneous recognition of where various sites or portions of sites fell? Lyon (1996:89) believes it was the former:

> Willey and Ford almost completed a draft for a report on the Greenhouse site in 1938, but sections had to be revised, and finally Ford alone wrote the report, publishing it in 1951. . . . The time between the excavation of the site and the publication of the final report allowed him to place the site more accurately in the culture history of the Southeast by making comparisons with work completed after the end of the WPA program. Ford was thus able to conclude that the site was not unique and was similar to sites throughout the Southeast. He compared the site to the Peck site near Sicily Island and the Troyville site at Jonesville excavated by Winslow Walker. Ford also saw similarities between Greenhouse and the West Florida sequence described by Willey in 1949.

Perhaps if we place special emphasis on the word "more" in this quote—that is, the elapsed time between excavation and publication helped Ford place the Greenhouse site *more* accurately in the culture history of the Southeast—then Lyon's comment is technically correct. Ford (1951a:5) himself pointed out that "Willey's [1949a, 1949b] work in Florida and Alex D. Krieger's [1946] researches in the Caddoan region have superseded the conclusions we were able to draw at that time [1938]." True, Willey's monograph was an elaboration of his earlier work, and Krieger's analysis of eastern Texas and northwestern Louisiana was sorely needed, but in a way this is quibbling; in reality, Ford and his WPA colleagues *immediately* knew the chronological position not only of the Greenhouse site but of all the sites they worked on in Louisiana. They knew as soon as the laboratory crew had washed and labeled the sherds that came in from the field.

We base this statement on various letters between Ford and Willey and later between Ford and Quimby, and also on what is contained in the one site report published during the course of the WPA program—that covering excavations at the Crooks site in LaSalle Parish (Figure 3.6) in 1938–1939 (Ford and Willey 1940). From a historical perspective, the report is invaluable because it documents that by June 1940—not quite two years after the excavation program started—Ford had added two new periods, Troyville and Tchefuncte, to the master chronological chart for the lower Mississippi Valley (Figure 3.7). Ford created Troyville by slipping it between the Marksville and Coles Creek periods, primarily on the basis of the new material from Greenhouse and previously excavated material from Troyville, Marksville, and Peck Village (Figure 2.2). On the basis of a series of excavations primarily at sites along Lake Pontchartrain in St. Tammany and Orleans Parishes (Figure 3.6), project personnel recognized a series of material— much of it undecorated—stratigraphically below Marksville marker types. This series, which was subdivided into several types (Ford and Quimby 1945), became the basis for creating the Tchefuncte period. Based on the wording in Figure 3.7, Ford knew that some of the material from Greenhouse, along with some from Peck Village and Troyville, resembled pottery from the Weeden Island complex in northwest Florida as well as pottery still being referred to as the Deasonville complex. Given who his coauthor was, why *wouldn't* he have made the immediate correlation between the Greenhouse material and the Weeden Island complex? Willey, along with Richard B. Woodbury, had recently completed a manuscript on several sites on the northwest coast of Florida, and, although it was not yet published (Willey and Woodbury 1942), Willey knew the region's chronology. Thus Ford did not have to wait until 1949, when Willey (1949b) published his "Archeology of the Florida Gulf Coast."

The Crooks Site

Ford and Willey suspected that Crooks, the most northerly of all the sites excavated during the WPA project and the only one north of the confluence of the Red River and the Mississippi (Figure 3.6), contained a Marksville component. This suspicion was based on the nature of the mounds at the site—one fairly high, conical structure, which was similar in shape and height to Mound 4 at Marksville, and one much lower mound, similar to several of the low mounds at Marksville. The resemblance was difficult to miss—a point understated by Ford and Willey (1940:9) when they noted, "The excavation of the Crooks site was undertaken because its superficial aspects indicated an occupation during the Marksville period." One didn't need sherds to tell the difference between a flat-topped "temple" mound, which indicated a later, Coles Creek–period occupation, and a conical Marksville-period burial mound (e.g., Ford and Willey 1941). And Marksville-period remains, because of their resemblance to Hopewell remains, were as much of a draw in 1938 as they had been in 1933 when Frank Setzler excavated the Marksville type site.

Stratigraphic evidence from the two mounds excavated at Crooks produced a pottery sequence that overlapped the one from Marksville as well as the chronologically earlier sequence from the Tchefuncte sites. Comparisons of type percentages from excavated levels at Marksville and Crooks led Ford and Willey to suspect that Crooks was slightly earlier than Marksville. In their comparison of

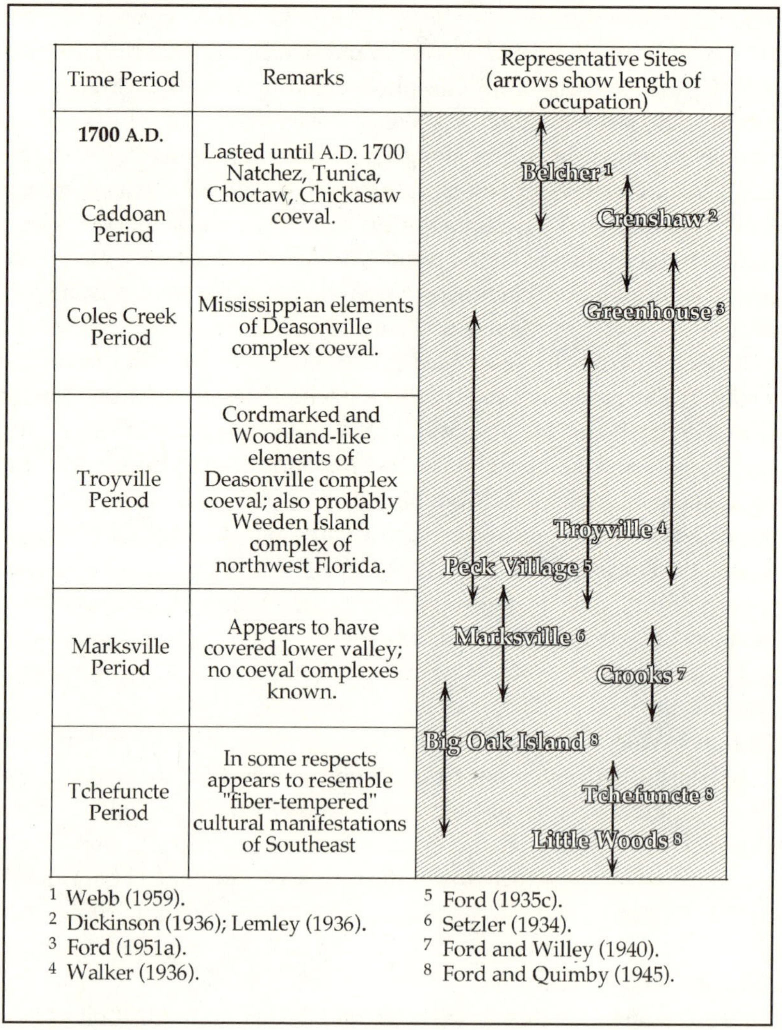

Time Period	Remarks	Representative Sites (arrows show length of occupation)
1700 A.D. Caddoan Period	Lasted until A.D. 1700 Natchez, Tunica, Choctaw, Chickasaw coeval.	Belcher [1] Crenshaw [2]
Coles Creek Period	Mississippian elements of Deasonville complex coeval.	Greenhouse [3]
Troyville Period	Cordmarked and Woodland-like elements of Deasonville complex coeval; also probably Weeden Island complex of northwest Florida.	Troyville [4] Peck Village [5]
Marksville Period	Appears to have covered lower valley; no coeval complexes known.	Marksville [6] Crooks [7]
Tchefuncte Period	In some respects appears to resemble "fiber-tempered" cultural manifestations of Southeast	Big Oak Island [8] Tchefuncte [8] Little Woods [8]

[1] Webb (1959).
[2] Dickinson (1936); Lemley (1936).
[3] Ford (1951a).
[4] Walker (1936).

[5] Ford (1935c).
[6] Setzler (1934).
[7] Ford and Willey (1940).
[8] Ford and Quimby (1945).

Figure 3.7. Ford and Willey's chart showing chronological periods applicable to the lower Mississippi Valley and occupation lengths of various sites in the region. Note that under the heading "Remarks," Ford and Willey conflated periods and pottery complexes. References to unpublished reports that appeared in the original figure have been updated (after Ford and Willey 1940).

pottery assemblages from Marksville and Crooks, Ford and Willey did not use the material from Setzler's 1933 excavations but rather sherd samples that Doran and Neitzel excavated in the spring of 1939 when high water forced them out of the Greenhouse site and up on the bluffs to Marksville. That work, consisting of the excavation of several long trenches, was never reported in detail, though Ford oversaw the eventual preparation of a short report in *American Antiquity* (Vescelius 1957).

The lack of a published report on the earlier work at Marksville created a difficult situation for Ford—not least because of his friendship with and respect for Setzler. Setzler had always intended to publish a report on his and Ford's 1933 excavations at Marksville, but he never completed it. Thus Ford was stymied as to how to incorporate elements of that work into the Crooks report without upsetting Setzler. He broached the subject in a letter of February 9, 1939, in which he described to Setzler some of the things coming out of Crooks: "I think you can see that it would be very useful to us in preparing our reports . . . to have a copy of your unpublished manuscript on the type site of the Marksville period. If it is at all practical I beg that you send us a copy." Setzler dragged his feet because he was embarrassed by the incompleteness of the report, but even at that he wrote back four days later, "It will naturally be a blow to me if you find it necessary to make a detailed report on the original Marksville site." Of course, Ford could not have done so even if he had wanted to because, as he told Setzler in a letter of February 23, "My memory of our discoveries is very incomplete." In that same letter, he told Setzler that "I am more sorry tha[n] I can tell you that it is going to be necessary for us to produce a report on a Marksville period site," and he let him know that despite the fact that Setzler was "the grandfather of Marksville" and that every effort would be made "to see that the proper credit is given to you," it would be impossible "to keep the traits of the Marksville period secret much longer."[14] Of course, by 1938 there was little "secrecy" surrounding those traits. It was well known, through Setzler's (1933a, 1933b, 1934) brief publications and Ford's (1935a, 1935b, 1935c, 1936a, 1938b) work, what the pottery looked like. Ford and Willey made only passing reference to other artifacts from Marksville in their report on Crooks.

The relative-dating technique for assigning sites to a chronological position would later be the focus of Ford's (1949) dissertation. Several statements in the Crooks report underscored Ford's reliance on similarity as a way of inferring phyletic connection and hence temporal closeness. For example, he and Willey noted, "In Louisiana, *Marksville Stamped* is ancestral to *Troyville Stamped*, a type of the Troyville period" (Ford and Willey 1940:74)—an evolutionary sequence based on similarities in design between sherds assigned to one type or the other.

14. Letters in LSU Museum of Natural Science archives.

On the opposite end of the time scale, they linked Tchefuncte-period sherds to those of the succeeding Marksville period:

> Certain features of the Crooks site suggest typological relation to the sites of the Tchefuncte period, which from recent evidences appears immediately to precede the culture of the Marksville stage in southern Louisiana. Five sherds of the Tchefuncte type *Tchefuncte Incised* were found in the fill of the burial platform and in the primary mantle of Mound A. Also some of the material listed as *Marksville Plain* shows very close typological relationship to *Tchefuncte Plain.* This is seen particularly in the fragments with tetrapodal supports, flanged bases, and notched rims. . . . The tendency for the Marksville type *Crooks Stamped* to increase in popularity early in Marksville time, as indicated by stratigraphic studies, is also of significance in light of the fact that where Marksville period types have been found in Tchefuncte sites, the type is relatively abundant. (Ford and Willey 1940:137–38)

One could quibble with Ford and Willey about Crooks Stamped being relatively abundant in Tchefuncte sites, since Ford and Quimby (1945) later listed a total of twelve sherds of that type from four of the Tchefuncte sites excavated during the WPA program (Figure 3.6). However, stratigraphic evidence consistently demonstrated that sherds of Crooks Stamped and of other types they assigned to the Marksville period were superposed over sherds of types assigned to the Tchefuncte period.

Of more importance here is the equivalence in Ford and Willey's scheme of periods, cultures, and stages: "Certain features of the Crooks site suggest typological relation to the sites of the Tchefuncte *period,* which from recent evidences appears immediately to precede the *culture* of the Marksville *stage*" (Ford and Willey 1940:137–38; emphasis added). It is clear that by 1940, Ford had completely turned to pottery types—not attributes or features of pottery but pottery types—to define not only periods but also cultures and stages. Throughout the 1940s, synonymous use of these three terms would become a hallmark of the culture-history paradigm.

Also of interest here is that Ford issued his first formal statement on diffusion in the Crooks report. Throughout the 1930s archaeologists debated the direction of movement of Hopewellian traits: had Hopewell been a southern phenomenon that moved north—the position apparently favored by Setzler (1933b)—or was it a northern phenomenon that moved south? Ford and Willey (1940:138–43) came down in favor of the former position, and the deciding factor was pottery:

> The pottery which is commonly referred to as the Hopewellian ceremonial ware [in the north] is very similar to the utility ware found at Marksville period village sites in Louisiana. The predominating pottery of Hopewellian sites in the various northern centers is a grit-tempered cord-marked ware, commonly referred to as Woodland. So far not a single cord-marked sherd has been found in a Marksville period burial mound, and only a few have been discovered in the top levels of the Marksville village site. However, a cord-marked type, *Deasonville Cordmarked,* is very common in the

Troyville horizon, which immediately succeeds the Marksville in Louisiana. (Ford and Willey 1940:139–40)

To set the stage for their scenario, Ford and Willey (1940:141) stated, "The very fact that a Hopewellian complex of features is firmly planted in such widely separated areas as Louisiana, Illinois, Ohio, New York, Michigan, Wisconsin, Iowa, and Missouri, indicates that all of these occupations are not of the same age. The basic resemblances of the culture are so great that it must have been distributed from a common center which consequently would be older." And where was that common center? The presence of large numbers of fancy stamped and incised sherds throughout the Crooks deposit and the absence of cordmarked "utility-vessel" sherds—meaning that Marksville peoples were using fancy pottery for everyday use as well as for grave inclusions—argued strongly for the interpretation "that the cultural influence which all the Hopewellian manifestations had in common, appeared first in the lower Mississippi Valley" (Ford and Willey 1940:141). As it spread north, somewhere "in the comparatively unexplored region between Louisiana and southern Illinois, this stream of cultural influence became thoroughly mixed with Woodlandlike culture, a fact demonstrated principally by the addition of cord-marked pottery" (Ford and Willey 1940:142).

Ford and Willey were not content to view the spread of Hopewellian traits by mere diffusion; rather, they concocted an elaborate scheme based on their reading of skeletal as well as artifactual evidence:

> The scanty physical evidence at hand[15] suggests that the Marksville period saw the introduction into the Lower Valley of a broadheaded people who practiced cranial deformation. The population of the preceding Tchefuncte period was cranially undeformed and dolichocephalic. . . . In several . . . Upper Valley areas, the period of Hopewellian culture saw the introduction of brachycephals into regions formerly held by longheaded peoples.
>
> Thus it is indicated that the northward drift of Hopewellian was not merely a movement of culture up the valley of the Mississippi; it rather was an actual movement of people. . . . Some mixing of peoples through absorption of the weaker groups may have taken place, and this may be what is indicated by the addition to the cultural complex of Woodland traits. However, since the simple hunting peoples who were being displaced probably had little to offer in the way of complex ceramic art, metal ornaments, smoking pipes, burial practices, or mound construction, it is not surprising that there is as much similarity in certain artifact forms as exists between the widespread manifestations. (Ford and Willey 1940:142–43)

Ford and Willey's statements on cephalic types at Crooks were based on "Preliminary observations made by the excavators in the field" (Ford and Willey

15. Scanty indeed, given that "Most of the skeletal material was in an extremely poor condition and, as a consequence, only a few crania and long bones could be saved for anthropometrical purposes" (Ford and Willey 1940:35).

1940:41). Further, those observations "suggest that at least some of the individuals are brachycephalic, or mesocephalic. The faces appear to be large. A few skull fragments indicate that cranial deformation was practiced" (Ford and Willey 1940:41). If at least some of the skulls were either brachycephalic (skull wider than it is long) *or* mesocephalic, then *some* of them were dolichocephalic (skull longer than it is wide). In other words, the Crooks mounds contained the full range of cranial types. This undermines Ford and Willey's evidence for a physically distinct Marksville population.

Ford and Willey's scenario for the development of Hopewell out of a Marksville base, which itself was seen as a "transplanted" culture—note their statement that the people responsible for Marksville were different from those responsible for the antecedent Tchefuncte—was interesting in how it appeared to accommodate available data. More importantly, it demonstrates that Ford, in contrast to his earlier explanations of the Peck Village materials as involving diffusion but also at least some in situ evolution, was by 1940 committed heavily to a diffusionist position, complete with population movements when he deemed it necessary. This apparent shift in thinking seems to have two proximate sources—the attempt to account for somatological as well as pottery data and Ford's earlier discarding of his paradigmatic classification system. The latter had allowed close monitoring of attributes and their varied combinations and frequencies as types. The system of naming pottery types that grew out of the 1938 Conference on Southeastern Pottery Typology resulted in a focus on types as discrete objects having particular attribute combinations and less attention on particular attributes. These two factors played a major role in Ford's first attempt at synthesis and significantly influenced how he later interpreted the archaeological record.

The 1941 Synthesis

Ford and Willey (1940:143) concluded their report on Crooks by stating, "The accumulated data on eastern archaeology is beginning to yield to synthesis and to outline a story of the distribution of cultures over a large part of the Mississippi Basin. . . . [A]fter a few more years . . . it should be possible to narrate in detail how primitive agriculturalists built a complex and thriving culture in the Eastern United States." By the time the Crooks report was published, they had already submitted a synthesis to *American Anthropologist* in which they outlined the "story of the distribution of cultures" not only in the Mississippi Basin but over the entire eastern United States. Although the article, eventually entitled "An Interpretation of the Prehistory of the Eastern United States" (Ford and Willey 1941), was coauthored, Willey (1969:67) later noted that the "vision and the bold conceptions were Ford's; my own role was a very junior one of formal organization and the injection of occasional cautionary and qualifying statements." Willey (1969:67) wrote that Ford originally titled the piece "A Key to the Prehistory of the Eastern United States," but Willey, without Ford's knowledge, substituted the word "interpretation" for "key" in galley proof. Ford apparently was not amused when he saw the published essay.

On the preliminary nature of ideas presented in the paper, Willey (1969:67) noted, "Ford felt that the impact of the ideas which the article carried were of greater importance to Eastern archaeology at that time than the negative circumstance of speculation outrunning factual proof." In truth, the article was rife with speculation and short on factual "proof," but the importance of the article in establishing the culture-history approach in the Southeast is difficult to overestimate. It stood as the only real archaeological synthesis of the region until Griffin (1946) published "Cultural Change and Continuity in Eastern United States Archaeology" a few years later.

The "Interpretation" was anchored heavily in the essentialist metaphysic. Ford and Willey's major objective in the paper was to arrange *cultures* in spatial and chronological order to show the direction of diffusion of various cultural "features" (Ford and Willey 1941:326). A series of cross sections, or "chronological profiles, analogous to geological profiles" (Ford and Willey 1941:327) along major river courses illustrated the positions of cultural units—each designated by a "cultural name in common use" (Ford and Willey 1941:331), such as Hopewell— and key archaeological sites. Lines of different slope, bounding what Ford and Willey referred to as "stages," crosscut the profiles, demonstrating the temporal distributions across space of the cultural features under investigation as well as the differences in rates of trait diffusion and/or population movement, given their view of absolute chronology, which constituted "frankly guesses" (Ford and Willey 1941:331). Figure 3.8—a cross section that runs northward along the Mississippi River from Baton Rouge to southeastern Iowa, then turns eastward to northern Indiana and north to Grand Rapids, Michigan—shows that Ford and Willey viewed most cultural features as occurring first in the lower Mississippi Valley and then spreading northward. The Archaic stage was viewed as ending in the Baton Rouge area between A.D. 700–800 but not in the Grand Rapids area until roughly A.D. 1100. It was succeeded by the Burial Mound I and II stages, the latter lasting much longer in areas north of Vicksburg, Mississippi, than in the region to the south, where the Temple Mound I stage, characterized by rectangular "temple" mounds, began at around A.D. 1150.

The Mississippi Valley chronological profile in some respects was the key to understanding eastern prehistory: "The Mississippi River and its tributaries form a great dendritic system of rich agricultural land through the central part of this region, providing an ideal artery for the dissemination of cultures based on an agricultural economy. The heart of the eastern cultural area is the immediate valley of the Mississippi River and the lower portions of the valleys of its tributaries" (Ford and Willey 1941:326). Hence, the Mississippi Valley was not only the center of a culture area but also contained a ready-made set of paths over which cultural traits might disperse. The similarity between Ford and Willey's notion and Clark Wissler's (1916b) culture-area and age-area notions (see Kroeber [1931b] for discussion and description) is striking, though Ford and Willey did not acknowledge the similarity or cite Wissler. They referred to Kroeber's (1939) rendition of the culture-area concept, but did not acknowledge it as the source of their ideas regarding the relations among culture areas, culture centers, and the distribution of culture traits.

By 1941, Ford and Willey recognized six periods in the lower Mississippi Valley, squeezing Plaquemine between Coles Creek and the historical period (Figure 3.8). In the Vicksburg-Memphis region, a different set of periods grew out of analysis of local decoration-based pottery types. There, the sequence contained an early Helena period (a designation that never caught on), followed by Early Baytown, which overlapped temporally with portions of the Marksville and Troyville periods to the south; then Late Baytown, which overlapped temporally with portions of Troyville and Coles Creek to the south; then Early Middle Mississippi, which overlapped temporally with portions of the Coles Creek and Plaquemine periods to the south; and finally the St. Francis period, which was more or less contemporaneous with the historical era.

Publication of Ford and Willey's synthesis set in concrete the notion Ford (1938b) had introduced a few years earlier and Ford and Willey (1940) had reinforced in the Crooks report—local diagnostic pottery types were to be used to create periods. Thus, "Cordmarking as a pottery surface treatment [an attribute] arrived in the Lower Mississippi Valley at the close of the Marksville period and achieved the peak of its popularity in the succeeding Troyville period" (Ford and Willey 1941:341), just as certain new decorative elements had originated somewhere other than the locations of his surface collections (Ford 1936a). Similarly, "The Troyville period in the Lower Valley gradually develops into that designated as Coles Creek" (Ford and Willey 1941:345), just as Coles Creek gradually replaced Marksville at Peck Village (Ford 1935c).

Since by this time Ford viewed cultural change as the result of not only diffusion but also migration, gone were the detailed studies of the phyletic evolution of various attributes of pottery types prominent in his earlier work (e.g., Ford 1936a:262–68). Similarly, diagnostic pottery types might still be analytical units of the ideational sort useful for measuring time and space, but, reverting to his 1935–1936 mode of thinking, he dropped his earlier disclaimer (Ford 1938b) that pottery complexes did not necessarily represent distinct cultures. As a result, his periods took on essentialist properties and were referred to as "cultures"—a practice begun in the Crooks report.

With regard to the northern spread of Marksville, "Whether this second wave entailed a movement of population or not, there is very good evidence that it

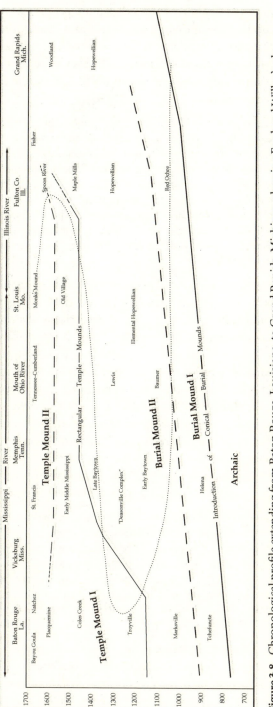
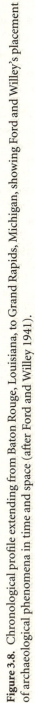

Figure 3.8. Chronological profile extending from Baton Rouge, Louisiana, to Grand Rapids, Michigan, showing Ford and Willey's placement of archaeological phenomena in time and space (after Ford and Willey 1941).

moved through and was assimilated by indigenous peoples who had already acquired a great deal of cultural virility, possibly as a result of absorbing the essentials of an agricultural economy from the preceding Adena stage" (Ford and Willey 1941:340). Agriculture and its spread were viewed as somehow allied with the introduction of other cultural features, with agriculture (an inference) considered as the prime mover:

> we have attempted to show how a set of strikingly unique cultural ideas, centering around a mortuary complex and cult of the dead, spread throughout the Eastern United States by way of the Mississippi Valley. . . . It seems likely that the real driving factor behind the spread of these new ideas [Tchefuncte-Adena and Marksville-Hopewell] was a basic horticulture. There are strong suggestions that these horticultural, mound building, coiled pottery cultural traits were introduced and promulgated by a new physical type, brachycephals who also practiced cranial deformation. This new population increment, and the new cultural complex, merged with the peoples and cultures of what has been referred to as the Archaic stage. (Ford and Willey 1941:343–44)

Important though population movement was to Ford as a mechanism of culture change, there was one "new idea" for which he did not invoke it as a mechanism—an "idea" that would later figure prominently in a classic dialogue about the prehistory of the Mississippi River valley. That "idea" concerned shell-tempered pottery, which became a hallmark of Ford and Willey's Middle Mississippi *period,* which they divided into two segments, early and late. With reference to the early Middle Mississippi period in the upper half of the lower Mississippi Valley, Ford and Willey (1941:348) noted that it "succeeds the Late Baytown in eastern Arkansas and western Mississippi. . . . It should be emphasized that the changes do not suggest a complete replacement of cultural features, but rather a development and an intrusion of new ideas." This is not so different from their earlier (Ford and Willey 1940) diffusionist statements—a blend of diffusion *and* in situ development—but notice what they had to say in the sentences immediately following:

> Shell tempering and the use of handles on pottery vessels are the most marked changes in ceramics. Clay-tempered polished vessels are gradually replaced by vessels of similar shapes tempered with finely ground shell. Red slipped bowls, ears on bowl rims, types of incised decorations, wide-mouthed bottle forms, round bottomed bowls, flat bottomed bowls with flaring sides, beakers, and many other ceramic features change but little. Rectangular mounds in plaza arrangement, small thin projectile points, elbow pipes, and pottery trowels all come from the Late Baytown of the same region. (Ford and Willey 1941:348)

In other words, there was a *gradual evolution* of the Baytown period into the early Middle Mississippi period rather than a disjunction. There might have been a few new ideas that filtered in, but in terms of the pottery, mounds, projectile points, and so forth, Ford and Willey saw the basis of early Middle Mississippi–period culture as being the preceding Baytown-period culture. Why is there no population movement or diffusion to explain this "transition" when they ostensibly explained every other "transition"? The most charitable way of putting it is to suggest that Ford was choosy about when to invoke those mechanisms in interpreting the archaeological record.

Confusion has always existed in the literature as a result of the myriad ways in which the term "period" has been used. Part of the confusion may have been fostered by Ford and Willey's (1941; see also Ford and Willey 1940) use of key terms such as "period" and "culture" without explicit definitions. They referred to units such as Coles Creek, Hopewell, Adena, and the like—shown in smaller font size in Figure 3.8—variously as cultures, horizons, periods, cultural periods, and cultural complexes. They referred to units such as Archaic and Burial Mound I—the larger font size in Figure 3.8—variously as stages, cultural horizons, cultural complexes, complexes of traits, and varieties of culture. The potential for conflation of these units was enhanced by their speaking metaphorically of "stages of a culture," such as Coles Creek, when they merely meant later sections of the time span occupied by the cultural unit. Also confusing was their mixing cultural traits—typically types of artifacts, many labeled with an inferred function—that supposedly were diagnostic of a particular cultural unit with those that were not diagnostic of any unit.

The absence of a logical structure of units of various sorts and scales in the synthesis is perplexing in light of the schemes then in use in the Southwest (e.g., Colton 1939; Gladwin and Gladwin 1934), where Willey was educated, and in the Midwest (e.g., McKern 1937, 1939)—schemes that both Ford and Willey were well aware of. We suspect that Ford's braided-stream notion of cultural change and the attempt to explain the archaeological record in ethnological terms resulted in the conflation of observations and units of measurement (his types) with interpretations and explanations. On top of that, any scheme that avoided focusing on time was anathema to Ford's way of thinking. Ford initially had trouble understanding not only the value of a classificatory system that disregarded time but also how such a system worked—hence Griffin's attempts in 1935 to explain it to him. Griffin wanted classificatory order; Ford wanted evolutionary sequences. Griffin didn't think Ford knew what he was talking about. A year and a half before the Ford-Willey paper appeared, Griffin wrote to Willey about Ford's evolutionistic tendencies and his speculative statements on diffusion:

> Regarding [Ford's] nose-thumbing at the McKern classification I am somewhat surprised at his lack of appreciation for a device which will enable him to save his face when his evolutionary sequences fall from their own hypothetical weight. Darned if I can see how he is going to develop the Archaic culture, Signal Butte I, and [Old Bering Sea culture] out of Marksville but I guess it can be done. The prehistoric Indians

sure must have been glad to get away from Louisiana and Mississippi the way they blossomed after they left the area. . . .

. . . . You talk as though you actually thought you had Hopewell sites down there in Louisiana. Are you going to express that in terms of the classification or will you have a nice genetic series worked out for that?[16]

Griffin expressed similar concerns in a letter written to Quimby later that year: "I heard that Ford is going to state that Hopewell developed out of Marksville. I hope he does not."[17]

The Aftermath of the Louisiana WPA Program

One by-product of the Louisiana WPA program—certainly evident in the Ford-Willey paper of 1941—was the abundance of information generated on the archaeological record of eastern Louisiana. Ford's sample of sites covered the known range of time as far as the ceramic period was concerned. Tchefuncte, Big Oak Island, and the Lafayette Mounds, for example, were selected because they appeared to contain pottery older than the Marksville period. Crooks was selected because it appeared to date to the Marksville period, and Greenhouse was chosen because it appeared to be a large Coles Creek–period mound group. Medora and Bayou Goula were identified as candidates to fill in the gap between Coles Creek and the historical period (Medora) and to provide material from the historical period (Bayou Goula). From those excavations had come hundreds of thousands of artifacts that provided not only chronological information but also a detailed inventory of elements of the material record other than pottery. The Louisiana WPA program ended officially in 1941, as it did or had done in other states, in advance of the storm clouds of war gathering in the distance (Quimby 1979). Federal funding began to be shifted toward defense measures, and archaeology was one area that was hard hit.

The obvious legacy of the Louisiana WPA program was its contribution to chronology—a contribution that was both immediate and long-lasting. Not all archaeologists, however, were happy with the chronological sequence put forward first by Ford and Willey in the Crooks report and then later refined in other WPA reports. Part of the irritation arose as a result of how some archaeologists of the period chose to view cultural periods—that is, as real things. Not all archaeologists succumbed to this temptation, but enough of them did so that when Ford and Willey (1940) proposed their new sequence of periods in the Crooks report, archaeologists used to the old sequence—the one without Troyville and Tchefuncte that Ford had used in the Peck Village (Ford 1935c) and surface-collection reports (Ford 1936a)—were angered. Maybe they could

16. Letter of June 16, 1939, from Griffin to Willey (LSU Museum of Natural Science archives).
17. Letter from Griffin to Quimby, November 6, 1939 (cited in Quimby and Cleland 1976:xxvii).

understand adding a sub-basement (Tchefuncte) beneath the older basement (Marksville), but why in the world would Ford slide a new floor—Troyville—between Marksville and Coles Creek, or, later, make matters worse by adding another floor—Plaquemine—between Coles Creek and the historical period (Natchez)? As Gibson (1982:271) put it, both Troyville and Plaquemine were

> transitional units. . . . carved out of ceramic complexes that had formerly been classified as something else. This confounded opponents who simply could not see how some cultural types could be Marksville or Coles Creek one day and Troyville or Plaquemine the next. These individuals apparently did not share Ford's view of culture as a gradually changing flow of ideas, with any one archaeological site encapsulating those elements which comprised a limited span of an unbroken continuum.

The manner in which Ford handled the criticism in the Greenhouse report (Ford 1951a) is perhaps his finest written statement against the notion that chronological periods were real, but we delay presenting it until Chapter 4, when we can place it in the context of how Ford used the Greenhouse data to bolster his earlier creation of the Troyville period. In 1940 and the years immediately after, Ford had another problem with which to contend regarding his chronology—the uncritical application of his chronological sequence to other areas. Whereas Ford saw the sequence as a local one, which had been designed to solve chronological problems specific to the lower Mississippi Valley, others took it as a regional sequence (or at least the basis for a regional sequence) designed to solve everyone's problems. Ford's sequence looked so good—and in several respects it was—that it became the anchor for most subsequent work in the Southeast (O'Brien 1998). Chronological sequences from areas outside the lower Mississippi Valley were constantly compared against Ford's sequence to determine the degree of fit between the two. Years later, in their classic book *Method and Theory in American Archaeology,* Willey and Phillips (1958:27) warned against this, noting that "we will assume for the sake of argument that local sequences remain local and that regional sequences are the result of correlating them—not combining them, be it noted, because in the process the original formulations are retailored to fit the wider spatial and (sometimes) deeper temporal dimensions." Interestingly, they used the Louisiana sequence as an example of what they termed the "osmotic tendency":

> One of the firmest sequences in North American archaeology is that established by James A. Ford and his associates in the southern portion of the Mississippi alluvial valley, centering approximately about the mouth of the Red River in Louisiana. . . . The unusual vigor of the "Lower Valley" sequence is manifested by a tendency to dominate in correlations with other sequences in neighboring regions, but it is important to point out that its strength derives from the hard core of stratigraphy at the center. If there is any valid criticism of this sequence, it is that it tends to take in too much territory. Workers in the delta of the Mississippi and adjacent coastal regions,

for example, have tried to fit their data into it, not without considerable strain, which is scarcely to be wondered at, considering the sharp environmental differences involved in such an extension. (Willey and Phillips 1958:27–28)

One might question the relevance of "sharp environmental differences" in chronological ordering, but Willey and Phillips were correct in pointing out that the "Lower Valley" sequence took in too much territory and also that ever since the ordering was developed archaeologists working in other areas had strained to accommodate their data within it.

By the time the Louisiana WPA program was up and running and the chronological picture in the lower Mississippi Valley was becoming clear, it was becoming obvious that that chronology was beginning to outdistance those in some parts of the Midwest and Southeast. At the 1939 meeting of the American Anthropological Association in Chicago—the same meeting at which Ford and Willey made their initial presentation of the southeastern synthesis—Ford, Griffin, and Phillips discussed the possibility of initiating a survey and study of the Mississippi Valley north of the Red River mouth that would eventually lead to a chronological ordering of remains in the region. This in turn would link the lower Mississippi Valley chronology to those in the upper Mississippi Valley and the Ohio Valley. Earlier, at the third meeting on archaeological needs sponsored by the National Research Council, Griffin and Setzler had argued for such a survey, primarily to determine what kinds of Hopewell-like remains might lie between Marksville and the northern Hopewell sites (Griffin 1976:27). The region north of the Red River and south of the junction of the Mississippi and Ohio Rivers at Cairo, Illinois, was in the late 1930s not exactly an archaeological no-man's land, but except for early work by Clarence Moore it had not witnessed any kind of reasonably sustained archaeological activity. It was to remedy this situation that the survey was devised:

The purpose of the Survey was to investigate the northern two-thirds of the alluvial valley of the Lower Mississippi River—roughly from the mouth of the Ohio to Vicksburg, Mississippi, an area long regarded as one of the principal blind spots in the archaeology of the Southeast. This is not altogether due to lack of work in the area, or to the character of such work, but rather to the fact that it had so far failed to reveal anything concerning the earlier pre-Mississippian cultures. The need for a comprehensive survey had been repeatedly voiced at Midwestern and Southeastern conferences and various suggestions made for carrying out such a project. (Phillips et al. 1951:v)

Although Phillips, Ford, and Griffin were interested in finding traces of pre-Mississippian cultures, they were particularly interested in those that perhaps had given rise to Mississippian culture:

There is general agreement among students of Southeastern archaeology that the climax of the late prehistoric cultures is the archaeological facies long recognized under the designation "Middle Mississippi." At a comparatively late date—A.D.

1400–1500 is probably not too late for its peak of development—this culture was firmly established over an immense area. . . . By 1939, when the present Survey was first discussed, an immense amount of data on Middle Mississippi had accumulated, but the problem of its origins and development appeared to be as far from resolution as ever. There was a general impression, shared by many students of Southeastern culture, that this was because the "central" Mississippi Valley, the assumed center of distribution of the culture, had not been sufficiently investigated. It was primarily to make good this lack that the present Survey was undertaken. (Phillips et al. 1951:39)

Although the survey-and-excavation program began in 1940, we delay discussion of it because much of what finally made it into the report was hashed out by Phillips et al. in the late 1940s. Importantly, Ford's method of presenting the pottery data—the bar graphs that later characterized his synthetic treatments of the prehistory of the lower Mississippi Valley (e.g., Ford 1951a, 1952a; Ford and Webb 1956; Ford et al. 1955)—first appeared in his dissertation on Peruvian archaeology, having grown out of his work in the Mississippi Valley. To put Ford's contribution to the Mississippi Valley survey in historical perspective, we need to first examine in considerable detail the work he did in Peru as part of Gordon Willey's Virú Valley Project.

4

Large-Scale Archaeological Surveys
1942–1951

As he had done when he left Louisiana to attend the University of Michigan, Ford put his fieldwork in the state on hold to return to graduate school, this time to Columbia University, in 1940. With the assistance of a Julius Rosenwald Fund fellowship, he was able to enroll in Columbia's doctoral program. A few years earlier, probably because of the background of his professors at LSU, Ford had figured he would end up at Berkeley when it came time for a doctorate—that is, if such a time ever came. Ethel Ford wasn't so sure, as she lamented to Jim's mother in May 1938:

> If I can just persuade him to begin work on his doctor's at the earliest possible date. At present he is balking at the idea of even thinking of the doctors. Competition in his field is getting keener and keener, and 15 years from now he will be glad he has it. I suppose I am too ambitious for him but if you and I are not ambitious for him, no one else will be. Jim has too big a future to let it be spoiled by lack of academic requirements, and the day is almost at hand when a man must have the doctor's degree to be considered an outstanding specialist in his field.[1]

Whether through his wife's prodding or of his own volition, Ford decided it was time to return to school. He must have felt that the WPA program in Louisiana, which was winding down anyway, could carry on in his absence.

Ford's move to Columbia reunited him with Gordon Willey, who had left the WPA project the previous fall to continue his own graduate studies. Not surprisingly, given his rural upbringing and matter-of-fact demeanor, Ford had a negative opinion of New York, although Willey (1988:61) thought that "underneath he was fascinated by the intensity and variety of the great city even though he was repelled by what he thought of as its falseness and its glitter." In a letter to George Quimby, in whose hands he had left the WPA project, Ford related that he and Ethel had

---

1. Letter of May 19, 1938, from Ethel Ford to Janie Ford (LSU Museum of Natural Science archives).

"settled down to untangling the mysteries of the subway and automatic elevators. Am picking up quite a bit of information but don't see what possible use there will be for it after we leave here."[2] And in another letter to Quimby, he noted, "Both Ethel and I are slowly developing the perverted point of view which is necessary to the proper enjoyment of this great metropolis. . . . I just gave my last 7 cents to a pretty maid who was collecting for the Youth Organization to Help Preserve Democracy by Keeping America out of the War. On the way home I passed a nice new Dodge [panel] body—make a fine field car. It was a Horse Watering Unit of the SPCA. Someone around here is nutz."[3]

New York was simply a place to be tolerated for the first-class education at Columbia, which in the previous four decades had turned out many of the top American anthropologists, many of them under the direction of Franz Boas. Among them were Margaret Mead, Ruth Benedict, Robert Lowie, Clark Wissler, Fay-Cooper Cole, Leslie Spier, and Edward Sapir—all well-respected scholars— but certainly the most prolific of Boas's students was A. L. Kroeber, who graduated from Columbia in 1901 and soon established the anthropology department at Berkeley.

From Willey's (1988) accounting, Ford had little or no trouble adapting to Columbia. He didn't have much use for required courses in social anthropology— Ruth Benedict's perspective, as Willey pointed out, had little in common with Leslie White's—but those simply were things to be put up with, albeit not without a degree of discomfiture, which Ford would occasionally summarize for Quimby in less than flattering tones:

> Am thoroughly disgusted with trying to get educated. Maybe I don't have what it takes although of course I think I do. Remember that I spent the winter at Michigan trying to uphold the Boa[s]ian point of view to White. Well, now that I am being fed Boa[s] in unadulterated form I can clearly see what Weslie [Leslie White] was talking about and there appear to be holes in this stuff big enough to drive a truck through. And Jesus—is Benedict mixed up. Am keeping my mouth shut pretty well but sometimes can't resist coming up for air and tripping her up.[4]

> Have just finished a little paper for Benedict on Anthropology and Science. She thinks anthro. is "the study of the mental life of man"—poor dope. That's all right tho—she won't tumble into her grave in her present benighted state—I'll save her. You know how it says in the Bible "and a little archaeologist shall lead them."[5]

At one point, Ford begged Quimby to send him some survey material to work on, because

2. Letter (undated, probably January 1941) from Ford to Quimby (LSU Museum of Natural Science archives).

3. Letter of January 31, 1941, from Ford to Quimby (LSU Museum of Natural Science archives).

4. Letter of November 1, 1940, from Ford to Quimby (LSU Museum of Natural Science archives).

5. Letter of January 1, 1941, from Ford to Quimby (LSU Museum of Natural Science archives).

In a month or so I shall have to start working on what Mead had to say about the [e]ffects of changing baby's diapers on the relationships of the individual to his culture. Maybe you don't know it but sphinct[e]r habits and early training in defacatory arts have a profound influence on personality development.—So please push those [survey] cards along and let me use them—not for what you think. Want to bury my head in a few graphs for a change and quit considering the importance of such anthropological problems as the solution of the mother-in-law problem by various prim[i]tives.[6]

Ford, like Willey, had William Duncan Strong (Figure 4.1) as his doctoral adviser. Strong, like Fred Kniffen, who had trained Ford, was another student of Kroeber's. It was no accident that by the late 1940s Ford's work took on a cast that showed the theoretical and methodological influence not only of Strong but of Kroeber as well.

Figure 4.1. Photograph of William Duncan Strong, ca. 1928 (negative no. 108960, photograph courtesy Field Museum of Natural History).

6. Letter of January 31, 1941, from Ford to Quimby (LSU Museum of Natural Science archives).

WILLIAM DUNCAN STRONG AND A. L. KROEBER

William Duncan Strong—"Dunc" to his friends and associates—received his graduate training at Berkeley under Kroeber, earning his Ph.D. in 1926. Kroeber had invented frequency seriation and no doubt influenced Leslie Spier, who tested, and in many ways perfected, the technique. Strong worked with Kroeber during the 1920s, when frequency seriation was still fresh in the latter's mind (e.g., Kroeber 1925c), producing or helping Kroeber produce several important studies on Max Uhle's Peruvian pottery collections (Kroeber and Strong 1924a, 1924b; Strong 1925). Kroeber was interested in the prehistory of Peru and Mexico "because he regarded these areas as the major sources of cultural influences spreading to the rest of the New World" (Rowe 1962:400). Strong, a senior at Berkeley when he and Kroeber began their studies of Uhle's collections in 1922–1923, was responsible for classifying the vessels and "was largely left to his own initiative in this part of the work, [though] Kroeber would drop in from time to time to see how the project was going and to make suggestions. When the classification was finished, Kroeber took over the results and wrote the report[s], adding Strong's name to [them] as co-author" (Rowe 1962:401).

Kroeber wanted to determine the chronology of Peruvian cultural manifestations by using Uhle's pots, which were well documented in terms of which grave lot they came from. The problem was to arrange the lots in chronological order, and to do this Kroeber and Strong used phyletic seriation—the same method Kidder (1917) had earlier used—as well as frequency seriation. They began with a procedure similar to that used by Kroeber (1916a, 1916b) when he seriated his pottery collections from Zuñi: they anchored their proposed chronology in the historical period based on the presence of "European articles" in certain graves, "thus affording a starting point for chronology" (Kroeber and Strong 1924a:9). In their initial analysis, they noted several things that would eventually become interpretive algorithms within the culture-history paradigm. For example, they noted that "reasonable numbers" of a pottery "style" in an area other than that where it was thought to have originated "suggests that it was the style rather than the pottery itself that was imported [to the former area], and that vessels of this type were manufactured on the spot" (Kroeber and Strong 1924a:12)—a statement not so different from what Ford (1935c, 1936a) said slightly more than a decade later.

Kroeber and Strong also grappled with what appeared to be temporally "intermediate or transitional" styles, recognized as those that displayed attributes— "influences"—of distinct cultures in muted form and/or mixed with apparently indigenous attributes (e.g., Kroeber and Strong 1924a:22–23). Transitional styles were characterized as such because the set of materials in which they were found contained "no forms or traits incisively peculiar to [the set]" (Kroeber and

Strong 1924a:47). The interpretive algorithm seems to have resided in Kroeber's essentialist notions that each "separate culture [would have] independent traits of its own" (Kroeber and Strong 1924a:48). Thus a so-called temporally transitional culture would consist of traits from the earlier one "beginning to break down and the [later, succeeding one] not yet [becoming] rigorously established" (Kroeber and Strong 1924a:48).

Grave goods would obscure the picture of the historical development of a cultural lineage, since they "do not necessarily represent momentary acts of a long homogeneous population, but probably represent in some instances a family record of several generations from variant elements [different social classes] in an *imperfectly assimilated population*" (Kroeber and Strong 1924a:49; emphasis added). Intermediate, or transitional, cultural phases were thus "expectable at a continuously inhabited site" (Kroeber and Strong 1924a:49). This was a rather clever attempt by Kroeber and Strong to reconcile the materialist notion of continuous culture development with the essentialist notion that each culture was a separate and distinct entity.

In their second study of the Uhle pottery collection, Kroeber and Strong (1924b:96–97) wrote, "Each of the seven [cultural] phases shows approximation of style to two others. They must therefore be construed as parts of a continuous development. In the absence of stratification, this continuity is of course of importance." This statement was a nod to phyletic seriation. They continued, "It will be observed that each style [of pottery] shares certain traits with those assumed to precede or succeed it, and differs from them in other traits. As the number of traits is considerable, and the number of vessels ranges from 19 to 173 for the various styles, averaging 85, the differentiation of the seven [cultural] phases is indubitable and their assumed succession highly probable" (Kroeber and Strong 1924b:103). This statement, too, reflects the fact that some of their seriations were of the phyletic sort, but they also performed a frequency seriation by converting absolute frequencies of pottery styles into percentages, concluding, "These percentage figures . . . are particularly impressive" (Kroeber and Strong 1924b:104). Although their percentages per cultural phase summed to greater than 100, it is worth noting Kroeber and Strong's (1924b:105–6) efforts to explain what was clearly an imperfect depiction of the popularity principle. Deviations from the model of a unimodal frequency distribution for each type were variously accounted for by claiming that some specimens were perhaps misclassified, some samples were too small to be reliable, some styles were not identical from phase to phase (indicating their types had group-like properties and were not atemporal, aspatial, immutable classes), or the majority of the materials were vessels made specifically for inclusion in graves rather than for ordinary use.

Although Kroeber and Strong (1924a, 1924b) used the terms "culture," "phase," "period," and "style" synonymously in their reports, Kroeber (1925a:229) later emphasized that "a distinct style is not necessarily proof of a distinct period. It is entirely possible that several styles can coexist in a given population in a given time." But Kroeber never defined what the term "style" meant or what a style was. Was it a class—an ideational unit—or a group—an empirical unit? That it was to him a class is clear from the discussion following his observation that multiple styles might be found to be contemporaneous. It was an "almost inescapable inference that the first specimens [of a particular style] in [a] debased manner must have been made after the pure manner [of the style] was established" (Kroeber 1925a:229). Thus, while a particular "style" might span a particular cultural phase or period, it might also be found to take either a pure or a "debased" expression, the former being early and the latter late in the history of the style. When two similar styles were not contemporaneous, they must "represent two overlapping or even distinct periods" (Kroeber 1925a:230). Here Kroeber imparted reality to his periods instead of viewing them as units imposed by the archaeologist. Neither could he escape the essentialist implications of his styles: when two similar styles were contemporaneous, they must "mainly represent different groups or strata of the population" (Kroeber 1925a:230).

By 1924 Strong had reached the point where he could begin working on his own (though still under Kroeber's supervision), and as his project he took on the analysis of Uhle's collection from the Ancón cemetery—a coastal Peruvian site that had been mined in the late nineteenth century for its fancy pottery (Reiss and Stüble 1880–1887; Uhle 1913). Strong (1925:137) indicated that his sorting of pottery specimens was "purely typological and based on careful consideration of all distinguishable characteristics—technique, shape, color, design, and combinations of any or all of these factors." After the material was classified, "the interpretive element of depth and layer of deposit [was] allowed to enter into consideration," and Strong (1925:137) noted that "the two methods of grouping [typological and depth] were found to accord in a way far too striking to be accidental." In particular, he found "a rather clear example of agreement between uniform pottery types and different layers of deposit," and thus he was "certain" that the "framework of cultural sequences [he derived] is correct as regards the main development and succession of cultural types" (Strong 1925:137). This was, in short, the essentialist notion of "culture types," reinforced by the apparent discontinuity evident in the pottery found within the discrete depositional chunks normally referred to as strata—a pitfall that culture-historians in general failed to avoid (Lyman et al. 1997a).

Strong (1925:159) divided the Ancón collection into five "periods"—Early Ancón, Middle Ancón I, Middle Ancón II, Late Ancón I, and Late Ancón II—"on the basis of color, design, shape, and other features" of the pottery. He then tallied the absolute and relative frequencies of "forty significant traits," or attributes, of the pottery within each period (Strong 1925:160). Strong (1925:164–65) devoted considerable space to the argument that each of the "forty significant traits" he considered "comes into slight use in one period, gradually increases to the height of its vogue, and then either fades out or disappears entirely." This, of course, was merely a restatement of the popularity principle, which his mentor had helped to establish (e.g., Kroeber 1909, 1916a, 1916b, 1919). Strong also argued that the five ceramic periods his typology suggested were in fact stratigraphically superposed (Strong 1925:166–80). Ford, as we discuss later, would reverse the procedure in his work on the pottery from the Virú Valley, using stratigraphy to build the chronology and seriation to supplement it. Strong (1925:184) followed Kroeber in noting that some types seemed to have "degraded" through time, suggesting his types, again like Kroeber's, were groups rather than atemporal classes. Strong (1925:184–85) also indicated that a mixture of pottery types in a grave represented "foreign influences" and the "result of a close amalgamation of at least two distinct cultures," indicating that, as with Kroeber, an essentialist metaphysic underlay his reasoning. Strong also enunciated some basic interpretive principles that came to characterize culture history, such as noting that geographic and/or physiographic isolation hindered the transmission of foreign influences and that while a cultural lineage may be temporally continuous, it would reflect "the waves of foreign culture or migrations [as] each left a mark to show the time at which it reached [the lineage under scrutiny]" (Strong 1925:185–86). Such influences would be reflected by the typological similarity—the shared attributes—of pottery in different areas. Ford (1936a) followed precisely the same interpretive algorithm in his analysis of sherds from Louisiana and Mississippi.

A final point to note regarding Strong's (1925:186) analysis is his suggestion that a "great depth and abundance of the deposits" characterized by a single pottery "ware" indicated "that this one period was of long duration." That is, while he knew that his ceramic periods provided a relative chronology, his desire to place absolute dates on those periods led him to offer the untenable suggestion that the thickness of a deposit was a direct reflection of the duration of time over which the deposit formed. This, as we will see, was also a pitfall that Ford (and others) failed to avoid.

Strong is remembered for his perfection of what came to be known as the direct historical approach (e.g., Strong 1935, 1936), which he also no doubt learned from Kroeber. Strong was a consummate culture historian who worked "from the [historically] known to the [prehistorically] unknown" (Solecki and Wagley 1963:1105), arguing that "it seems evident that any anthropological or sociological approach which ignores or underestimates the importance of time perspective is open to . . . criticism" (Strong 1935:300). Ford would echo such comments throughout his postdoctoral career. Strong also was well aware of organic evolution, having begun his college career as a biologist (Solecki and Wagley 1963; Willey 1988), and he perceived parallels between organic evolution and the historical development of cultures. Like Kroeber and Boas, Strong (e.g., 1953) thought there might eventually be some value to schemes such as Leslie White's resurrected version of universal, progressive cultural evolutionism, but he preferred to postpone judgment until particular historical sequences were known and documented. Parallels in Ford's thinking on this topic are apparent.

THE FIRST SOUTH AMERICAN TRIP: CALI, COLOMBIA

Ford hadn't been at Columbia University long enough to become much influenced by anyone when he received an opportunity to work in Colombia as part of a ten-unit team headed to the Andes with money provided by the U.S. State Department to the Institute of Andean Research, which was housed in the American Museum of Natural History in New York. The project was the brainchild of George C. Vaillant of the American Museum, who had worked through his friend Nelson Rockefeller, coordinator of Inter-American Affairs in the State Department (Willey 1988:117), to secure the funding. Vaillant enlisted archaeologists from several leading institutions, including Columbia and Yale, to assist in the field effort. Strong was one of them, and he selected Willey as his assistant for the Peruvian unit. He suggested that Ford ask Wendell Bennett of Yale if he could work with the Colombian unit. Bennett agreed. Ford surveyed and excavated in the Cauca Valley outside Cali from July to December of 1941. He then spent the next four months analyzing artifacts and preparing his part of the report (Ford 1944), the first part of which was by Bennett (1944), on a survey of Colombian pottery. As one might expect from a short field stint in a country with which he was previously unfamiliar, Ford's report is simply a straightforward, descriptive account.

Ford didn't delude himself into thinking that the report contained much in the way of novel information:

Haven't done so hot in archaeology this year. Surface collections have not paid off. The material is scarce and doesn't vary worth a damn. On the basis of tomb collections have outlined two horizons for a small section of the central [Cordilleras] but [neither] seems to be very old. Haven't good evidence for their temporal position but am making a guess. Damned if I know where the ancient Andean connections are.[7]

At present am putting figure numbers and commas in my report. It isn't very long, very informative, or very profound. If I were Bennett I would throw the Mss. away and publish the illustrations.[8]

By far the most interesting information on the Colombian expedition comes not from Jim Ford's report but from letters Ethel wrote to their families back

---

7. Letter of March 10, 1942, from Ford to Quimby (LSU Museum of Natural Science archives).
8. Letter of April 16, 1942, from Ford to Quimby (LSU Museum of Natural Science archives).

in the States. Given the focus of this book, we don't discuss Ethel very much, but through her eyes and pen one gains a much better picture of her husband's personal side and of what it was like to do archaeology in remote areas, whether in Louisiana or the mountains of Colombia. Ethel accompanied Jim on all his trips to Latin America, and through her letters she vividly described not only the trials of doing archaeology in a foreign country but also the other side of the coin—the natural beauty of the areas in which they worked and the nature of the people with whom they came into contact. Ethel Ford would have made a heck of a good ethnographer. She possessed excellent powers of observation, especially when it came to people; she also had an even temperament and a kind spirit, all of which gained her access to situations from which she otherwise would have been barred. If she ever complained about the inhospitable nature of the environments in which she found herself, she never did it in her letters. Below are excerpts from a letter posted from Cali after a two-week stay in the mountains of western Colombia:

> What the archeology consists of is going by car on until the road ends in the direction Jim is working. It usually ends abruptly where the valley ends and the mountains begin. There we get horses and ride back to some finca where the people have previously agreed to take us in the house or to let us put up our tent in the yard and where they have agreed to feed us. These people are the poorest of the poor in [Colombia. Their] farms bring small yields, clothing is scanty, and for the children usually consists of one garment. Some of the men wear shirts that have been patched as long as they will hold together. . . .
>
> A man here may not enter the kitchen where the women are working. Wendy [Wendell Bennett] and Jim want me to make some studies of what life is like around the houses so I stick around and talk with them as best I can and am learning how to make friends with them more rapidly. . . .
>
> Due to the fact that you are a North American means that you are rich, and there are many things that give you away—the fact that you brought several kinds of medicine, have a toothbrush, and have clothes of such good quality. As you all know, ours are Sears Roebuck but they show up too favorably here. Some [women] have refused to let me even see the kitchen on the basis that it is too ugly. With these setups it is impossible to talk with the women at all for they work in the kitchens all day long. My best progress so far has come through being constantly genial and nonchalant about the things they seem to expect me not to like. By offering medicine to the sick and doctoring them. This latter item breaks the ice better than anything else. My next move is to wear a dress. I am going out this afternoon to get some thread and a crochet needle. As much as I loathe crocheting, I have to have some excuse of a friendly nature to sit long hours in the kitchen and talk and see what goes on.

THE WAR YEARS

By the time the Fords returned to New York in May 1942, the United States was heavily involved in the war effort against Germany and Japan, and Jim entered the army in the summer of that year. He served until 1945, spending almost all his time designing and testing equipment and clothing for Arctic conditions (Figure 4.2), often working closely with the noted polar explorer Sir Hubert Wilkins (Willey 1988:63). Given his previous trips to Alaska as Henry Collins's assistant and his "knowledge of the north and of Eskimo life, his flair for practical skills of all kinds, his ranging physique, and his adventurousness," Ford not only was prepared for the work but apparently enjoyed it, though he "secretly chafed to get back to archaeology" (Willey 1969:64). With the war's end in 1945, Ford returned to Columbia in the fall, passing his Ph.D. examinations early in 1946 (Willey 1969:64). He then became involved in what would be one of his most significant contributions to Americanist archaeology.

THE SECOND SOUTH AMERICAN TRIP: THE VIRÚ VALLEY, PERU

The project that eventually played itself out in the Virú Valley, one of a number of coastal valleys that extend down the west side of the Peruvian Andes to the Pacific Ocean, had originally been conceived in 1945 by Willey, Bennett, and Julian Steward (Willey 1988:132), though other archaeologists, including Strong, were soon brought into the discussions. Funding for such projects was still available through the Institute of Andean Research, though it initially was unclear to the original proposers even where such a project should take place. Finally, more as a result of Bennett's familiarity with the area than of anything else (Willey 1988:63), the Virú Valley was selected. Fieldwork took place in 1946. Although Willey's name more than anyone else's is associated with the Virú Project, it generally is acknowledged (e.g., Willey 1988) that Wendell Bennett was the initial force behind the program. His vision was to establish an interdisciplinary project where archaeologists could collaborate but still feel free to pursue their own interests independently.

As anyone who has ever assembled a team of archaeologists knows firsthand, only two words can describe the eventual outcome—successful or disastrous. Either people are going to get along, which often means holding one's ego in check, and contribute toward a common goal, or they're going to destroy the entire effort. At the start, the Virú Valley Project had all the markings of a disaster, as Willey (1988:92–93) pointed out:

> As might have been anticipated, the complexity of the arrangement carried with it problems for coordinate action—especially smooth and happy coordinate action on the part of individualists like archaeologists. A certain amount of wrangling started even before we had left the States. Who was really to be the boss? Duncan [Strong] was at the time the President of the Institute of Andean Research and felt that the mantle of "Head" should descend upon him, but the rest of us felt that the presidency of that rather pro-forma body did not automatically confer such a distinction. To our way of

Figure 4.2. Photograph of James A. Ford, ca. 1943. The tag accompanying the photograph reads, "Mr. James A. Ford, senior design specialist, Office of the Quartermaster General, Washington D.C." (photograph courtesy W. G. Haag).

thinking, the Viru Committee, the *ad hoc* body which had conceived and set up the program, should constitute the directorate. This hydra-headed committee, consisting of Bennett, Strong, and myself, had a hard time sorting things out, and I found myself in a tough spot being called upon frequently to cast the deciding vote between my two senior colleagues.

Since Willey had already received his doctorate from Columbia, in 1942, he probably felt fairly safe in voting against his former adviser, Strong.

Willey noted that it wasn't only the individualistic personalities of archaeologists that tended to make things difficult but also the multi-institutional nature of the project: "University presidents and deans, museum directors, the officers of the Smithsonian—all such persons had made it clear that they expected 'their man' to have a prominent role in whatever was done" (Willey 1988:133). As it turned out, researchers from seven institutions took part—Yale, Columbia, Cornell, the Smithsonian, the American Museum, the Field Museum of Natural History in Chicago, and the Museo Nacional de Arqueología in Lima.

As problematic as institutional control and personal disagreements over leadership were, "easy collaboration was even more seriously jeopardized by Duncan bringing Jim Ford along as his assistant" (Willey 1988:93). Willey was wary of the match between Strong and Ford, containing as it did built-in trouble because of the different personalities of the two men. As well, Ford was not exactly a novice graduate student: "[T]he role of 'assistant,' for the brilliant and highly independent Jim, at age 35, looked like a mistake. He was far too advanced to play such a part" (Willey 1988:93). The project had its rough moments—Ford had spent too much time in hostile environments, where he had had to make do with what he had, not to comment on Strong's inabilities in such areas as getting Jeeps unstuck from mud holes (Willey 1988:93). Although he was Strong's assistant, at least in title, Ford ended up teaming with Willey in the field, which probably eased the situation somewhat.

True to Bennett's vision, project members conducted their own research programs, though the individual pieces were supposed to mesh. Strong and his other assistant, Clifford Evans, began an excavation project (Strong and Evans 1952), while Willey and Ford began looking for sites and making surface collections at those they found. Ford's task from the beginning was to work out a chronology of the sites, which by the end of the project totaled more than three hundred (Ford and Willey 1949:18). The research formed the basis of his Ph.D. dissertation (Ford 1949). During this work he developed and perfected the graphing techniques for which he is often remembered. The Virú Project is typically remembered for its seminal study of settlement patterns (Willey 1953b)—a topic suggested to Willey by Julian Steward; Ford's (1949) methodological and chronological contributions are less often cited.

In his dissertation, published as *Cultural Dating of Prehistoric Sites in Virú Valley, Peru* (Ford 1949), Ford outlined his reasoning and his methods for testing the reliability and validity of the chronological implications of the surface samples. Some of his statements echoed those of a decade earlier (Ford 1935a, 1935b, 1936a, 1936b, 1938b), but some were new. It is difficult to track the sources of some of Ford's early ideas because of the consistent lack of references in his published work, with the exception of those he coauthored (e.g., Ford and Willey 1940, 1941). As an exercise in citations analysis, we compiled what we take to be the major pieces of literature on Americanist archaeological and anthropological method and theory that were cited by Ford between 1935 and 1949 (Table 4.1). Even in the later years,

Ford tended to reference only relevant substantive literature and to bypass the methodological and certainly the theoretical literature. The two exceptions, and even they are not too exceptional, are the short piece in *American Antiquity* on chronology (Ford 1938b) and his dissertation (Ford 1949). In the dissertation, he at least cited some of Kroeber's work in the Southwest, along with Spier's (1917) "An Outline for a Chronology of Zuñi Ruins."

Maybe it was Strong who made Ford include references to the work of Kroeber and others. Regardless, as with Kniffen, we think Strong contributed substantially to Ford's methodological sophistication. To fully appreciate the significance of what Ford accomplished in his Virú Valley research, we must provide some background not only to see *where* Ford might have derived some of his ideas but also *how* he derived them.

Frequency Seriation in the 1940s

Strong and Kroeber's use of frequency seriation was part of a developing tradition that began in the second decade of the twentieth century (Lyman et al. 1998). The method is based entirely on changes in the frequencies of artifact types, which, if properly defined, provide a way to measure the passage of time. Historically, many researchers have been more comfortable with stratigraphically superposed collections than with seriated collections as measures of time. Even Kroeber and Spier, who developed and perfected the method, believed that the chronological implications of seriated collections should be tested via excavation. Percentage stratigraphy was used by Nelson, Kidder, and Spier to provide an appropriate test of seriational orderings. Though sometimes used to provide preliminary indications of possible temporal relations, frequency seriation never truly attained the same status as a chronological tool as did stratigraphic excavation (and to a much lesser extent percentage stratigraphy).

In fact, after about 1920, very few archaeologists—Erich Schmidt (1928) and George Vaillant (1930, 1931) were among those few—used percentage stratigraphy. Most archaeologists trained in North America simply collected artifacts from

Table 4.1. Analysis of Citations in Ford's Early Articles

Ford 1935	Ford 1936	Ford 1938	Ford and Willey 1941	Ford 1944	Ford and Quimby 1945	Ford 1949
none	none	Kidder and Kidder 1917 Nelson 1916	Cole and Deuel 1937 Holmes 1903	none	Cole and Deuel 1937 McKern[a]	Brew 1946 Kroeber 1916b, 1917, 1919, 1925a, 1925b Richardson and Kroeber 1940 Rouse 1939 Spier 1917

[a]Ford and Quimby (1945:1) referred to the "McKern classification" and indicated that "Tchefuncte is an aspect composed of three or more foci," but they did not reference any of McKern's articles on the Midwestern Taxonomic Method.

superposed contexts and then labeled the aggregates of materials "cultures" or the like (e.g., Gamio 1924; Harrington 1924; Kidder 1924; Kroeber 1925a, 1925b; Loud and Harrington 1929; Roberts 1929). Gerard Fowke (1922:37) remarked, "The intermittent character of occupancy is . . . shown by the distinct segregation of numerous successive layers of kitchen refuse." In other words, each artifact-bearing depositional unit, or stratum, was thought to contain the remains of *a culture.*

Archaeologists have long viewed visibly bounded chunks of the depositional continuum as the results of disjunctions in the continuum of cultural development—disjunctions that can be explained through anthropological mechanisms such as migration, diffusion, and the succession of one culture by another (Lyman and O'Brien 1998; Lyman et al. 1997a). Frequency seriation was unnecessary if superposed collections were available, or else it might be used simply as a check on superposition to ensure that artifacts were indeed in the correct order. It escaped notice that frequency seriation fit comfortably within the materialist epistemology, whereas the conception of superposed assemblages as components or cultures was couched within an essentialist metaphysic. But precisely *because* this escaped notice, the desire to study culture *change* was doomed to be unfulfilled once superposition dominated excavation methods.

Attempts to perfect frequency seriation were limited prior to the early 1950s. So far as we know, no one used statistics to actually help seriate or sort collections until the mid-1940s, just prior to Ford's work with the Virú Valley pottery. In 1945, the results of the Rainbow Bridge–Monument Valley Expedition in northeastern Arizona were published (Beals et al. 1945). In that study, typical procedures such as phyletic seriation and superposition (e.g., Beals et al. 1945:58) were used to build a chronological sequence of pottery types. Broken-stick graphs (Beals et al. 1945:18–19) similar to those used by Kidder and Kidder (1917) and Amsden (1931) were employed to illustrate the shifting proportions of pottery types through time (Lyman et al. 1998). Divisions of the sequence into distinct cultural periods were perceived to be "arbitrary," but this fit the notion that a culture sequence was a continuum, and it allowed as well for "the presence of various time spans impossible to classify under existing period definitions" (Beals et al. 1945:149). That is, the unclassifiable materials were "transitional" (Beals et al. 1945:164) between, or intermediate to, various periods.

Archaeologists of the 1940s were searching for a technique to illustrate the waxing and waning of a type's popularity in an intuitively obvious fashion that was also somehow quantitative. Until the late 1930s, this had been largely restricted to presenting tables of proportional frequencies of types. Important exceptions include Paul Martin's (1938, 1939) efforts to depict graphically such waxing and waning (see Lyman et al. 1998). Ford would, in his Virú study, contend with graphing techniques in significant fashion.

Ford and Seriation before Virú

Prior to his work with the Virú Valley collections, Ford had used percentage stratigraphy with pottery from Peck Village (Ford 1935c), Crooks (Ford and Willey 1940), and the several sites that represented the Tchefuncte "culture" (Ford and Quimby 1945). He had not, however, performed a frequency seriation in the sense of Kroeber and Spier, though he was surely aware of the technique, given Kniffen's (1938) use of it. But it seems to us that it was precisely Ford's technique for presenting the *results* of percentage stratigraphy that led to the frequency-seriation technique for which he is remembered. In studying the Peck Village materials, Ford set a methodological precedent when he used a bar graph to illustrate the fluctuations of the relative frequencies of pottery marker types across the superposed collections. This was a marked departure from the work of his predecessors, all of whom used tables of percentages. A few years later, the vertical distribution of percentages of pottery types at Crooks was arranged by Ford and Willey (1940) as a set of rectangles, the width of each rectangle representing the relative frequency of a type. Each rectangle was centered in a typologically unique column. The Crooks type percentages were compared to those from Marksville, and Ford and Willey (1940:137) concluded that the initial occupation of Crooks occurred before that of Marksville. Here, then, is an indication that Ford was aware of how different sites might be related chronologically based on the relative frequencies of their shared pottery types, and of how those sites could be visually ordered on a graph (Lyman et al. 1998). He had come to an analogous conclusion in his earlier work at Peck Village when he noted that the western portion of that site appeared to predate the eastern portion (Ford 1935c:23).

It is the Tchefuncte report, however, that presents the clearest examples of the bar graphs for which Ford would shortly become famous. Bars were centered in a typologically unique column and arranged by vertical provenience (Figure 4.3). These graphs not only revealed "the trends of popularity of the pottery types of the Tchefuncte period . . . but also [indicated] the relative temporal position of the Tchefuncte complex" (Ford and Quimby 1945:74). Further, the relative temporal positions of the various Tchefuncte sites were suggested—that is, site-specific collections with similar relative frequencies of types were similar in age. Some types variously were said to be "indicative" (74–77), "representative" (81), or "characteristic" (84) of particular cultures and periods, indicating that Ford was still thinking, as he had in the mid-1930s, of marker types.

Particularly within the analyses of Crooks (Ford and Willey 1940) and the Tchefuncte sites (Ford and Quimby 1945), one can perceive the growth of Ford's thinking on how chronologies were to be worked out. The flowing, braided stream of culture development was monitored by the popularity of pottery types. These would display unimodal frequency distributions through time. Thus, one could track at least the history of pottery types by measuring their relative frequencies.

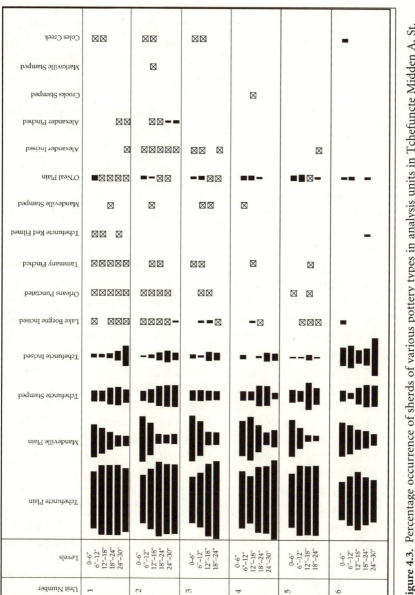

Figure 4.3. Percentage occurrence of sherds of various pottery types in analysis units in Tchefuncte Midden A, St. Tammany Parish, Louisiana. Boxes marked with an X represent small samples (after Ford and Quimby 1945).

Tables of numbers representing those frequencies demanded some study to detect the waxing and waning of a type's popularity, and it was difficult to see such trends in broken-stick graphs, though Beals et al.'s (1945) version was a minor improvement. While other archaeologists used bars of varying widths to represent percentages of pottery types by level, they were usually difficult to read, especially when many pottery types were involved. Ford's innovation was not that he used bars but in how he arranged them; thus in referring to Ford's (1949) dissertation, Bennyhoff (1952:231) mentioned Ford's "ingenious graphic presentation of data." Such graphs were readily popular because one could actually *see* the growth and decline of a type's popularity through time. They seemed to eliminate the need for statistically aided seriation such as had been done by Beals et al. (1945)— a point that would later result in a notable debate between Ford and one of his contemporaries. That Ford's bar graph technique could be used with equal efficiency and effect to seriate surface collections *and* to illustrate percentage stratigraphy was demonstrated conclusively in his dissertation.

Method and Theory at Virú

Ford (1949:31) began his report on the Virú Valley ceramic chronology by noting that there was no technique for measuring absolute time, and thus "the principal basis for reconstructing Peruvian prehistory must remain a relative scale in which time is measured by cultural change. This means, principally, ceramics." He noted that stratigraphic excavations provided one way to measure time and argued that these should be in midden deposits such as he had excavated at Peck Village (Ford 1935c) rather than in tombs. Echoing Strong's earlier concern about pottery from Ancón, Ford noted that "refuse materials are not consciously selected as are grave goods and can be expected to allow cultural change to be measured both qualitatively and quantitatively. Also, accumulations of any appreciable depth can be excavated by levels, to give a reliable basis for determining cultural change" (Ford 1949:31–32). The Peruvian cultural chronology in place in the 1940s (e.g., Bennett 1946; Kroeber 1944; Strong 1948) had been founded largely on grave lots such as Strong and Kroeber had dealt with, and Ford was concerned that such artifacts were often difficult to correlate or associate with architectural features. And he, like Strong, distrusted vessels that had been manufactured solely for placement with the dead. Ford (1936b:102) had, in his first programmatic piece, cautioned that artifacts "thrown away as garbage . . . represent a better cross section of that phase of the material life of the people than the artifacts which were selected to accompany the dead." We do not know whether this thought originated with Ford, but clearly he held this belief prior to his association with Strong. On a more practical level, grave-lot pottery was rare in virtually all Virú Valley collections because few tombs were excavated during the project. Also, the grave goods forming the basis of the existing chronology consisted of "beautiful pottery" rather than the "domestic ceramics" that Ford (1949:41) had to deal with. Thus he concluded "the already known ceramic chronology promised to be of little assistance in the dating of dwelling site refuse."

Ford (1949:32) viewed his task as involving a two-step procedure:

> First, it was necessary to assemble a time scale showing both the qualitative and quantitative aspects of refuse dump ceramic styles. As far as . . . possible, this time scale would be based on the evidence provided by vertical stratigraphy. Where this kind of evidence was not available, the method of seriation of surface collections was used. . . . The second step was to gather and classify collections from all the sites which were to be examined by Willey. The results of these classifications were then to be compared with the time scale to determine the ages of the occupation areas.

This quotation includes the first use of the word "seriation" by Ford in any of his publications. In his master's thesis Ford (1938a:11, 69) used "serration" to refer to what we are calling percentage stratigraphy. He also used "serration" (Ford 1938a:68) to refer to what we are calling frequency seriation. This is what Gordon Willey (pers. comm. 1998) said about Ford and "seriation":

> The word and concept do bring back memories of Jim. Sometime in the late thirties I had an argument with Jim about the word itself. Jim in his *sui generis* way insisted that it was "serration" and that it referred to a sawlike graph line that would describe a series of chronologically arranged types with their overlapping modes. I told him no and cited Leslie Spier and Kroeber and their southwestern pottery studies. At that time, Jim must not have read these papers. He had, however, picked up some seriational principles, probably from Fred Kniffen, the cultural geographer at LSU who had taken courses with Kroeber at Berkeley, and he had also seen Collins seriating harpoon points in Alaska with successive beach lines giving chronological direction to the seriation. Eventually, Jim must have gotten around to reading these papers, but we never referred to our "seriation"-"serration" argument again.
>
> This wasn't a case of Jim not wanting to give other people credit. On the contrary, he was quite generous this way. It was, rather, the old "pioneer woodsman's spirit," with its accompanying indifference to, and possibly even scorn of, the "establishment."

For Ford, stratigraphy—something that was "second nature to Jim's thinking" (W. G. Haag, pers. comm., 1996)—would provide the ultimate chronological control. But archaeological deposits at many sites in the Virú Valley tended to be shallow, so Ford and Willey turned to surface collection as an artifact collection method. Although the general feeling at the time was that stratigraphic excavation led to a more trustworthy chronology than seriation did, apparently in Ford's mind this applied only to sites with thick deposits: "[I]t is doubtful whether an excavated collection in a thin site is in any way superior to a surface collection for dating that site" (Ford 1949:34).

Ford's description of his field methods reflected his concerns about sample bias. Surface collections were made by workmen who were instructed (a) not to select certain sherds over others for collection, (b) to fill a "required number of bags," and (c) not to gather all sherds from one spot (Ford 1949:35). Collected areas at each site tended to be "no more than 100 meters in diameter" (Ford 1949:35). Further, "Each locality was carefully examined in an effort to determine whether there were any variation in the types and proportions of material exposed on the surface in the different parts of the site. Where there was any reason to suspect such differences, two or more collections were made" (Ford 1949:35). To circumvent the possibility that surface materials postdated a structure, "strata cuts" (Ford 1949:44) were excavated in deep sites.

A major problem was to determine the age of a site when "material from separated time periods is mixed on the [site] surface" (Ford 1949:35). Such "reoccupied sites" were often, but not always, recognized by the presence of structures that had been remodeled. Ford was also concerned with obtaining representative samples; to determine the "desirable size of a collection" he made duplicate collections at different times from five sites—the same as he had done at some of his surface-collected sites in Louisiana (Ford 1936a). He then calculated the relative abundances of pottery types within each sample from each site and compared site-specific sample pairs on a bar graph.

On the basis of his duplicate samples, Ford (1949:35) noted several things, including the fact that relative abundances of types fluctuated most dramatically in small samples. Further, even the relative abundance of types that made up more than 10% of a collection tended to differ between samples. But Ford (1949:36) suggested that the "popularity" of types would be fairly well reflected by samples of at least 200 sherds and be within 10% of the actual, or site-specific, value. He concluded that "a random collection of over 100 sherds [is] fairly dependable, and anything over 50 sherds [is] usable for rough dating" (Ford 1949:36).

Ford also dispensed with the notion that different-sized pottery vessels would produce different numbers of sherds and potentially lead to errors in dating. He argued that

> Vessel size and thickness changed with time, as did other cultural features, and were subject to as strict stylistic control. A percentage increase of a type due to the vessels becoming larger or thinner is as good a measure of time change as it is when it reflects greater popularity of that type. The primary aim of a chronological analysis of ceramics is to provide a time and space scale by means of which other and more important cultural elements may be ordered, thus making possible a reconstruction of culture history. To provide a "true" qualitative and quantitative history of ceramics is of lesser importance, if not impossible of accomplishment with the type of data that can be obtained from refuse deposits, and the fact that such uncontrolled variables as those just described are hidden in the pottery counts is not of much concern. (Ford 1949:37)

Ford was acknowledging, without using the terminology, that although his percentage-stratigraphy analyses and frequency seriations employed an interval scale of measurement, the resulting arrangement of collections was best interpreted in ordinal-scale terms. He cleverly suggested that changes in certain dimensions of vessels, such as size and wall thickness, might lead to more sherds being incorporated into deposits, but by treating those dimensions in the same way as decoration, he revealed the discipline-wide, commonsense understanding of style: they were simply things that changed in form and/or frequency through time; *why* they changed was not considered in any theoretically rigorous fashion (e.g., Schapiro 1953).

Evolutionary Underpinnings

In words reminiscent of Kroeber (e.g., 1931a, 1943) and Strong (e.g., 1925; see also Strong 1953), Ford suggested that culture change and biological evolution resembled one another because the two processes were gradual: "Change in culture occurs by only two processes: first, combination of ideas already available in the cultural environment [recombination]; and, second, discovery [mutation] and adaptation to cultural purposes of new phases of the natural environment" (Ford 1949:39). But on the same page, in words reminiscent of what Brew (1946) and Steward (1944) had said (Lyman and O'Brien 1997), he argued that culture change and biological evolution were fundamentally different:

> [T]he relationship ties in a cultural history weave back and forth between the different cultural categories in a bewildering fashion entirely foreign to the history of living organisms, and only the strongest and most easily detected can be traced with any assurance. These evidences of relationships are to be expected, but in dealing with the materials that will be used to form a hitherto unknown cultural chronology, they must be set aside and carefully ignored. Assumptions as to relationship are impossible until the chronological factor is completely under control. (Ford 1949:39)

In other words, biological history has the appearance of culture history at only superficial levels. The former has a branching appearance, whereas the latter has a reticulate appearance. This is so because genes flow only downward through generations, speciation is a process of branching or divergence, and species do not interbreed; ideas flow upward as well as downward between generations and also flow between individuals within a generation, and cultures interact or interbreed. As Steward (1944:99) had remarked a few years earlier, "Biological types fall into genera, families, and phyla that do not and cannot cross with one another, whereas associations of cultural elements continually fall apart and recombine in all sorts of ways." The influence of an essentialist metaphysic and the resulting typological thinking is evident here, as is the equation of a biological taxonomic unit with an ethnographic unit typically termed a culture. Through the years, biology has gradually shifted to the more materialistic, populational thinking (e.g., Davis 1996) in which the appropriate unit for study of phylogenetic history is a population rather than a taxon (Ghiselin 1966, 1974, 1981; Mayr 1976, 1987), and branching as well as reticulate lineage histories are possible; no such shift has yet occurred in anthropology (e.g., Dunnell 1982; Lyman and O'Brien 1997; O'Brien 1996c; O'Brien and Holland 1995b; Rambo 1991).

As a result of equating a culture with a biological species—both conceived in essentialist terms—Ford argued that determination of phylogenetic relations between archaeological—read *cultural*—units must await the establishment of their chronological relations. Ford was not clear in his dissertation about why or how a known chronology would aid in writing a phylogenetic culture history; his master's thesis indicates the notion rested on the commonsense understanding that an ancestor must precede a descendant in time. In modern paleobiology, this is of course only one issue that must be addressed. One must also know, for example, whether formal similarity is of the analogous or homologous sort as well as the ages of the similar phenomena (e.g., Smith 1994), another point that is clear in Ford's thesis but not in his dissertation. This latter issue often was more or less accidentally circumvented as Americanist archaeologists focused on decorative attributes of pottery, which theoretically are for the most part adaptively neutral and thus largely homologous (Dunnell 1978; O'Brien and Holland 1990, 1992). When functional attributes—ones that influence selective fitness and thus are not adaptively neutral, such as the kind of temper used in pottery (e.g., Dunnell and Feathers 1991; O'Brien and Holland 1990, 1992; O'Brien et al. 1994)—were employed to build historical types, distinguishing such instances of analogous similarity became paramount but was seldom remarked (see Rouse [1955] for a notable exception).

Typology

Ford (1949:38–43) commented at some length on classification, arguing that the utility of any artifact-classification scheme resided strictly in its ability to measure "culture history in time and space. . . . to measure culture and trace its change through time and over area" (Ford 1949:38). Any classification "must be tested by the question of how well it serves [its] end purpose" (Ford 1949:38). These statements echoed those made by J. O. Brew (1946:46) a few years earlier in his monograph "Archaeology of Alkali Ridge, Southeastern Utah," which was cited by Ford. As he had before, Ford argued that the notion that a correct classification was one which approximated the types envisioned by ancient artisans was "highly questionable." He believed that "the apparent order [resulting from classifying] has been imposed on the material either by chance circumstances or, more commonly, by the classifier himself"; thus "the same group of archaeological material may be classified in an almost unlimited number of ways, each equally valid from an empirical point of view" (Ford 1949:38). Ford (1949:39–40), like some of his contemporaries (e.g., Brew 1946; Krieger 1944; Rouse 1939), never said that artifact types *didn't* reflect to some degree the ideas or cultural norms of the people who made the artifacts. What he said was that archaeologists need not concern themselves with such speculation, "for these [norms] will be more or less reflected in the classification system" of the archaeologist (Ford 1949:40). In some cases, "Each type established will . . . grade insensibly into other materials" (Ford 1949:40), but in other cases divisions between some types will be quite sharp "and inherent in the material" (Ford 1949:67).

Nowhere did Ford make the point more forcibly that types were arbitrary than in a letter to George Quimby concerning design evolution as seen in Louisiana pottery: "Different arrangements of brushing are widespread in [the] Caddoan [area. The type] Hardy is just another of those cases of developing or evolving types—you have got to draw a line somewhere between Hardy and C[oles] C[reek] Inc[ised]. While Hardy and CC Inc. were undoubtedly coeval at one time it is obvious that Hardy is replacing CC. Inc. Hope you are beginning to realize that 'there ain't no such thing as a pottery type'—you have to manufacture them yourself. This is true in the same sense that there is no such thing as a period in a culture history—Marks[ville], Troy[ville], CC., etc. are all products of our imaginations.—that is enough Plato for this time."[9]

The admittedly loose correlation between cultural norms and archaeological types later led Ford into an argument with one of his contemporaries, but it was critically important to his reasoning, as it provided the warrant for types to display a particular distribution in the archaeological record. And that distribution should approximate a normal-frequency curve:

> In consequence, when the relative *popularity* of a type is measured through time the resultant graph will resemble a normal distribution curve. The type will appear to have been made first in very small quantities. As time passes it reaches its period of maximum *popularity*, more or less great. Then it declines in *popularity* and finally vanishes. This apparent life cycle of a type is misleading, for it is really created by the act of classification. (Ford 1949:40–41; emphasis added)

But how could an archaeological construct—a type—somehow be prehistorically "popular"? It must somehow reflect cultural norms, but for Ford that reflection did not have to be perfect because the desired result was a chronology of *types*, not of norms. As he had noted, a " 'true' qualitative and quantitative history of ceramics" was no doubt impossible to attain (Ford 1949:37). Further, the norms and ideas of a culture were constantly and gradually changing, so slicing out an arbitrary chunk of that continuum, using ideational units such as Ford's types, would naturally produce a unimodal frequency distribution of specimens (see Kidder 1936b:xx). This was so because pottery was a flowing continuum— one of the trickles of the cultural stream—ever varying through time: "Each type established [by the archaeologist] will be found to grade insensibly into other

9. Letter of January 19, 1941 (LSU Museum of Natural Science archives).

materials that were made coevally or particularly those that preceded or followed. This will lead to 'drifting' of the type concept in the mind of the classifier unless it is guarded against by strict definition of the type limits" (Ford 1949:40)—precisely the reason Ford had one person, C. H. Hopkins, sort all the pottery from the WPA project in Louisiana. The crucial point here is that Ford, like his contemporaries, lacked a theoretical rationale for the normal frequency distributions displayed by his types, and thus he was forced to fall back on common sense: "No two pottery vessels made during . . . history were exactly alike. . . . Yet all this material that represents any one time level is clearly imprinted with the prevalent cultural ideas or styles. . . . Ancient potters conformed to prevailing ideas exactly as we do in everyday practice. The several different styles of pottery that may have been in use at any one time are due to the difference in function of the vessels or origin of stylistic ideas" (Ford 1949:40).

With no theory to guide unit construction in his attempt to use types to write culture history, Ford, like his contemporaries, was forced to resort to trial and error. A "type" was an arbitrary chunk of the ceramic continuum and thus a construct of the archaeologist. Yet each chunk could be

> given a type name and . . . defined . . . with very rigid boundaries which the classifier expected to observe as consistently as possible. The types thus set up were guesses. In each one the classifier was guessing that the observable differences would be significant temporally or areally, or would be the coeval results of different function or of distinct cultural influences. These types were not final; all were held on probation until analysis should prove whether or not they would be useful in determining culture history. (Ford 1949:41)

Provisional types sometimes were lumped into one type and sometimes split into more than one type after their utility as time-space measuring devices was determined. Types that could be seriated successfully were thought to be useful constructs, but stratigraphic excavation of sites containing some of the thicker deposits "served as a more detailed basis for the evaluation of the type divisions" (Ford 1949:42). A Fordian type was an ideational unit, the definition of which was extrinsically derived on a trial-and-error basis until a type definition was found that produced a unimodal frequency distribution of empirical specimens through time. "Setting up new types, merging, or breaking up of old types was done in cooperation after considerable discussion. The stratigraphic excavations which the other workers [e.g., Strong and Evans] were analyzing carried much of the weight of the evidence used in these processes" (Ford 1949:43). Ford's ideas were not all that different from those of other archaeologists, including Alex Krieger. For Krieger (1944:272), types had "demonstrable historical meaning" and thus occupied "a definable historical position, that is, [a type's] distribution is delimited in space [and] time" (Krieger 1944:277). Types useful for the "retracing of cultural developments and interactions" (Krieger 1944:272) should have continuous distributions across one section of the temporal and spatial continua (Krieger 1944:280).

That historical types should display the kind of distribution specified by Krieger fit well with the notion of development of cultural lineages as a flowing, braided stream. Brew (1946:48) spoke of the "continuous stream of cultural events," as had Nelson and Kidder in preceding decades. Ford (1949:38) cited Kroeber's (1917) position that culture was a superorganic phenomenon and defined culture "as a stream of ideas that passes from individual to individual by means of symbolic action, verbal instruction, or imitation." Internal cultural change was perceived as normally gradual—"the accumulation of variations resulted in slow shifting of the norms" (Ford 1949:39). Thus, abrupt or rapid change must have been "forced by external pressure" (Ford 1949:39). Large-scale change did not have a source within the culture tradition or lineage under study; rather, it had an external source and represented the intersection of two or more trickles in the braided stream of culture history. This position was essentially the same one Ford outlined in his surface-collection monograph (Ford 1936a) and that was implicitly stated in the paper he coauthored with Willey on eastern prehistory (Ford and Willey 1941).

Despite their lack of theoretical grounding, Ford and some of his contemporaries displayed tremendous insight into various critical issues. For example, Ford noted that how types were constructed might produce less-than-perfect normal curves—a point later emphasized in a review of Ford's substantive results (Bennyhoff 1952). Ford (1949) also recognized that every archaeological phenomenon represents a span of time at some scale (see Brooks 1982). As a result, some of the predicted fluctuations in frequency curves (Kroeber 1919; Neiman 1995) will be muted by the diachronic nature of the samples (e.g., Teltser 1995b). Further, sampling error might create inexplicable features in the curve (see also Bennyhoff 1952), as could disturbance to the deposits producing the samples. As it turned out, these problems were of no great concern to Ford.

Results

Ford had planned to use frequency seriation to build his chronology for the Virú Valley, but "the excellent results that were appearing from the stratigraphic cuts . . . soon made it obvious that vertical stratigraphy would be available to carry the weight of the evidence for a site-dating background" (Ford 1949:44). As a result, Ford used percentage stratigraphy, just as he had when analyzing the artifacts from the Tchefuncte-period sites in Louisiana (Ford and Quimby 1945). Ford (1949:45–47) used fourteen strata cuts (seven by Collier, six by Strong and Evans, and one he had excavated) in ten sites as the basis for the chronology. Ford examined seven other strata cuts but omitted them from the analysis because they either duplicated the evidence used or compressed the represented time span into what he perceived to be too thin a depositional unit and thus mixed early and late pottery types.

Ford noted that gaps in the occupational history of any site could be detected by a "sudden shift in pottery type proportions" (Ford 1949:44)—in other words, by a change in tempo of the slowly moving stream of culture. Since no single site contained the entire valley-wide history of occupation, Ford had to interdigitate (Lyman et al. 1998) various site-specific results:

> The basic assumption that guided this process was that each pottery type selected by the classifiers from the ceramics made in Virú had undergone a popularity cycle through time that resembled a normal distribution curve. . . . The quantitative history of each type differed from every other, so that when all types were considered a pattern was formed. Each strata excavation, when analyzed, revealed a portion of this pattern. Thus inspection of the [bar] graphs, giving consideration to the percentage trends indicated for each type, the actual percentage of each type present in the various [excavation] levels, and the relative vertical positions of the peaks of popularity of each type provided the basis for a judgment as to the time covered by each excavation as compared with the others. (Ford 1949:45)

All site-specific percentage-stratigraphy graphs were then arranged on a single graph. Interestingly, Ford (1949:45) noted that because "It is obvious that refuse heaps cannot be expected to accumulate at exactly the same rate," he "felt at complete liberty either to expand or compress either parts or the whole of [a site-specific percentage-stratigraphy] graph in order to make it fit the others." An apparent gap in the resulting synthetic master graph was partially filled by placing eighteen surface collections in the graph. This perhaps is the weakest portion of his analysis, as there is a clear discontinuity between the eighteen collections and re-lated excavated samples—all of which Ford placed early in the valley chronology—and the collections arranged on the basis of percentage stratigraphy—placed late in the chronology. The resulting graph, or master chronology (Figure 4.4), was "presented as the story of the popularity of the pottery types described in the Virú Valley."

Ford was aware that spatial variation—what he referred to as "differences between the communities of the prehistoric peoples of Virú" (Ford 1949:47)—might be reflected in the graph, but he indicated that he and his colleagues had "assumed a high degree of similarity of the culture in all parts of the valley at any one moment in the past." In other words, he believed this source of variation was minimal. Of some interest here is how he treated the resulting master-chronology graph in terms of its measurement of time. Ford was aware that his ordering based on percentage stratigraphy provided a relative—that is, an ordinal-scale—chronology, but that he was using an interval-scale measure—relative frequencies of pottery types—to derive that chronology. But he conflated the two measurement scales when he noted that some ceramic periods appeared to be of longer or

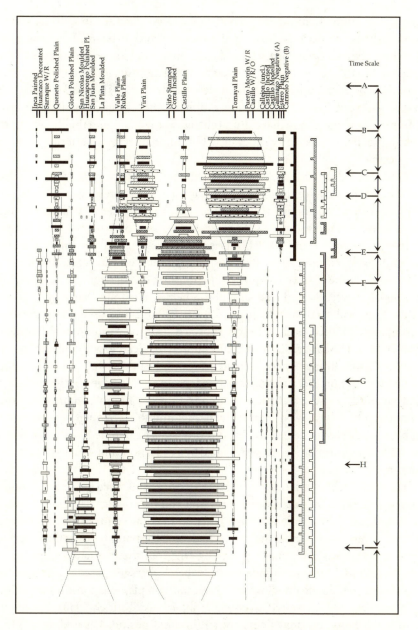

Figure 4.4. A portion of Ford's master summary graph of the Virú Valley chronology based on stratigraphic excavations and seriation of surface collections. Levels of the several strata excavations are indicated by staffs on the right side of the diagram. Relative frequencies of the pottery types named at the top of the diagram are shown by the lengths of the horizontal bars. The type frequencies are smoothed, as shown by the dotted lines. Both the arbitrary time scale, which is used for dating site collections, and period names are listed at the right. Ford included four earlier ceramic periods, but they are deleted here (after Ford 1949).

shorter durations than others: "The suggested acceleration in cultural change from early to late periods probably did occur" (Ford 1949:48). Ford was aware that the thickness of a deposit was not a good measure of its age, but he nonetheless suggested that "the amount of midden accumulation suggests that [two earlier] periods were several times longer than [several later periods]" (Ford 1949:48). We suspect that contributing to Ford's suggestions of absolute time was his unwavering subscription to the notion that cultural change was *gradual,* and thus he attempted to interpret his graphs of frequency distributions in interval-scale terms from that perspective.

Once the valley-wide master-chronology graph was completed, "the curves indicated for the percentage popularity of each type were drawn [Figure 4.4]. This smoothing was done by eye, and an effort was made to strike an average between the variation shown by the several collections covering the same sections in the chronology" (Ford 1949:49). It is our impression that this smoothing was meant to serve two purposes. First, it underscored the various factors that Ford believed made the observed frequency distributions diverge from perfectly smooth unimodal curves. Second, the smoothing helped illustrate that each type was of the historical sort—a style, in Ford's words—and thus useful for measuring chronology. As such, each type was expected to display a unimodal frequency distribution. The bar graphs sometimes showed that feature with minimal clarity, and Ford's smoothing "by eye" helped bring out the underlying (expected) shape of the distribution. Because of his dependence on percentage stratigraphy, Ford had no need to use a statistical technique to order his collections. His visual smoothing merely showed what the expected unimodal frequency distributions of types would look like had the various problems he outlined—how types were created, variation in time span represented by a collection, and so on—not infected his samples.

Ford (1949) followed the lead of his predecessors and sliced the ceramic continuum into periods, then described the ceramic complex of each. Horizontal lines—each designated by a unique capital letter, as in some of his earlier work (Ford 1935c)—were drawn across the graphs to denote the boundaries of those periods (Figure 4.4). Slices were made by noting where in the frequency graphs some types began to decline in abundance and where others increased. This technique was similar to his earlier designation of ceramic complexes as constituting unique combinations of pottery types (Ford 1938b; see also Kniffen 1938), but for the Virú graph Ford also drew lines across it in other positions as well, in an effort to provide a series of "[s]hort spans of time to which each collection might be referred" (Ford 1949:49). This procedure reflected Ford's materialist notion of the cultural continuum, and the notion that periods of that continuum were arbitrary. Given his method in 1949, Ford could speak of a C-D period, a G-H period, and the like. The resulting sequence of periods provided an "arbitrary scale to which the dating of surface collections [could be] referred" (Ford 1949:49).

After building the master chronology largely on the basis of percentage stratig-raphy, Ford attempted to plug the surface collections into their proper positions in the sequence based on the relative proportions of ceramic types. A strip graph representing the relative frequencies of types in a surface collection was "matched with the smoothed graph of the valley chronology until the point was found at which the percentages of all the types in the surface collection came nearest to fitting the curves of the master graph. This point was considered to be the mean cultural date of the surface collection" (Ford 1949:51). One result of this technique was that "mixed collections representing sites that had been occupied at two widely different periods became quite obvious. The nesting of the more popular types has brought these types close together on the summary graph" (Ford 1949:50). If several types marked a particular period but were found in a collection containing a set of different types that marked another period, then clearly the collection was mixed and the "two complexes of pottery types" represented "simple re-occupation" (Ford 1949:50)—an interpretation that was a far cry from what he had proposed years earlier for sites in Louisiana (Ford 1935c, 1936a). Placing a collection that seemed to represent a single occupation into the master chronology represented assigning an age to that collection that "must be considered at best as a *mean* cultural date" (Ford 1949:51; emphasis added). That is, Ford was well aware that a surface collection so placed had an unknown temporal duration, and the constantly shifting frequencies of pottery types within it were averaged over that duration by considering the collection as a single unit. Interestingly, Ford (1949:52) also noted that collections that had been excavated from vertically bounded units also represented such time-averaged samples.

The recognition that sets of artifacts, however sets were identified, represented time-averaged collections—founded in the materialist metaphysic—would never receive much recognition in Americanist archaeology. This problem has been recognized in paleobiology for some time and is referred to as "time averaging" (e.g., Behrensmeyer 1982; Peterson 1977; Schindel 1980). The significance of such recognition for studies of culture development and evolution would largely be dismissed in the 1950s, when culture historians, without recognizing that they were doing so, wholeheartedly adopted the essentialist metaphysic. The notions of palimpsest and coarse-grained assemblages—introduced by the "new archae-ologists" of the post-1960s era—while related, had a rather different origin and meaning. Palimpsest assemblages derive "from a variety of events and actions by both man and [natural processes]" (Binford 1980:9); coarse-grained assemblages are "the accumulated product of events spanning an entire year and [thus] the resolution between archaeological remains and specific [human-behavioral] events is poor" (Binford 1980:17). Ford was interested in the historical continuum of pottery and the development of cultures rather than in specific human activities. But slicing the temporal continuum of culture history into discrete periods, as Ford and others (e.g., Kroeber, Kidder, Willey) did, forces one away from monitoring the differential persistence of variant forms through time—explicable in Darwinian evolutionary terms—to comparing the contents of temporal units of various durations and explaining their differences in transformational—historical and ethnological—terms (O'Brien and Holland 1990; Teltser 1995b). The ultimate reason for the slicing resides in the explanatory system implicitly held by culture historians—common sense informed by anthropology and ethnology (Dunnell 1982). This sense-making system used essentialist categories such as villages, occupations, and cultures for analysis, and it facilitated communication between Americanist archaeologists by using such categories with more or less agreed-upon meanings (Lyman et al. 1997a). Ford sliced up the continuum at Virú just as he had done from the time he started doing archaeology in the 1930s (e.g., Ford 1935c, 1936a, 1938b).

Reviews

Ford's (1949) statements on culture change and how it could be measured were misconstrued by the new archaeologists of the 1960s as "normative theory" and characterized as an "aquatic view of culture" that could offer no more of an explanation of culture change than to suggest that the flowing stream of ideas "periodically 'crystallized' . . . resulting in distinctive and sometimes striking cultural climaxes which allow us to break up the continuum of culture into cultural phases" (Binford 1965:204). Ford's aquatic view is apparent in his writings, but the normative aspect—expressed as periodic crystallization producing discrete cultural phases—decidedly is not. Ford recognized that his decoration complexes and types were arbitrary constructs—ideational units—meant to measure the flow of culture; his master chronology for Virú—founded largely on percentage stratigraphy and to a minor degree on frequency seriation—showed the current. And he explicitly noted that his types *might*, but did not necessarily, reflect the "ideas in the minds of the prehistoric culture bearers" (Ford 1949:40). That was of little concern to Ford; the only thing that mattered was that the types allowed him to measure the flow of time. Further, and this is important, he *never* suggested that cultural norms "crystallized" into units—phases, foci, or whatever—because that would, of course, have contradicted his view of culture as a *constantly* flowing stream. Rather, periods were either arbitrary or, as was usually the case, "eyeballed" chunks of time created by the analyst.

Clifford Evans (1951:271) was impressed with Ford's (1949) "fundamental contribution to theoretical and applied archaeological methodology." James Bennyhoff (1952:233) was impressed as well, noting that Ford's "procedure represents one of the foremost advances in American archaeology." But Bennyhoff was also concerned that readers understand that Ford's ascription of a "mean cultural date" to a surface collection did not necessarily date a site. In particular, Bennyhoff (1952:232) worried that when reviewing Ford's assignments of a surface collection to a ceramic period, "The casual reader may gain the impression that this ceramic period represents the average (longest) period of occupation of the site," and thus he cautioned that Ford's technique did not date the site "but only the surface sherds." After examining Ford's data, Bennyhoff (1952:232–33) concluded that "the 'mean cultural date' reflects the terminal occupation of the site" and that "surface sherds from any deep deposit will not reflect the average period of occupation of the site." In his response, Ford (1952b:250) noted that Bennyhoff overlooked the point that the "evidence used was selected—rather carefully selected," as well as the point that although surface collections might have yielded terminal dates for some of the sites, that fact had no bearing "on the great majority of shallow sites that I tried to date by this means." In other words, the *ceramic* chronology was correct; the chronology of *site occupation* was another matter.

Willey (1953b:9–10) was very explicit about potential dating problems when he used Ford's ceramic chronology to derive a chronology of *sites* in the Virú Valley. Calling his use of Ford's data "associational dating," Willey (1953b:10) noted that even if it were assumed that "Ford's pottery collection dates [are] 100 percent correct, we are still left with the problem of how valid are the associations of collections and sites. [In short, m]ultiple ceramic period components are found at many sites, and in each case there is the question of which component dates the structural features on the site." Willey was well aware of the problems with indirect dating. Thus he emphasized that "Ford stands responsible only for the seriational dating of the Virú *pottery collections.* I must accept the responsibility for applying those dates to the *sites*" (Willey 1953b:10).

Among his other concerns, Bennyhoff (1952) had problems with Ford's substantive conclusions. He noted that despite Ford's use of percentage stratigraphy and frequency seriation (the latter a misnomer, since all Ford did was to align surface-collected assemblages against percentage-stratigraphy data from excavated sites), "the ceramic periods proposed by the Virú project are still defined by the presence or absence of diagnostic decorated types. Many surface collections have been dated by these fancy time-bearers rather than by the quantity of plain wares found, even though the domestic pottery should be the best indication of the occupation period" (Bennyhoff 1952:233). Bennyhoff's claim that Ford overlooked the value of plain wares now seems a bit ironic in the face of what some of Ford's chroniclers have said about him. For example, Evans (1968:1164) stated that Ford "revolutionized Peruvian archeology by classifying the plain pottery into types and demonstrating their utility in the seriation of surface collections." In a similar vein, Willey (1988:65) recalled arguments between Ford and Strong over types: "Duncan, whose Peruvian archaeology began to take form for him with his study of Uhle's grave lot collections in the museum at the University of California, was not entranced by the idea of classifying the thousands of plain red, brown, or black sherds that came in from the Virú Valley surface collections or refuse digging.

He wanted to rely only upon the fragments of Moche modelled or Tiahuanacoid painted types. Jim would listen to Duncan's ideas on this in smoldering silence. Then he would grumble, 'Dunc, we've got to have a scientific method in this stuff. We're not collecting antiquities.' "

To substantiate his claim, Bennyhoff first indicated there were three different techniques of firing represented in the Virú pottery and that the techniques could be arranged in a temporal sequence "on the basis of a quantitative analysis of undecorated pottery" (Bennyhoff 1952:233). He then demonstrated that "The dating of sites on the basis of decorated sherds often places the associated plain wares out of context within the firing periods, and sometimes shifts the plain wares into a completely different firing period. Therefore, at a significant number of sites the claimed significance of the present plain ware frequencies has not been utilized" (Bennyhoff 1952:234). Second, he noted that size differences of vessels in several plain wares had prompted Ford and colleagues to designate multiple types, but Bennyhoff lumped them together and reordered Ford's collections using only those with samples of at least 130 sherds. Sixteen of the forty-six collections Bennyhoff (1952:234–36) ordered were "placed in a different ceramic period from that assigned by Ford," and he remarked that his "rearrangement does satisfy the theoretical principle of quantitative analysis better than Ford's."

Not surprisingly, Ford took exception to this criticism, noting that

> The rearrangement of the dating of late sites is based upon the assumption that the seriation of surface collections which Bennyhoff has made after merging several of the types, reflects culture history more accurately than does the stratigraphic excavation I used. A number of such seriations of surface data were made in Peru before the stratigraphic data became available, and although they have a more handsome appearance were discarded in favor of the information from strata cuts. (Ford 1952b:250; see also Ford 1949:44)

Bennyhoff identified two of the problems inherent in the culture-history toolbox in general and in Ford's use of some of the tools in particular. First, Bennyhoff noted that the technofunctional attribute of firing could be used to measure time—something Ford may have been unaware of. But Bennyhoff also presumed that the sequence of firing periods was unilinear, beginning with one technique, passing through another, and ending with the third. Functional attributes, because they concern adaptation and fitness, need not behave that way at all (Dunnell 1978; O'Brien and Holland 1990, 1992). The conflation of stylistic and functional traits—those that reflect homologous and analogous relations, respectively—plagued the study of culture history from the start, and it continues to plague Americanist archaeology today. Second, whether Ford's or Bennyhoff's arrangement of collections more closely matched the tenets of the popularity principle—the frequency distributions are unimodal—cannot be determined without statistical tests—another point that would a few years later lead to a debate between Ford and one of his contemporaries.

Ford did not hesitate to draw conclusions of an anthropological sort from the ceramic history he had written. Thus he spoke of types, traits, and "[cultural] influences" spreading geographically; of types being "received" in an area; of the "careless" application of paint and slips; and of ideas being "imported" (Ford 1949:59–61). He also concluded that "while the utility ceramics were made by the common people, the manufacture of ceramics for use as burial goods was already in the hands of specialists" (Ford 1949:62). As Evans (1951:271–72) later remarked,

> The only part of Ford's cultural interpretations that might not meet with the approval of some of the other authorities on Peruvian archaeology [was] his concept of "burial cult ceramics" [introduced by Ford] to account for the great deviation between the utilitarian ware traditions and the elaborate wares most typically found in the cemeteries. Ford sees this separation as the result of the development of a "class of priest-potters" who must have been engaged only in the manufacture of special wares for burial purposes.

Ford (1949:66) actually went further, suggesting the priest-potters were "identified with the ruling class," given the apparent trend "throughout the history of Virú [toward] an increase in population and an accompanying trend towards centralization of political control. This control was strongly religious in nature." Here Ford referred to evidence that would be presented by Willey (1953b), and it is difficult to determine how much of what Ford was saying originated with him and how much with Willey or someone else associated with the project. Nonetheless, it is clear that Ford desired to do more than merely build a chronology of ceramic types.

THE LOWER MISSISSIPPI ALLUVIAL VALLEY SURVEY

There are several striking similarities between Ford's (1949) contributions to the Virú Valley Project and to a project known officially as the Lower Mississippi Alluvial Valley Survey (Phillips et al. 1951) but commonly referred to in southeastern archaeology as PF&G after the codirectors—Philip Phillips, Ford, and James B. Griffin. The monograph that resulted from the project has been termed "a landmark volume in the development of our knowledge of the prehistory of the eastern United States" (Willey 1996:41; see also Dunnell 1985a). The similarities between it and Ford's Virú work are not so surprising when one realizes that Ford worked on the Virú project between 1946 and 1948 (Ford and Willey 1949) and on the Mississippi Valley project sporadically between 1940 and 1948 (Phillips et al. 1951:v–vi). Many of the arguments Ford outlined regarding the utility of surface collections and the continuous and gradual flow of culture through time in his contribution to the Mississippi Valley volume thus echo those he presented in his dissertation. In some cases, the dissertation is more carefully and thoughtfully worded than the monograph, undoubtedly because the latter was a collaboration.

Project Background

The Mississippi Valley survey was initiated by Ford as a result of the constant late-1930s suggestion that the valley between the mouths of the Red and Ohio Rivers was archaeologically unknown relative to the areas to the north and south. Despite some efforts by the University of Arkansas Museum (Dellinger and Dickinson 1940; see also Hoffman 1981), the central Mississippi Valley was still considered to be one of the "principal blind spots in the archaeology of the Southeast" (Phillips et al. 1951:v). Although Ford's sustained efforts appeared to be resulting in a solid "reconstruction of prehistory in the southern part of the Lower Valley [it] had reached the point of need for verification farther north" (Phillips et al. 1951:v). Initially, the project team consisted of Ford and Griffin. Phillips learned of the project and wrote Ford about joining them in the venture: "The announcement that you are planning to work in eastern Arkansas and Missouri is good news. Could you use a voluntary assistant? I am anxious to learn more about your methods of survey, pottery stratigraphy, etc., and would consider myself well paid if you would let me tag along. Don't hesitate to say so if you think it would be a nuisance."[10] Phillips's involvement could hardly have been viewed by either Ford or Griffin as a nuisance. As a result of his dissertation research (Phillips 1939), Phillips was more familiar with portions of the archaeological record in western Mississippi than were either Ford or Griffin, and his experience was valuable. Too, there was a lot of unknown territory to cover, and a third member could make things go that much more quickly.

Gordon Willey at one time planned to join the team, but Strong, his adviser at Columbia, initially axed any institutional involvement, as Willey related to Ford:

> Cooperation of Phillips, Griffin, you and I would be swell. From my own standpoint I would profit immensely in learning something about [Middle Mississippi culture] from both of these chaps who probably are better informed on it than anyone else. Also it offers a big but coherent and planned problem of research which is probably the most important line of attack at the present time in the Southeast. Strong realizes all these things, and is perfectly congenial with all parties concerned . . . but he doesn't want to get Columbia involved in too ramified a scheme which will stretch out perhaps for several seasons and over several people and institutions. He is more than willing for me to pursue the thing personally but without Columbia's moral or financial support. This last virtually blocks me as I could not raise 40 dollars let alone 400 on my own resources.[11]

10. Letter of October 24, 1939, from Phillips to Ford (LSU Museum of Natural Science archives).
11. Letter of November 23, 1939, from Willey to Ford (LSU Museum of Natural Science archives).

Willey, however, was determined to find a way to join the survey, and he asked Ford to write Strong and give him a clearer idea of how the project was institutionalized. Ford did, and Willey soon wrote back, saying "Strong . . . is just about sold on the idea now." One of the conditions was that two Columbia students accompany Willey to the field—a condition Willey accepted, though he asked Ford if they could split them up: "If I am going to have to tackle [Middle Mississippi] I wouldn't like to have the three guys who know all about it in one camp and me with two green students in another."[12] That certainly wouldn't be any fun.

While Ford was waiting to see if Willey would be able to join the venture, he circulated to Phillips and Griffin a proposal he titled "Plan for an Archaeological Survey of the Central Mississippi Valley." The proposal clearly was constructed to investigate the origin of Middle Mississippi culture:

> One of the major questions awaiting solution at the present stage of knowledge of the pre-history of the eastern United States is that of the origin of the Middle Mississippi culture. At a comparatively late date—1500 A.D. is a probable estimate—this remarkably homogeneous culture had spread from Wisconsin to Louisiana and from eastern Oklahoma to central Georgia.
>
> . . . the central Mississippi Valley, the region in which the primary developments from an earlier cultural stage into Middle Mississippi must have taken place, has received little [archaeological] attention. . . .
>
> Cultural materials recently found in southwestern Arkansas seem to reflect an evolutionary development of culture from the Marksville into the Middle Mississippi stage. If this did occur, there should be sites in the central Mississippi Valley which will demonstrate this process in detail. As yet such transitional sites are unknown, and the question of the possible origin of this late culture is unanswered. (Ford 1939b:1–2)

The institutions then supporting the three investigators—Harvard (Phillips), Louisiana State (Ford), and the University of Michigan (Griffin)—contributed the salaries of the three, but salaries didn't pay for vehicle rental or gasoline. Ford needed a federal agency to help with these and other aspects of the project, and what better agency to approach than one that was planning a parkway across much of the area of interest? Thus he pitched the proposal to the National Park Service, specifically to A. R. Kelly, who came through with what Phillips et al. (1951:vi) later referred to as "not only the moral support of the National Park Service, but material assistance as well."

Fieldwork, which eventually took place without Willey, was conducted over seven months between 1940 and 1947; Ford apparently contributed field time only during 1940 (Phillips et al. 1951:v). During that period, 385 sites were located, sherd collections were made at almost all of them (Figure 4.5), and 11 sites received minor excavation. In the early days of the project, material was shipped to the WPA laboratory in Baton Rouge for washing and cataloging, since Quimby had a

---

12. Letter of December 18, 1939, from Willey to Ford (LSU Museum of Natural Science archives).

workforce that could process the sherds in a timely manner. The fieldwork caused some concern on the part of members of the WPA advisory board, including Setzler and Strong, because the WPA was sponsoring work in Louisiana, not in Arkansas,[13] where the majority of survey work was taking place. Ford offered the WPA a supplementary proposal that would allow the laboratory to process material from both states, and work apparently continued uninterrupted until the laboratory was shut down when WPA archaeology in Louisiana came to a close in 1941.

The resulting report of the survey-and-excavation project, published as *Archaeological Survey in the Lower Mississippi Alluvial Valley, 1940–1947* (Phillips et al. 1951), was a collaborative effort by Phillips, Ford, and Griffin—a fruitful collaboration, according to Griffin (1985:7), "even if some lemons appeared in the publication." The authors noted in the preface which of them was ultimately responsible for which sections. The section on typology was written by Ford and revised by Phillips, "with many suggestions by Griffin" (Phillips et al. 1951:vi). The section on seriation was written by Ford and the section on stratigraphy by Phillips. As interesting as those sections are, in our opinion the major value of the monograph is found in the "Summary and Conclusions" section, "written by all three authors and patched together in consultation" (Phillips et al. 1951:vi) during a meeting the three had one week in Phillips's apartment in Cambridge, Massachusetts (J. B. Griffin, pers. comm., 1996). This section is a dialogue among the three men, and their differences of opinion—founded in conflicting metaphysics—reveal the conflict within the culture-history paradigm in general (Lyman et al. 1997a). These differences appear as well in various sections of the report and underscore the problem culture historians had in assimilating different views of culture change. Simply put, there was no universally agreed upon algorithm for producing a history of a culture or cultures. The differences among the authors ultimately led to Phillips and Griffin rejecting some of Ford's analyses and conclusions, forcing him to publish them in a separate monograph (Ford 1952a). To place the disagreements in context, it is important to briefly note the experiences of the one coauthor—Phillips—that we have not talked much about. Our lack of discussion should not be taken as an indication that Phillips was not an important figure in Americanist archaeology prior to 1951, but neither had he attained the same level of recognition that his coauthors had. That would change in the 1950s.

Philip Phillips—Diffusion and Southeastern Archaeology

Phillips (Figure 4.6) was one of those rare individuals whom everyone respected, for his demeanor as well as his accomplishments. Neither of us ever met

13. Letters of February 9, 1941, and undated (probably January 1941) from Ford to Quimby (LSU Museum of Natural Science archives).

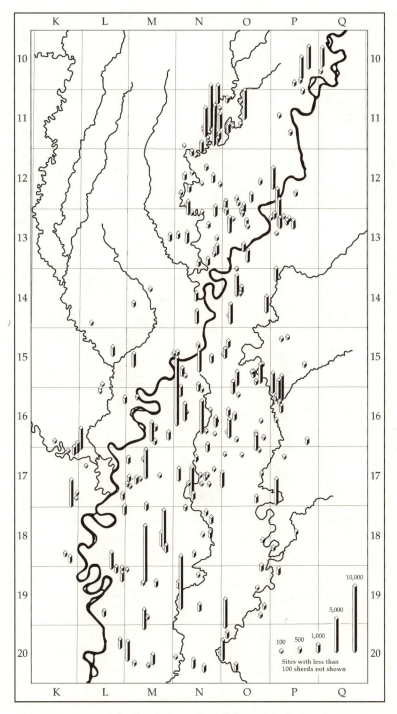

Figure 4.5. Sizes of sherd samples collected from sites during the Lower Mississippi Valley Survey (after Phillips et al. 1951).

Phillips, but over the years we have never heard a single disparaging remark about him, though we have often heard him described as a "gentleman." Griffin (pers. comm., 1996) described him as "a wise, compassionate gentleman who could tolerate the two Jims [Ford and Griffin] at the same time. No mean feat. It was a great pleasure to work with him. A man who could have been director of the Peabody Museum, but having money, was able to build a mini-research center just outside of Boston. I can't recall any instance of irritation or crudity between us or between him and Ford. One simply did not do that with Phil."

If one associated "gentleman" with Phillips, then one also associated "Peabody Museum" with him, because throughout his life he maintained the same institutional link with which he began his career. Phillips came to the museum in 1937 as an assistant curator of southeastern archaeology. Having earned undergraduate

Figure 4.6. Photograph of Philip Phillips, ca. 1940 (photograph courtesy W. G. Haag).

and master's degrees in architecture, he turned to archaeology after the stock market crash of 1929, entering Harvard in 1930 and earning his doctorate in 1940. His adviser was the great Mesoamericanist Alfred M. Tozzer (Figure 1.2), but Phillips chose as his specialization the lower Mississippi Valley (Willey 1996:40). Phillips's dissertation, *Introduction to the Archaeology of the Mississippi Valley,* is, unfortunately, unpublished, but is said to have "had a strong influence on many scholars working in the field" (Stephen Williams, quoted in Willey 1996:40).

We can gain an appreciation of Phillips's archaeological reasoning by noting several of his more revealing statements prior to the culmination of the Lower Mississippi Alluvial Valley Survey. Phillips used diffusion as an explanatory mechanism virtually from the start of his career, examining, for example, the possibility of detecting contact between pre-Columbian Mesoamerica and the Southeast (Phillips 1940; Willey and Phillips 1944)—a topic that later occupied Ford. Some of Phillips's most revealing statements on his view of archaeology during the 1940s are found in his review of William Webb and David DeJarnette's (1942) monograph "An Archaeological Survey of Pickwick Basin in the Adjacent Portions of the States of Alabama, Mississippi, and Tennessee," which stemmed from a large project funded by the Tennessee Valley Authority in the 1930s. In his review, Phillips (1942) focused on the fallacy of too strong a subscription to the Midwestern Taxonomic Method. To him, weaknesses in the Pickwick Basin monograph lay "almost wholly in the domain of interpretation and are the result of mixing the stratigraphic and analytic (McKern [Midwestern Taxonomic]) methods."

Phillips was not enthusiastic about Webb and DeJarnette's use of stratigraphy to document culture development represented by "a single occupance over a long period of time," during which "radically new elements [read *culture traits*] [were introduced, and] older types persisted." Given this interpretation, Webb and DeJarnette could not "account for stratigraphy" and were placed in what Phillips saw as the untenable position of having the entire culture history of the basin being represented as a single focus in the sense of McKern (1937, 1939). In Phillips's view, the source of the problem was, again, reliance on the Midwestern Taxonomic Method: "This is the important point. Your archaeologist unhampered by a classificatory bias [such as that provided by the Midwestern Taxonomic Method], would find no trouble at all in breaking the series down into sequent periods, each marked by the appearance of a new type of material. Persistence of the older types [such as was perceived by Webb and DeJarnette] would not bother him at all. But a unit in the McKern classification has to be set apart by differences, and if the differences are outnumbered by the similarities due to persistence then your classifier is helpless" (Phillips 1942:198).

The problem extended into what Phillips (1942:199) perceived to be the "most interesting [of several] teasing problems": what was the "position of the clay tempered group of pottery types"? Phillips (1942:200) felt that a long cultural succession in which new "features" were introduced "without corresponding loss of old ones [was] what one feels to be a true picture of normal cultural development." In short, culture change was slow and gradual. Clay-tempered pottery preceded shell-tempered pottery in time, but what, Phillips wondered, was the precise *historical*—as opposed to merely chronological—relation of the two? Were they "connected" in some implied ancestor-descendant manner, or were they "separated," in which case a " 'new people' can be brought in to account for [the relationship]" (Phillips 1942:201)? Phillips thought that stratigraphy would provide the requisite evidence for answering such questions. It is not surprising, then, that his major contribution to the Lower Mississippi Alluvial Valley Survey was stratigraphic excavation. Nor is it startling to find that the one issue Phillips wrestled with more than any other during the survey-and-excavation program was the historical connection between users of clay-tempered pottery and users of shell-tempered pottery. What *is* surprising, given Ford's predisposition to viewing the appearance of new traits in the archaeological record as the result of diffusion and/or migration, was that in the end Ford took the opposite position from that held by Phillips.

Phillips et al. on Typology

The discussion entitled "Classification of Pottery" in the survey report is a remarkable example of the conflation of the materialist and essentialist metaphysics, of empirical and ideational units, and of archaeology and anthropology. It is a classic example of the materialist paradox—the use of essentialist units within a model based on materialist conceptions of change (Dunnell 1995:34). The various conflations are exacerbated by Phillips et al.'s (1951:61–68) constant fluctuation within the text between their discussions of types as archaeologically useful units and types as somehow anthropologically relevant units. For example, in the second paragraph of the pottery section they noted that within the study of archaeological materials there are "two basically divergent interests: (1) interest in objects as expressions of the ideas and behavior of the people who made and used them and (2) interest in objects as fossils for the determination of time and space relations" (Phillips et al. 1951:61). Unfortunately, in the remainder of their discussion they failed to keep the two interests distinct. We have attempted to structure our review of Phillips et al.'s discussion of types as if they had written two such sections, one on types as archaeological constructs to be used as measurement tools and the other on types as anthropologically meaningful units.

Types as Archaeological Constructs

Phillips et al. (1951:65) conceived of type construction as demanding "hairsplitting," arbitrary decisions. They thought this because they believed there was a "ceramic continuum" that represented a "three-dimensional flow" of variation in pottery (Phillips et al. 1951:63). In short, "Techniques of manufacture, surface finish, shape, and decoration constantly, but slowly changed" (Phillips et al. 1951:62), not only through time but over space as well. To draw an analogy, we can use a biological species, which is not a static entity through time, since it may evolve, eventually, into another species. Although we speak in colloquial terms of a species evolving, we have to make it clear that what actually is evolving is a population of individuals that at any one time, and strictly for analytical purposes, we label as a species. Thus, a species, like an archaeological type, is actually an arbitrary chunk of an evolutionary continuum. But just as biologists for years missed this critical point, so too did many archaeologists. Ford was an exception.

Phillips et al. (1951:62) were well aware of what an "evolutionary series" represented, but they apparently did not like the "phylogenetic implications" of such arrangements, probably because of Ford's (1949) earlier suggestions that one must work out the temporal relations of phenomena before attempting to determine phylogenetic relations. Thus they noted that "when it becomes clear that related types have the same distribution in time and space, it may be preferable to lump them together as a single type whereupon the concept of 'series' becomes superfluous" (Phillips et al. 1951:64). This suggests that they did not completely understand the concept of "series" as originally developed by archaeologists in the Southwest (e.g., Colton and Hargrave 1937; Kidder 1917), or that Ford's (1938a, 1940) earlier approval of such notions had either changed to disapproval or he was overruled by his colleagues.

The authors indicated that when a group of several discrete pottery types, "each of which may have a separate history," was found "in a site, or level in a site," it was conveniently referred to as a "complex" (Phillips et al. 1951:64). They further noted that such a "pottery complex in a given situation is usually described in terms of percentages of the several component types and, where so described, gives a useful measure for comparison with other cultural situations" (Phillips et al. 1951:64). Ford's (1938b) complexes of a decade earlier had been founded only on the presence or absence of types, especially marker types. Phillips et al. cautioned that a complex was not a "more inclusive" taxonomic unit than a type, but because it sometimes took on such a connotation, they avoided using the notion.

Phillips et al. (1951:63) illustrated the ceramic continuum, admittedly in "crude diagrammatic form," as shown in Figure 4.7. The three dimensions of the flow, or continuum, are represented by the circles, which themselves represent the formal *and spatial* dimensions of variation in a "type," and the cylinders, which represent the temporal dimension. To Phillips et al., then, types were arbitrary chunks of the continuum; thus from this perspective types were ideational units. Such a conception clearly had a precedent in Ford's work.

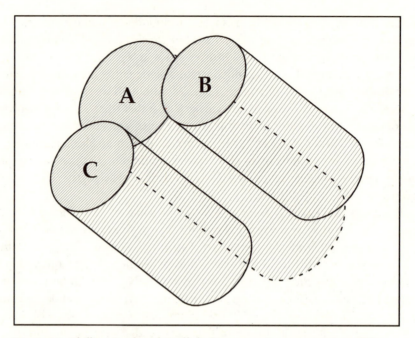

Figure 4.7. Phillips, Ford, and Griffin's diagrammatic representation of the concept of the pottery type. Each letter represents a type and the circle containing the letter the range of variation in the type. The length of a cylinder corresponds to the amount of time a type was in existence. In the figure, three closely related types are shown to overlap (after Phillips et al. 1951).

If types were arbitrary constructs of the classifier, what dictated how the chunks were to be delineated? For Phillips et al. (1951:61), "the choice of methods of classification is governed . . . by the predilections and general attitudes of the classifier, and particularly by the ends which the classifier has in view." As noted, there were two possible purposes to classification—to get at the ideas and behavior of the artifact makers, and to determine time-space relations. Since those purposes are founded in completely different metaphysics, each requires different kinds of units. This point was largely unrecognized in 1951. In the first stage of analysis, Phillips et al. (1951:61) were interested in time-space relations, arguing, "Until a certain amount of order has been achieved in respect to time-space relations on a regional scale, it may be questioned whether satisfactory cultural inferences can be drawn from any archaeological materials" (Phillips et al. 1951:61). They wanted their types to be tools that would allow them to perform some analytical work. The time-space boundaries of those units, as indicated by empirical specimens, were supposed to be limited in order to allow them to write culture history—specifically, to measure time-space differences, similarities, and relations.

They sought to select those attributes that were

the most [culturally and historically] sensitive—and at the same time most recognizable—characters as guides or "constants" in the process of classification. In Southeastern pottery generally, these are features of surface treatment and decoration, and thus it has come about that what may for convenience be called the Southeastern classification employs a binomial system of nomenclature in which the second term or "constant" is descriptive of surface treatment or decoration, as in Mulberry Creek *Cord-marked* or Indian Bay *Stamped.* (Phillips et al. 1951:65)

But how does one choose "sensitive" attributes, the combinations of which compose types useful for determining culture history? In lieu of a theoretically informed choice, "in the initial stages of classification one seizes upon *any* feature that will serve to distinguish one group of sherds from another" (Phillips et al. 1951:65), and thus the preliminary sorting of sherds was "done in the time-honored way . . . by piling the whole mass of sherds into one terrifying heap, and sorting them as many ways as possible" (Phillips et al. 1951:66). A sort of guide to the choice of attributes was provided by previous experience, such as the use of tempering agents—having been previously shown elsewhere to have some culture-historical significance (Griffin 1939)—for the "primary breakdown" (Phillips et al. 1951:66).

In short, the type *definitions* were extensional accidents of what had been collected. Subsequent to later field seasons, some early types were abandoned and new "preliminary type descriptions" were written in light of new material (Phillips et al. 1951:67). Those categories thought to already have the status of types—and how this was determined is unclear, though we suspect that it involved assessing the utility of the types for writing culture history—were identified in the final report by describing the "'central' [average?] material of the type and the variations in terms of this assumed 'center'" (Phillips et al. 1951:67). Ultimately, then, the types were extensionally defined units initially formulated through trial and error and later refined in the light of new material and their demonstrated utility for measuring time and/or space: such types are often referred to as historical types (e.g., Steward 1954).

Types as Anthropological Units

Phillips et al. (1951:61–62) emphasized, "fanatically," that they viewed types as tools, but they also noted that despite their attempts to maintain this view, there was an inevitable tendency to eventually conceive of a type as "an entity," at which point "the classification ceases to be a 'tool.'" This inevitability resided for the most part in how they rationalized their model of the ceramic continuum; that rationalization was founded in the notion of cultural development as a flowing braided stream of ideas, and pottery reflected those ideas:

Each community that had reached a certain level of sophistication in pottery-making will be found to have been maintaining side by side several different vessel styles. These are normally closely related [read *formally similar*], particularly in the matter of construction, paste, and surface finish, and seem to mark vessels made for different purposes or vessel ideas derived from different sources. If any one of these particular styles is examined at a single place and a single point in time, it will be seen that, while each vessel varies in minor detail, such variations tend to cluster about a norm. This norm represents the consensus of community opinion as to the correct features for this particular kind of vessel. Variations from the norm reflect the individual potter's interpretation of the prevailing styles, and the degree of variation tolerated is also culturally controlled. With the convenient hindsight of the archaeologist, we can divide such variations into two classes: those which were not followed by the rest of the community, and those that were. The latter are, of course, significant as the means by which ceramic development was accomplished. (Phillips et al. 1951:62)

Shifts in ceramic features were "no doubt partly the result of new ideas" but also the result of "play on the potentialities of current forms and styles" (Phillips et al. 1951:62)—that is, to extend the genetic metaphor, mutation and recombination, respectively. Vigorous centers of ceramic production "impress[ed] their ideas on less enterprising neighbors," "popularity centers will be seen for certain styles," and "Between these centers, styles vary and trend toward those of other centers in rough proportion to the distances involved, subject of course to ethnic distributions and geographic factors" (Phillips et al. 1951:62).

The modeled ceramic continuum "was a hopelessly crude approximation" because it did not show cylinders and circles (Figure 4.7) that were "irregular in shape, expanding, contracting, branching, and coming together, so that no two horizontal cross sections would be the same" (Phillips et al. 1951:63). In other words, the modeled continuum was a poor reflection of the flowing, braided-stream model of ceramic change. Like Krieger (1944), whom they cited with approval (Phillips et al. 1951:62), and others with similar views, they reverted to a commonsense rationalization of their types:

Whether, among the primitive communities of the Mississippi Alluvial Valley, groups or classes of pottery were recognized, and whether such entities, if we may speak of them as such, were conceptualized in terms anything like those with which we define a pottery type, are intriguing and by no means unimportant questions. We need not go into them here, however, because by reason of the very nature of the material to be classified [archaeological sherds *versus* cultural vessels] the possibility that our and their conception of a given type might coincide is so remote as to be negligible. [However, just because our typology] cannot be expected to show any strong relationship to cultural "reality," it does not follow that such relationship is precluded now and forever. To a certain extent, the characters we select as criteria for type definition, however dictated by expediency, not to say necessity, are bound to correspond to characters that might have served to distinguish one sort of pottery from another in the minds of the people who made and used it. We should, of course, make every possible effort to increase this correspondence. (Phillips et al. 1951:63)

This was a typical rationalization of the culture-history paradigm, similar to what Ford had written in the Virú Valley monograph and in his master's thesis. Archaeological types *might* conform to prehistoric stylistic norms, but they might not and probably did not, at least initially. Types would "finally achieve cultural meaning" if and when they showed "some correspondence to ethnographic distributions in time and space" (Phillips et al. 1951:64; see Lipo et al. 1997). Once one "knew" what a piece of Natchez pottery looked like, it became an index fossil. And how did one know a piece of pottery was Natchez? Because it came from a Natchez site. This is a classic example of circular argument—neat, from all appearances, but epistemologically weak. How could the archaeologist test the suspected correspondence of his types with prehistoric groups? In short, it was impossible.

Although Phillips et al.'s types were arbitrary constructs, they were rationalized as stylistic norms—as chunks of the braided stream of cultures. How could the stream's flow be measured? "The separate characters of paste, surface, form, and decoration change . . . in time and space, and not all at the same rate. Each separate character has its own history and each history will provide a more or less sensitive register for the history of the culture as a whole" (Phillips et al. 1951:64). Thus, "the norm of style, which we measure by means of pottery types, shifts both areally and chronologically in a manner so gradual that we are hard put to say at what point in either dimension one type leaves off and another begins" (Phillips et al. 1951:64). Phillips et al. (1951:65) thought they could detect, if only approximately, these norms:

> Type "A" let us suppose has been defined on the basis of what appears to be the "norm" at what appears to be a [geographic] "center". . . . As we go away from that center in space—the same thing happens in time . . . —the characters that we have selected as determinants for the type gradually shift, the all-too familiar phenomenon of "creep," until at some point we can stretch our original type definition no further and have to consider whether material "X" more closely resembles Type "B," already established at another center, or whether it is not sufficiently like either "A" or "B" and must be given an independent status as Type "C."

This wording was pure Ford, similar to the wording in the Virú Valley report. However, the whole notion began to unravel when they admitted that the " 'centers' are often only such because they first attracted our attention, or because of our ignorance of the intervening spaces" (Phillips et al. 1951:65). In other words, their "stylistic norms" were accidents of sampling (see Lipo et al. 1997). Epistemologically, that types might "creep" reveals such units were conceived as empirical and real rather than ideational (inches don't creep). This was, simply, essentialism couched in the anthropological jargon of culture.

Phillips et al. and Seriation: Assumptions

The section of Phillips et al. (1951:219–36) on seriation, although it outlines their views on the method, misrepresents what they ended up doing. As we noted earlier with respect to Ford's work in the Virú Valley, seriation was used to refer to the practice of placing surface-collected pottery assemblages in chronological ordering by matching type percentages against a master ordering based entirely on percentage-stratigraphy data (Lyman et al. 1998). In the section, the authors addressed several aspects of seriation, especially the significance of the spatial dimension, not found in such detail in Ford's earlier works. First, it was assumed that because the people in the area "were presumably agriculturists," there was a "comparative stability of peoples"; in other words, "the people who carried the cultural traits we are studying were probably relatively stable geographically and that for the most part population changes were slow gradual ones" (Phillips et al. 1951:219). Second, it was assumed that most of the sites from which pottery was collected "were occupied for a short time in proportion to the entire chronology" because such "short time-span collections [are] essential if the method of seriating surface collections is to be successfully applied" (Phillips et al. 1951:219). Phillips et al. (1951:219) were concerned that collections representing long spans of time— what we earlier termed "time-averaged"—were mixed, meaning they represented different "complexes." Some sites appeared to have multiple complexes, and Phillips et al. noted that they made multiple collections from those sites: "A cross section of the ceramic styles in vogue at these different sites at one instant in time would have been the ideal material for seriation purposes, but that, of course, is an unattainable goal" (Phillips et al. 1951:220).

Third, as discussed under their section on classification, Phillips et al. (1951:220) assumed "that in any large area cultural continuity in both time and space is to be expected as the normal state of affairs. A gradual change of feature with the passage of time and across the area, when it is viewed on any one time horizon, was our very idealized concept of the cultural history with which we were dealing." While admitting they did not preclude the possibility of such things as replacement of one human population or cultural tradition by another, they began by assuming that this had not occurred, and thus "did not begin analysis with any assumption that changes in ceramics, such as the shift from clay- to shell-tempering, necessarily indicate[d] any abrupt cultural or population replacement" (Phillips et al. 1951:220). Fourth, as noted above, they assumed that their types were of the historical sort.

The fifth assumption revealed yet again the commonsense rationalization of their types and the conflation of the materialist and essentialist metaphysics. It was

> not a basic assumption but rather a logical derivative of the preceding
> [assumptions]. . . . If our pottery types are successful measuring units for a

continuous stream of changing cultural ideas, it follows that when the relative popularity of these types is graphed through time, a more or less long, single-peak curve will usually result. Put in another way, a type will first appear in very small percentages, will gradually increase to its maximum popularity, and then, as it is replaced by its succeeding type, will gradually decrease and disappear. (1951:220)

As a warranting argument for this rephrasing of the popularity principle, Phillips et al. (1951:221–22) made up an example of the frequency distributions of modern artifacts, noting that they could have derived actual data but that it was "easier to make up our illustration than to dig it out of the census." Their example, which illustrates changes in kinds of transportation popular in Ohio between 1800 and 1940, is shown in Figure 4.8. Correctly, in our view, they proposed that the frequency curves for each kind of transportation will "be different in each part of the area on each time horizon, and a distinct pattern will appear when each part of the area is viewed through time" (Phillips et al. 1951:223) because each type had its own, independent history and those histories varied across space. The importance of the made-up example is that it shows how Ford (1949) and Phillips et al. (1951) could date sites relative to one another. The basic assumption was that "the popularity curves of the various constituent types will form a pattern. Each portion of this pattern will be peculiar to a particular time and area"; in other words, each synchronic slice of the quantitative continuum was "a unique thing" (Phillips et al. 1951:221). More emphatically, "systematic classification of cultural data representing a particular range of time creates in each case a characteristic quantitative pattern" (Phillips et al. 1951:222). Thus, once a master arrangement is constructed, it can serve as a key into which each new collection can be placed, based on the notion that it will fit most validly in terms of its relative age in the position where the least amount of violence is done to the overall unimodal frequency distributions of all types included. This is what Ford had done with his Virú Valley graphs.

That their example of the popularity principle in action was imaginary is less worthy of comment—Kroeber's (1919) example (see also Richardson and Kroeber 1940) was not made up and could have been used with virtually equal effect—than is the fact that Phillips et al. (1951:220–21) stated, "We have not discovered a natural law operating independently of our own humble efforts. This peculiar characteristic of type popularity distribution through time is something we have helped to bring about through our own conceptualization of the pottery types that manifest said behavior. How the curves come out is partly controlled by how the types are defined." In one sense, this is correct: the *precise* shape of a type's frequency-distribution curve will be a function of how that type is defined. But how can the second sentence possibly be correct, especially when types "manifest said behavior"? There must be some sort of "natural law" at work, else the whole notion that one can seriate the frequencies of types in collections collapses. One

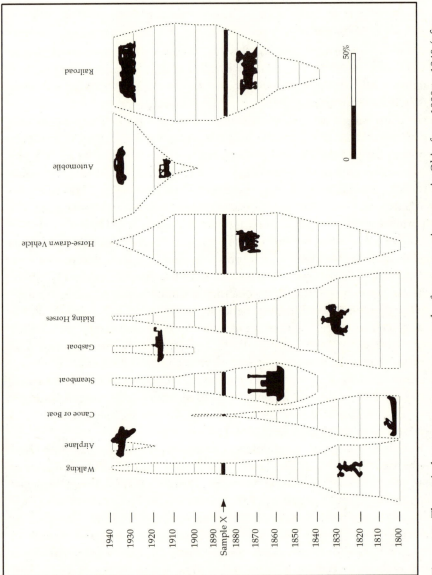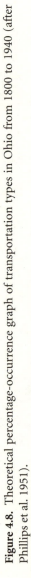

Figure 4.8. Theoretical percentage-occurrence graph of transportation types in Ohio from 1800 to 1940 (after Phillips et al. 1951).

might argue that the law at work here is what we have termed the *popularity principle.*

When Phillips et al. suggested that there was no law at work, they seem to have been referring to the fact that what they chose to measure—the history of pottery—didn't actually take the form of a unimodal frequency distribution because types are artificial constructs of the archaeologist, whereas the pottery itself changes continuously as modeled by the ceramic continuum. One cannot, of course, *see* the continuum in the empirical specimens without knowing the precise time-space position of each type; in lieu of that, one examines change in the continuum by charting fluctuations in the frequencies of ideational units we call types. But this conflates essentialism and materialism—variation between empirical specimens is merely real (emic-like) *difference,* even when their time-space loci are known. *Change* can only be measured as fluctuations in the frequencies of empirical representatives of ideational units, and such units make difference *definitional* and thus an *artificial* product of the classifier (etic-like) rather than somehow real. The popularity principle is a law *only* because of how we choose to measure the ceramic continuum; it is not a "natural" law. Using statements about cultural norms as warranting arguments for types and the popularity principle only confuses the matter further.

Phillips et al. (1951:223) required two other assumptions of their seriations. They assumed that their samples were representative of the entire time span of the chronologies they constructed, such that "no large time gaps remain unrepresented." They also assumed that "a random sample of over fifty sherds [was] sufficient to indicate the proportionate type frequencies existing in the refuse from which the material was collected." The first could be tested, as Ford (1949) had done, by seriating all collections and looking for gaps in the continuous frequency distributions of types. The second grew out of Ford's (1949) study of duplicate collections from sites in the Virú Valley.

Phillips et al. and Seriation: Operations

In a nod to the importance of controlling spatial variation when using types to measure time, Phillips et al. (1951:223–24) mapped out the "percentage frequency of [each] type at each site" and found that "Regional specialization [of types] tended to increase with the passage of time so that late complexes from the northern and southern ends of our Survey were more unlike than were the early." They refrained from drawing "iso-ceramic lines" and instead divided the valley into five arbitrary subareas on the basis of the distribution of pottery types dating to the latest period; to return to the metaphor, they arbitrarily defined five trickles of the braided stream at one point in time. They already knew the basic "outlines of the ceramic chronologies in the region," based on antecedent work by others (e.g., Jennings 1941; Webb and DeJarnette 1942) and on their own stratigraphic excavations (Phillips et al. 1951:226). In fact, those excavations were explicitly used "as guides" to chronology building because they could easily be arranged on the graph in proper temporal order, given that "the order in which they had come from the ground" was known and because they "immediately showed the frequency patterning for the time covered by [a stratigraphic] cut" (Phillips et al. 1951:226). In other words, just as in Virú, percentage stratigraphy was used from the start to build the chronology; seriation of surface collections played a supplemental role. Why? Probably because the superposed collections more clearly reflected the passage of time than the seriated surface collections did: "Vertical arrangement of the material in the ground gave some control over the collections from the stratigraphic pits, and we knew that the collections from the lower levels had to be older than those from the upper. However, for the surface collections we had no such guide" (Phillips et al. 1951:226–27). Thus seriation is merely an ordering technique; it does not tell us which way time is going (assuming an arrangement measures time in the first place).

Surface-collection graphs "were taken one at a time and compared to the beginning that had been made with the stratigraphic material. . . . These surface-collection graphs were shifted about in vertical relation to one another until patterning was developed" (Phillips et al. 1951:227). "If [the surface-collection graphs] fitted somewhere along the time represented by the excavations [in the percentage-stratigraphy graphs], the graph was fastened down to the backing sheet [containing the percentage-stratigraphy graph] with paper clips." This must be the source of Ford's (1957:figure 4; 1962:figure 8) famous illustration of two hands fitting a strip into place (Figure 7.2). The result was a set of what were called "seriation graphs" that in truth combined surface collections and percentage stratigraphy into a "chronological column" for each of the five "seriation areas" they had delineated (Phillips et al. 1951:227). The resulting patterning of type frequencies was good—the frequency distributions approximated what were later termed battleship-shaped curves (Ford 1952)—prompting the authors to suggest their assumption that "most surface collections represented relatively short lengths of time" was correct (Phillips et al. 1951:227; see Lipo et al. 1997). Collections that did violence to the form of the curves were deemed to contain early and late types "in a fashion that showed either that the sites had been occupied for a long time, or there had been reoccupation" (Phillips et al. 1951:227). These collections—eighteen in number—were removed from the graphs. The procedure for setting up time periods involved moving the graph for each geographic area up and down "until the same [artifact] types showed comparable relative quantities" at the same vertical position across all graphs (Phillips et al. 1951:228). At such positions, a horizontal line was drawn to break the graphed continuum into segments.

The plethora of compromises that had to be made to ensure that all of the several graphs had the horizontal lines drawn in similar positions relative to type frequencies (Phillips et al. 1951:228) underscored the arbitrary positional character of the dividing lines or slices. Precisely the same technique was being used in paleobiology at that time. The boundary between ancestral and descendant species was drawn by "select[ing] some feature or features of essential importance characterizing a genus or species and [drawing] the line where this character becomes dominant or universal in the evolving population," but this procedure was not easily applied (Simpson 1944:172–73).

Subscription to the notion that culture change could be modeled as a flowing, braided stream is apparent in the slices made through the graphs. The authors warranted the compromises necessary to make the slices, for example, by noting, "The groups of ideas to whose products have been tagged such names as Mazique Incised did not spring up simultaneously all over the area. They moved from one part to another, and that took time" (Phillips et al. 1951:229; see Lipo et al. 1997). Further, the time periods designated by the slices were "the smallest time divisions which we felt justified in making in the chronologies" (Phillips et al. 1951:231). The units that would become known as cultures or phases—for example, Baytown and Mississippian—might contain one or several of these periods. This is a significant point, for it underscores the differing epistemologies of the authors—differences that would ultimately rend the fabric of their discussion. We will return to this topic, but to understand its source we need to first review Phillips et al.'s discussions of stratigraphy.

Phillips et al. and Stratigraphy

In the seriation section, authored by Ford, it was noted that the collection from each arbitrary excavation level was treated as if it were a separate surface collection and that no attempt was made to resolve the levels with the actual sedimentary stratigraphy (Phillips et al. 1951:228). Thus it was noted that "whether the evidence indicates that there was a break in the deposition between the Baytown refuse characterized by clay-tempered pottery and the shell-tempered Mississippian deposits" could not be resolved; Phillips's "judgments" contrasted with Ford's "guesses" on this issue (Phillips et al. 1951:228). Both sides apparently agreed that if the human population had not been stable, if there had been "sudden and frequent movements of populations so that the cultural change in any one locality would have had little semblance of order," then "cultural periods would have been developed which were clearly delimited, one from the other" (Phillips et al. 1951:231). Instead, Ford perceived continuity in his "seriation graphs" and argued that had there been two separate populations there should be " 'pure' deposits of [Baytown overlain by pure deposits of Mississippian] which would illustrate the break in cultural continuity"; none had been found (Phillips et al. 1951:232). Phillips in particular perceived something else in Ford's graphs and thus in the stratigraphy.

Ford did not use data from sites he perceived to contain mixed deposits as a result of slow sediment deposition, and through his alignment of surface collections believed to represent short time spans he confirmed his perceptions that some sites were "mixed." He argued that to view seriation with "an attitude of suspicion and doubt" and to favor vertical stratigraphy displayed a "misconception of the phenomena of cultural change and the part that typology plays in measuring that change, or a lack of understanding of the seriation technique" (Phillips et al. 1951:231). In reading the Mississippi Valley survey volume, one gets the feeling that Ford somehow didn't trust the stratigraphic data; we suspect this was because Phillips and Griffin didn't care much for Ford's arrangement of surface collections. Ford noted that because the surface collections were not an "instant cross section of the ceramic content of the culture . . . a certain 'fogging' [read *time averaging*] of the quantitative history" was admitted to his graphs, but he quickly added that this did not invalidate assigning each site a "mean date" (Phillips et al. 1951:231–32, 234). And while such a dating assignment tended to " 'flatten out' the cultural evidence which accumulated during the occupation span that each collection represents" (Phillips et al. 1951:234), this did *not* mean the ceramic histories documented in the graphs were somehow invalid.

In his section on stratigraphy, Phillips took a decidedly different stance. Although he cautioned that the notion that "stratigraphic analysis is a more 'accurate' and sure method of dating than seriation . . . is by no means certain," he also revealed his preconceptions when he noted that the periods in Ford's graphs were "strictly chronological division[s], as devoid of typological significance as can be, being based on differences in percentage frequencies rather than differences in constituent types" (Phillips et al. 1951:239–40). The word "typological" here has precisely the meaning Ernst Mayr (1959:2) gave it in the context of biological evolution—"there is no gradation between types, gradual evolution is basically a logical impossibility for the typologist. Evolution, if it occurs at all, has to proceed in steps or jumps. [This is so because f]or the typologist, the type is real and the variation an illusion." A typologist, in other words, thinks in essentialist terms.

Phillips's typological thinking is particularly clear in his discussion of excavation methods. Excavations were done in 10-cm-thick arbitrary levels, and thus the critical issue was obvious:

> The crucial operation in the interpretation of [the] stratigraphic data [provided by such excavations] is the correlation of pottery distributions with soil stratification. . . . In a homogeneous deposit without observable profiles [read *strata*] you have to take the pottery distribution at face value so to speak, assuming that the changes or lack of changes from [arbitrary excavation] level to level mean just what they say. Where stratification has been recorded, however, an opportunity is given to evaluate such

changes a little more realistically. . . . Thus, two distinct phases of interpretation are involved: (1) interpretation of [stratigraphic] profiles for what they may reveal of events on the site, or that particular portion of it; and (2) interpretations of pottery distributions in the light of such events. (Phillips et al. 1951:242)

Two things are noteworthy in this statement authored by Phillips. First, it is not intuitively clear why natural strata would be more "realistic" than arbitrary levels, nor is it clear of *what*, precisely, strata are more realistic. Second, the order of interpretive phases underscores Phillips's personal bias.

Returning to the problem of matching up the arbitrary levels with the strata, Phillips et al. (1951:242) chose to construct for each site a composite profile showing all four vertical faces exposed in an excavation unit, and to superimpose on that profile a bar graph showing fluctuations in relative frequencies of pottery types (Figure 4.9). Interestingly, while they admitted that the composite profiles had the effect of "exaggerating incongruities," they also argued that "the resulting errors of interpretation are more likely to be on the side of safety" (Phillips et al. 1951:242). Safe or not, the net result was to increase the probability of disposing of "transitional" collections (Phillips et al. 1951:291) as stratigraphically mixed and thereby to simultaneously enlarge the body of empirical evidence that suggested a cultural discontinuity and decrease the body of empirical evidence for gradual continuous cultural change. Thus a "mixed site" was simply a stratified site that had been reoccupied (Phillips et al. 1951:291).

Whereas Ford (e.g., 1935a, 1949) conceived of culture change as gradual and steady, Phillips, and perhaps Griffin, conceived of the flow as more discontinuous or jerky. This view emanated in part from the priority ascribed to the inherent discontinuity of a column of stratigraphic units (Phillips et al. 1951:428); thus the breaks in the cultural flow that Phillips and Griffin perceived tended to correspond to stratigraphic boundaries. But this is how they *expected* the archaeological record to be arranged—nice, orderly units with highly visible discontinuities between them. Such units underscore their essentialist viewpoint. Ford's view was different, and clearly materialistic. For Ford, pottery

> was developing in a continuum throughout its entire history in the Mississippi Valley, that whether new types evolve by modification of older ones or come in as new ideas from the outside, they take their place in an uninterrupted cultural flow. The logical consequence of such a view is that, in most cases a "mixed" pottery complex represents a single brief span of time on the continuum, an "instant" for all practical purposes, when both elements of the mixture were being made and used side by side. The importance of this postulation for the seriation method [as well as for percentage stratigraphy] can hardly be exaggerated. Ford does not deny that mixed complexes sometimes do result from reoccupation of sites. Such collections he frankly banishes from his graphs and says so. . . .

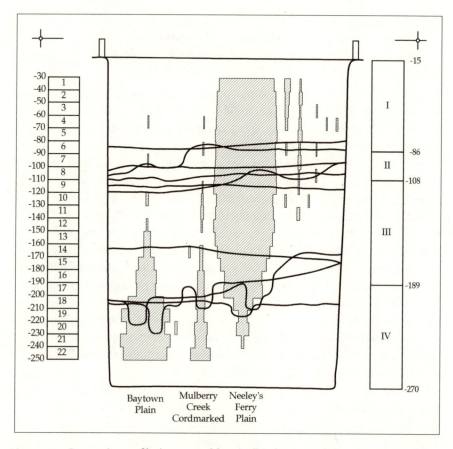

Figure 4.9. Composite profile (average of four walls) diagram of Cut A, Rose Mound, Cross County, Arkansas, with relative percentages of pottery types by excavation level superimposed. The negative numbers on the left correspond to depth (in cm) below the top of the excavation stakes (upright rectangles at the edges of the graph). The numbers in boxes refer to 10-cm excavation levels. Roman numerals I–IV represent idealized strata obtained by averaging the four walls of the 2-m² excavation unit (from Phillips et al. 1951).

   Griffin and Phillips, on the other hand, while not rejecting the general theory of continuity, are inclined to feel . . . that there are more instances of mixture through reoccupation of sites than Ford has recognized. In particular . . . they have tended to see indications of at least one significant break in the otherwise placid stream of pottery continuity at the point where the tempering material shifts from clay to shell, in other words between the Baytown and Mississippi periods. They feel that, by including mixed collections on the graphs, Ford has effected a spurious transition that seems to prove his continuity hypothesis, but in reality leaves the question open. (Phillips et al. 1951:427)

Phillips and Griffin's essentialist notions of "abrupt cultural change" demanded, in the end, that sites be viewed as stratigraphically "mixed" when they showed no abrupt change (Phillips et al. 1951:291–92). Similarly, the surface collections were viewed as mixed and thus when seriated consisted of false "transitional" collections "that are actually the result of reoccupation" (Phillips et al. 1951:292). How Phillips and Griffin *knew* the surface collections and the collections from their stratigraphic tests were mixed highlights their essentialist stance. They could not empirically test such an inference except to cite those cases of clear stratigraphic separation of types as accurate reflections of reality and to discount cases where the types were stratigraphically associated as mixed. This point draws a clear contrast between the epistemological positions of Phillips and Griffin on the one hand and Ford on the other.

An excellent example of Phillips and Griffin's perspective is given in the discussion of the pottery from the Rose Mound site in Cross County, Arkansas. There they excavated a single 2-m-square unit in twenty-two arbitrary 10-cm-thick levels. The authors noted, "The stratification of this [unit] has a particularly important bearing on the interpretation of the pottery stratigraphy" with regard to the shift from sand-tempered to shell-tempered pottery, or what was then termed Baytown to Mississippian pottery (Phillips et al. 1951:286–87). A graph of the type percentages constructed as a bar chart of the kind for which Ford is famous was superimposed on a composite stratigraphic profile that showed the boundary between the two lowest stratigraphic units. A simplified version is shown in Figure 4.9. Phillips concluded that

> the effect of this slope [of strata boundaries] on the pottery stratigraphy is to introduce a spurious transition of a new and insidious kind. . . . The resulting pottery graph could not fail, therefore, to show a smooth transition in [pottery types]. To judge correctly the stratigraphic relationship between [the two stratigraphic zones, the five arbitrary levels containing the boundary between the strata] would have to be eliminated from consideration. *The resulting conclusion is that there was an abrupt shift from a pure Baytown to an equally pure Mississippi pottery complex.* (Phillips et al. 1951:288–89; emphasis added)

While Ford might have agreed the five levels were mixed, he did not agree, given his percentage-stratigraphy and seriational data, with the "resulting conclusion."

Ford might not have agreed with a lot of what Phillips and Griffin thought, but he let them have their day in court, as they allowed him to have his. The handling of the disagreements created a document that chronicles the struggles they went through in attempting to write the culture history of a complex region. As Haag (1953a:275; see also Haag 1953b) observed in his review of the monograph, "The psychological and personal circumstances under which the work was prepared is a rare accomplishment and an object lesson for the student of American archaeology." Similarly, Steen (1953:57) noted, "It would be impossible to achieve complete unanimity among three competent archaeologists on a project so extensive, and this public airing of differences of opinion [in the summary and conclusions] is excellent." In a larger sense, the survey report documents the battle between continuity and discontinuity that was fought repeatedly by culture historians, as it does the different perspectives on archaeological units that have existed. By the time the report was published in 1951, Phillips, Ford, and Griffin had been able to resolve some of the issues over which they disagreed initially, but many of them remained unresolved.

Ford and Phillips continued to collaborate after 1951, but Griffin had drifted off to the north to continue surveying the central Mississippi Valley (Griffin and Spaulding 1952) and had become more involved with midcontinental archaeology. Ford and Phillips's collaboration did not signal an end to the conflict in metaphysic that had set them at odds intellectually during the alluvial-valley survey. In fact, it did not end with Ford's death in 1968, because two years later Phillips got the last word in with his two-volume synthesis of the prehistory of the Mississippi Valley from the Ohio-Mississippi confluence to the Gulf of Mexico (Phillips 1970). Phillips had a few things to say that bear directly on our discussion, not the least of which was his personal perspective on how Ford imparted chronological control over the archaeological record. The conflict in metaphysic that led to the separation of Griffin and Phillips into one camp and Ford into another comes through loud and clear in the survey report (Phillips et al. 1951), but it is stated most eloquently by Phillips in explaining how Ford came to add the Troyville period to the lower Mississippi Valley sequence. To put Phillips's comments in historical perspective, we have to preface them with some notes on Ford's analysis of the Greenhouse site in Avoyelles Parish, Louisiana, which had been excavated as part of the Works Progress Administration–sponsored program.

A CONTINUING CONFLICT OF METAPHYSICS: GREENHOUSE AND THE TROYVILLE PERIOD

Greenhouse, in the bottomland below the Avoyelles Prairie bluff and about a mile northeast of the Marksville site (Figure 3.6), was excavated in 1938–1939, but the report was not finished until 1950 and not published for another year (Ford 1951a). The most prominent features on the site were three large flat-topped mounds and four smaller mounds. Greenhouse was selected for excavation principally because it appeared to be a Coles Creek–period mound center, but during the course of analysis, which Ford and Willey completed in 1939, Ford decided to divide the sequence into two periods—an earlier Troyville period and a later Coles Creek period. As we pointed out in Chapter 3, brief mention of this was made in the Crooks report (Ford and Willey 1940), wherein it was also mentioned that two other sites, Peck Village (Ford 1935c) and Troyville (Walker 1936), both in Catahoula Parish (Figure 2.2), also were occupied during the Troyville period. Ford and Willey proposed that Peck Village and Troyville were initially occupied slightly earlier than Greenhouse, during the waning years of the Marksville period (Figure 3.7). Greenhouse was occupied until the end of the Coles Creek period, Peck Village was abandoned somewhat earlier during that period, and the terminal occupation of Troyville didn't quite make it to the middle of the Coles Creek period.

Ford maintained this chronological arrangement in the final Greenhouse report. There he produced his usual series of percentage-stratigraphy graphs from different "analysis units"—horizontal sections of excavation units selected to omit stratigraphic mixtures within the 3-inch-thick arbitrary levels (Ford 1951a:26)— showing the alignment of relative frequencies of sherds in each pottery type and how various units correlated with one another. One of the graphs, showing the alignment of three analysis units from excavations in Mound E, is illustrated in Figure 4.10. Ford smoothed the type-frequency bars, as he had for the Virú Valley data (Ford 1949) and the data presented in Phillips et al. (1951), to derive nice, orderly distributions. More importantly, along the right edge of the graph Ford drew in the portion of the master chronology represented in the analysis units. The letter "D," which separates the Troyville and Coles Creek periods, corresponded to the "D" in the Phillips et al. (1951) report, which signified the beginning of the last third of the Baytown period.

Some archaeologists grumbled when Ford and Willey added two new periods to the previously established sequence in the Crooks report (1940)—Tchefuncte and Troyville—and yet a third—Plaquemine—in their synthesis of eastern pre-history (1941). This grumbling persisted in some quarters throughout the 1940s, especially with regard to Troyville, and in the Greenhouse report Ford fired a shot across the bow of the complainers:

> The [WPA] excavation program has made possible the expected subdivision of the rough time scale that I presented in 1936 [Ford 1936a]. New classificatory terms have been interposed between each of the time-period names previously set up, thus giving a more accurate measure of the chronology in verbal terms. Of considerably more importance, however, is the fact that the stratigraphic data have produced a picture of quantitative change of ceramic styles. The sequence of period names "Marksville," "Coles Creek," and "Natchez" presented in 1936 was actually the limit of our control over ceramic chronology in this region at that time. While we were aware that these were probably gross divisions of a changing cultural continuum, this could not be demonstrated and had no more validity than a reasonable assumption deduced from experience with culture history in other areas where details were better known. Some of the ignorance that makes such a neat and "air-tight" classification possible has now been dispelled, and the expanded list of period names can be presented as nothing more than convenient labels for short segments of a continually changing culture history.

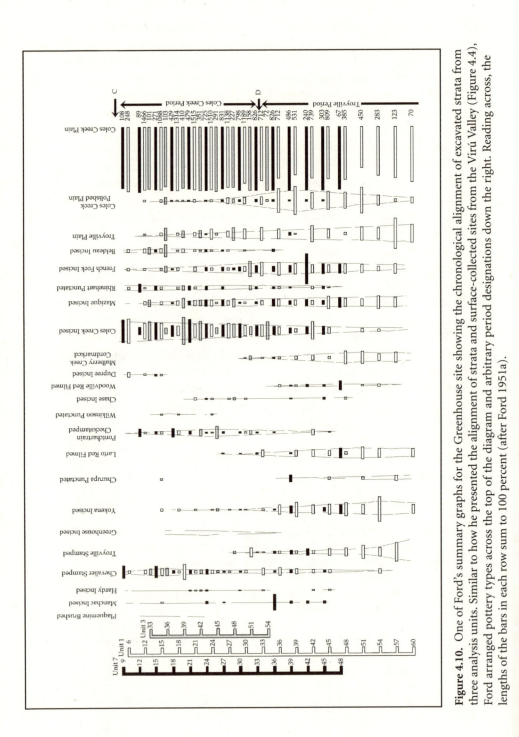

Figure 4.10. One of Ford's summary graphs for the Greenhouse site showing the chronological alignment of excavated strata from three analysis units. Similar to how he presented the alignment of strata and surface-collected sites from the Virú Valley (Figure 4.4), Ford arranged pottery types across the top of the diagram and arbitrary period designations down the right. Reading across, the lengths of the bars in each row sum to 100 percent (after Ford 1951a).

The old and new period names correlate as follows:

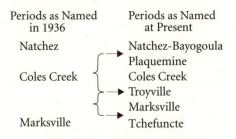

Periods as Named in 1936	Periods as Named at Present
Natchez	Natchez-Bayogoula
	Plaquemine
Coles Creek	Coles Creek
	Troyville
	Marksville
Marksville	Tchefuncte

   This readjustment of the named divisions for the time scale in this area seems to have puzzled a few of the archaeologists working in the Mississippi Valley, even some of those who have been best informed as to the field-work which led to this rearrangement. Complaints have been made that pottery types that were formerly classified as Coles Creek in age are now assigned to the Troyville Period. Discussion develops the opinion that if this latest chronological arrangement is correct then the former must have been in error. The adoption of new names for all the periods in the more recent arrangement may have avoided some, but not all, of this confusion. These serious and earnest seekers after truth really believe that we have *discovered* these periods and that this is a more or less successful attempt to picture the *natural divisions* in this span of history. This is obviously an incorrect interpretation. This is an *arbitrary* set of culture chronology units, the limits of each of which are determined by *historical accident,* and which are named to facilitate reference to them. Had the Marksville Site excavated by Fowke and Setzler produced cultural evidence from the middle of the span of time we now call "Marksville" to the middle of the period named "Troyville," then it is certain that the arbitrary lines we have drawn in this history would have been differently placed. (Ford 1951a:12–13; emphasis added)

Although his statement was written in 1950 (or earlier), Ford had adhered to it throughout his work in Louisiana: use pottery as the basis for creating temporal units, the dividing lines between which will continually shift as more work is done. There's nothing "real" about them. If truth seekers wanted to impart an empiricalness to the units, that was their problem, not his.

Phillips's Belated Response

   One person who wanted to do just that was Phillips, who in 1970 was still as wedded to cultural discontinuities marking the boundaries of periods as he had been two decades earlier. Look at what he had to say about Ford's notion of a Troyville period. We quote from him extensively, because the original thoughts are too important to abbreviate:

The concept of a Troyville "period" in Lower Mississippi archaeology has been a target of criticism since it was first launched by Ford and Willey (1940). Many students have felt uneasy about it. Others have flatly stated that they could not use it in their particular area of interest (McIntire, 1958; Saucier, 1963). The reasons for this almost universal discomfort lie, I believe, in the peculiar nature of Troyville as an archaeological formulation.

It is important to remember that Troyville was a departure in *theory* from Ford's earlier unit concepts such as Marksville and Coles Creek, but I am not aware that this was made explicit by Ford or anyone else at the time. In his writings previous to 1940—and even later, in the Tchefuncte report (Ford and Quimby, 1945)—Ford's periods were conceived as intelligible culture-historical units in the usual sense, *i.e.,* they were defined by reference to features whose initial appearance marked the beginning of the period as their disappearance (somewhat less definitely) marked its end. This is what Ford meant by his "marker" types in the 1936 report. . . . [14]

By 1940 Ford's theory of archaeological culture as a unity[—]a continuum in time and geographical space arbitrarily sliced up by the investigator[—]freed him from the necessity of defining his periods in cultural terms; hence there is no more talk of "marker" types.[15] The classic archaeological method of coincidence of period beginnings with significant cultural changes is abandoned because there are no significant cultural changes. In Ford's view change itself is continuous and proceeds at a more or less unvarying rate which can be "measured" in terms of slowly shifting popularity of long established styles of pottery decoration.

The purpose here is not to take issue with this theoretical point of view, although I don't agree with it. But like all innovations, its impact on existing nomenclature was not fully appreciated, even by its author. Other students, expecting an archaeological unit and finding nothing to characterize it by, were inclined to question its existence (Jennings, 1952[a], p. 264 [see also Jennings 1952b]). It is instructive to compare the reception of Troyville with that of Plaquemine, another insertion in the Louisiana sequence, made some years later. Both arose as necessary refinements of the existing sequence. Plaquemine offered no difficulty because it was simply a subdivision of Coles Creek, entirely within that period as previously defined. There are some new types that could readily be singled out as markers. At the same time there was no question about the continuity that obtained between Coles Creek and Plaquemine. Many Plaquemine types are to a considerable extent only variations upon older Coles Creek types, the sort of thing that normally occurs with increasing typological refinement.[16]

Troyville is different. At first it also seemed to have been sliced out of Coles Creek (I have only just realized this lately, on rereading Ford and Willey, 1940), but it soon

14. Close study of Ford's analysis of Peck Village clearly indicates this is not at all what he meant. Marker types were those for which the peaks in frequency could be used to denote a period, but this certainly did not mean such types never occurred in other periods. Similarly, his slightly later "type fossils" (Ford 1938b:263) could occur in one or more periods and simply served to "distinguish the passage of time."

15. Marker types were never referred to by Ford in Phillips's "cultural terms," nor were ceramic complexes, especially after 1938 (Ford 1938b).

16. Compare what Phillips was saying with what Ford said in the Peck Village report (Ford 1935c) and the surface-collection monograph (Ford 1936a); they sound identical. For Phillips, the continuity in terms of not only design but also tempering (clay) and other paste characteristics was a clear signal of a smooth transition between Coles Creek and Plaquemine, "punctuated" only by the appearance of a few new types—a classic case of essentialism.

developed that it was also sliced out of Marksville (Ford, 1951[a]). But this could only work if there is a clear case of continuity between Marksville and Coles Creek. If there is discontinuity (and who can doubt it in this particular case?), that discontinuity would be automatically incorporated in the new Troyville phase. In my opinion it is, but the fact is not brought out in Ford's (1951[a]) description of the Troyville complex. It seems to be nothing more than a mixture of two separate and distinct complexes. Ford would say this is because these two complexes were defined first and we got used to them—if Greenhouse had been dug first, etc. I disagree. My position is that Troyville is an important cultural-historical phase in the Lower Red River region, needing only to be described as such (by someone who knows the material better than I, let me hasten to add).

To conclude this digression into methodology, in setting up Marksville and Coles Creek in 1936, Ford was following the classic method of starting new periods with the appearance of new forms. Later it became necessary to subdivide these periods. If Troyville had continued to be simply a division corresponding to early Coles Creek (as Plaquemine to late Coles Creek), which is about what it was as originally defined by Ford and Willey in 1940, there would have been no difficulty. The "natural" (a word which Ford would not allow me to use) line of separation between the old Marksville and Coles Creek would have remained in place. But Ford's description of 1951, in failing to accent the new forms that belong specifically to Troyville, makes it appear to straddle this line. Actually, he is using a new criterion in marking off chronological divisions. Instead of coinciding with the appearance of new features and the disappearance of old, lines of separation are determined by their maximum occurrence. For example, Troyville Plain, Coles Creek Polished Plain, and French Fork Incised extend approximately through both Troyville and Coles Creek [Figure 4.10], their maximum frequencies falling on or near the line separating the two periods. If Ford were desirous of demonstrating his break with classic archaeological method he could do no better than to point to these examples. (Phillips 1970:908–9)

We find it interesting that Phillips in several places referred to Ford's break with "classic" archaeological method. In reality, he didn't break with anything. In the Peck Village report (Ford 1935c) and in the surface-collection monograph (Ford 1936a), he did discuss "decoration complexes," and he also discussed the evolution of designs, using them to work out a sequence of pottery types. That the fancy Hopewell-like decorations dropped out and were replaced by overhanging lines and other things was certainly noticed by Ford, and he used that relative point in time as a period boundary—Marksville below the boundary, Coles Creek above it. Given correlations made between decorations and historical tribes, Ford had a convenient late period with which to cap his sequence.

Phillips liked the Marksville–Coles Creek boundary as well as that between the Coles Creek and Plaquemine periods (the latter being presented for the first time in Ford and Willey [1941] on the basis of work at Medora [Quimby 1951] and Bayou Goula [Quimby 1957]). Even Ford's Tchefuncte period (Ford and Quimby 1945) was one of those "intelligible culture-historical units in the usual sense"

(Phillips 1970:908). At this point, we have to ask ourselves, "When did Ford change his mind?" The designations "Tchefuncte" and "Plaquemine" as periods—both "intelligible" units—appeared in print in 1940 and 1941, respectively, though the notion of a Plaquemine period—what Ford referred to as "a good transitional stage between Coles Creek and Caddoan"[17]—was in the making a year earlier. Tchefuncte even made its initial appearance in the same publication as Troyville—the Crooks report (Ford and Willey 1940). So when did Ford have time to change his approach? Of course, he hadn't; the problem was that Phillips was fooled by, or didn't read closely enough, Ford and Willey's chronological chart (Figure 3.7).

If, Phillips later lamented, Ford hadn't toyed with the sacred Marksville–Coles Creek boundary and had just split the Coles Creek period into three pieces—Troyville (early Coles Creek), Coles Creek (middle), and Plaquemine (late)—everything would have been fine. But no, he had to ram the Troyville period between the two periods with which everyone was comfortable—Marksville and Coles Creek—in the process squashing them into shorter periods by squeezing them against either the solid basement period, Tchefuncte in the case of Marksville, or the equally solid ceiling period, Plaquemine in the case of Coles Creek. Neither of those two anchor periods was going to budge, so Marksville and Coles Creek took the brunt of the force. This apparent "rearrangement" threw everything out of whack because everyone but Ford was looking for discontinuities in the archaeological record. Certainly he might *use* an apparent discontinuity as a means of establishing a period boundary, as he did when he used the disappearance of fancy decoration to end the Marksville period, but he didn't *rely* on them. It just so happened that in almost every case he *had* used highly visible artifacts or designs to mark period boundaries, but this was simply coincidental to his real purpose—to cut up the continuum into a sufficient number of short-term periods to allow the measurement of time and the writing of culture history.

Hence, Phillips was just plain wrong when he stated that Ford had broken with classic archaeological method—if we understand Phillips's notion of what that means—because Ford was never allied with it in the first place. When, during his analysis of the Virú materials, he developed the graphic techniques for which he would become famous, and when he applied those techniques to collections from the Mississippi Valley survey (Phillips et al. 1951) and from Greenhouse (Ford 1951a), he really was doing nothing more than he had always done—simply *reading* a chronological order of arbitrary periods from the archaeological record as opposed to searching endlessly for clues as to the *natural* jointedness of things. As we've already seen and will certainly see more of, some of his colleagues were not particularly amused with Ford's method—one unceremoniously compared him to a butcher running through the Southeast with a meat cleaver in hand.

17. Letter of May 5, 1940, from Ford to Willey (LSU Museum of Natural Science archives).

At the very least, this type of reaction shows that archaeologists working in the region, like Phillips, preferred their prehistory in a natural fashion.

To Ford, his method—"Die Methode," as he labeled it in a letter to Quimby in 1948—had a long and illustrious history in archaeology. In fact, it was simply another evolved "culture trait" that characterized Americanist archaeology:

> [The method] has a history which explains its present form like all other cultural traits. Component parts of the scheme have passed from individual to individual and have welded together to form what might be called a "new" idea (or culture trait) that can be most clearly viewed as though humans didn't exist. As one of the dogs who is passing along this evolving strain of fleas I am aware that the particular variety which I am supporting at present resulted from the mating of the ideas of Kroeber as practi[c]ed by [Spier] (Analysis of Zuni Ruins) and the graphic techniques used by [Emil] Haury and [E. B.] Sayles in the Snaketown Report (fig. 48 for example). Kroeber's study of Dress Styles is basic to the whole concept.[18]

"Sure," Ford added sarcastically, "I've invented this scheme just like Howe invented the sewing machine and Watt the steam engine." And perhaps because he was fed up with some ribbing he had been taking about the graphic method, he told Quimby, "For the love of God don't refer to this as the 'Ballo[o]n Method'—the name that ass Carling Malouf has tacked on it through a seminar he gave this year at Columbia. There have been enough snide remarks about hot air without inviting such."

18. Letter of January 22, 1948, from Ford to Quimby (LSU Museum of Natural Science archives).

5

Ford on the Defensive—Types and Diffusion

1952–1956

Published reviews of Ford's work in the Virú Valley and in the lower Mississippi Valley generally were favorable toward his methods (e.g., Bennyhoff 1952; Evans 1951), though some of the substantive results of both studies were criticized (e.g., Haag 1953a, 1953b; Steen 1953). The tenor of comments made by the discipline at large, though, was different. In reality, most archaeologists didn't understand where Ford was coming from theoretically and methodologically—Phillips certainly didn't, and he worked with Ford—and while they might have accepted his methods on visual grounds (Ford did, after all, produce pleasing graphics) they couldn't make the connection between the continuous flow of time and the arbitrariness of how you cut the continuum into pieces. One who could, however, was Gordon Willey:

> A classification is an arbitrary procedure; the grouping or categorizing of phenomena reflects the attitudes of the classifier toward his data rather than any inherent "truths" in the materials themselves. . . .
>
> In establishing the culture "periods" as the major classificatory device of this report we are operating with the basic assumption that culture changes through time. The culture period is the means of measuring and describing cultural forms, both material and non-material, as these have existed in a time continuity. . . . [W]e have defined these culture periods by their own content. . . .
>
> The primary method by which the culture continuum has been arranged and given direction from early to late has been stratigraphy. This has been continuous rather than discontinuous stratigraphy and has effected a correlation between arbitrary depth in refuse deposits and cultural succession. . . . [E]ach of the culture periods . . . was first established upon the presence of certain pottery types and upon the percentage configuration of these types in particular stratigraphic depth context. By this it is meant that the simple presence of a pottery type is not always enough to denote a

specific period; its association with other types and its percentage relationships with these types in context were more often significant factors.

It will be seen from this that the culture periods, as they were first defined, were essentially ceramic periods. . . . The concept of the [pottery] type as used in this report follows procedures of definition which are current in the archeology of the southeastern United States. The function of a pottery type is as an historical tool. It is conceived as an abstraction based upon a specified range of constructional and artistic variables which are recognized in a group of pottery specimens. To be of value in the solution of historical problems each type must have a definable time and space position. (Willey 1949b:3–5)

Willey had used percentage stratigraphy in his earlier work in Florida—his report, "Archeology of the Florida Gulf Coast," was completed in 1945 (Willey 1949a)—and he used it again in his synthesis (Willey 1949b) to build his chronology of culture periods. There he not only aligned percentage-stratigraphy graphs from different excavation units into a site-wide chronological ordering (Willey 1949b:80–84), but also developed a regional chronology by correlating site-specific chronologies using bar graphs of type frequencies based on percentage stratigraphy (Willey 1949b:figure 14). The regional graph is virtually identical to Ford's graphs for the Virú Valley and the lower Mississippi Valley survey. Willey did not label his culture-period boundaries with capital letters, as was Ford's habit, but his periods appear to be precisely identical to Ford's arbitrary units. In his synthesis, Willey was not explicit about how he carved these periods out of the continuum, but in his other Florida monograph, he remarked that

The ceramic stratigraphy or indications of sequence observed . . . is of a continuous kind. Although identifiable physical strata were discernible in cross section of the midden, the field report and laboratory analysis of materials do not give any cultural correlations with physical changes in the appearance of the refuse. Cultural changes, as are implied in the distribution of the pottery types in the midden, seem to have been effected gradually. They are demonstrated by percentage shifts in pottery type frequencies from level to level. (Willey 1949a:62–63)

Willey (1949a:71) broke the sequence into two periods, distinguished by what he called "the sudden appearance" of one pottery type, the "dropping out" of other types, and the "diminished" frequencies of still other types. Examination of his data indicates that the sudden appearance of the new type was not as sudden as Willey's wording suggested, and thus we conclude that Willey used a method and criteria similar—but not identical—to Ford's for carving the temporal continuum into periods. This is somewhat surprising in that Willey would, a few years later, with Phillips, produce a major programmatic statement on culture-historical method (Phillips and Willey 1953). That statement retained little of the materialism evident in Willey (1949b) and had a much more essentialist tone.

Willey seems to have been an exception in agreeing with Ford theoretically and methodologically. Surprisingly, in his review of Willey's (1949b) synthesis of

Florida prehistory, Phillips (1951:108–9) found much to recommend "the method of combining two or more stratigraphic cuts on the same site in an interpolated se-riation," though obviously by the latter he meant percentage stratigraphy (Lyman et al. 1998). This was, of course, precisely what Ford (e.g., 1949, 1951a; Phillips et al. 1951) had done. But Phillips (1951:109) misunderstood the arbitrary nature of Willey's culture periods and indicated that "By 'period' is designated the familiar concept elsewhere more often termed 'phase' (Southwest and Middle America), 'focus' or 'aspect' (Eastern U.S.)—a definable unit of culture occupying a certain position in the space-time continuum." It is not at all clear in Willey's writings that this is what he meant. But herein no doubt resides the origins of Phillips's (1970) distaste for Ford's constant modification of the sequence of periods for the Southeast. Periods were, in Phillips's view, *not* arbitrary chunks of the time-space continuum; they were real cultural units that in some situations could be equated with phases, foci, and the like. As such, once they were recognized, they were immutable. Such an essentialist perspective forces one to speak of "change" in transformational terms, just as Phillips (e.g., 1970) did.

Griffin was another who disliked some of what Ford was doing, and apparently it was primarily he who was responsible for the publication in a separate monograph of a portion of Ford's research that grew out of the Lower Mississippi Valley Survey (Ford 1952a). That separate monograph would ultimately result in the initiation of one of the most heralded debates within the culture-history paradigm—a debate attributable in part to Ford's failure to maintain a distinction between the essentialist and materialist metaphysics. While Ford prior to 1952 might often have spoken metaphorically of prehistoric cultures, at other times he clearly viewed them as discoverable. For example, in a review of some archaeological work in Florida that had resulted in the distinction of two time periods (Goggin and Sommer 1949), Ford (1951b:118) observed that "the numerous traits shared by both [periods] suggest that these are time divisions of the same culture." Given his own approach to slicing up the time-space continuum, it is not surprising that Ford made no comment on the division of the continuum into two periods. What is surprising, given his unabashedly materialist approach to the continuum of culture and how to measure it, is that he indicated the two periods represented "the same *culture*." This indicates that yet again Ford had one wheel stuck in the essentialist sand. Shortly after Ford's review of Goggin and Sommers's work was published, he would get the entire vehicle stuck.

Recall our discussion in Chapter 4 of Ford's reference to types as more or less closely reflecting cultural norms. If Ford could not know or show that his types held such cultural implications—which he admitted but dismissed as irrelevant to his focus on time—then how could similarities of trait lists be construed as reflecting *a culture*, when those traits consisted of type designations? Simply put, they could not. Such failure to avoid the pitfall of the materialist-essentialist paradox ultimately led to a rather scathing review of Ford's work and the initiation of debates between him and an archaeologist who perceived this weakness.

CORRELATING AND EXPLAINING LOCAL CHRONOLOGIES

The monograph Ford (1952a) published as "Measurements of Some Prehistoric Design Developments in the Southeastern States" was begun as a section to be included in the Phillips et al. volume, but it was not published there because it "contained a number of errors, and the drawings were not so well done as is desirable"; new information was becoming available that needed to be incorporated; and "Griffin objected to the section as prepared in both detail and principle" (Ford 1952a:313). In the monograph's introduction, Ford (1952a:317) expressed general agreement with Walter Taylor's (1948) recently published polemic that archaeology should be more than the reconstruction of a detailed culture history. What Ford had in mind was making a contribution to "the developing science of culture," but he also noted, "This does not mean that such objectives as discovering chronological sequences and more complete and vivid historical reconstructions will be abandoned; rather these present aims will become necessary steps in the process of arriving at the new goal" (Ford 1952a:318). As he had stressed from the beginning of his career, Ford perceived chronological control of the archaeological record as a requisite first step to any other research endeavor.

Ford argued that the new goal of archaeology, as with anthropology, was *culturology,* the term Leslie White (1949:117) used to label "the science of culture." Archaeology, in Ford's view, had two roles in culturology: first, it should document the historical development of cultures, and second, it should "provide basic data for a closer examination of general principles, of causes, speed, inevitability, and quantitative aspects of culture change over long periods of time" (Ford 1952a:318). In the terms used by those who in the 1960s had a vision of what a "new" archaeology should look like, archaeological method should provide the time depth necessary to understand cultural processes and the general principles by which cultures operate and evolve. Thus, we agree (Lyman et al. 1997a) with Ford (1952a:318) that he was following the lead of his contemporaries (e.g., Caldwell 1959; Phillips and Willey 1953; Willey and Phillips 1955, 1958), but we also agree with him (Ford 1952a:318) that he was correct in implying his work was "slightly in advance of the majority."

Ford (1952a:318) characterized his study of pottery-design developments as consisting of two parts—a "conventional contribution [consisting of] an effort to align ceramic chronologies in adjacent geographical areas somewhat more accurately than has been done previously" and a less conventional contribution that he thought might reflect "possible future interests of archaeology." The first part was basically the same sort of approach to the archaeological record that he (e.g., Ford 1949; Phillips et al. 1951) had used in both the Virú Valley and the lower Mississippi Valley and that Willey (1949b) had used in Florida. Ford (1952a:319) acknowledged that his method of chronology building "may become unnecessary in a few years, when numerous dates are available from measurements of radioactive carbon." As it turns out, this was a surprisingly prophetic observation (e.g., Ford 1966, 1969). The second part was concerned with tracking changes in pottery and attempting "to trace evolving [pottery] strains through time and across space and measure them qualitatively and quantitatively" (Ford 1952a:319). The wording may sound familiar, but it actually revealed a marked departure from his earlier work. From his "culturological" point of view, Ford (1952a:319) perceived "the specific forms of ceramic variables [to be] controlled by the attitudes and ideas that were held by the makers of the vessels. These ideas, transmitted from individual to individual, are the cultural trait that is studied." Suddenly, and virtually without warning, all of his previous cautions that archaeological types might or might not reflect cultural norms or ideas were gone. His types—which themselves hadn't changed a bit in terms of name, description, or anything else—now apparently reflected those norms and ideas accurately and precisely. This might have been acceptable to some of his contemporaries, such as Irving Rouse, who since virtually the beginning of his career had suggested that archaeological types *might loosely* reflect cultural norms (e.g., Rouse 1939) but who never really pursued the matter analytically. The notion clearly was not acceptable to everyone.

Why would Ford change his tune? Or did he really? In reading Ford's writings to this point in his career, we gain the distinct impression that *culture* history was what he was ultimately after. From his start in the 1930s he had simply used pottery as the tool for measuring time and building a chronology of arbitrary culture—or, more correctly, ceramic—periods. This was a materialist's approach to the archaeological record. But once the chronology was worked out, then what? The braided-stream model of cultural evolution as well as the ceramic-continuum model derived from it (Figure 4.7) had served Ford well in allowing him to approach such issues as classifying pottery by using ideational units—albeit extensionally derived. That model also forced him to slice the cultural continuum into arbitrary chunks. But these were all merely analytical tools developed to ultimately allow the study of the history—the tempo and mode—of *cultural* development. Ford had known the basic chronology for the Southeast since 1935, merely refining it over the next fifteen years by slicing it into thinner and thinner pieces. By the early 1950s, it was time to get on with the more important issue—the actual writing of a culture history now that the chronology was sufficiently well known.

When we say that Ford virtually abandoned his earlier cautions that his types did not clearly reflect cultural norms, we emphasize the word "virtually" because there are, in fact, earlier hints that he was comfortable thinking his types in *some* instances reflected cultural norms sufficiently clearly to allow him to trace individual streams of ideas. For example, Ford (1935c:30) early on observed that the Marksville-period pottery from Peck Village was "decorated in practically an identical manner [to pottery] from mounds of the Hopewell Culture in southern Ohio. [Thus, it] seems fair to assume that there is cultural connection between these two areas." The form of that assumed cultural connection was postulated a few years later by Ford and Willey (1941) when they suggested that Hopewell had originated from a Marksville ancestor. Likewise, in a section of the Mississippi Valley survey monograph written by Ford, we read revealing statements such as, "The groups of ideas to whose products have been tagged such names as Mazique Incised did not spring up simultaneously all over the area. They moved from one part to another, and that took time. For example, the idea of red slipping on clay-tempered vessels (Larto Red Filmed) apparently was moving from south to north through the region, while cord-marking on clay tempered pots (Mulberry Creek Cord-Marked) was moving from northeast to south" (Phillips et al. 1951:229).

Although Ford acknowledged historical mechanisms such as innovation as a source of new phenomena, that particular mechanism was in his view more difficult to detect in the archaeological record than other mechanisms such as diffusion and migration, which could be tracked empirically over time and space based on typological similarities. Perhaps the discussions of these mechanisms within anthropology (e.g., Goldenweiser 1925; Kroeber 1931; Steward 1929; Wallis 1925, 1945) influenced Ford's thinking, but he had the annoying habit of seldom citing the literature that might have influenced his views. Whatever the case, it is clear that by the late 1940s and early 1950s, Ford was ready to do something a bit more anthropological than he had previously done.

Methods

Ford (1952a:320) believed that archaeological data generated over the previous fifteen years in the Southeast had finally made it possible "to study a long span of the history of a segment of culture over a fairly extensive geographic area. This segment of culture is ceramics." He focused on the region bordered by Tallahassee, Florida, in the southeast, the upper Neches River in eastern Texas in the west, the Mississippi River delta in the south, and northeastern Arkansas in the north (Figure 5.1). Basic chronological data from all areas in the region (e.g., Newell and Krieger [1949], east Texas; Phillips et al. [1951], northeastern Arkansas; Willey [1949b], Florida) were founded in stratigraphic excavation and percentage stratigraphy, supplemented by frequency seriation of surface collections. In using such purely chronological information to trace out the details of the braided stream of culture in the region, Ford (1952a:321) reiterated his view of culture history and the importance of types:

> Cultural material is constantly changing in all its aspects, and the ways in which temporally significant divisions can be made in ceramics, for example, based on changes in form, or surface finish, or decoration, size, or many other categories are limited only by our abilities to perceive differences. . . . [To be validly correlated, area-specific] typologies must be directed towards the solution of the same problems. Measurements of cultural influence become difficult if not impossible when one of the measuring devices, the type, is defined to include two or more of the streams of prehistoric cultural concepts that have been isolated in an adjacent region.

Here Ford was underscoring that variation in the construction of typologies could result in incomparable types. But he failed to make clear that incomparability could reside in two arenas. Types as ideational units could be *definitionally* different, and types as empirical, essentialist units could have various degrees of accuracy such that some of them would measure "cultural influence" less well than others. Thus Ford conflated the essentialist and materialist metaphysics. Because of his familiarity with the typological system he and others had developed and used in the Southeast, Ford indicated that Willey (1949b), whose data Ford used in his monograph, "was able to design the northwest coast of Florida classification system so that it not only controlled time change there but also measured the common cultural connections between that region, Georgia, and Louisiana" (Ford 1952a:321). In simplest terms, Ford was, without using the words, employing what Willey (1953a:363) would later refer to as an "axiom" of culture history—"typological similarity is [an] indicator of cultural relatedness"; as Willey (1953a:364) noted, this axiom held the implication of "a common or similar history" for archaeological units. Ford (e.g., 1938a) had, of course, subscribed to this axiom since the start of his career.

Why did typological similarity exist? For Ford it existed because the development of cultures in an area was conceptualized as a braided stream—a series of variously intermingling and diverging streams of ideas. Willey's "common history" between cultural lineages was reflected by their intersection and resultant exchange of ideas—Ford's "cultural influences." The mechanisms that resulted in such intersections were diffusion and migration. As Ford emphasized, on the one hand, organic evolution involved only branching (speciation); on the other hand, cultural evolution was reticulate—the lineages "grew back together as readily and frequently as they separated" (Ford 1952a:322). Such hybridization of cultural lineages was an "unhandy phenomenon [that was] as equally valid for a small segment of culture, such as ceramics, as for culture as a whole" (Ford 1952a:322). Thus, given this conceptualized structure of culture history, Ford (1952a:322) noted that he could not "pretend to measure and trace all of the streams of cultural influence that have left their mark on [the ceramics]. . . . It is impossible to follow all the branches [trickles of the braided stream] simultaneously, and consequently a selection must be made. Thus it cannot be pretended that an attempt to depict

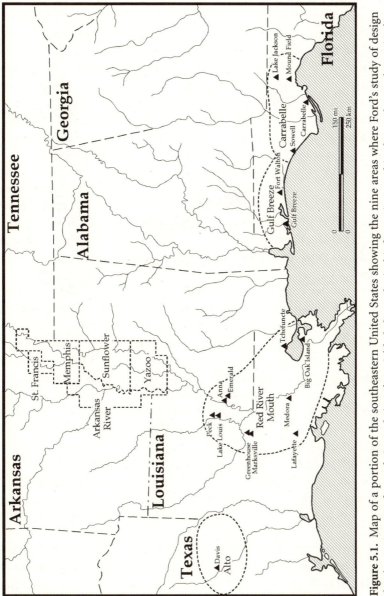

Figure 5.1. Map of a portion of the southeastern United States showing the nine areas where Ford's study of design developments was focused. Several sites that yielded chronological information used in the study are shown in the four southernmost areas. Too many sites contributed to the five area chronologies in Arkansas and Mississippi to be indicated at this scale (see Figure 4.5) (after Ford 1952a).

a history of ceramic development is anything more than a more or less successful attempt to follow some of the more prominent streams of ideas."

Ford's braided-stream conceptualization of culture change helps us to understand how he thought the archaeological record might be explained in anthropological terms—that is, by calling on ethnologically documented mechanisms such as diffusion and migration. But from an archaeological perspective, this leaves at least two questions unanswered. First, if formal similarity is the key to detecting the intersection of two streams of ideas, how similar is similar enough? How similar must two sherds be to be considered typologically the same? Ford played rather fast and loose with this question, probably because his type definitions were extensionally derived and because of his notion of the ceramic continuum. But the second question is perhaps even more important: how did Ford know that mere formal similarity—of whatever degree—was homologous similarity and not analogous similarity? Simply put, he didn't—not that he ever worried about it. This problem was never addressed satisfactorily by culture historians, despite it being pointed out about once every decade virtually since the beginning of the paradigm (e.g., Kroeber 1931a, 1943; Rouse 1955). Precisely this flaw in the paradigm was noted during the birth of processual archaeology in the 1960s (Binford 1968a:8).

Ford conceded some of the practical problems with what he sought to accomplish. For example, given that ceramic "history was a continuous flow of cultural ideas in the two coordinates of space and time, it is obvious that it cannot be clearly stated and that only a slightly better approximation can be achieved through pictorial representation" (Ford 1952a:322). That is, the continuity was graphed discontinuously. Thus, the continuous flow of the ceramic continuum illustrated in his graphs was shown by "small picture frames, which when coordinated constitute the full-length film, as it were," and therefore provided information on the fluid nature of the culture continuum in the form of "static abstractions" (Ford 1952a:322). Finally, as Ford had cautioned in his earlier writings (e.g., 1949; Phillips et al. 1951), the quantitative data concerning type frequencies surely was only approximately correct and did not "conform to the proportion of the different kinds of pottery made and used by the Indians" (Ford 1952a:322), yet this was of minimal concern to him, as he believed that any included errors would probably cancel each other out.

Interestingly, Ford (1952a:323) rather briefly indicated that the graphic method he would use was (a) founded on the study of type frequencies as established by Kroeber (1916a, 1916b) and Spier (1917); (b) derived from his own efforts directed toward developing similar methods since his efforts at Peck Village—characterized by him as a "slow and painful process of crystallization" (Ford 1952a:323); and (c) borrowed from the graphic style originally used by E. B. Sayles in his 1937 study of stone artifacts from the Hohokam site of Snaketown in Arizona. Ford (1952a:323) suggested that Sayles "may have adapted this graph style from paleontology," but Sayles did not reference any paleontologist as the source of inspiration for this form of graph or in any other context (Lyman et al. 1998).

The similarities between Sayles's style of graph and Ford's earlier graphs is less apparent to us than Ford's wording suggests. Sayles used what is clearly a form of phyletic seriation in some of his graphs (Lyman et al. 1998)—a technique not used by Ford since the surface-collection monograph (Ford 1936a). Ford's graphs were meant to show the changing frequencies of types through the time span represented, with a type's frequency denoted by the bars' width and time by its vertical position. In short, Ford's graphs were different, and they were complicated. This lack of simplification, combined with the visual smoothing by Ford of the type frequencies, would leave his graphs susceptible to criticism. Ford, unlike Sayles, included on several of his graphs (e.g., Figure 5.2) drawings of the types for which he plotted frequencies, stratigraphic data in the left column, and sample size data in the right column. Other graphs (Ford 1952a:figures 4, 5, and 7) consisted of bars denoting type frequencies, contained stratigraphic data in the left column, and carried the denotation of temporal periods along the right margin, as the graphs in his earlier work had (e.g., Ford 1949; Phillips et al. 1951). Several of Ford's graphs (Figure 5.3) were composites of multiple sites in multiple areas and were meant to show the basic chronological history of different pottery types in those areas. Such an arrangement allowed Ford to trace the history of the cultural streams he sought.

Ford correlated his areal chronologies just as he had correlated site-specific chronologies in the Virú Valley and in the lower Mississippi Valley survey: "[C]hronological graphs representing neighboring areas [were] laid side by side on a table. Then, bearing in mind that we have no absolute time control over either the entire span of each chronology or of its segments, the parts of the chronologies are shifted upward or downward, until the best agreement is achieved between the patterning formed by corresponding or closely related types" (Ford 1952a:328). There was, he admitted, a problem with such a procedure when dealing with such a large expanse of space: "it is not to be expected that temporally corresponding sections will resemble one another completely" (Ford 1952a:328). Why not? Simply put, "Cultural influences take time to move across geographical areas. . . . One certainty when comparing types in different regions is that they do not represent the same instant in time. This means that it is to be expected that identical types or types that have been defined on the basis of the same stream of cultural influence will shift their relative positions in the neighboring chronologies, depending on the direction in which they are moving" (Ford 1952a:329). This is the Doppler Effect, the archaeological significance of which was demonstrated a few years later by James Deetz and Edwin Dethlefsen (1965) and which still influences how archaeologists think and explain the time-space distribution of types (e.g., Beck 1995).

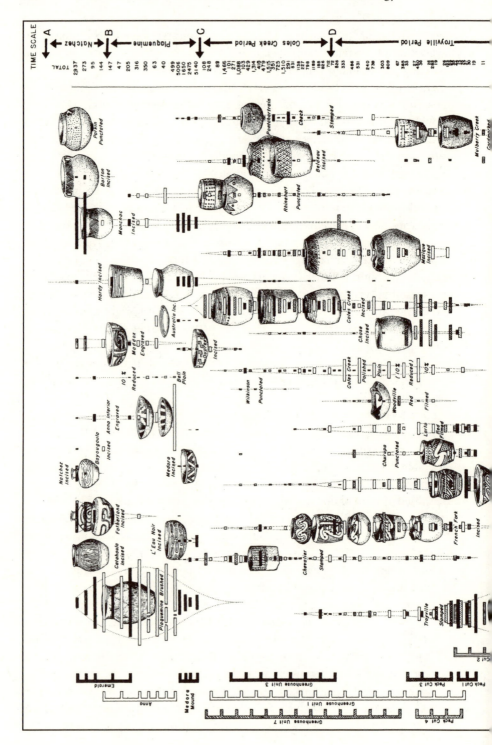

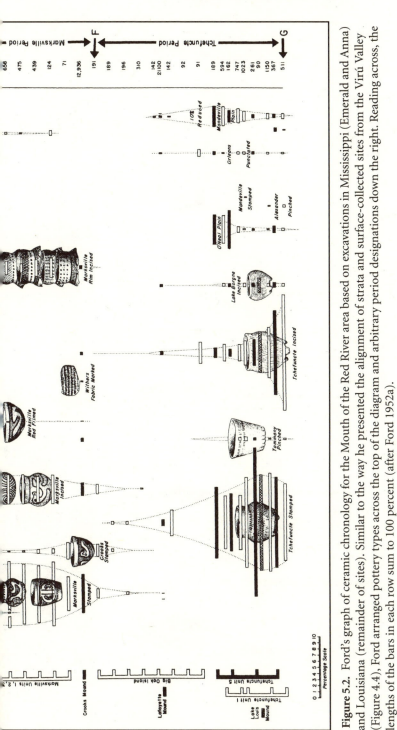

Figure 5.2. Ford's graph of ceramic chronology for the Mouth of the Red River area based on excavations in Mississippi (Emerald and Anna) and Louisiana (remainder of sites). Similar to the way he presented the alignment of strata and surface-collected sites from the Virú Valley (Figure 4.4), Ford arranged pottery types across the top of the diagram and arbitrary period designations down the right. Reading across, the lengths of the bars in each row sum to 100 percent (after Ford 1952a).

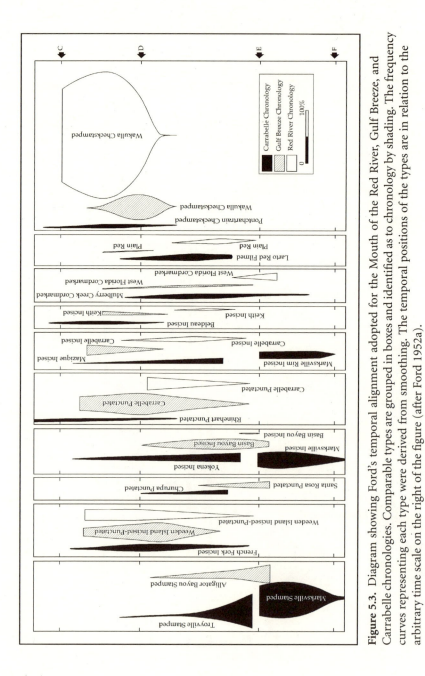

Figure 5.3. Diagram showing Ford's temporal alignment adopted for the Mouth of the Red River, Gulf Breeze, and Carrabelle chronologies. Comparable types are grouped in boxes and identified as to chronology by shading. The frequency curves representing each type were derived from smoothing. The temporal positions of the types are in relation to the arbitrary time scale on the right of the figure (after Ford 1952a).

Diffusion takes time, and given the chronological resolution available in his graphs, Ford believed that only slow, diffusion-related processes could be detected "with any confidence." He added, "This factor of time lag of similar types in adjacent areas makes it necessary to draw conclusions as to the direction of movement of influences when the columns [showing the relative frequencies of types] are being aligned" (Ford 1952a:329). To assist in making such inferences, Ford produced what we here reprint as Figure 5.4. On the basis of that figure, Ford (1952a:330) argued that the direction of diffusion could be determined in two ways. First, a "geographical frequency center" would emerge for each type (Ford 1952a:329), and he treated such centers as real in his discussion (e.g., Ford 1952a:360). Not only would each type have a single-peak frequency through time, it would have a single-peak frequency across space, occurring more frequently in its area of origin than in an area to which it had diffused. But Ford had minimal faith in the validity of this notion, probably because it presumed something about how completely a new idea would be accepted in an area, though he was not explicit on this point. He also failed to notice that the notion was fundamentally flawed because his types were extensionally defined units and as such were historical accidents, the nature of which depended on the materials examined. Although he did not mention it in the design-element monograph, the concept of typological "creep" played a role here, and thus Ford's idea was plagued by the question of how similar was similar enough. Centers emerged precisely where one first looked—a point recognized in the Phillips et al. study but apparently forgotten by Ford in his rush to do culturology.

The other way Ford determined the direction of diffusion—which he found to be more "reliable" than the first—called for a determination of the ancestry of a type. A type should have ancestral types (in a phyletic sense) in its area of origin—denoted by the A' and the B' in Figure 5.4. The recognition of such ancestral types rendered the "direction of diffusion . . . obvious" in Ford's view, but he did not elaborate on how one was to establish such direct lines of ancestor-descendant relations. We suppose it would involve what it did at Peck Village in 1935—stylistic similarity between superposed types that differed in only one or two of the multiple attributes considered. But the important point is that typological similarity for Ford was purely and simply of the homologous sort; the potential for types to be analogously similar was not mentioned. He was perhaps correct in this unremarked assumption, given that he was largely concerned with decorative elements, but such an assumption would undergo some scrutiny a few years later (e.g., Rands 1961; Rands and Riley 1958).

Ford recognized that the use of different quantitative units by different researchers would hinder his analysis of the frequency history of types. For example, tallying the number of sherds in a collection provided a set of frequencies that could not legitimately be compared with values for the number of vessels represented

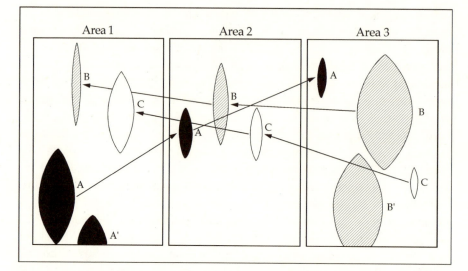

Figure 5.4. Diagram illustrating Ford's conception of quantitative change and time lag in diffusion—phenomena that he believed must be considered in making temporal alignments of relative chronologies (after Ford 1952a).

by the sherds in a collection. Similar problems exist in archaeology today (e.g., Grayson 1984; Lyman 1994), even in the analysis of pottery (e.g., Orton 1975). Ford (1952a:338–40) spent some time reworking the data from the Davis site in the Caddoan area of eastern Texas presented by Perry Newell and Alex Krieger (1949). This displayed his awareness of some of the practical issues of doing archaeological research, and although he correctly recognized that his procedure of reworking the data did *not* "affect the relative frequencies of the types in the different levels and other proveniences of the Davis Site," he erroneously believed that a "beneficial effect of this procedure is to make possible direct comparison of the rate of type frequency change in the Davis Site evidence with that of the other Southeastern chronologies" (Ford 1952a:338–39). This belief could not be correct because regardless of whether sherds or vessels were tallied, Ford's arrangements of type frequencies were merely *relative* dating tools. Thus the tempo of change could not be determined, though such a belief permeated Ford's other work, such as his analysis of the Virú Valley collections.

Finally, Ford (1952a:331) correlated the various chronologies by "focusing attention on the patterning formed by type maximums and by placing less weight on the apparent starting and stopping points of type occurrences." Recall that he sometimes drew the boundaries of his temporal periods through the peak of a type's occurrence (Phillips et al. 1951) and that he also referred to ceramic collections as providing a "mean ceramic date" (e.g., Ford 1949). Why? It is never explicit in his earlier writings why he did this, but in 1952 he made it clear. In a brief paragraph, Ford (1952a:344) noted he had long recognized that it was obvious that the end points in the temporal range of a given type might be obscured by various processes such as mechanical mixing of types in a vertical column of sediments and that seriating mixed surface collections might produce a too-long temporal range for a type. And recall, too, that Ford was very aware of the problems with small samples. In short, given these problems, the actual end points of a type's distribution in time and space were obscure. Thus, in 1952 Ford noted, "For these reasons, it seems best to place more weight on the temporal position of the type maximum than on the apparent vertical position of its initial [or final] appearance" (Ford 1952a:344). The type maximum was likely to provide the best approximation of perhaps the type's modal age rather than of its mean age as a result of sample sizes, mixing, and other processes that influenced the apparent positions of the end points of the type's temporal range.

If Phillips had recognized this in 1970, perhaps he would have had less to say about how Ford carved up the temporal continuum. But in coming to recognize why Ford spoke of mean ceramic dates and why he focused on peaks of popularity for identifying where he would slice the temporal continuum, we also have come to see that to understand Jim Ford and the conclusions he reached, one must read *everything* he wrote, for in no one article or monograph does he spell out his entire analytical program. His initial programmatic statement (Ford 1936b) is too short, and his knowledge at that time too superficial, for this paper to be of much use in figuring out his thoughts sixteen years later. His later writings provide only bits and pieces of his overall logic, and perhaps this is why his work in methods is typically characterized as "seriation," because he spoke of it as such, even though almost all of it technically was percentage stratigraphy instead. Perhaps this is also why his work in the design-elements monograph (Ford 1952a) was so open to criticism; to accurately evaluate and fairly review his analytical results, you had to have read more of Ford's work than just the monograph.

Results

Constructing the areal ceramic chronologies for the Southeast was the easy part. They were largely founded on percentage stratigraphy—an important point apparently missed by one reviewer of the monograph (Spaulding 1953a). Ford smoothed the resulting bar graphs by eye for the same reasons he had smoothed the Virú Valley and Mississippi Valley collections: accidents of sampling, variation in pottery fragmentation, and other uncontrollable factors made the frequency distributions fluctuate and diverge from perfect unimodality. That the frequency distributions were nonetheless chronological was clear from the superpositional relations of the arranged collections. The visual smoothing served to show how

Ford thought the curves would appear—that is, they would reflect the "popularity" history of each type—were it not for the various factors that caused the observed frequency curves to fluctuate. Ford then correlated the various areal chronologies, explicitly acknowledging (Ford 1952a:343) that the final arrangement was probably not exactly correct but that there were probably no "major errors," and begging the reader's acceptance of the arrangement for purposes of discussion. He had made the same pleas in the Virú Valley and Mississippi Valley monographs.

Once the areal chronologies were worked out and correlated, Ford (1952a:343) chose to examine the history of "eight ceramic decorative traditions," each representing a "selected stream of ideas across space [that had developed] through time." These historical streams were extracted from the chronological charts and graphed in a series of fourteen illustrations (Ford 1952a:figures 8–21) (Figure 5.5) that showed the classic " 'battleship' frequency curves" (Ford 1952a:344) for which Ford was now well known, the arbitrary time scale denoted by capital letters he had first used in 1935 and 1936, drawings of examples of each decorative type, and the spatial positions of the decorative types. Ford then devoted twenty-seven pages of text to discussing the decorative traditions. In those pages, he detailed the formal, spatial, and temporal dimensions occupied by each tradition, noting such things as where a particular *expression* of a type first appeared, where it next appeared and in what relative frequency, if it appeared in the same form and if not how it differed from the original, and so on. The heart of the matter was what the graphs meant in terms of the history of particular idea streams—this was the new part of his analysis that was "slightly in advance of the majority" (Ford 1952a:318).

It would take us as many words as it did Ford to describe the particulars of what he thought his graphs meant, and we would still need to reproduce all of his figures to clarify the description. What is perhaps more worthy of our attention here is Ford's wording to explain the appearance of his figures. In discussing the distributions of the design elements in each of the eight ceramic traditions, Ford (1952a) spoke of one design type leaving "no direct descendants" (347), of one design type evolving from another (350), and of particular design types and elements displaying "close kinship" to one another (355). In other words, formally similar types were phylogenetically related—that is, their similarity was homologous. This is precisely the way Colton and Hargrave (1937) had explained the apparent history of southwestern pottery fifteen years earlier—a procedure Ford (1938a, 1940) had viewed with apparent favor. What made Ford's wording different was his explicit referral to the braided stream of cultural ideas as a warrant for his interpretations; Colton (a biologist by training) and Hargrave (a quite knowledgeable avocational biologist) had used no such commonsense warrant in their discussion and instead spoke of pottery types as if they were species of organisms with various ancestral-descendant and collateral relationships, leading

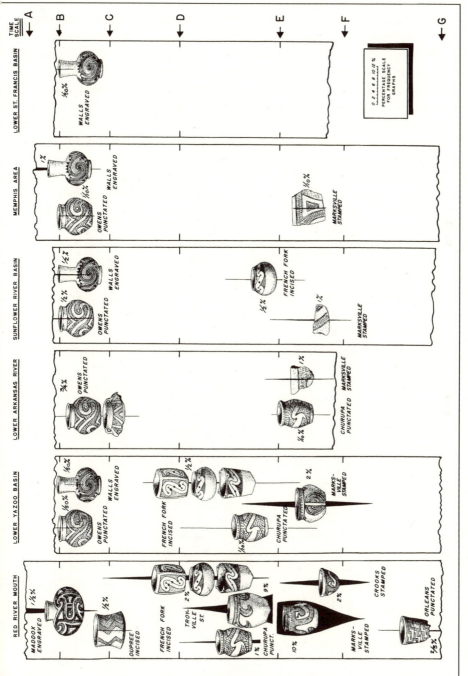

Figure 5.5. South-to-north profile showing Ford's reconstruction of the history of decorations featuring contrasting roughened and smoothed vessel surface (after Ford 1952a).

Brew (1946) and others to discard their procedure on the grounds that pots don't interbreed and exchange genes.

Given Ford's braided-stream-of-ideas model, the mechanisms by which the manifestations of those ideas—the actual sherds—came to have the distributions they did were obvious: diffusion and migration, processes that were ethnologically and historically visible mechanisms of idea movement. Of course, to employ such mechanisms as explanatory devices demanded that his design elements and ceramic types accurately reflect cultural *ideas* or norms. Ford had argued for years that this was unlikely because his types were arbitrary chunks of the ceramic continuum. No wonder his explanatory efforts received some rather devastating criticism. But it is important to note that some culture historians (e.g., Rouse 1954) found his substantive results and his methods of producing them to be acceptable. Others who disliked or disagreed with the particulars of some of the substantive results had less to say about how Ford did his analysis than about how he chose to interpret various aspects of the data. One of these was Krieger (1952), whose main complaint was that Ford placed Krieger's Alto-focus material from east Texas late in time, whereas he (Newell and Krieger 1949) placed it early in the Caddoan developmental sequence. Ford's notion was that the Texas pottery looked like the Plaquemine-period pottery from southern Louisiana, so it must date in the same range—a classic case of suspected homologous similarities being used to reconstruct phylogeny.

Several years earlier, Ford had become aware of the discrepancy between his chronology and Krieger's, and in a letter to Quimby in 1949 he warned him to hold up submittal of his paper on the Plaquemine "culture phase" until Krieger's monograph (Newell and Krieger 1949) was published:

> When I read his previous paper and the Mss. of this one I was impressed with his arguments [on the temporal positions of types in the lower Mississippi Valley and in the Caddoan area], but since I have started working on [Greenhouse] have begun to accumulate some doubts. In his latest paper he wants to place Alto equal in time with Marksville which makes it necessary that nicely polished pottery like his *Holly Fine Engraved* be confined to the NE Texas–NW La. area for a long period of time. The polishing trait reached the mouth of Red River later as Coles Creek Pol[ished] Pl[ain] but engraving [didn't arrive] until even later in Plaquemine.
>
> Take a look at his [decorated types] and compare them to your Plaquemine types. If my memory serves me correctly there is considerable resemblance—so much so that it seems probable that somebody is wrong. [Either] Plaquemine is earlier than we have supposed in our relative chronology (which seems impossible!); [Krieger's] Alto Focus is considerably later than he thinks it is both relatively and actually;—or the La. chronology about the mouth of Red River covers a lot more time than we have thought and Alto (and Plaquemine) date from 500 A.D. That is hard to take also.[1]

1. Letter of March 21, 1949, from Ford to Quimby (LSU Museum of Natural Science archives).

As radiocarbon dating eventually showed, the Alto focus *was* a lot later than Krieger thought; any resemblance between decoration on Caddoan pottery and Marksville pottery was entirely fortuitous.

Despite the criticism leveled at Ford, almost no one explicitly noted that given Ford's apparent desire to determine the history of particular streams of cultural ideas, he had failed to use units—types—that ensured he was measuring such streams. There was, however, one individual, Albert Spaulding, who did note this problem. That only *one* person observed this reflects the characteristically commonsense culture-history approach to the archaeological record (Lyman et al. 1997a)—virtually *all* archaeologists, including Ford, figured their types more or less loosely reflected cultural norms or ideas.

THE FORD-SPAULDING DEBATES

The literature generated as a direct result of Ford's (1952a) monograph includes a number of items, and without a reference guide, the situation becomes confusing. The chronology of the writing and publishing of those pieces is summarized in Table 5.1. A quick look at the table shows how difficult it would be to review the items in strict chronological order, and thus we adopted an easier approach. We begin by considering Spaulding's review of Ford (Spaulding 1953a), followed by a discussion of Ford's (1954b) response and Spaulding's (1954a) reply. Then, we turn to the crux of Spaulding's review: what, exactly, is a type? The often heated exchanges became known as the Ford-Spaulding debate (e.g., Thompson 1972:36), though it actually was a series of debates. A few other individuals also jumped into the fray (e.g., Evans 1954; Steward 1954). Few histories of Americanist archaeology have explored the roots of the debates, although they arguably were some of the most important ever to have taken place in the field. The debates illuminate rather succinctly—if not as lucidly as one might hope—the materialist-essentialist paradox (Lyman et al. 1997a).

On the Measurement of Design Developments

Spaulding was not impressed with Ford's efforts in the design-element monograph. In Spaulding's (1953a:589) view, Ford's measurements consisted of "counting and ranking" of pottery types, which was neither measurement nor scientific. Thus, while apparently agreeing with the assumption underpinning Ford's criterion for sorting collections—"that two assemblages which resemble each other closely are not far removed in time" (Spaulding 1953a:589)—Spaulding (1953a:590) found Ford's sole use of "graphical methods" lacking in methodological rigor and sophistication, and thus highly questionable. Ford, in Spaulding's (1953a:590–91) words, could "only assert that his final ordering is the best possible under the circumstances and reproduce the graphs to substantiate the assertion.

Table 5.1 References Relevant to the Ford–Spaulding Debate

Reference	Date of Completion	Date of Publication or Circulation
Design Elements		
Ford 1952a	August 1951	February 1953 [a]
Spaulding 1953a	?	October 1953
Ford 1954b	?	February 1954
Spaulding 1954a	?	February 1954
What is a type?		
Spaulding 1953b	August 1952	April 1953
Ford 1954a	May 1953	April 1954
Spaulding 1954b	November 1953	April 1954
Ford 1954c	?	February 1954

[a]This date denotes when the University of Missouri–Columbia library received a copy of the monograph.

The absence of any mathematical expression of degree of fit leaves the skeptical reader with no recourse other than reproducing the component histograms and trying new arrangements himself, a task which is made difficult by the absence of the original counts on which the percentages were calculated." Thus, Ford's visual smoothing of curves seemed to represent a "bloody amputation" (Spaulding 1953a:591). That Ford's graphs of sorted collections were founded in percentage stratigraphy and *not* in seriation escaped Spaulding's notice; it also apparently escaped Ford's notice because he failed to make this point in his response (Ford 1954b), though he did indicate why he thought such visual smoothing was appropriate (see also Ford 1949; Phillips et al. 1951). Spaulding might have been reacting to the manner in which Ford correlated his various areal chronologies— that is, how he stacked them up against one another. That *did* have the appearance of capriciousness, given that the chronologies were all *relative* ones rather than absolute ones. Spaulding did not make this clear.

In his response to Spaulding's review, Ford (1954b:110) noted that "measurements" was not his wording but rather that of the editors. In typical Fordian style, he said that he wanted to entitle the monograph "Through the Prehistoric Southeast with Slide Rule and Ink Pot" but that the editorial staff at the American Museum wouldn't let him. While conceding he perhaps should have used a mathematical means of ordering the data in some of his analysis—he referred specifically to the Brainerd-Robinson technique—he argued that technique was unnecessary "to demonstrate what appears to be obvious by inspection" (Ford 1954b:110), "cannot take into account areal variation in type frequencies" (Ford 1954b:110), and produced coefficients that do "not distinguish between frequency agreements that are to be found at either end of the time span of a type" (Ford 1954b:111). The first point underscored Ford's lack of methodological sophistication; to him, such sophistication was unnecessary because the solution was obvious. Here we suspect the obviousness resided in the battleship-shaped curves reflecting a type's popularity; otherwise, Ford would have mentioned that the curves were founded largely on percentage stratigraphy. The second point identifies Ford's misunderstanding of the Brainerd-Robinson technique; the *analyst* selects the assemblages to be sorted regardless of whether those assemblages are sorted visually or, as in the Brainerd-Robinson technique, with coefficients of similarity. The third point indicates that Ford did not understand that a Brainerd-Robinson coefficient measures the *total* similarity of two assemblages based on the complement of the sum of the differences between relative frequencies of *multiple* types. The probability of finding his dreaded "frequency agreements" at either end of the duration of a type is so minute as to be considered nonexistent.

In his reply to Ford's (1954b) response, Spaulding (1954a:113) reiterated that "Ford simply does not know what the word 'measurement' denotes." He continued, noting that "in scientific usage it . . . definitely does not include ranking [read *sorting* or *seriating*]" (Spaulding 1954a:113). Thus, Spaulding, using "ranking" as a synonym for sorting or seriating, was pointing out that although Ford's arrangement provided some form of ranked (against time?) order of collections, it did not "measure" anything. To Spaulding (1954a:113), "In ordinary usage [measurement] refers to comparison with a scale subdivided into equal units of specified size, and in scientific usage it has a considerably more technical meaning which definitely does not include ranking." Thus, what today would be termed ordinal scales of measurement were not, in Spaulding's view, *scientific* scales of measurement.

Spaulding (1954a:113) also argued that "time relationships were in large part inferred by means of relative frequencies of ceramic types [but] trait [read *type*] counts and locus, not time, were the empirical data of the study. [Thus a] general murkiness of exposition, of which the infelicitous use of measurement is an example, is a persistent stumbling block in understanding the arguments advanced" by Ford (1952a). This very complex statement is *the* key to the Ford-Spaulding debate. Spaulding was suggesting that one cannot measure geographic distance with units such as years, that one cannot measure time with units such as kilometers, and that one cannot measure cultural ideas with *arbitrary* units called types (see also Spaulding 1957, 1960). Thus, Spaulding was questioning the *warrant* for the inference that Ford's arrangements of type frequencies in time and space measured the temporal flow of streams of cultural ideas. Ford (1954b:110) indeed had no theoretical warrant for such an inference and could only suggest that Spaulding's criticism was founded on "a lack of familiarity with certain characteristics of the *mechanics of cultural development and diffusion* which were used as basic assumptions" (emphasis added). Such commonsensical warrants— the popularity principle in this case—of course characterized the weaknesses of the culture-history paradigm in general, and, in conjunction with his model of culture change as a braided stream, of Ford's interpretations of the results of his graphs in particular. The question that immediately comes to mind is whether Spaulding could provide a stronger warrant.

Prelude to Essentialist Artifact Classification

Until the early 1950s, most archaeologists were content to worry about the chronological placement of the types they constructed. These units *might* reflect cultural norms or customs, as Ford (1938a), Rouse (1939), Krieger (1944), and Phillips et al. (1951) indicated, but such suspicions were merely commonsensical rationalizations for the units. They were not empirically testable save in a tautological manner, such as in Brainerd's (1951a) rendition that the popularity of norms produced normal frequency distributions of types through time, and thus empirical manifestations of such frequency distributions denoted that the seriated types reflected norms or customs. Nonetheless, lacking theory, the commonsense understanding that types were somehow "real"—read "emic"—units grew stronger. In 1953, Spaulding published a paper describing a technique for discovering "real" types (Spaulding 1953b). Ford (1954a) responded, Spaulding (1954b) replied in kind, and Ford (1954c) finally produced a more programmatic statement concerning his views of classification. It is necessary to digress yet again to bring this portion of the Ford-Spaulding debates into sharp focus. To do that, we must understand Spaulding, and to understand Spaulding, we need to sketch the epistemology of someone who had a significant influence on him.

George W. Brainerd

At the same time that Ford (1949, 1951a, 1952a) was perfecting his graphical technique for measuring the passage of time, attempts were being made to render the technique of ordering more "objective" (Brainerd 1951a:303). Early attempts to use statistical techniques of ordering focused on a select few of the numerous historical types, or known index fossils (e.g., Beals et al. 1945:166–67). How could all the data be considered simultaneously? With the help of statistician W. S.

Robinson (1951), Brainerd (1951a)—who had been involved in the Rainbow Bridge–Monument Valley project in Utah—developed a mathematical technique for measuring the *similarity* of pairs of assemblages: "[C]ollections with closest similarity in qualitative or quantitative listing of types lie next to each other in the time sequence" because of the "concept that each type originates at a given time at a given place, is made in gradually increasing numbers as time goes on, then decreases in popularity until it becomes forgotten, never to recur in identical form" (Brainerd 1951a:304).

The rationalization for arranging collections based on their similarity was the typical one of *popularity*. What was new was the explicit statement that similarity was measurable in quantitative terms. As Robinson (1951:293–94) put it, "similarity of percentages of different types of pottery in use is evidence that the deposits are close together in time, and dissimilarity of percentages is evidence that the deposits are far separated in time." The mathematical "indexes of agreement" (Robinson 1951:294) that result from the quantitative measurement of similarity are known as "Brainerd-Robinson coefficients."

In his discussion, Brainerd (1951a:302) echoed Ford's statement regarding the importance of sound chronologies to writing culture history and reconstructing cultures. Brainerd (1951a:302–3) indicated—correctly, in our view—that typologies need not be functionally oriented if one seeks to measure the temporal dimension with artifact form, and he implied that such "cultural interpretation" of artifacts as provided by functional typologies might weaken the validity of any chronological implications derived from such typologies. But Brainerd originally rationalized types using common sense: "Each [type] must be of such complexity in number and organization of attributes that the presence of an artifact belonging to it suggests that its makers lived in the same cultural milieu as that of makers of all other artifacts classified into the same sorting group; thus all artifacts classified from one group must have been made at approximately the same time and place" (Brainerd 1951a:304). In other words, types, to Brainerd, reflected "cultural standards" if they were marked by the presence of a "constant combination of [complex] attributes" (Brainerd 1951a:305). This constant recurrence of attribute combinations was to become the cornerstone of Spaulding's (1953b) "emic type" two years later. Brainerd conflated the typical extensional definition of types with the empirical, essentialist meaning: the archaeological utility of types was to be evaluated on the basis of their "sensitivity and reliability" for distinguishing temporal-spatial differences, with "sensitivity" depending on "the judgment of the typologist" (Brainerd 1951a:303). He would elaborate this rationalization a few months later (Brainerd 1951b).

Fordian types—that is, ones constructed for purposes of culture history—were theoretical units initially formed extensionally by trial and error, and tested to ensure that they measured time. With no theoretical foundation, such types had an arbitrary appearance—admitted by Ford and others—and certainly had no clear sociobehavioral meaning. This was, to some, an unsatisfactory state of affairs. Spaulding (1953b) formalized the growing dissatisfaction by providing an explicit alternative. In his early writings on typological nomenclature, Spaulding (e.g., 1948a, 1948b) never mentioned how type units might be constructed, but he hinted at what he desired. He wanted a classification technique that omitted the problem of transitional assemblages and "expressed at one stroke the classifier's opinion of the cultural relationship and the chronological position of an assemblage," as such a technique would allow "a combined presentation of [the] independent units of chronological position and cultural affinity in either narrative or chart form" (Spaulding 1949:5).

The form of the classification technique was apparently unclear to Spaulding in 1949–1950, but it was identified for him in 1951 at a conference on archaeological method sponsored by the Viking Fund and held at Spaulding's home institution, the University of Michigan. Spaulding (1951) presented a paper at the meeting, which indicates he was in attendance. Brainerd also presented a paper, published as "The Use of Mathematical Formulations in Archaeological Analysis" (Brainerd 1951b). Brainerd had just published his landmark paper (Brainerd 1951a) on objectifying the sorting procedures of the seriation technique—a paper with which Spaulding (1953a, 1954a) clearly became very familiar (Spaulding did not cite it in his review of Ford [1952a], but we suspect he had it in mind in that review). In his seldom-cited "Mathematical Formulations" paper, Brainerd made two important points. First, he indicated that "Archaeological taxonomy [read "typology"] is in itself a generalizing procedure which ultimately depends for its validity upon the archaeologist's success in *isolating the effects of culturally conditioned behavior* from the examination of human products" (Brainerd 1951b:117; emphasis added). His second point is extremely important, and thus we quote it in full:

> The first step of procedure in artifact analysis is usually the formulation of types, groups of artifacts, each of which shows a combination of similar or identical attributes or traits. . . . If [the observation quoted above] is acceptable, the systematics used must have cultural validity in that they must mirror the culturally established requirements met by the artisans. In his search for these tenets of the unknown group it behooves the archaeologist as a scientist to work objectively, free of a priori conceptions. The attributes used in sorting artifacts into types should thus be *objectively chosen as those which occur most often in combination in single artifacts.* Criteria based upon subdivisions of an attribute which occurs in a continuous range through the material are preferably used only when the distribution curve of the attribute in the archaeological samples shows binodality, and *the dividing line for sorting should be drawn between the nodes.* By use of the above requirements for type attributes, the archaeologist can *objectively describe the cultural specifications followed by the artisans. Statistical procedures for the formulation of, and sorting of specimens into, types satisfying these requirements are feasible,* and may in some cases be useful. It seems conceivable

also that mathematical studies of attribute combinations may demonstrate more finely cut cultural differentiation without the use of the intermediate concept of types, for types are, after all, simplifications to allow qualitative division of the material into few enough categories to permit inspectional techniques of analysis. (Brainerd 1951b:118–19; emphasis added)

Brainerd (1951b:122) argued that his suggested use of mathematical and/or statistical techniques would eliminate one of the problems with the Midwestern Taxonomic Method noted by Spaulding (1949)—that of transitional collections. Brainerd (1951b:123) also indicated his suggested techniques would eliminate the problem of existing typologies falling "far short of full utilization of archaeological materials for the recovery of information on culture." In short, "In such analyses, it is conceivable that a bridge may be found uniting the objectivity of the taxonomist to the cultural sensitivity of the humanist. Cultural intangibles can, if they exist, be made tangible. *Better technique is the solution*" (Brainerd 1951b:124; emphasis added). Thus, the other problem identified by Spaulding (1949) of getting at culture and cultural relations via the study of artifacts could be eliminated by better technique: statistics. Pretty heady stuff, this, if your name was Albert Spaulding. Here, in one package, was the solution to the two problems he had identified in 1949.

Spaulding-esque Types

Spaulding's "Statistical Techniques for the Discovery of Artifact Types" (1953b) addressed both problems. His statistical approach to constructing types provided a warrant for rendering sociobehavioral meaning from types, and it eliminated the problem of transitional collections. Further, his statistical technique appeared to eliminate the trial and error and arbitrariness of the Fordian approach. Finally, his definition of a type as "a group of artifacts exhibiting a consistent assemblage of attributes whose combined properties give a characteristic pattern" (Spaulding 1953b:305) was compatible with earlier definitions, including Ford's (e.g., 1938a), because of the recurrence of attribute combinations, and thus no one argued this point—including Ford (1954c). The important difference was that for Spaulding, recurrence was *empirically* (statistically) determined; for Ford, recurrence was definitional, or ideational.

The key issue to Spaulding was the apparent arbitrary and capricious nature of Fordian types: empirical generalizations expressed in commonsense terms were needed to explain the time-space distributions of Ford's types. Fordian types were extensionally defined recurrent combinations of attributes with limited temporal and spatial distributions and thus were theoretical units that, upon (deductive) testing and refinement, measured time. Those types might or might not have cultural significance. Spaulding's types, however, were of an entirely different sort. To Spaulding, following Brainerd (1951b), types were real and inherent in the specimens; in other words, they were essentialist, empirical units. Hence, "Classification into types is a process of *discovery* of combinations of attributes *favored by the makers* of the artifacts, not an arbitrary procedure of the classifier" (Spaulding 1953b:305; emphasis added). Because types are inherent in the data, they can and must be discovered, and inductive statistical techniques, as suggested by Brainerd (1951b), provided the objective means of discovering which attributes regularly—that is, more often than random chance would allow—co-occur on specimen after specimen. To Spaulding, who, like his contemporaries, viewed artifacts as products of human behaviors, the discovery of recurring attribute combinations denoted *the discovery of human behavior concerning which attributes should be combined to produce a normal, or favored, specimen.* Spaulding's technique was designed to receive input only from the specimens themselves, and thus it, like Brainerd's (1951b), left unresolved the issue of attribute choice.

Because Spaulding's units were empirical, they had time-space locations—that is, they occurred in single components. Application of his method was restricted to one assemblage—a time- and space-bound unit—at a time. This eliminated the problem of transitional assemblages. Fordian types, on the other hand, were theoretical, and thus had measurable distributions in time and space and could be found in more than one component at a time. Transitional collections were a predictable result only if one believed that types of artifacts or larger units such as foci or phases were somehow real, which was a belief held by many, including Spaulding. Ford's orientation was narrow—types were analytical tools that the archaeologist constructed in such a manner as to permit chronological ordering of assemblages—but his attempts to explain culture history in terms of the model of culture development to which he subscribed were "badly muddled by a conflation [of] the definitional and interpretive meanings attached to type[s] and by frequent recourse to intuitive rationales necessitated by the lack of any truly theoretical justification for the culture-historical position" (Dunnell 1986b:172). That is, Ford never clearly distinguished between his theoretical units and his interpretations of them *as* empirical units. His theoretical types were definitional and thus immutable; their empirical frequency distributions characterized culture change. That they might have sociobehavioral meaning was not at all clear, and this was, in Spaulding's view, the fatal flaw in Ford's (1952a) interpretations of the time-space distributions of pottery decorations.

Ford (1954a) protested that Spaulding's approach was "amazingly naive" because it only suggested cultural norms; it did not help write culture history. Such a protest was predictable, given both Ford's model of the ceramic continuum (Figure 4.7) and the fact that Spaulding's units could have only locations rather than distributions. In other words, since they were not ideational units, they could do little analytical work. In his response to Ford's protestation, Spaulding (1954b:393) noted that Ford had not "challenged the validity of the techniques

[Spaulding] used to discover [attribute] clusters" and underscored the procedural murkiness in Ford's constructions of "attribute combinations." Spaulding's (1954b:392) "attribute clusters" were proclaimed by him to be "functional types" in the sense that because they "include inferences as to the behavior of the makers of the artifacts," they are "culturally meaningful" in an emic sense. Thus the debate was about not only the meaning of types but also their utility as tools for performing analytical work. That Ford's units were useful devices for measuring time and space was clear; what could Spaulding's types do?

Faced with the question of the utility of his units and the lack of a nontautological test of their interpretive meaning, Spaulding was forced to turn to his method as justification, much as had been implied by Brainerd's (1951b) suggested use of the division of types by identifying "nodes" or, more correctly, statistical modes, and drawing a line between them. The legitimacy of the claim that discovered attribute combinations reflected human behavior and thus were culturally meaningful had to come from the method used to detect them—the statistically significant patterning of the attribute combinations—as there was no other place from which it could come. Such combinations were clusters of attributes that reflected "the cultural specifications followed by the artisans" for Brainerd (1951b:118) and a "social behavior pattern" for Spaulding. Their types must therefore have a restricted distribution in time and space (Spaulding 1954b:392); their utility resided only in the fact that they allegedly held sociobehavioral meaning and accurately reflected cultural norms. The warrant for such presumed human-behavioral meaning was that the artifacts existed as human creations and that they were sortable into recognizable (discoverable, empirical, essentialist) sets; thus, they *must be* real. They could, however, do no analytical work for culture-historical interests in the way that Ford's seriable types could. In Ford's view, that was only part of the problem.

Defending Fordian Types

Ford's "On the Concept of Types: The Type Concept Revisited" (1954c) was published as a direct result of the debate with Spaulding and was written not only to refute Spaulding's claims but also to clarify his own position on types. On the first page, Ford expressed doubt that Spaulding's (1953b) statistical method would allow the discovery of a "cultural type" because such types simply were shorthand devices for both anthropologists and the makers of artifacts. The heart of Ford's discussion focused on the fictitious Gamma-gamma people who occupied the Island of Gamma, and on the types of houses they constructed. Ford's discussion of Gamma-gamma architecture clearly reflected the Phillips et al. (1951) ceramic-continuum model (Figure 4.7) as well as his model of culture as a braided stream. With regard to the former, Ford's (1954c:46) figure 1, reproduced here in Figure 5.6 (left), was merely the end of one of the cylinders of the continuum model and showed the variation contained within the circle; his figure 2, also reproduced here in Figure 5.6 (right), was a slice through the continuum showing the ends of several cylinders. Ford referred to the "fluid process" of cultural change, to "streams of thought," and to "one stream of cultural development [being] replaced by another" (Ford 1954c:51). Although it is relatively easy to see that Ford's thinking regarding types was the same in 1954 as in the late 1930s—culture and its manifestations are always changing, and archaeologists merely slice arbitrary chunks out of that continuum—his discussion of the type concept as used by culture historians was not very convincing because of his use of an ethnographic example.

Cultural, or emic, types certainly exist, Ford thought, as the houses on the Island of Gamma and on nearby islands indicated. But what Ford (1954c:52) wanted were "type groupings consciously selected [by an archaeologist to produce] a workable typology. . . . designed for the reconstruction of culture history in time and space." Unfortunately, just as Spaulding might have predicted, Ford never specified how such groupings were to be extracted from the flowing, bubbling conglomeration of his constantly changing braided cultural stream. In particular, he never spelled out what a type "designed for the reconstruction of culture history in time and

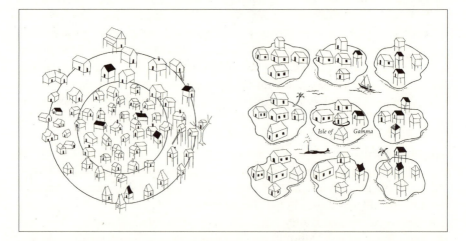

Figure 5.6. Diagrams representing Ford's conception of types (left) and spatial variation in types (right). The left-hand diagram shows types of housing on the fictitious Island of Gamma, with the "average" house at the center of the inner circle. The farther one moves away from the center of the diagram, the more variable the houses become. The right-hand diagram shows types of housing on the fictitious Island of Gamma and on eight neighboring islands. Ford was attempting to show that the more one moves away from the "average" house type (represented by the ringed house in the center of the Isle of Gamma), the more variation increases (after Ford 1954c).

space" should consist of or how one knew one had such a type. That variation might "tend to cluster about a mean, which [the ethnologist could] visualize as the central theme of the type [read *the type definition*]. [But] the ethnologist cannot rely upon the culture bearers to define this central theme. They may or may not be aware of it. . . . The cultural trait [read *type*], then, is an abstraction made by the ethnologist and derived from the cultural activity" (Ford 1954c:45). Although an artifact—be it a house or a potsherd—might "illustrate the aborigine's ideas as to the proper ways to construct dwellings" or ceramic vessels (Ford 1954c:47), it comprised a constellation of *alternate* ideas about how things might be done—it was only a shorthand description—and thus it was clear that a type perceived by an anthropologist of whatever stripe was "not a natural cultural unit" (Ford 1954c:48). The ethnologist or archaeologist might choose the wrong scale of idea combinations to examine—house form as opposed to how a roof was thatched— or the wrong combination of attributes.

In Ford's view, discontinuities along the temporal and/or spatial dimensions of the archaeological record gave the archaeologist a sort of natural (in no way to be confused with cultural or essentialist) seam by which the time-space continuum could be broken into chunks. Thus types were accidents of the samples available: "[T]he particular locality where an archeological collection chances to be made will be one of the factors that determines the mean and the range of variation that are demonstrated in any particular tradition in the culture that is being studied" (Ford 1954c:49). Chance samples of the continuum would provide only discontinuous snapshots, and as such, "Types are easily separable and they look natural [read *emic* or *real*]" (Ford 1954c:52). This was because types were extensionally defined. To Ford, the significance of this observation was that Spaulding's argument was flawed because his type definitions were founded on the discontinuous nature of the samples generally available to archaeologists.

From Ford's perspective, given his views on the ceramic and cultural continua, there were also two problems associated with the observation that available samples dictated type definitions. First, types might appear emically real because the archaeologist was unaware of "the favor performed by the chance geographic [and, we might add, stratigraphic] separation of samples" (Ford 1954c:49–50). The second problem was that too much data in the hands of a novice typologist would result in an "overlapping of types [and] a meaningless conglomeration" of such units: "Permitting sampling chance to determine typology operates very well so long as the archeologist has only a spotty sampling of the culture history" (Ford 1954c:52). Too complete a sample would result in typological "creep" and a smearing and blending of type boundaries if the typologist didn't pay close attention.

In the end, Ford's strategy for refuting Spaulding's position backfired because his vague allusions to cultural customs and standards and his discussion of a (fictional) ethnographic example gave Spaulding's types something of a claim to such meaning. Thus, some individuals later bought Spaulding's arguments hook, line, and sinker. In discussing the type-variety system, Gifford (1960) suggested, on the one hand, that a variety represented individual or small-group social variation within a society, much as Kroeber had done thirty-five years earlier and Phillips (1970) would do a decade later. A type to Gifford (1960:343) was "the material outcome of a set of fundamental attributes that coalesced, consciously or unconsciously, as a ceramic idea or 'esthetic ideal'—the boundaries of which were imposed through the value system operative in the society by virtue of individual interaction on a societal level. These ceramic ideas occurred in the brains of the potters who made the ceramic fabric that constitutes a type, and they are not by any means creations of an analyst."

Spaulding's types, then, were essentialist: "They presume[d] that significant variation occurs as more or less discrete packages and that variation not assignable to such packages lack[ed] explanatory significance" (Dunnell 1986b:181). Comparison of Spaulding's types must therefore be qualitative and focus on *differences* between and among types. Fordian types stem from a materialistic conception of reality—variation in form is continuous across space and through time. In the absence of theoretically informed unit construction, the division of that continuity into types is a trial-and-error process, the success of which Ford chose to evaluate with the historical-significance criterion. This did not ensure that Ford's and others' types were stylistic (Dunnell 1986b:173) in the sense that the types so identified were selectively neutral variants (Dunnell 1978; O'Brien and Holland 1990), though they were *dominantly* stylistic (Dunnell 1986a:31), given that Ford examined decorative attributes. For Ford to suddenly shift his focus from measuring time to studying diffusion and related processes—that is, to tracking streams of cultural ideas—without changing the kind of types he used or providing a stronger theoretical warrant that his types in fact clearly reflected cultural ideas was his downfall.

In the end, the Ford-Spaulding debate was something of a catalyst for the new archaeology of the 1960s. Spaulding's view (rooted in Brainerd's work) represented an entirely new approach: appropriate *methods* would allow one to detect emically significant properties of the archaeological record—properties that revealed human behaviors (e.g., Binford 1968a:23). The new archaeologists wanted to study *culture* and *cultures,* not just to measure the time-space continuum by detailed classification of artifacts. Ford's response would have been that you couldn't do the former without first doing the latter; his mentors, Kroeber and Strong, would have agreed. What many of Ford's contemporaries, as well as some of the new archaeologists, couldn't accept was Ford's approach to rendering anthropological and cultural meaning from the archaeological record—the very aspect of his research that so incensed Spaulding.

The Ford-Spaulding debates were over just about as quickly as they started. Spaulding went on about his business, in his mind, as well as in the minds of many impartial observers, having bloodied Ford a bit in their tussle over types. Part of Ford's problem, as his friends have admitted, was that he couldn't always express himself the way he wanted—or at least so that other people could understand what he was saying. Another part of the problem, we suspect, was that Ford's heart wasn't really in the argument, especially when it came to quibbling over types. In his mind his position had been clear since the 1930s; why rehash it yet again? His real interest lay in digging up sherds and plotting their frequencies, not in explaining his reasoning to all comers. In the early 1950s, Ford saw there was still a lot of work that needed to be done in the Mississippi Valley, and lots of problems still to solve.

CULTURAL DISCONTINUITY IN THE MISSISSIPPI VALLEY

One problem still around in the early 1950s was what to do about reconciling the Louisiana chronology—what Ford (1952a) referred to as the Red River Mouth chronology—to the Lower Mississippi Alluvial Valley chronology—an unfortunate misnomer, since the survey (Phillips et al. 1951) that produced the chronology went only as far south as about Yazoo City, Mississippi. The Phillips et al. survey discussed differences between the two chronologies in terms of where period boundaries should be drawn. Ford (1952a) attempted a realignment based on pottery decoration, though his efforts to reconcile various details between the two were only partially successful (O'Brien 1998). Thus in the mid-1950s there was still concern about which chronology to use in the large expanse of the Mississippi Valley south of Yazoo City and north of the northern limit where Ford drew his border around the Red River Mouth chronology (Figure 5.1). This chronological no-man's land included the lower reaches of the Sunflower, Yazoo, and Big Black Rivers in Mississippi and the Tensas River basin in northeastern Louisiana.

Phillips realized that several years of fieldwork would be required in the unknown region before chronological problems could be addressed adequately, and in the early 1950s he initiated a survey-and-excavation program sponsored by the Peabody Museum (Harvard) that he named the Lower Mississippi Survey. One of the program's first projects that had a direct bearing on chronological issues was Robert Greengo's excavation in 1954–1955 of several sites just north and south of Vicksburg, Mississippi, which formed the basis for his dissertation. It was almost a decade later (in 1964) before Greengo published a monograph in which he summarized the ceramic data, though most of the information had been circulated among archaeologists for several years. Concomitant with the initial stages of Phillips's project were excavations sponsored by the National Park Service at three sites just northeast of Natchez, Mississippi—Emerald (Cotter

1951), Anna (Cotter 1951), and Gordon (Cotter 1952), the last of which was the original Coles Creek type site (Ford 1935c, 1936a).

Two somewhat related problems had grown out of the inability to correlate completely the Red River Mouth and Lower Mississippi Valley chronologies. First, the continued proliferation of pottery types that had begun as early as the late 1930s had created a very unstable situation with regard to the placement of plain-surface sherds. Phillips et al. (1951) had treated this topic in their survey report, but the situation reached epidemic proportions in the mid-1950s. Decoration had long been used to create easily recognized "index" types, but what did one do with the tens of thousands of plain sherds that occurred in collections? The answer was to create new types. Thus, as new sites were excavated in the Mississippi Valley, new pottery types were created to fill in perceived gaps in the chronologies—types that were extensionally defined based on the materials at hand. This, as we will see, created considerable confusion.

The second problem, which also was addressed by Phillips et al. (1951), was how best to explain the appearance of new features in the archaeological record. Did one invoke the notion of gradual replacement of traits, or, alternatively, the notion of abrupt replacement, which was visible in not only shifts in pottery types but also abrupt changes in the sedimentary record? Under the Phillips and Griffin view, a cultural disruption as significant as the introduction of shell tempering should be visible in terms of a stratigraphic break between the earlier Baytown-period deposits and the later Mississippi-period deposits. If one bought into this replacement scenario, was the replacement a result of diffusion of traits/ideas or the result of population movement? Phillips and Griffin viewed it as the result, at least in part, of population movement, specifically the infiltration of the valley by shell-tempered-vessel users. Ford held out (in this case) for continuity, though it is clear he admitted that some traits which showed up in the Mississippi-period archaeological record came from outside the valley—a natural part of slow, steady cultural development. But even in Ford's normally peaceful flow of culture, there were a few times when the tempo picked up significantly as a result of fast-running side streams entering the main river. At the scale at which Ford usually operated, such changes were difficult if not impossible to see, but there were those rare occasions where one would have had to be blind not to see it. The Marksville-Hopewell connection postulated by Collins and Ford was one such occasion, and by the early 1950s there was about to be another one.

Jaketown

An apparent opportunity to link the Red River Mouth and Lower Mississippi Alluvial Valley chronologies presented itself in 1950 when Bill Haag, then at the University of Mississippi, learned that the Mississippi State Highway Department was tearing into several mounds just north of Belzoni in Humphreys County. The mounds had been visited by C. B. Moore (1908:581–82) early in the century, but he did no digging in them. They were visited again by Griffin in 1941 during the Lower Mississippi Valley Survey, in which he collected more than 4,000 sherds from the surface. The collection "had everything," as Phillips et al. (1951:273) later put it, and Phillips returned to the site in 1946 and excavated a couple of 2-m-square units in what turned out to be thick midden deposits. The site, which by then was called Jaketown (Figure 5.7), for several reasons figured prominently in Phillips et al.'s (1951) discussion. First, it was one of the few sites which suggested there might be a discontinuity between the Baytown-period clay-tempered sherds and the Mississippi-period shell-tempered sherds. Second, Jaketown contained sherds of Tchula-period pottery types as well as Poverty Point objects, a term derived from the site of the same name in West Carroll Parish, Louisiana (Figure 5.7) and used to refer to fired-clay lumps of myriad shapes that were used as heating elements in earth ovens and possibly in other cooking and/or heating activities (Gibson 1974, 1975, 1985; Pierce 1998). By 1951, when Phillips et al. wrote their survey report, the objects were suspected to date in large part to the preceramic period (Webb 1944, 1948). Based on the earlier work, it appeared that there also was a discontinuity between Poverty Point–period levels and Tchula-period levels at Jaketown. To understand the importance of the Jaketown report in Ford's evolution of thought, we need to examine briefly what Phillips et al. (1951) had to say about the deposits excavated in 1946.

In their discussion of Jaketown, Phillips et al. (1951:274) noted that the superpositional arrangement of sherds by types spoke for itself, with "most of the types falling into their proper places as though through orders"—that is, the majority of Tchula-period sherds (e.g., Tchefuncte Stamped, Lake Borgne Incised) were stratigraphically below most of the Baytown sherds (e.g., Marksville Stamped, Coles Creek Incised), which were below most of the Mississippi-period (shell-tempered) sherds. Here Phillips et al. were using period designations from the Lower Mississippi Alluvial Valley chronology and type designations from the Red River Mouth chronology. Despite the perceived accuracy in vertical positioning of the pottery, they felt there was little to say about the posited Baytown-Mississippi discontinuity because there was no "soil stratification to serve as control for the pottery stratigraphy" (Phillips et al. 1951:276). Since there was no sedimentary break—no visible change in color, texture, or kind of sediment—similar to what the authors claimed to have found at Rose Mound in Cross County, Arkansas, they were forced to concede that if a discontinuity was there, they didn't see it.

Their efforts were rewarded at the other end of the vertical column, where Poverty Point objects underlay Tchula-period sherds of various types. As Phillips et al. explained, this superpositioning was not viewed as anything novel, since by 1951 everyone knew, or at least assumed, that Poverty Point objects predated the introduction of pottery in the lower Mississippi Valley. But what Phillips et al.

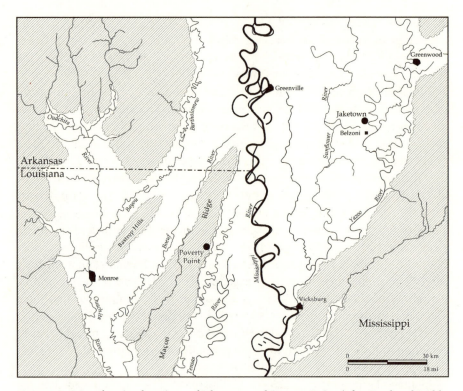

Figure 5.7. Map showing locations of Jaketown and Poverty Point (after Ford and Webb 1956).

(1951:280) wanted to be able to establish was "the hypothesis that the Poverty Point objects represent a pre-pottery, hence pre-Tchula, *period*" (emphasis added). Cut A (Figure 5.8) showed the trends in pottery and Poverty Point objects clearly; what it did *not* show was an "apparent change in the character of the deposit coinciding with" the changeover from one to the other (Phillips et al. 1951:280). The authors, at least Phillips and Griffin, were so tied to the notion that sedimentary boundaries equaled points of culture change that they could make the following statement:

> The dotted line in the right-hand column at -185 cm. [Figure 5.8] simply represents an arbitrary point which might be regarded as the bottom of the midden. The change in color from almost black midden soil to the olive-brown sub-soil began at -155 cm, and was complete at -225 cm. Minus 185 cm. is thus only a kind of average. The bulk of the Poverty Point objects in Levels 15 and 16 lay in soil, therefore, that scarcely differed from the sterile sub-soil. It gave no appearance whatever of being an occupation level distinct from the overlying midden. All of which makes it very difficult to imagine how they got there. (Phillips et al. 1951:280)

Presumably they got there by the same process or processes that led to deposition of the ones higher up, but Phillips et al. never considered this. To them, if it wasn't a midden—clearly distinguishable from underlying sediments—then artifacts didn't belong there.

Cut B, however, *did* show evidence of a discontinuity, though there was a slight problem with the data—the presence of a few sherds in the lower deposits and a few Poverty Point objects in higher deposits (Figure 5.8). These problems weren't so severe that they couldn't be overcome. First, zone II (Figure 5.8) was said to be mound fill, "containing material from the older portions of the site" (Phillips et al. 1951:280). Then, sherds in zone V were explained away as having been in later pits that intruded into earlier deposits. What interested Phillips et al. in cut B was zone V and the fact that it "gave evidence of being an occupation level, or a series of superimposed levels separated by thin lenses of sterile soil, probably water-laid." Here, then, was evidence of discontinuity between the Poverty Point period and the succeeding Tchula period, defined on the basis of shifts in artifact frequencies

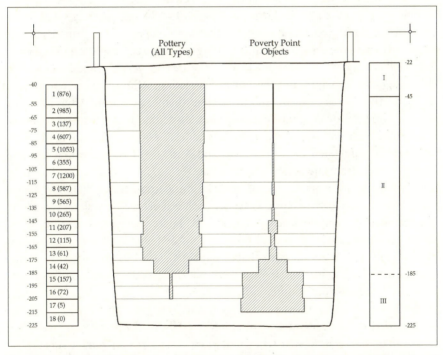

Figure 5.8. Stratigraphic diagram showing vertical distribution of pottery (all types) and Poverty Point objects in cut A at Jaketown, Humphreys County, Mississippi. See Figure 4.9 for explanation of letters and numbers (after Phillips et al. 1951).

and, just as importantly, changes in the sediments bearing the artifacts—exactly what Phillips et al. thought they saw between the Baytown- and Mississippi-period levels at Rose Mound. What better way to separate cultures than on the basis of lenses of water-laid sediments?

The 1951 Excavations

Ford and Phillips planned to return to Mississippi in the spring of 1951, though their plans did not call for working at Jaketown. However, Haag told them that after cleaning some of the Jaketown profiles exposed by the highway department, he had found the same thing recorded in 1946: beneath a thick midden containing the entire ceramic sequence was another thick refuse layer, but without pottery. The layer contained artifacts similar and in some cases identical to those from Poverty Point described by Clarence Webb (1944, 1948). From an area on the site's southern edge, Haag had also collected hundreds of small chert microblades, retouched blades, and small cores that had produced the blades—artifacts that again were identical to those Webb had found at Poverty Point (Haag and Webb 1953). Because of the discoveries, Haag had "little difficulty in reviving [Ford and Phillips's] interest in the Jaketown Site" (Ford et al. 1955:14).

Phillips, given the two field seasons (1949–1950) he had recently spent in the lower Yazoo Basin, welcomed any large sherd sample, especially from a site that appeared to have the correct superpositioning of pottery types. Although Jaketown didn't fall exactly in the "no-man's land"—the area between the Red River Mouth chronology to the south and the Lower Mississippi Alluvial Valley chronology to the north—it was close enough to warrant further attention. After all, if one wanted to tie the two chronologies together, a site that had produced sherds of types from both areas—for example, Tchefuncte Stamped, Tammany Pinched, and Orleans Punctated from the south and Mulberry Creek Cordmarked and Baytown Plain from the north (Phillips et al. 1951:277)—would appear to be an ideal candidate. Even better, the 1941 excavations demonstrated that most lower-valley types at Jaketown behaved as expected: sherds of the known later types were concentrated in the upper levels and dwindled in percentage the deeper one went, while the known early types were primarily in the lower levels and dwindled at higher levels. This was a situation that Phillips et al. (1951:276) described as being "almost too good to be true. If Ford had built this midden with his own hands, he would not have done it differently."

Work was conducted between February and May 1951. In a reversal of roles, Ford carried out the excavations, and Phillips analyzed the pottery and wrote the first draft of that section. Here we are not interested particularly in the substantive work carried out at the site but rather in the major issue alluded to earlier—discontinuity—and the related issue of typology. For ease in presentation, we take those issues in reverse order, and for reasons that will become obvious in a moment, in examining the issue of typology, we focus almost exclusively on plain-surface sherds and the types created to house them.

The 1951 excavations at Jaketown mirrored the stratigraphy and superpositioning of index types found in the excavations of 1946. If one glances through the report on the earlier excavations (Phillips et al. 1951:273–81), it is easy to overlook the fact that only two "plainware" types—Baytown Plain and Neeley's Ferry Plain—were included in the stratigraphic diagrams. We can ignore Neeley's Ferry Plain because it was barely represented, and focus on Baytown Plain. Why did its curve, when sherd percentages were graphed by depth, take on a "boxey" look, meaning that there was little difference in relative frequency from top to bottom? This seems odd for a site with a known long sequence, but Phillips's discussion in the Jaketown report explains why Baytown was represented the way it was:

> It must be confessed that we have gotten our Lower Mississippi plainwares into a muddle. We are not apologizing for it, because we have at least tried to deal with them, which is more than many archaeologists have done. In any case, explanations are in order, particularly in respect to the dominant clay-tempered types. In the Red River sequence [six] clay-tempered plain types have been distinguished. . . . In the Lower Mississippi Survey only one clay-tempered plain type was set up, Baytown Plain. This illustrates two equally unsatisfactory methods of dealing with plain pottery. In the first, a type was set up for every time period, more or less, and it was freely admitted [Ford 1951a:71] that in most cases only typical pieces could be sorted. In the second, the sorting difficulty was eliminated, but the type had such wide variability and range in time and space as to be virtually useless for comparative purposes. (Ford et al. 1955:76–77)

Phillips certainly was correct: neither method of dealing with the plain pottery was satisfactory. We might well ask why anyone would intentionally establish a series of types, knowing that only a few sherds—the ones used to form the types initially—could be placed in them accurately. The answer is that as archaeologists moved from site to site, each of which was found through the use of index types to date to a different time period, they had to do *something* with the plain-surface sherds they encountered, so they created new plainware types. And, as Phillips noted, they created one or more for each time period.

Willey had pointed out the plainware problem in a letter to Ford in 1938, written when Willey was worried about how to sort the thousands of undecorated sherds pouring into the WPA laboratory in Baton Rouge:

> *Sherd trouble.* Undoubtedly, as we have *decoration transition* at AV-2 [Greenhouse] we have *plain ware* transition also. The differentiation between Coles Creek & Marksville Plain was beginning to be vague. Hence, only definite sherds of each, on old description basis, are to be so classified. We are making out type cards in pencil on "(Transitional) Plain" and holding all the material out for your inspection next Tuesday. We can then redistribute it to Marksville, Coles Creek, or a new type plain

ware. The amount of odd looking decorated stuff is also amazing. Looks like [a] perfect transition.

The plain ware trouble is by far the worst. It will be unfortunate if we screw up our Coles Creek—Transitional—Marksville percentages with wild judgements on this undecorated stuff. A lot of it is almost Marksville in thickness; Coles Creek (inferior) in surface finish; and a little to the Marksville side in paste cross-section except that it is a little too hard.[2]

Given these admitted problems, look how Phillips attempted to deal with them, remembering that one of the reasons Jaketown was so attractive in 1951 was its location between the centers of the two competing chronologies:

Our problem here is how to deal with the plainware at Jaketown. The site is near enough to the Louisiana area and covers enough time so that any of the above-listed types [see above quote] might be expected to appear. However, except for Tchefuncte and Coles Creek Polished Plain, we have not attempted to segregate them. . . . For the rest, we have fallen back on the Survey catch-all, Baytown Plain. It comprises the overwhelming majority of sherds in all levels, except the very earliest and the very latest. It is not, however, quite so difficult to pin down as that. At Jaketown, the interval corresponding to the Plaquemine Period is almost unrepresented, so we have very little if any plainware that would (in another context) be called Addis Plain. (Ford et al. 1955:77)

And how was it known that the Plaquemine period was almost unrepresented? Because index types used to define the period were missing. Notice what Phillips was saying: in another context—one where sherds of Plaquemine-period index types were present—the same sherds that he was tossing in Baytown Plain would be tossed in Addis Plain. However, since he knew there was almost no Plaquemine period represented at Jaketown, the sherds couldn't very well be placed in Addis Plain, since that would signify that the Plaquemine period *was* represented. Quite a sticky situation, and one in which Phillips found himself with regard to plainwares from earlier time periods:

The late Baytown Period, corresponding to Coles Creek, is also lightly represented so the quantity of Coles Creek Plain, if we could sort it, would be small. Troyville Plain has turned out to be a kind of regional specialization, "an abortive trend toward crudeness in ceramics" that is perhaps commoner in Coles Creek than in Troyville times [Ford 1951a:68]. It is somewhat easier to sort; if it occurred in any strength at Jaketown, we probably could do so. Our assumption is that it did not range so far up the Mississippi Valley. With all these factors considered, it seems that the bulk of the sherds we are here calling Baytown Plain is the local equivalent to Marksville Plain, and to a lesser extent Coles Creek Plain, in Louisiana. (Ford et al. 1955:77)

Look at that statement carefully. There were only a few (or no) late Baytown-period index-type sherds at Jaketown, which means that that period, which corresponded to the Coles Creek period farther south, was only lightly represented.

2. Letter of December 21, 1938, from Willey to Ford (LSU Museum of Natural Science archives).

Phillips couldn't really sort out sherds of the type Coles Creek Plain from any of the other plainware types, but that was all right because the number of Coles Creek Plain sherds was small anyway, given that the Coles Creek period was only lightly represented. Thus Phillips was left with the obvious conclusion that Baytown Plain was the equivalent of Marksville Plain and, to a lesser (unspecified) extent, of Coles Creek Plain.

Maybe, as Phillips suggested in the pottery section of the Jaketown report, archaeologists *had* gotten their lower Mississippi Valley plainwares "into a muddle," but at the same time, couldn't the other types—the ones based primarily on decoration—be used to address the second issue—the existence or nonexistence of a cultural as well as a stratigraphic discontinuity at a site? Yes, they could, and Ford et al. tried to match Tchula-period sherds from Jaketown against sedimentary evidence to demonstrate a discontinuity between the Poverty Point and Tchula periods. Phillips et al. (1951) stated that such a discontinuity existed in cut B made in 1946, but in one part of the later report, Ford et al. (1955:151) modified this conclusion, saying that such a break was "indicated but not proved." In another part of the report (Ford et al. 1955:114), they stated that there indeed *was* a break between Poverty Point and Tchula—an interpretation based on the almost perfect segregation of sherds and Poverty Point objects in different levels (Figure 5.9). With regard to a break between Tchula and Baytown, they were forced to conclude that if there indeed were a break, "it cannot be demonstrated on present evidence; consequently, we adhere to previous assumptions of continuity for these early ceramic phases of Lower Mississippi prehistory" (Ford et al. 1955:151).

What about the Baytown-Mississippi transition—the point that earlier had caused Phillips and Griffin to adopt one stance and Ford the other? Was it the result of continuity or disruption? Based on the vertical positioning of sherds by type, in one part of the report the authors of Ford et al. (1955:117) were reserved, noting, "The 1946 tests indicated an 'abrupt replacement of Baytown by Mississippi types,' without accompanying soil change; the 1951 excavations had the same result." But then a few sentences later they got a bit braver: "The combination of a late date [based on the presence of sherds from known late-occurring types], thin deposits, and a weak showing of the preceding Late Baytown types suggests almost certainly a break between the Baytown and Mississippi occupations of the site" (Ford et al. 1955:117). This statement occurs in the section of the report entitled "Stratigraphy," which was written by Phillips. We know who the author was from a series of letters exchanged among the three authors in which two of them complained to the third about his heavy-handed editing. For example, Phillips wrote Ford in April 1954, pointing out that

> I confess that (on the assumption that you were not merely kidding) the picture of
> you and Bella Weitzner [the technical editor at the American Museum of Natural
> History] "plowing slowly through the Jaketown Mss. cutting it to pieces" is one that I
> cannot contemplate without alarm. I was under the impression that we had finished it

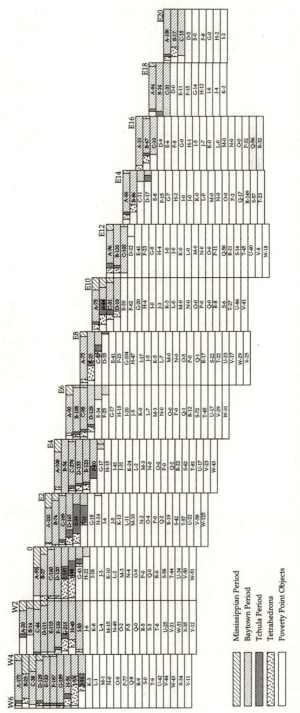

Figure 5.9. Stratigraphic section along north wall of 26-m-long trench 5 at Jaketown, Humphreys County, Mississippi, showing vertical positioning of Mississippi-, Baytown-, and Tchula-period objects. Letters and numbers at the top of each excavation unit refer to horizontal provenience; letter-and-number designations within the excavation units refer to individual 6-inch levels (after Ford et al. 1955).

off in Baton Rouge and from there on [it] was just a question of the normal editorial preparation for the printer. If there is any rewriting to be done in my sections, I shall certainly want to be the one to do it. Otherwise you may expect screams loud and long.[3]

Ford didn't see the message Phillips penned on the top of the copy of the letter he sent to Haag: "Dear Bill: I am sending this to you as a warning. We know what Jim's 'editors' are capable of doing when they 'retype.' . . . I resent Jim's attitude that there is only one way to do these things and that's his way." Ford admitted "doing the hatchet work myself,"[4] but he pleaded his case on grounds of grammar and syntax. In comparing the final manuscript against rephrasing that Phillips demanded, it is evident that Ford eventually backed down and let the stratigraphy section stand pretty much as originally written.

By the "Conclusions" section of the Jaketown report, Ford et al. (1955:151) were pulling no punches as to how they viewed the Baytown-Mississippi transition: "The final period is represented by a thin veneer of Mississippi culture that we have reason to think is late with reference to that tradition as a whole. This and other circumstances suggest a discontinuity in the sequence between Baytown and Mississippi, and we are inclined to think that this reflects a strong invasion of new ideas into the region, and possibly a new people" (Ford et al. 1955:151). Ford had always had "cultural-disruption" leanings, especially when he couldn't explain a piece of the archaeological record any other way, but never to the extent he showed in 1955. It was almost as if he had been converted to religion—one hell of a conversion in our opinion, since he soon out-disrupted his fellow disruptionists to such a degree that even Phillips had to distance himself from Ford and his newly found stance. To understand where that stance came from, we need to turn attention to the other large site in the greater Mississippi Valley that caught Ford's attention in the early 1950s.

Poverty Point

In 1948, Clarence H. Webb, a pediatrician and respected amateur archaeologist from Shreveport, Louisiana, reported that the large mounds known as Poverty Point (Figure 5.7) were preceramic in age. Not until Webb began working there in the 1930s did it become clear that the site predated the earliest use of pottery in the lower Mississippi Valley. It wasn't until the early 1950s that archaeologists discovered the nature and extent of the Poverty Point earthworks—a partial octagon comprising six concentric ridges, each 4 to 6 feet high and about 150 feet from crest to crest, dissected by aisles that pass from outside the rings to the open area in the center. The diameter of the octagon from outer ridge to outer ridge

3. Letter of April 22, 1954, from Phillips to Ford (LSU Museum of Natural Science archives).
4. Letter of June 24, 1948, from Ford to Haag (LSU Museum of Natural Science archives).

is slightly less than 4,000 feet. Until aerial photographs housed at the Mississippi River Commission Cartographic Laboratory in Vicksburg were examined (Ford 1954d), the geometric arrangement was unknown, because it was too large to be recognizable at ground level. Ford's (1954d) published tracings of the earthworks are fairly accurate but impressionistic. The plan map of the site and the contour maps included in the final monograph (Ford and Webb 1956) are better. In 1983 the site was mapped professionally using aerial photogrammetry (Gibson 1984).

Why, one might ask, would a site known to contain large quantities of surface artifacts and several large mounds—one of which was roughly 70 feet high, thus making it the highest mound in the South—not have been examined in systematic fashion before the 1950s? Maybe it was because archaeologists took Gerard Fowke at his word when he declared the mounds as being natural rises (Fowke 1928), but more probable was the reason given by Ford and Webb (1956:14):

> For a number of years after [C. B.] Moore's report appeared, archeologists working in the South were fully cognizant of the unusual nature of the site and of the artifacts to be found there. Although the locality was visited a number of times, no one was prepared to undertake additional work. Other problems more readily solvable were too numerous for much time to be spent on a unique culture that did not fit into the gradually clarifying outline of Southeastern prehistory.

The reason it did not fit was because of the apparent absence of pottery: how could a large site containing mounds *not* contain pottery? Ford's view of the mound was no exception: "I too am not convinced that the large mounds on the Poverty Point and Medley Plantations were man-made. According to my geologist friends at Louisiana State, there are two possibilities: either they are erosional remnants which have been projected up above the flood plain since the latter part of the Pleistocene, or, possibly, they are the remains of a dome that was pushed up by a salt plug."[5]

Ford, accompanied by Stu Neitzel, began working at Poverty Point in the spring of 1952, and together they excavated three 5-foot-wide trenches across the ridges at various points. The artifacts subsequently were analyzed by Phillips and Haag, and, as Ford and Webb (1956:21) pointed out, "the results were already known to us as we finished writing the report on the Jaketown Site." Ford and Neitzel returned to the site for two weeks in 1953 and mapped and cored the large Poverty Point Mound (Ford 1954d). They returned again in February 1955, this time accompanied by Junius Bird of the American Museum, and worked through May, during which time they excavated six additional trenches, explored Mound B, and made a contour map of the Motley Mound.

Thousands of items were recovered from the test units (only the fill from Bird's trench 4 was screened), including numerous complete projectile points,

5. Letter of September 26, 1950, from Ford to Haag (LSU Museum of Natural Science archives).

tiny bladelets of the type earlier described by Webb (1948), and steatite-vessel fragments; thousands of Poverty Point objects; and, unexpectedly, fifty-three pottery sherds. The presence of sherds was surprising, since none had been found previously. Twenty-one of the sherds were described as having "the clay-tempered paste, color range, thinness, and rather good firing that is characteristic of Coles Creek Period ware" (Ford and Webb 1956:105). Since the Troyville–Coles Creek–period site known as the Jackson Place (Moore 1913) adjoined the Poverty Point earthworks at the southern end, Ford and Webb (1956:105) noted that "the well-known small boy could have picked up fragments from the rather rich sherd-bearing midden there and sailed them onto the Poverty Point earthworks." Maybe this would explain the majority of the clay-tempered sherds recovered, but Ford and Webb were hard-pressed to explain the presence of several sherds deep in the deposits, being "reluctant to believe that Coles Creek–like pottery was made in Poverty Point times" (Ford and Webb 1956:106). The other thirty-two sherds were fiber-tempered, and the presence of one sherd deep in trench 8 suggested to Ford and Webb (1956:106) that "fiber-tempered pottery is not a late addition to the cultural equipment of the people who lived at the Poverty Point site."

Since there was almost no pottery at the site, Ford turned to the fired-clay objects to align the excavation units chronologically. Although Poverty Point objects are excellent Late Archaic–period markers (ca. 1500–600 B.C.), some were still being made into later periods (e.g., Dunnell and Whittaker 1990; Huxtable et al. 1972). They occur over a wide area of the greater Mississippi Valley from southern Missouri (Dunnell and Whittaker 1990; Hopgood 1969; Klippel 1969; Marshall 1965; Pierce 1998; Whittaker 1993) south to the Gulf of Mexico (e.g., Ford and Quimby 1945). Figure 5.10 shows one of Ford's percentage-stratigraphy graphs, on which he plotted relative frequencies of objects in each of eight form-related types. As impressive as the graph appears, Ford and Webb were concerned because the trends noted at Poverty Point in terms of an increase or a decrease in specific fired-clay-ball types were the inverse of what was found when they plotted similarly organized data from trench 5 at Jaketown. They didn't know what to make of the discrepancy: "Whether the difference is attributable to areal variation, or whether one or both sets of data are faulty, are questions that we shall have to leave for the future investigator" (Ford and Webb 1956:49).

The authors also dedicated considerable space to describing the 2,365 projectile points that came from their work and from decades of collecting by avocationalists. Being a pottery person, Ford had never devoted much energy to the analysis of projectile points, perhaps because "Typing projectile points is much more difficult than typing other cultural material—pottery, for example. Because of the limitations imposed by the material, there is not much room for variation in the different practical ways to chip flint. Limitation is also imposed by function, as every projectile point must have a tip; a stem, though optional, is very useful, and

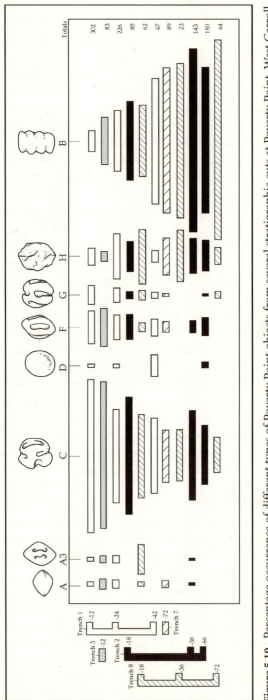
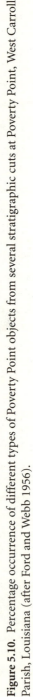

Figure 5.10. Percentage occurrence of different types of Poverty Point objects from several stratigraphic cuts at Poverty Point, West Carroll Parish, Louisiana (after Ford and Webb 1956).

the utility of barbs probably was very apparent to the makers" (Ford and Webb 1956:50). This is a very weak argument since material limitations have nothing to do with whether a class of objects is useful for chronological purposes. In fact, Ford and Webb (1956:50) contradicted themselves, admitting that "it is obvious that the projectile points of the Eastern United States changed form in response to cultural influences and in a broad way are extremely useful markers" (Ford and Webb 1956:50).

By 1950, typological classification of ceramic materials in Americanist archaeology had far outdistanced the classification of lithic artifacts. Archaeologists such as Ford and Griffin were preconditioned to regard pottery as integral both to descriptive archaeology and to the chronological ordering of archaeological deposits. In addition, as Ford had pointed out in his earliest publications (e.g., Ford 1935a), pottery is abundant on sites in the central and lower Mississippi River valley (as it is in the Southwest), and it was natural that it would assume a place of primacy in archaeological analysis. Projectile points, on the other hand, are rarer occurrences on most sites.

Culture historians, whether dealing with pottery or projectile points, rarely considered focusing on dimensional change in sets of artifacts rather than on artifact-type replacement as a way of tracking time. And as with pottery, typological systems built around projectile points have come and gone over the decades. Prior to the 1950s, one practice was to identify groups of points based on the presence of specific form-related criteria such as location of notches, but in many cases the characteristics were more general in nature and were embedded in general descriptions of groups of objects. A rather inclusive description of a group was put forth, and all objects that generally fit that description were included in the type.

One of the first large-scale efforts to standardize projectile-point categorization on a panregional scale was Dee Ann Suhm, Alex D. Krieger and Edward B. Jelks's "An Introductory Handbook of Texas Archeology," which appeared as volume 25 of the *Bulletin of the Texas Archeological Society* (Suhm et al. 1954). The volume, which contained synopses and trait lists of the recognized cultural complexes of Texas as well as descriptions of pottery and projectile-point types, quickly sold out and was later reissued as "Handbook of Texas Archeology: Type Descriptions" (Suhm and Jelks 1962). The handbook not only reorganized an expanding list of named pottery and projectile-point types from Texas and neighboring regions into coherent units but also listed the known geographic range of the types and, when known, date ranges. The handbook's success can be linked directly to its appeal to amateurs and collectors as well as to professionals. Anyone who wanted to know what kind of point a certain specimen was could open the book and find a similar, *named* specimen among the photographs. The authors had drastically reduced the confusion over what a specimen of a particular shape should be called—a confusion created in part by the proliferation of point types in the late 1940s and early 1950s (e.g., Bell and Hall 1953; Krieger 1947) as more archaeologists started creating their own types without searching the literature to see if similar points already had been named.

The Texas handbook was not yet available when Ford, Phillips, and Haag wrote the Jaketown manuscript, and their categorization was a hybrid of formally named types—two created by Newell and Krieger (1949) based on their work at the George C. Davis site in Cherokee County, Texas, one by Edward Scully (1951) based on specimens from northeastern Arkansas and southeastern Missouri, and one they created themselves—and what for lack of a better term we can call nonformally named types. The authors were clear about why they used a hybrid system: "In classifying the points from Jaketown, we attempt to follow the system of assigning names to clearly recognizable groups. . . . We are fully in sympathy with this trend, but hesitate to assign formal names to certain ill-defined groups until we are more certain of their chronological and areal significance" (Ford et al. 1955:127). Despite making such a cautious statement, the authors didn't mind taking a formally named unit such as Newell and Krieger's Gary Stemmed type and carving it up on the basis of such things as width and thickness into more types with names like "Broad Gary Stemmed," "Thin Gary Stemmed," "Small Gary Stemmed," "Long Gary Stemmed," and even "Typical Gary Stemmed." There is nothing in Ford et al.'s descriptions of these types to suggest that any of them had more chronological or areal significance than Gary Stemmed did.

For the projectile points from Poverty Point, Ford and Webb either used types included in the Suhm et al. handbook or created new types. They were able to place 1,863 of the 2,365 points from the site into named types, with the vast majority of the others being so fragmented or reworked that they could not be placed. Rather than using the point types to discuss intrasite age differences as they had with the Poverty Point objects, Ford and Webb attempted to place the entire Poverty Point projectile-point assemblage in time by comparing percentages of point types with those from other sites in the Southeast. As shown in Figure 5.11, they used assemblages from four sites in Louisiana (Crooks Mound, Tchefuncte, Mooringsport, and Albany Landing), one in northeastern Mississippi (Bynum Mounds), and one in Alabama (Pickwick Basin site CT°27). Site CT°27, in Colbert County, had received considerable excavation in connection with the Tennessee Valley Authority–sponsored Pickwick Basin project (Webb and DeJarnette 1942). It was a deep midden and had produced a large quantity of artifacts, including more than a thousand projectile points. The site report did not include information comparable to the type descriptions used to categorize the Poverty Point artifacts, but William S. Webb supplied Ford with the needed information.

In our opinion, this is one of the sloppiest analyses Ford ever conducted. He patched together a comparison of points that were classified at different times and by different investigators using entirely dissimilar systems. The descriptions

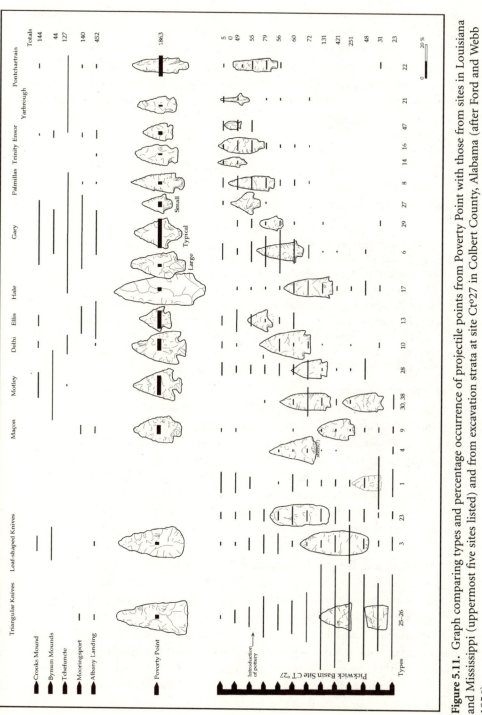

Figure 5.11. Graph comparing types and percentage occurrence of projectile points from Poverty Point with those from sites in Louisiana and Mississippi (uppermost five sites listed) and from excavation strata at site Ct⁰27 in Colbert County, Alabama (after Ford and Webb 1956).

supplied by Webb for the Alabama points supposedly allowed Ford to go back into the Pickwick Basin report and figure out which points came from which levels in the site. Once he tallied the number of points in each descriptive type by depth, he arranged them in ascending order by age (Figure 5.11). Then, he decided which Alabama types matched which Poverty Point types (again, Ford and C. H. Webb were using types described by Suhm et al. [1954] as well as new types Ford and Webb described) and aligned them in the same order in which the Alabama points were arranged.

Given certain rigid controls, there was nothing illogical about what Ford was doing. What made this particular analysis problematic was the lack of comparability among collections from Poverty Point and Alabama in terms of how the points were classified. Ford knew this:

> It is not to be expected that the groupings can be directly comparable, for the classifications were set up without reference to one another. If the Pickwick material were reclassified with the Poverty Point categories as a basis, it is certain that a portion of Pickwick Type 8, for example, would fall into our class Palmillas, and another portion into Pontchartrain. If [the Pickwick] system were applied to the Poverty Point collections, a similar rearrangement would result. The question of which system is correct is not well founded; at this stage of our knowledge of the prehistory of projectile points, one system is as good as the other. The object of this discussion is to make it clear that an exact direct comparison based on the two systems is not possible. (Ford and Webb 1956:72)

One look at the artifact drawings in Figure 5.11 will demonstrate the lack of comparability between the Pickwick types and the Poverty Point types. Some are close, but most are not. Ford's discussion of the graph shown in Figure 5.11 is a confusing and poorly conceived post facto justification for the resulting assemblage alignments, full of language about spatial and regional variation but never offering an explanation that could be backed up by the data. Curiously, in light of earlier considerations he gave to potential biases inherent in surface collections (e.g., Ford 1936a), he never addressed the matter relative to the Louisiana points, many of which had been collected unsystematically.

Discontinuity and Poverty Point Culture

In the concluding section of the Jaketown report, Ford made a trial run at explaining the origin of Poverty Point culture in the Mississippi Valley—a preliminary statement fleshed out more fully in the Poverty Point report, which was published a year later. By the mid-1940s there was growing suspicion that despite its size and complexity, Poverty Point was a preceramic site, though the thought that a large mound center had been built before the Tchefuncte period was disconcerting to say the least (Ford and Webb 1956:14). A few small mounds were known to date as early as the Tchefuncte period—Ford and Willey (1941) had included these in their summary of eastern prehistory—and the Marksville period had its conical burial mounds and circular earthworks, but it wasn't until the end of that period that the construction of large mounds such as those at Troyville and Greenhouse kicked into high gear.

Large-earthwork construction obviously required the participation of lots of people as well as lots of food to feed them. Ford and Willey (1941) discussed the connection between food and people in their summary of eastern prehistory, noting that the initial development of mound construction in the East must have been tied to both pottery manufacture *and* horticulture. Linking mound construction to horticulture seemed logical, since it was assumed that a horticultural base not only freed a population to do such things as build mounds but also was more stable in the long run than, say, hunting and gathering were. The earthworks-horticulture connection led Ford to his conclusion about the appearance of Poverty Point culture in the Mississippi Valley—a scenario so unfounded on evidence that not even his coauthors on the Jaketown report, Phillips and Haag, would have anything to do with it. But Ford only outlined it there, saving the clincher for the report on the Poverty Point site.

Ford's arguments—more so in the Poverty Point report than in the Jaketown report—were based in part on radiocarbon dates. Radiocarbon dating was still in the experimental stage when the dates were run on organic samples from Poverty Point and Jaketown. By 1955, one could choose among several university laboratories when it came time to submit a sample—those at Chicago, Columbia, and Michigan were the best known—or, if one had a friend at Humble Oil and Refining Company, as Ford and Haag did in geologist Harold Fisk, you might get your samples run there. Alternatively, one might get a hobbyist with a homemade apparatus to run a couple of dates, as Fred Schazman of Highland Park, New Jersey, did for Ford and Haag.

By the time the Jaketown report was written, two radiocarbon assays were available from the site, both coming from charred-post fragments found more than 10 feet deep in the deposit and less than a foot above a sandbar that underlay the midden. Two runs were made on the charcoal, producing dates of 2400 ± 150 and 2300 ± 150 radiocarbon years before the present (Ford et al. 1955:154). Averaging the dates, as Ford et al. did, produced a mean date in calendar years of roughly 400 B.C. We are leaving out a significant discussion by Ford et al. of the incongruity between that date and Fisk's (1944) dating of former river channels that abutted Jaketown, but suffice it to say that there was about a thousand years' difference between the two, with the radiocarbon date being later than the channel date. Fisk later was proved wrong.

Ford et al. (1955:154–55) stated, "If the radiocarbon date of about 400 B.C. obtained at Jaketown proves to be correct, and if the majority of dates that have been obtained for the Hopewellian culture of Illinois and Ohio are accepted

[Griffin 1952b], then the Poverty Point culture would be approximately contemporaneous with at least the earlier phases of Hopewellian. The evidence cited [in this report] strongly suggests a cultural connection between the Poverty Point cultural complex and Hopewellian." The "strong" connection comprised primarily the resemblance in Ford's mind between the octagonal earthworks at Poverty Point and the geometric earthworks in the Ohio Valley—this plus the fact that the large Poverty Point mound in outline resembled a bird in flight (Ford 1954d). And, of course, birds commonly graced the exteriors of Hopewellian jars and bowls.

It wasn't only the largest mound at Poverty Point that Ford reported as resembling a bird. In a brief communiqué to *Science* (Ford 1955a) and in a longer piece in *Natural History* (Ford 1955b), he reported that the Motley Mound also was constructed to resemble a bird in flight. Amazingly, he could also tell the directions in which the birds were flying: "the giant bird represented in the large mound at Poverty Point appears to be flying due north, while the bird of the smaller mound is headed due west" (Ford 1955a:551; see also Ford 1955b:471–72). Willey (1957:199), in his review of the Poverty Point report (Ford and Webb 1956), claimed that "an examination of their excellent contour maps does not convince on the matter of the effigy interpretation."

Ford and his coauthors also saw a connection between the Poverty Point–period material culture at Jaketown and elements of what Griffin (1952a:355–56) had termed the "Late Archaic" in the Midwest to refer to artifact assemblages that appeared to just predate the arrival of pottery. They also noted similarities between the Poverty Point–period assemblage from Jaketown and early pottery cultures such as Tchefuncte-Tchula in the Mississippi Valley and Adena in the Ohio Valley. These similarities were convenient because it now made it appear as if Poverty Point–period artifacts, and by extension Poverty Point culture, could be slid between the Late Archaic and Tchefuncte-Tchula periods. There was one slight problem with this configuration—what to do with Hopewell, which postdated Adena in the Ohio Valley just as Marksville, the southern equivalent of Hopewell, postdated Tchefuncte. Ford et al. (1955) took care of that problem by simply calling Adena early Hopewell. This is where Phillips and Haag left things, but not Ford:

> Ford, with a typical lack of reasonable caution, wishes to register a guess. The preceramic Poverty Point culture may possibly represent an early southward thrust of the mid-continental Hopewellian [Adena] culture. Perhaps the rather sophisticated bearers of this culture invaded the Lower Mississippi Valley in small numbers, conquered the local Archaic peoples, and set up a class-structured society with themselves as the ruling class. Certainly such an arrangement would have been necessary to have permitted the construction of such large geometrical earthworks as those at Poverty Point. (Ford et al. 1955:155)

Ford based this guess on the presence at Jaketown of the hundreds of small chert microblades, retouched blades, and small cores that had produced the blades—the artifacts that had drawn Ford to Jaketown in the first place and that were identical to what Webb had found at Poverty Point (Haag and Webb 1953). By 1954, if not earlier, Ford was convinced those objects were Hopewellian, and he modified Haag's portion of the final report to reflect that belief. Haag wouldn't have any of it. In reviewing the galleys for the monograph, he noted what Ford had done. He wrote Ford and told him, "It is not that the data are not factual and interesting but it is the tone of their presentation; it seems as though it is written by someone who is trying to show that there is a strong connection between Poverty Point microflints and Hopewell. That someone is certainly not ole W[illiam] G H[aag]."[6] Ford changed some of the wording, probably not in small part because of Haag's later comments in the letter: "Now, James, I love you like a brother and will not be angry if you don't change a thing. . . . [I]f you are sick and t. of looking at it just forget it—I'll write a short article for A[merican] A[ntiquity] or A[merican] A[nthropologist] . . . and make us all out liars."

In the end, Phillips and Haag let Ford be Ford and make some of his outlandish statements about invaders. As if those statements were not speculative enough, Ford even proposed where the Jaketown invaders had come from: "This possible interpretation would, in turn, conform to the accumulating body of evidence that suggests that the 'Hopewell Culture,' 'Woodland Culture,' or 'Burial Mound Stage' (however one may choose to designate it) was derived from some as yet unidentified part of northeastern Asia by routes that also remain unknown" (Ford et al. 1955:155). Ford might have been technically correct—the people responsible for "Hopewell Culture" *were* the descendants of people who had migrated from northeastern Asia thousands of years earlier. But that's not what he meant. He meant that the Hopewellian peoples were recent immigrants. As he pointed out, not in the Jaketown report but rather in an article in the popular journal *Natural History* (Ford 1955b:467),

> We know that 10,000 years ago, Indians were living here who had a chipped-stone culture somewhat resembling the Solutrean techniques of the Old Stone Age in Europe. This was at the time of the beginning of the retreat of the last Pleistocene ice sheet in North America. Early in the first millennium B.C., the inhabitants of eastern North America began to produce a number of new things, such as dome-shaped mounds as tombs for the dead, stone tools that were ground instead of being chipped, pottery, and techniques of working copper. These things are suspiciously similar to tools used about the same time by people living in central Siberia. The techniques may have been brought into eastern North America by a new wave of immigrants. However, connecting links are lacking over the thousands of miles that lie between.

6. Letter of June 11, 1954, from Haag to Ford (LSU Museum of Natural Science archives).

The second major change in the cultures of eastern North America occurred about 900 A.D. The influence in this case seems definitely to have come from Middle America, where the highly evolved civilizations of the Mayas and others were in the making. This wave brought the bow and arrow, intensive agriculture, and a new religion that led the Indians to build rectangular pyramids of earth as bases for temples. However, the ancient people of Poverty Point lived and died long before the cultures of Middle America made themselves felt in eastern North America. This settlement is rather to be identified with the cultures that stemmed from Asia by way of Bering Strait. The intervening distance and the time interval are both great, but evidence supporting this includes fragments of tubular pipes. These are similar to tubes that have been used for magical cures in northeastern Asia for several thousand years.

In short, there had been several waves of Asian immigrants to the North American continent, the last one made up of folks from central Siberia who, once they arrived in the midcontinent, settled down and eventually became Hopewellian peoples. And what was the evidence for such a claim? The presence of burial mounds, groundstone tools, copper items, and tubular pipes. Ford would later use those traits, along with others, to argue that Mexico was the source of inspiration for Poverty Point.

If we want to pin down the point at which Ford made the final turn to diffusionism and cultural discontinuity—something that would later completely dominate his thinking—then we can point to the time of his work at Jaketown and Poverty Point. It is interesting that Ford, in prefacing the invasion scenario in the Jaketown report, characterized himself as exhibiting "a typical lack of caution," because there is very little in his prior published work, perhaps with the exception of the design-element monograph (Ford 1952a), that even came close to the outlandish speculation of his Jaketown conclusion. But the Jaketown report and the popular account of Poverty Point (Ford 1955b) were only the set-ups for his interpretive statements the next year in Ford and Webb's (1956) Poverty Point monograph. Since that monograph was written by Ford *and* Webb, one might think it would be difficult to sort out who said what, but this is not so. The concluding section, "Interpretations Based on Cultural Data"—appropriately titled because it was nothing if not interpretive—was pure Ford, and he picked up right where he had left off the previous year in the Jaketown report.

As in the Jaketown report, Ford used radiocarbon dates to support his scenario. By the time the Poverty Point report was published in 1956, nine additional dates had been secured on bone, shell, and charcoal from suspected Poverty Point–period deposits at Jaketown and Poverty Point. This made a total of ten dates— four from Jaketown (Ford and Webb [1956:121] reported the original two dates as one averaged date; we follow that designation here) and six from Poverty Point. Ford graphed those dates and their one-sigma ranges (Figure 5.12) relative to other radiocarbon assays available from the lower Mississippi Valley. He obviously was pleased with the date ranges for the Plaquemine, Coles Creek, and Troyville periods, but he thought all but the earliest of the six Tchefuncte-period dates were too late. As for the Poverty Point–period dates, Ford thought they probably were in the ballpark, ranging in calendar years as they did from 1200 ± 120 B.C. to 200 ± 110 B.C., though he was unwilling to believe that Jaketown and Poverty Point were occupied over an 800-year period. He based this unwillingness on the fact that Poverty Point–period artifacts at Jaketown were incorporated within a natural levee alongside what Fisk (1944) had called a former channel of the Ohio River: since "natural levees at any one locality are built in the course of a very few years," the occupation couldn't have spanned more than a few centuries (Ford and Webb 1956:124). Thus, "If we must choose probable dates for the culture out of this embarrassing wealth of dates, we will select the time between 800 B.C. and 600 B.C. as most probable" (Ford and Webb 1956:124). Why Ford selected this date range rather than any other will be obvious in a moment.

Notice in Figure 5.12 that Ford selected eight Adena and Hopewell dates from sites in Kentucky, Ohio, and Illinois for comparison with the lower Mississippi Valley dates. Ford admitted this was a selective sample,

> for we have chosen to ignore other determinations for these cultures that date as late as 800 A.D. As in the local chronology, a choice must be made in the rather scattered dates that result from these assays, and the majority of the dates, as well as the cultural probabilities, favor the earlier group. The dates [selected] for the Adena and Hopewell cultural phases . . . appear to place these phases in the sequence archeologists have long thought to be correct. (Ford and Webb 1956:128)

Ford was correct: the dates he *selected* did place Hopewell and Adena in more or less correct position. In those days, Hopewell was often considered a period, conforming more or less to what today is termed the Middle Woodland period (ca. 250 B.C.–A.D. 450); today, it is considered a "tradition" that lasted from about the birth of Christ until around A.D. 100–200. But the dates did something else as well: "They also suggest that at least the early phases of this comparatively high cultural development were contemporaneous with the Poverty Point Culture" (Ford and Webb 1956:128). Ford was reluctant to use that alignment as an interpretive base without corroborative evidence, but "[i]n this case, the cultural and radiocarbon evidences seem to be in agreement and to warrant an elaboration of a thesis that was suggested in a previous paper [Ford et al. 1955]" (Ford and Webb 1956:128).

Ford argued that given the sheer size of Poverty Point in both area and amount of dirt in the mounds and rings, a sizable population had to have been involved in the construction, probably several thousand people, if not more. And, unless that population had had a stable food supply nearby, they wouldn't have been living in a large group to begin with. According to Ford, only two easily gathered foods would have provided the necessary supply: shellfish from the Tennessee River in Alabama, and agricultural products. Since there was almost no shell at

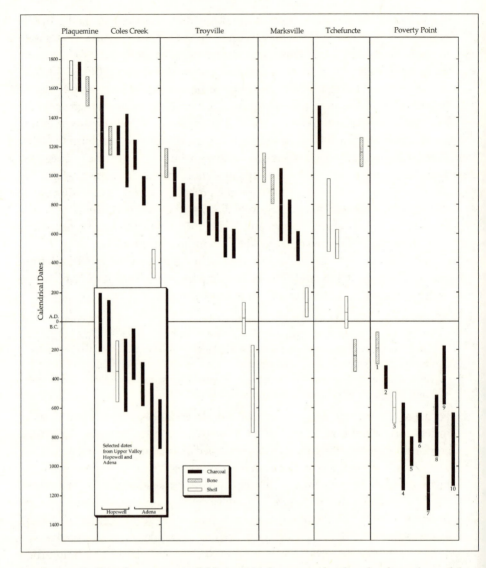

Figure 5.12. Radiocarbon assays available in 1956 that were related to the chronology of the lower portion of the Mississippi Valley. One-sigma range of probability is indicated by the length of the bars. Selected dates from Hopewell and Adena sites in Ohio, Illinois, and Kentucky are included for comparison. Dates 1–4 are from Jaketown, and 5–10 are from Poverty Point (after Ford and Webb 1956).

Poverty Point, the residents must have been agriculturists. Ford made a critical assumption at this point, namely that without a "stable basic food . . . certainly the *surplus labor* necessary to undertake constructions on the scale accomplished by these people would not have been available" (Ford and Webb 1956:129; emphasis added). This notion of surplus labor, along with the question of who controlled it, was central to Ford's remarkable scenario of the founding and evolution of not only the Poverty Point site itself but also Poverty Point culture in general. It is worth presenting his argument more or less in its entirety:

> The second, rather obvious conclusion to be drawn from the arrangement and scale of these earthworks is that this community must have been rather strictly organized. While a religious motivation may ultimately explain the large amount of earth construction, this effort was obviously well controlled. . . . It is difficult to visualize how in a loosely organized society this quantity of essentially non-productive labor could have been expended.
>
> The basic culture of the Poverty Point people conforms to the characteristics of the latter parts of the Eastern Archaic stage [yet t]he identity of the postulated organizing element in the population at Poverty Point is suggested by the cultural resemblances to Hopewell and related cultures in the upper drainage of the Mississippi Valley. (Ford and Webb 1956:129)

Thus Ford was saying that although the "basic culture" of the Poverty Point people was equal to that of Archaic peoples in the East, there were enough similarities—earthworks and bird motifs—to identify an "organizing element." That element was the same as he had postulated in the Jaketown report, only this time he explained the full developmental sequence, including the decline of Poverty Point:

> Diffusion of ideas might have produced the cultural situation that made possible construction of this complex site. It is possible, but rather difficult to visualize in the light of what usually happens when elements of a more advanced culture diffuse to people with a simpler way of life. Generally, items of obvious practical utility are accepted and adapted. However, complex traits that have no obvious utility and that are very expensive in terms of community effort are generally resisted until they are imposed by conquerors backed with military force, or by missionaries supported by the prestige and the appurtenances of their superior culture.
>
> This pyramid of speculation supports the hypothesis that the Poverty Point Site was constructed and occupied about 800 B.C. to 600 B.C. by a people living in a class-structured society. The culture of the lower class seems to have belonged to a late phase of the Eastern Archaic. The ruling class was probably invaders from the upper drainage of the Mississippi Basin where the Hopewellian cultures were beginning to evolve.
>
> This hypothesis may explain the rather selective nature of the Hopewellian-like traits found in the Poverty Point complex. . . .
>
> When a people of less advanced societies have been forcibly organized and set to labor on projects that suit the goals of their masters, the situation is liable to become somewhat unstable. Subject people rapidly learn military techniques and organization,

but, unless there is a continuing cultural pressure, they do not necessarily accept the imposed religious ideas and goals. If the Poverty Point culture was the result of actual invasion by a limited number of early Hopewellian people, we need not expect to find a large number of sites representative of it, nor need the invasion have lasted any great length of time. On a very modest scale this may have been similar to the invasion of Britain by the Romans. . . .

As stated above, the Poverty Point Culture seems to have flourished from 800 B.C. to 600 B.C. A breakdown of this culture and at least a partial regression to a more typical Archaic mode of existence may explain the apparent gap that exists between Poverty Point Culture and the appearance of the Tchefuncte-Tchula cultural stage. The earliest radiocarbon date for the latter is about 250 B.C., but the other dates are substantially later. River channel associations seem to be not earlier than Stages 5 or 6. There are a number of different channel positions between Stage C_1 and Stage 5. This type of evidence suggests an even longer span of time intervening between Poverty Point and Tchula-Tchefuncte cultures than do the radiocarbon dates.

The people of the succeeding Tchula-Tchefuncte cultural stage lived in relatively small villages and made a rather poor variety of pottery which seems to combine traits derived from Early Hopewell of the Illinois Area, from Alexander Complex of the Lower Tennessee River Valley, and from the fiber-tempered wares of the Southeast. Artificial cooking stones were still made, mostly of the biconical shape. Their mounds were modest conical or dome-shaped tombs for the dead. Geometrical earthworks similar to those at Poverty Point were unknown and, so far as we know, nothing resembling the Hopewell earthworks of Ohio was ever again constructed in the Lower Mississippi. Also, the core and blade industry that was so prominent a feature of the Poverty Point complex is not represented. The variety of chert materials, hematite, magnetite, and large quartz crystals that were imported from the north in Poverty Point times, was no longer used. Projectile points were made of local material.

The Tchefuncte Period may represent the first normal diffusion of developmental Hopewellian elements into the Lower Mississippi. This stream of influence was intensified in the succeeding Marksville Period, when the ceramics became very similar to those made in fully developed Hopewell times. This later diffusion of traits seems to include very little that could be a retention from the Poverty Point Culture. (Ford and Webb 1956:129–30)

Gordon Willey reviewed the Poverty Point monograph in *American Antiquity,* and, perhaps because of his friendship with Ford, was kind in his comments on the invasion scenario: "The Ford and Webb report is a job of high technical quality. . . . All that is now available to know is here. Unfortunately, it is not enough to provide a substantial basis for many of their interpretations about the Poverty Point culture. Let me add that these interpretations are as good as anyone could offer with present data, but Poverty Point remains something more of an enigma than most Southeastern archaeological sites" (Willey 1957:198–99). However, in ending the review, Willey (1957:199) added his own opinion on the matter: "It is still a possibility, I think, that an early stimulus for mound building came into the lower Mississippi Valley from the south, that is from Middle America, and that the Poverty Point mounds and embankments are earlier than those of the Ohio Valley." He was right on the second count and wrong on the first. It now is generally accepted that the lifespan of the Poverty Point site was roughly 1700–700 B.C. or so, though archaeologists tend to argue about when construction of the earthworks reached its zenith (see Gibson 1980; Jackson 1986; Webb 1968a, 1977). There is no evidence of Mesoamerican influence, though within a decade Ford had swung around to Willey's way of thinking.

FORD'S CONVERSION TO DISCONTINUITY

What was it that caused Ford to adopt diffusionism wholeheartedly, specifically so-called migration theory, in an attempt to explain Poverty Point—not only the site itself but also Poverty Point "culture"? While he had not necessarily eschewed the notion of migration—recall some of his early comments on Marksville and Hopewell—before publication of the Jaketown report in 1955, he had consistently emphasized continuity over disruption. One could argue that the two views— continuity and migration—are not disconsonant, that one can perceive time, and culture for that matter, as a gradually flowing stream but which at some point receives a jolt that changes the tempo. Perhaps there *is* some middle ground between constant disruption and no disruption, but we don't think this is where Ford fell. Rather, we think there was an abrupt change in his thinking relative to the flow of time, and it came between the publication date of the Greenhouse report (1951) and that of the Jaketown report (1955). Somewhere between those years, Jim Ford bought into the idea that there indeed were huge discontinuities in the archaeological record. With that switch, diffusion in general and migration in particular naturally became weapons in his explanatory arsenal. To be even more precise, we believe it was directly as a result of Ford's no longer being able to deny the role of migration and diffusion in shaping the archaeological record that he was forced to search for, and to find, discontinuities in the record.

If we ignore all mention of diffusion and migration in the Jaketown report and concentrate only on discontinuity, several things stand out, principally the almost schizophrenic discussion of stratigraphy, which might be a result of Ford's fiddling with what Phillips wrote originally—though not to such an extent that Phillips would notice. The report contradicts itself in several places, perhaps the most significant one being the issue of a Poverty Point–Tchula break. Was there one, or wasn't there? The answer depends on which section of the report one happens to read. First, there is a lengthy discussion as to how all of the sherds, except for a few strays, were positioned above the Poverty Point objects—a situation that indicated "a significant break in the history of the Jaketown Site" (Ford et al. 1955:114). Later, there is a statement that the break was only "indicated but not proved" (Ford et al. 1955:151).

Was Ford concerned that he was going too far by changing his lifelong stance against discontinuities? Was he waffling because he was unsure? Probably not, given that he apparently had no problem in spinning the completely unfounded interpretive yarn about northern peoples invading the lower Mississippi Valley. More likely, he didn't even realize the change in thinking he was going through at the time. Interestingly, it was Ford who was in charge of the excavations at Jaketown. One would have to go back to Peck Village to find another site in the valley that he was in charge of excavating. Did he direct the excavations because he was actually *looking for* discontinuities between periods, or did he start to see discontinuities once he was in the field rather than sitting in the laboratory analyzing sherd distributions? This appears to be another of those questions that is lost to history, but the answer really doesn't matter. What *does* matter is that by 1956 Jim Ford was a confirmed diffusionist—a position he kept for the remainder of his life.

6

The Nature of Culture and
the American Formative

1957–1969

The monograph that Ford and Webb produced on their excavations at Poverty Point was the last of Ford's great works on the prehistory of the lower Mississippi Valley. The two monographs produced after 1956, both of which summarized excavations Ford undertook in eastern Arkansas, were lackluster, almost mechanical recitations of what was done and what was found. Gone was the spark that had characterized his earlier publications, as were the in-your-face quips and barbs designed to get a rise out of any contemporary with whom he happened to be quarreling at the time. Ford was having trouble sustaining his interest in anything, and he bounced from project to project rather aimlessly. With the addition of the Poverty Point report to his stack of publications, the search for chronological order in the lower Mississippi Valley was essentially over, at least for the span of time that was of interest to Ford. What he needed was another grand-vision type of project.

During the mid-to-late 1950s, he became involved with a number of projects, few of which resulted in publications. He returned to Peru in July 1958 and worked there until August 1959, mapping several large sites and developing a ceramic chronology for three valleys on the northern coast (the Chira, Piura, and Lambayeque), but he produced no report on the work. Another project that was never written up—and which could have produced spectacular results if Ford had sustained his interest in it—was a National Science Foundation–sponsored study of physiographic changes in a portion of the Mississippi Valley and of how those changes related to patterns of human settlement.

Up until the late 1950s, most archaeological work in the alluvial valley had been focused on the ceramic periods, with little attention paid to the long span of time that preceded them, which even then was known to encompass at least

271

6,500 years and perhaps a lot more. Mastodon bones—obvious index fossils of the Pleistocene epoch (pre–11,000 years ago)—occasionally were found in the valley (e.g., Williams 1957), as were fluted projectile points that in the West, at least, dated near the Pleistocene-Holocene (post–11,000 years ago) boundary. Much more common than fluted points were specimens of a type known as *Dalton,* which by the 1950s was suspected of having followed on the heels of the fluted points. Dalton points were then thought to date ca. 7000 B.C.; they are now considered to date pre-7900 B.C. (Goodyear 1982; O'Brien and Wood 1998). The ubiquity of Dalton points made them excellent index fossils, and Ford's plan was to plot their locations relative to former river channels and related features such as point bars and levees.

By the early 1960s, it was obvious that Harold Fisk's (1944) classic geological study of the lower Mississippi River valley, the centerpiece of which was the dating of former Mississippi and Ohio River channels, was grossly inaccurate once one moved back in time beyond the historical period (geomorphologist Roger Saucier was a few years away from pointing out the inaccuracies in print [Saucier 1968]). One could, however, assume that Fisk's *relative* chronology of floodplain features was correct, but what better way of checking that chronology than through archaeology—exactly what Ford and Kniffen had started doing in Louisiana back in the 1930s? Ford had worked back and forth between archaeology and geomorphology at sites such as Jaketown and Poverty Point, using artifacts of known age as a check on Fisk's sequence. In similar fashion, there was every reason to expect that the presence of Dalton points on a landform would provide a minimal age for it, unless the points had been washed in from somewhere else or picked up and reused by later peoples.

For whatever reasons, Ford's interest in the project flagged, and he turned it over to Alden Redfield, then a graduate student at Harvard. Redfield later produced a series of notes on the project (Redfield 1971) as well as a doctoral dissertation and a brief report on the Lace Place, a Dalton-period site in the L'Anguille River drainage of northeastern Arkansas (Redfield and Moselage 1970).

THE POINT BARROW MONOGRAPH

The most significant project in which Ford was involved in the late 1950s was the preparation of a comprehensive monograph on his years of work in Alaska. Ford returned there in the summer of 1953 for his fourth and final archaeological trip, joining a Harvard-sponsored team working at sites near Point Barrow, but the trip produced little in the way of new data. Of much more importance were the materials that had been collected in the 1930s, and shortly before he left for Alaska, he obtained on loan from the Smithsonian all his notes and artifacts from his earlier expeditions. The monograph he eventually produced, *Eskimo Prehistory in the Vicinity of Point Barrow, Alaska* (Ford 1959), is more or less a compilation of all his pre-1953 work. Ford originally approached his old friend Henry Collins about collaborating on the project, since Ford had worked for Collins when the collections were made. "Do you want this study to be a collaboration," he wrote Collins,[1] "or would you prefer that I try to clean up the mess, along with your advice of course?" In that letter, Ford also voiced some agitation with the Smithsonian that had been festering for a long time:

> However, whichever way the work is done there probably is going to be some difficulty from the administration. I would naturally prefer to see this report come out in the American Museum series. For one thing, I think we have a much better format and preparation of illustrations is a lot easier. For another, I am still just a little griped that [Alexander] Wetmore did not provide funds for working up the collections soon after the field work was done. I do not see why at this point the American Museum should pay me to prepare a publication for the Smithsonian. This is the old credit fight of course and I am not much interested in it, but have no intention of "sacrificing" my valuable efforts for Wetmore's edification. I am still, as you know, burned up about the way in which Gordon Willey's and my attempted collaboration on the Viru papers came out, and that is further reason why I am not inclined to prepare this paper for the Smithsonian.

Seven years eventually passed between the time Ford received the artifacts and notes from the Smithsonian and the report's publication—by the American Museum—but the important thing was that it finally appeared. In the report, he stated for the record, "Had it been possible to study and report upon these collections soon after the completion of field-work, I would have been able to present this study as a substantial contribution to the unraveling of Eskimo prehistory. However, since the early 1930's, excellent studies of the archeology of the Arctic Coast of Alaska have been made. . . . This, then, is in the nature of a mopping-up job" (Ford 1959:16). Privately to Collins,[2] Ford lamented, "The Point Barrow paper is in the last stages of writing and I am frantically casting about for something to conclude. Nearly all conclusions have been drawn for me, and I find myself writing such statements as '. . . . on this point I must agree with Giddings who agrees with Larson who agrees with de Laguna who follows Collins in concluding that. . . .' "

Two features of the Point Barrow monograph are of brief interest here. The first is the way Ford handled the chronological positioning of harpoon heads from the sites. As one might expect, it didn't matter to Ford whether he was working on pottery or on bone harpoon heads: "It is well recognized that in the study of Eskimo prehistory harpoon heads serve much the same function of 'key fossil' as do ceramics for cultures in a Neolithic stage of development" (Ford

1. Letter from Ford to Collins, January 7, 1952 (LSU Museum of Natural Science archives).
2. Letter from Ford to Collins, September 24, 1957 (LSU Museum of Natural Science archives).

1959:93). Based on the work of Collins (1937) and others, a general sequence of harpoon-head types had been worked out for the Arctic, and Ford was able to place the materials from his four excavated sites within the sequence, in the process developing a chronological ordering of the assemblages (Figure 6.1). Then, in a move reminiscent of his early work in Louisiana (Ford 1935c, 1936a), he gave the chronological sequence an evolutionary significance by showing the "probable evolution of forms" (Ford 1959:95).

Although common practice had long before established harpoon-head "types" for use in Arctic archaeology, and Ford certainly used those, the novel feature of his work was in his use of attribute replacement as a means of creating an evolutionary sequence, as he had used design changes on pottery to establish his early Louisiana sequence:

> In addition to relative quantities, this diagram [Figure 6.1] has been arranged to bring together the varieties of harpoon heads that seem to be typologically related, thus providing a basis for deductions as to the evolution of forms. It appears obvious that the popular early harpoon head, Birnirk, has developed into the type named Natchuk by elimination of the single stone side blades (sometimes replaced by an ornamental groove) and by the reduction in the number of points on the spur to one. Similarly, it seems clear that the Thule 2 Type, which reached its maximum popularity of 32 per cent at Nunagiak, evolved from Natchuk by the addition of a second barb to replace the lost stone side blade of the preceding type, Birnirk. (Ford 1959:96)

For Ford, here as elsewhere, formal similarity was homologous and thus denoted ancestral-descendant relations. The possibility that the replacement of a stone blade with a barb might be a functional change apparently never entered Ford's mind, but such was not unusual among culture historians (Lyman et al. 1997a).

The second feature of interest in Ford's work was his use of traits to examine the derivation of Birnirk culture—the label assigned to the complex of sites in the Point Barrow region. Continuing a trend evident from about 1951, Ford badly mangled the handling of units such as periods and cultures, in some places referring to Birnirk as a period, as a culture, and as a phase. In still others he referred to Birnirk as a cultural stage. We wouldn't bother discussing his phyletic reconstruction if it were not for his comments regarding the use of traits and the problems involved therein. Trait diffusion was at the center of Ford's attention during most of the 1960s, but in his major treatment of the topic (Ford 1969), he was less clear than in the Point Barrow monograph about the difficulties in selecting traits for examination:

> The process of listing cultural traits which at first consideration may seem to be very simple is, in reality, quite a difficult task. Two decisions must be made for each trait. First, should the unit of comparison be the artifact, features of artifacts, or categories of artifacts? Trait lists may be extended considerably by making finer distinctions, but the significance of similar clusters of features is lost in the process. The second decision is that of the degree of similarity that is to be considered significant. (Ford 1959:238)

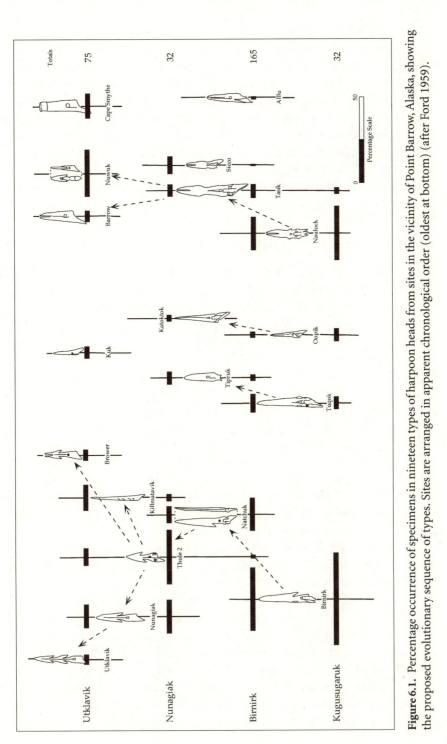

Figure 6.1. Percentage occurrence of specimens in nineteen types of harpoon heads from sites in the vicinity of Point Barrow, Alaska, showing the proposed evolutionary sequence of types. Sites are arranged in apparent chronological order (oldest at bottom) (after Ford 1959).

Ford created a long list of traits to use in his chrono-phyletic reconstruction and then examined artifact assemblages from sites placed in various periods/phases/cultures to derive the number of individual traits that linked various units. For example, thirty-two traits linked Okvik and Birnirk, but only twelve linked Ipiutak and Birnirk. In turn, forty-six traits linked Birnirk and Thule. The conclusion of this analysis was obvious to Ford: Birnirk culture grew out of both the Okvik and the Old Bering Sea cultures, and in turn, Birnirk and cultures contemporary with it but located in other parts of the Arctic gave rise to Thule culture. Ford would use similar reasoning, though not so well thought out, in postulating an American Formative that took in vast chunks of the Western Hemisphere.

THE ARKANSAS MONOGRAPHS

In the spring of 1958, either just prior to or just after completing the Point Barrow manuscript, Ford returned to the Mississippi Valley, this time to assist the National Park Service in excavating the Menard site on the lower Arkansas River in Arkansas County, Arkansas (Figure 6.2). The site had enjoyed a place of prominence in Americanist archaeology beginning with cursory examination by Edward Palmer, one of Cyrus Thomas's Bureau of American Ethnology field agents (Thomas 1894; see also Jeter 1990:133–40), and continuing through excavations by C. B. Moore in 1908 (Moore 1908) and Philip Phillips in 1941 (Phillips et al. 1951:265–70). The site's prominence was due to the exquisite pottery it had produced over the years—plus the long-held assumption that Menard was the location of Osotouy, a Quapaw settlement near Arkansas Post, which was established by Henri de Tonti, a member of the La Salle expedition, in 1686. Ironically, as Ford (1958:133) pointed out, Phillips and Griffin wanted to assign pottery from the upper levels of the two test pits Phillips excavated to the Quapaw, but Ford had his "stubborn doubts." He changed his mind after his 1958 excavation, deciding the evidence supported the notion that Menard *was* the location of Osotouy.

As with his Point Barrow analysis, we might make only passing reference to Ford's work at Menard except for one point he raised in his monograph. After examining the vertical distribution of sherds of various types both in his trenches and in the test units Phillips excavated in 1941, Ford suggested the stratigraphy was telescoped. Notice in Figure 6.3 that there is an overall tendency for sherds of Baytown Plain to increase in relative frequency with depth and for sherds of Neeley's Ferry Plain to decrease—which is what sherds of those types were supposed to do if the chronology developed by Phillips et al. (1951) held up. But also notice that not all late types as defined by Phillips et al. decreased in relative frequency with depth. For example, Wallace Incised—which Ford was willing by 1958 to assign to the Mississippi period (probably Quapaw), just as Phillips

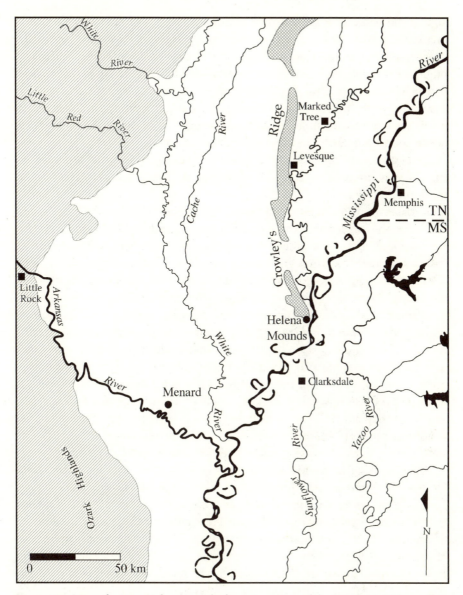

Figure 6.2. Map of eastern Arkansas and adjacent portion of the Mississippi River valley showing the locations of the Menard site and Helena Mounds.

and Griffin had earlier suggested (Phillips et al. 1951)—should have decreased dramatically with depth (given the large percentages of Baytown Plain in the lower levels), as should several of the other late types. Instead, they fluctuated randomly throughout the excavation columns—a result, Ford argued, of mixing, in which "the earlier cultural materials moved upward and later materials moved downward by the overturning of the soil, the digging of pits, post holes, and so on, either in aboriginal times or later. Soil brought in for the preparation of new house floors doubtlessly contributed" (Ford 1958:152).

This was not the only time Ford used the "telescoped-deposits" argument to explain away nonperfect patterns in excavated samples of artifacts. He did it in the Point Barrow report (Ford 1959:95–96), just as Phillips, perhaps with Ford's "editorial assistance," had done in the Jaketown report (Ford et al. 1955:104). In both cases, the reader was referred to the volume by Phillips et al. (1951:232–33) for elaboration. There, in what was called a discussion of the use of stratigraphic data in seriation but that was in reality a discussion of the use of percentage stratigraphy (clearly written by Ford), Phillips et al. outlined how to take care of the problem of telescoped deposits: "The control which we have over this accidental upward weighting of midden-deposit evidence is the comparison of such unusually slow-growing [deposits in those] cuts with the results of other excavations in the same area. A still better check is the comparison of these cuts with seriated short time-span surface collections" (Phillips et al. 1951:233). This was and still is a reasonable practice, but for Ford—and things are really not much different today—what it really boiled down to was this: he knew some types were later than other types, and when they didn't "behave" stratigraphically—that is, when they didn't fall "into their proper places as though under orders" (Phillips et al. 1951:274)—he explained the deviant behavior through reference to stratigraphic mixing.

While working at the Menard site, Ford visited a site that he, Griffin, and Phillips had found in 1940 during the course of their Mississippi Valley survey. Ford (1963:5) wrote, with just a bit of an air of authority, that "Local residents were unaware that this was a prehistoric site, an understandable error, because the five mounds that then composed the group were situated on the southeastern edge of Crowley's Ridge, and the loess soil that caps this ridge has eroded into deep gullies, leaving narrow rounded ridges that in some cases resembled mounds. The archeological surveyors, however, were very much impressed." Perhaps, but Griffin (pers. comm., 1996) remembers the event a little differently: "In the spring of 1940 as PF & G were driving north along the east side of Crowley's Ridge, I called attention to the Helena Mds and said that if those humps were in the Illinois River area they would be mounds. Hell no [Ford responded], they were erosional remnants. One day we went up there and you know, they were mounds."

The site, termed Helena Crossing, sat on the southeastern edge of Crowley's Ridge, an erosional remnant that extends nearly 200 miles from the head of the

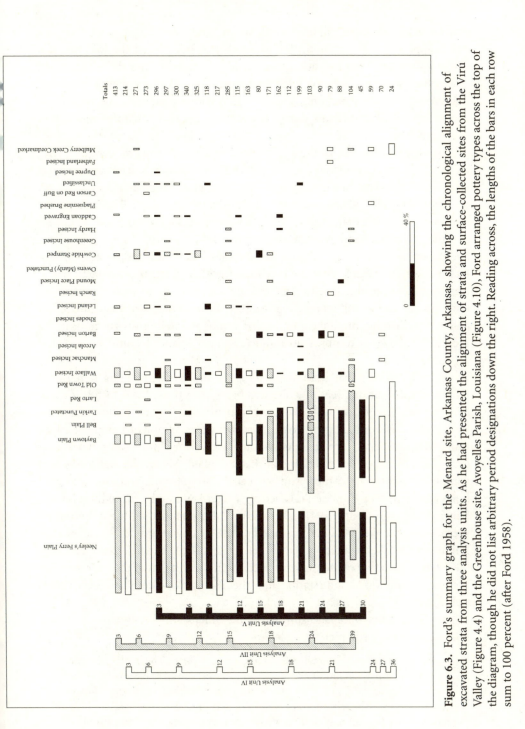

Figure 6.3. Ford's summary graph for the Menard site, Arkansas County, Arkansas, showing the chronological alignment of excavated strata from three analysis units. As he had presented the alignment of strata and surface-collected sites from the Virú Valley (Figure 4.4) and the Greenhouse site, Avoyelles Parish, Louisiana (Figure 4.10), Ford arranged pottery types across the top of the diagram, though he did not list arbitrary period designations down the right. Reading across, the lengths of the bars in each row sum to 100 percent (after Ford 1958).

alluvial valley at Cairo, Illinois, south in an arc to Helena, Arkansas, on the Mississippi River (Figure 6.2). Phillips et al. (1951:50) listed the location as a "large village site," but the site actually held five mounds and little if anything else in the way of an archaeological signature. When Ford revisited it, he found that recent road construction had destroyed two of the mounds and that house construction had disturbed a third. He excavated the two remaining mounds in the fall of 1960.

The Helena Mounds, as the site is more commonly known, were attractive archaeologically because they appeared to be similar to Hopewell mounds in western Illinois, based on their arrangement, location, and shape—five closely spaced, conical-to-rounded structures, sitting on a ridgetop and slope. The mounds lay almost in the middle of the 400-mile gap between the Hopewell mounds of Illinois and the Marksville mounds excavated during the 1930s and 1940s in Louisiana, and if they *were* Hopewellian, they offered what Ford, Willey, and, earlier, Collins, had wanted: the means to tie the two areas together in terms of artifacts, burial treatment, and the like. True to their appearance, the mounds were Hopewellian. One mound contained a single log tomb with the remains of two individuals inside, but the other mound contained five tombs and numerous skeletons in the mound fill above the tombs. Four radiocarbon dates ranged from A.D. 30 ± 150 to A.D. 335 ± 150.

One might think that if an archaeologist stated in the opening remarks of a monograph that one reason a site was being investigated was to fill in a gap between two regions, he would at least compare the artifacts against materials from both areas. Ford didn't do this; rather, with the exception of a single sherd, he assigned the pottery from the Helena Mounds to various lower-valley types—for example, Tchefuncte Stamped, Indian Bay Stamped, Marksville Stamped—and completely ignored any comparison between those types and numerous decorated types Griffin had long since established for western and west-central Illinois (e.g., Baker et al. 1941; Griffin 1941, 1952c). Ford also classified all the undecorated sherds as Marksville Plain, never addressing the "plainware muddle" discussed by Phillips in the Jaketown report (Ford et al. 1955:76–77). And he did not compare the internal structure of the two excavated mounds with that of mounds in either Louisiana or Illinois, despite stating that "the Illinois excavations have been rather well described" (Ford 1963:47).

Ford ended his one-page summary-and-conclusions section on a cryptic note—one that we will pick up on later:

> No attempt at extensive comparisons is made in this paper. The entire subject of the widespread Hopewell culture needs a review. In this, considerable attention should be given to the question of origin. For some years it has been clear that Hopewell must in some way be related to the Middle American "Formative" and to the basic culture of the Andean region of South America. The radiocarbon dates available at

present make it appear that these influences entered the Mississippi Valley from the south. This is one of the principal questions in North American archeology, and the complete answer is not yet in sight. (Ford 1963:47)

It might not have been completely in sight in 1962, when Ford probably wrote that statement, but it was becoming clearer in his mind all the time. If the monograph on the Helena Mounds has any historical value, it might be in the fact that it contains one of the first, if not *the* first, mention by Ford of an American Formative. This was an idea that had been boiling around in his mind for a long time, and it would set his research agenda for the rest of his life.

FEUDING OVER CULTURE: THE BARRANQUILLA PAPER

Closely allied with Ford's notion of an American Formative was his view of culture and how it changed. Until the early 1960s, he never produced an extended statement on what culture actually is and how and why it might change through time or vary across space. Instead, he tended to provide, beginning with his first article in the *Louisiana Conservation Review* (Ford 1935a), only brief statements. By stringing these together in the chronological order in which they were published, one can detect threads of continuity in his thinking but also a sort of intellectual growth. Ford (1935a:9) early on defined culture as "the component of the customs and styles of languages, handicrafts, arts and ceremonials practiced by any particular group of people at any one time. Culture is in reality *a set of ideas* as to how things should be done and made" (emphasis added). Ford (1935a:9) followed this definition with the statement, "[culture] is in a continuous state of [gradual] evolutionary change since it is constantly influenced both by inventions from within and the introduction of new ideas from without the group." This was Ford's major axiom, and to exemplify and provide a warrant for it, he wrote, "Perhaps the best present illustration of one of the more rapidly changing modern cultural elements is the way in which women's dresses, though all slavishly alike at any one time, change from season to season" (Ford 1935a:9) The choice of women's dresses as the "best present illustration" is interesting, because it is precisely this "cultural element" that Kroeber (1919) had used in his early discussion of change in cultural elements. Ford did not, however, cite Kroeber's paper.

Three years later, Ford (1938b) listed Kroeber's (1919) study of women's dresses at the end of his paper on chronological methods, but he did not cite it in the text. Interestingly, at that time he was apparently unsure about how one was to distinguish cultural influences "from within" and those "from without" (Ford 1938b:262). His publications from the early and middle 1940s are essentially silent on the topic, save for comments such as the following concerning pottery-decoration complexes in different regions of the Cauca Valley of Colombia: "The cultural contrast of these two adjacent regions is caused by one of two factors:

isolation of cultures or temporal difference. Even a guess at the solution of this problem is not possible on the basis of the evidence at hand" (Ford 1944:73).

In his report on pottery from the Virú Valley, Ford (1949:38) defined culture as "a stream of ideas, that passes from individual to individual by means of symbolic action, verbal instruction, or imitation." This was, apparently, the first time he actually used the stream metaphor. Where did it come from? Ford (1949:38) explicitly attributed the notion to Kroeber's (1917) conception of culture as a "superorganic" phenomenon. Kroeber's statement was that "civilization [read *culture*] is not mental action but a body or stream of products of mental exercise" (Kroeber 1917:192). Culture was, then, something above the organic: "The mind and the body are but facets of the same organic material . . . the social substance . . . the thing that we call [culture] transcends them for all its being rooted in life" (Kroeber 1917:212). Culture was, in short, something that "had passed beyond natural selection, that was no longer wholly dependent on any agency of organic evolution" (Kroeber 1917:209).

Ford clearly paid attention to what Kroeber had to say in 1917 about culture as a superorganic phenomenon, but he unfortunately did not pay attention to what Kroeber later said about the parallels between organic and cultural evolution (e.g., Kroeber 1931a, 1943). Thus, although Ford acknowledged that two such radically different kinds of similarity might exist, he presumed, as we argued earlier, that all similarity was of the homologous (common ancestry) sort. Perhaps that was because Kroeber (1919:239) had indicated in his paper on women's dresses that stylistic phenomena are those that do not "vary in purpose." Maybe Ford thought that if he examined artifact styles, particularly decoration, he would in the process be studying idea streams rather than something that was a functional necessity— the result of adaptive convergence or analogous similarity—and thus not a good measure of the history of idea streams. We really don't know because Ford didn't discuss the matter.

To Ford, what should be important to archaeologists is determining the histories of streams of cultural ideas. The question, then, was that if culture is ideas, and culture change can be conceived as a flowing stream of ideas, how was culture to be studied? Ford (1952a:319) indicated that "it is impossible to study culture until it has been expressed in some material form." In his view, artifacts were "useful as recorders of cultural influence" (Ford 1949:38). He usually studied pottery, but other objects, such as fired-clay balls, harpoon heads, and even projectile points, would do. On the one hand, these were all "material culture," and on the other hand, they were also all an archaeologist could study: "all else has usually been destroyed by the passage of the centuries" (Ford 1936b:102).

In his publications, Ford went on at length about archaeological "culture*s*," such as "Hopewell culture," "Tchefuncte culture," and the like, but his discussions of *culture* were, as we have indicated, brief. This changed in 1962 with the publication of a series of notes and handouts made for a seminar that he and two friends at the Smithsonian, husband and wife Clifford Evans and Betty Meggers, held at the Universidad del Atlantico in Barranquilla, Colombia, in the summer of 1961. The seminar, sponsored by that university and the Organization of American States, was held to train young archaeologists from Central and South America in modern archaeological analysis (Figure 6.4). Ford pulled together a variety of teaching aids and assembled them in a notebook that subsequently was revised and published by the Pan American Union (Ford 1962). This kind of publication today would not attract much attention, perhaps receiving brief mention in the book notices section at the back of a journal. Ford's compilation of notes and charts *was* reviewed, however, and the reviews were deadly.

Ford decided the seminar was the perfect venue in which to present his first extended discussion of culture. Even that might not have prompted much response from reviewers, for much of what he said could be found scattered in his earlier writings, just as was his discussion of archaeological methods. But in this short monograph—the published text is a mere sixty pages—he also made very explicit his views on what he termed the "culturological point of view" (Ford 1962:6). He paid for his remarks at the hands of an anthropologist whose sympathies were not in that camp.

Ford's opinions on culture directly underlay his study of the American Formative, and as we argue below, they had to. From a historical perspective, it is clear why he presented his most lengthy statement on culture just before he turned attention to the topic that was to concern him for the remainder of his life. It might seem odd that he picked a paper with the title "A Quantitative Method for Deriving Cultural Chronology" as the place in which to express formally his views on culture, but remember that for Ford, as for most of his contemporaries, cultural chronology was just that—a temporal ordering of *cultures*. Recall, too, Ford's (1952a:319) statement that "it is impossible to study culture until it has been expressed in some material form." Ford (e.g., 1954c) was skeptical that even ethnographers could study sets of ideas because the idea bearers were, in Ford's view, more or less unaware of those idea sets. *Empirical* expressions of those ideas— be they the human behaviors of marriage, residency, or interpersonal interaction (e.g., kinship, sociopolitical organization) studied by ethnographers, or the potsherds studied by an archaeologist—were thus required. Notice that Ford said it was impossible to study culture until it had been expressed in material form. This is not a matter of semantics; he wrote the phrase exactly as he meant it to be read. If one could order the material remains of cultures properly, one could monitor not only the flow of time but also the evolution of those cultures—the flow of the idea stream. He expressed this most vividly in an illustration (Figure 6.5) he borrowed from a paper he had earlier published in Colombia (Ford 1957). The message in the diagram is abundantly clear: the continuous march of time

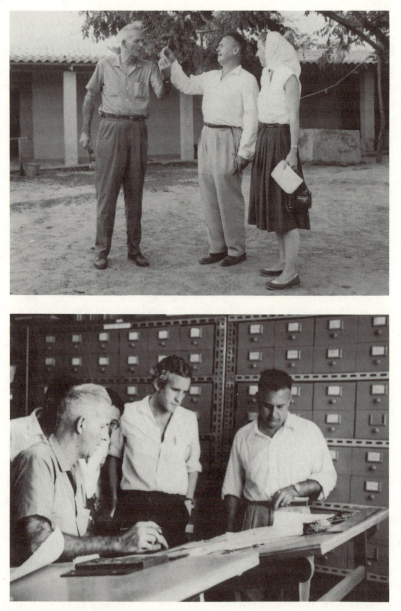

Figure 6.4. Photographs of (top) James A. Ford, Clifford Evans, and Betty J. Meggers in Barranquilla, Colombia, 1961; (bottom) Ford, left, and Evans, right, explaining the finer points of archaeology to Latin American students (photographs courtesy W. G. Haag).

can be captured in material culture, in this case pottery vessels. The caption is equally clear: archaeological types are accidents of history, entirely dependent on the entry point of the archaeologist into the sequence.

In short, Ford was thinking in materialist terms when he attempted to monitor the developmental history—evolution, if you wish—of cultural lineages, even though they might have a reticulate pattern rather than the simpler dendritic pattern of organic evolution. However, he, like his contemporaries, fell into the pit presented by the materialist-essentialist paradox precisely because he wanted to study culture rather than the archaeological record (Lyman et al. 1997a). Those who reviewed his quantitative-method paper found much on which to comment in both arenas.

A Quantitative Method for Deriving Cultural Chronology

Ford's (1962) discussion is perhaps most easily considered if it is broken into two portions, one dealing with archaeological methods and the other with culture. We can thus dispense with methods rather quickly before turning to culture. Ford's discussion of archaeological methods was largely a reiteration of many of the points he had made in the late 1940s and throughout the 1950s. In some cases his treatment of particular topics was abbreviated, such as his consideration of the requirements of and problems inherent in the seriation method (Ford 1962:41–42). In other cases, he was much clearer than he had been in previous treatments, perhaps because of the brevity of his discussion. His section on "Making a Typology" (Ford 1962:14–16) is an excellent example, for here, while he referred the reader to Ford (1954c) for "more complete discussion," he did not get bogged down in polemic and warranting arguments. Instead, he quickly discarded the notion that the types of the archaeologist are "cultural [read *emic*] types" (Ford 1962:14): "The makers of buildings, graves, pots, tools, and weapons that are the subject matter of archaeology are all dead, but even if they were alive they could not tell the archaeologist what he needs to know [the *ideas* regarding the proper and best ways humans should behave]. These people lived in their cultures as securely and unconsciously as fish live in the sea; that culture is an evolving phenomena and has a history surely never occurred to most of them" (Ford 1962:11).

Ford (1962:14) nonetheless argued, "This temporal and spatial [cultural] drift [read *flow of ideas over space and through time*] tends to be a gradual process, and the history of these changing [artifact/idea] forms is *exactly what we would like to discover*" (emphasis added). One discovered that history (which the culture bearers themselves were incapable of knowing) by constructing types—cutting chunks out of the ceramic continuum—that allowed the measurement of time and space. The chunks should be tightly defined to avoid typological creep or a type that would "run" (Ford 1962:14), and Ford noted that the best way to define

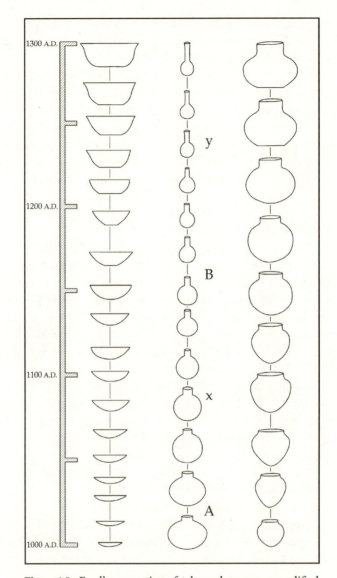

Figure 6.5. Ford's conception of culture change as exemplified in material culture. Note the constant gradation in the three forms through time. Ford also used the diagram to reinforce the arbitrariness of types. If a type A is set up in the water-bottle tradition as shown, then the classifier has to select the next type in this tradition at least as far away as B in order to differentiate among types consistently. The examples midway between these "typical" type examples are the difficult borderline cases. Alternatively, if the first type established had been set up at x, then the second type would have to be as far away as y. In this arrangement, the forms that were typical for type B of the first system become the doubtful specimens of the second (after Ford 1962).

such chunks was by "trial and error" (Ford 1962:16), which involved placing on a single table all "the sherds from sites representing as many different time levels as can be secured; stir thoroughly and then simply sort into groups the sherds that look alike" (Ford 1962:19). Alternating this procedure with testing to see if the resulting groups distinguished different time-space loci would eventually produce a useful set of extensionally defined types. Seriable types, or types that fell in different stratigraphic positions, were desirable.

In his review of Ford's handbook, George Cowgill (1963:697) noted that when Ford said his types were "arbitrary," he apparently meant that the boundaries of such units were arbitrary (given the ceramic continuum, for example), as indicated in Figure 6.5. Robert Ascher, in his review, suggested that Ford's definition of a type—"the product of a set of customs of manufacture and decoration that were practiced for a shorter or longer period of time by a people living in a relatively small geographical area" (Ford 1962:27)—"will be acceptable to most" (Ascher 1963:570). Importantly, Cowgill (1963:697) noted that "the Spaulding and Ford views about the discoverability of artifacts types are not contradictory, but are complementary." In Cowgill's view, both men sought clusters of attributes that occurred "oftener than we would expect if attributes were randomly associated," and once found, they both could then "proceed to specific and verifiable statements about patterning of attribute combinations" (Cowgill 1963:697). The difference was one of method, Cowgill (1963:697) reasoned, because "Spaulding's 'statistical technique' presupposes that the unit of analysis is the single component [whereas Ford's technique examines simultaneously] many closely related components." The root of the difference in method was ultimately ontological. Ford was here a materialist who viewed cultural evolution as a continuum with no natural joints or seams; Spaulding was an essentialist who believed there were natural seams and thus sought such joints or breaks in the continuum. Cowgill (1963) failed to note this fundamental difference, as did Ascher (1963).

Given these unrecognized differences in epistemology, perhaps it is not surprising that Ascher (1963:570) didn't like Ford's (1962) use of words when referring to sherds—words such as "descendants," "ancestral forms," and "parallel lineages." No less a luminary than A. V. Kidder (e.g., 1915) had used similar terms, but that fact apparently escaped Ascher's notice. Of Ford's use of such words, Ascher noted (1963:570), in terms reminiscent of J. O. Brew's (1946) evisceration of Colton and Hargrave's (1937) and Gladwin and Gladwin's (1934) so-called "genetic-chronological" model (Willey and Sabloff 1993:122), that "Sherds were never alive: is it not time to drop denotative diction derived from questionable analogies?" But Ford, like Kidder, Gladwin, Colton, and others, was speaking metaphorically—he never argued that sherds exchanged genetic material. Many individuals used what we have termed phyletic seriation to seriate collections of artifacts (e.g., Beals et al. 1945; Kidder 1917; Sayles 1937), but they were not the subject of such misplaced criticisms. The problem with Ford's thinking was, however, deeper than this, and it concerned his views of culture.

Ford on Culture and Culturology

Since virtually the beginning of his career, Ford had emphasized that types were arbitrary groups of things that existed within arbitrary chunks of the time-space continuum. His types allowed him to measure that continuum because they were ideational units, the empirical representatives of which displayed each type's distribution across space and through time. But Ford wanted to study *culture* history, not artifact history. That is, he wanted to track the flow of streams of cultural ideas, and to do that, he had to firm up the linkage between his types and his use of them to measure streams of ideas. Such a linkage could be established, Ford apparently thought, by arguing that culture consisted of ideas, and that ideas could have material expressions. None of his reviewers disputed the first point, and none really doubted the second, as Ascher's (1963) and Cowgill's (1963) reviews indicate. What these two reviewers, plus a third, took exception to was Ford's additional comments on culture and culture change.

Ford's (1962:6–9) comments can be summarized as follows:
- Culture is a nonbiological phenomenon and thus cannot be explained in terms of biology or genetics. Cultural anthropologists and archaeologists study culture, not people as biological organisms.
- Cultural forms are not created by genius; new forms—whether of social customs, religion, or pottery—"can only come from preceding forms." [This is the "culturological point of view."]
- The potentials of the human mind and body (along with the environment) set limits on what *can* be accomplished, but they do not dictate what *is* accomplished.
- Cultural change is slow, continuous, and gradual and is never "simultaneous" because there are always old forms contemporary with new forms. Change, especially among primitive people, is "usually almost unconscious and unnoticed," as people choose particular forms to duplicate. [The popularity of a form is measured archaeologically by its frequency in a collection.]
- There are only three ways that innovations might appear within a cultural tradition: invention, discovery, or borrowing. Invention involves combining extant ideas in a new and unique way; discovery involves finding some new "item" that can be put to use; and borrowing involves "the geographical diffusion of traits [and] is the most common way in which cultural inventories are increased and also one of the most common phenomena the archaeologist has to deal with."

Ford (1949:38) had earlier written in a footnote that "it is understood that individuals do not 'create' ideas. The concept of 'free will' seems to have no place in science. Individuals receive ideas from other humans, sometimes combine them, less frequently discover them in the natural world about them, and almost always pass them along to others." Thus his 1962 statements were expansions and elaborations of this early phrasing, and were not that different from what Kroeber (1917) had said. A flattering review might point out two things about Ford's thinking. First, in removing what might be called biological/genetic determinism from the equation, Ford was trying to parrot Kroeber's (1917) observation that because culture was "superorganic," organic evolution—and all processes entailed thereby, such as inheritance and natural selection—was *unlike* cultural evolution. This was Ford's "culturology." Remember too that Ford had studied at Michigan and no doubt was influenced by Leslie White (e.g., 1949, 1959a, 1959b), who throughout his career had argued that culture was "extrasomatic" and had written such statements as "the biological factor of man is irrelevant to various problems of cultural interpretation such as diversities among cultures, and processes of culture change in general and the evolution of culture in particular" (White 1959b:12). It is thus perhaps easy to see where Ford obtained his notions, but it is equally easy to see that he did not fully understand Kroeber's or White's reasoning and thus incorrectly perceived people as mere flotsam on the stream of culture history.

The second point that might be made by someone sympathetic to Ford's view is that perhaps he was attempting to remove what we would today refer to as human *intentions* from the archaeological study of cultural evolution by dismissing the relevance of "free will" to scientific archaeology. Rather, we suspect his point was that *individuals* might have free will to express themselves as they wished, but societal censure would not allow new cultural forms to originate from such a source because of cultural conservancy and a desire to maintain the status quo. Thus he argued that while culture is constantly changing, "This change usually occurs by small mutations, by the recombination of features already available in the cultural inventory or borrowed from neighbors. Normally, the changes will be so small that an observer will see the sum effect as a gradual drift, either slow or fast" (Ford 1962:9).

Ascher (1963:570) did not like that Ford presented his thoughts on culture and culture change not "as assumptions nor hypotheses, but as evident conclusions." This was serious in Ascher's view and led him to observe that some of Ford's seriations and his interpretations thereof were circular precisely because they depended on his concepts of culture change. Ford (1962:54) had admitted this when he wrote that inferring migrations from seriated collections was "a neat example of circular reasoning. Chronologies are aligned according to conclusions about directions of diffusion; once aligned, they may be used to 'prove' the directions in which complexes moved." Ford was, unfortunately, rather vague about how such tautological reasoning was to be avoided.

Cowgill (1963:698) noted that Ford's notions of culture and culture change "are taken as axiomatic and are used only in justifying the assertion that change is gradual and in denying the possibility of abrupt and drastic change brought about by exceptional individuals." Cowgill had no apparent difficulty with those notions as long as the goal of archaeological analysis was to build a chronology. The problem was that such notions of culture change precluded, in Cowgill's (1963:698) view, study of "cultural process or ecological interpretation" and of "fluctuation in rates of change." He thus remarked that "Ford's methods do not lend themselves to these or to many other problems because there is no systematic approach to the question of how and in what ways different types resemble one another, or of the extent to which transitional specimens are actually found. . . . Ford has been satisfied to stick with a method of processing ceramic data tailored very closely to the needs of chronology alone" (Cowgill 1963:698). The problem was that Ford assumed that all formal similarities documented in similar types denoted homologous similarities, and he was sloppy in deciding which types were formally similar because he did not worry about the question of how similar was similar enough. In Ford's view, transitional specimens would not be found except by the careless typologist who did not actively seek to avoid typological creep, which, of course, was a result of the extensional nature of his type definitions.

It wasn't the archaeologists who reviewed Ford's monograph who dug in their heels and asked the really difficult questions. Instead, it was Morris Opler, a cultural anthropologist, who in an unsolicited comment pointed out what he perceived to be serious errors in Ford's thinking about culture and culture change. Opler (1963:897–98) didn't like Ford's "catatonic fixation on culture" as characterized by his statement that archaeologists and cultural anthropologists did *not* study people but rather only culture (Ford 1962:6), Ford's mischaracterization of the history of evolutionism within anthropology (Ford 1962:3–4), or the strange melding of the first two points into one that held humans to be "passive recipient[s] of whatever cultural evolution brings" (Opler 1963:901). In short, Opler (1963:902) simply could not agree with Ford's position, which he characterized as holding that "man has developed his enormous and intricate brain, his powers to remember and record the past, his abilities to probe the minute and the remote, his capacity for invention, communication, and planning, in order to remain a supermoron fit only to fetch and carry for Mother [cultural] Evolution." The following year Opler published a longer article entitled "The Human Being in Culture Theory" (Opler 1964b) in which he took on both Kroeber and White for their derogation of the importance of the individual.

White's position on the subject (e.g., White 1948) was as well known as Kroeber's, and Opler was no fan of White's. Neither was Opler a fan of anyone who adhered to White's notions on the roles played by energy and technology in cultural evolution. In one of the most openly hostile and vicious attacks ever made in American anthropology, especially given the general mood of the time, Opler had this response to Betty Meggers's (1960) comments made in a volume honoring White: "Apparently the 'practical tool kit' Dr. Meggers urges upon the field of anthropologists is not quite so new as she represents, and its main contents seem to be a somewhat shopworn hammer and sickle" (Opler 1961:13). Anthropologists, even those who normally weren't too sympathetic to the Whiteian point of view, immediately condemned Opler for his stupid and libelous remark.

In his response to Opler's comments, Ford (1964:400) admitted that cultural and biological evolution are analogous but separate processes. Thus, when noting that Opler attempted to integrate organic and cultural evolution, Ford wondered if he had suggested that people intentionally developed a big brain. Ford wanted to omit such mechanisms as the human mind, free will, racial genius, and the like from attempts to explain cultural evolution, implying that these were irrational forms of explanation. Opler (1964a:404) replied that variation in thinking, whether by a few or many people, was the source of much cultural development, and he dispensed with the notion of cultural evolution "if by the phrase is meant a one-directional movement over time, independent of human beings" (Opler 1964a:403). Ford (1962:3) had mentioned Leslie White as "com[ing] to the rescue of [the] central fact of human history" that cultures did evolve, but he didn't cite any of White's writings nor present any of White's ideas other than to suggest that a Whitean form of cultural evolutionism implied that "man's culture is not produced by the 'human mind.' " Instead, Ford (1962:3) argued that a culture "came from a preceding culture in a manner analogous to, but by no means identical with, the generation of living forms" and then suggested that Kroeber's (1917) statement on the superorganic was "a clear statement to this effect." As Cowgill (1963:698) astutely observed, this meant that "culture [was] the cause of culture."

Why Ask Why?

What was Ford thinking? *Why* was he thinking what he was? It seems to us that Ford's ontological position never really changed. He began, in 1935, with the notion that culture—ideas—changes continuously and gradually, and by 1949 he had adopted Kroeber's metaphor of an evolving culture as a flowing stream of ideas. The most common way new ideas were introduced into a cultural stream was by diffusion, at which point the stream became braided. That model of cultural evolution, in short, was the source of Ford's explanations for the temporal, spatial, and formal variation in the sherds, projectile points, and harpoons he studied. Cultures usually were rather conservative, thus the flow was gradual. Different empirical forms of ideas slowly gained and then lost popularity, as his types showed. His conceptual model *had* to fit the empirical record. Observations on his own culture and those made by ethnographers relative to other cultures provided a commonsense understanding. Cultures had evolved—why else study time via archaeology—and common sense provided the understanding. It was thus difficult for Ford to deal with those who held a different commonsense understanding. All he could do was argue, "If the theoretical bases for the techniques described [and used by him] were faulty, it seems improbable that the techniques would work" (Ford 1964:399).

Importantly, Ford now had the foundation laid for the work that was to become his final major contribution to the discipline. Diffusion was the major source of change in the flowing streams of ideas—the trickles intersected and diverged with remarkable frequency. Formal similarity of sherds, harpoons, and fired-clay balls was, therefore, of the homologous sort. He had as early as 1936 abandoned detailed study of formal variation in favor of a binomial system of pottery nomenclature. In many ways this precluded detailed study and consideration of the crucial question of how similar two sherds, for example, had to be to consider them members of the same type unit. Ford had for so long worked with seriation and percentage stratigraphy as relative dating techniques that the radiocarbon revolution seems to have had little influence on his thinking. In 1961 he was well aware of what people such as Meggers and Evans were proposing relative to long-distance diffusion and its role in shaping the prehistory of the Americas, and he was well prepared—preadapted, if you will—to enter the game himself. That is, we suspect, why he devoted so much space to his view of culture and culture change in his 1962 monograph. He had to establish a foundation for what he was about to attempt.

DIFFUSION, MIGRATION, AND THE AMERICAN FORMATIVE

Diffusion (the movement of things and/or ideas) and migration (the movement of people) have long been central to interpretations of the archaeological record. These were the processes of change called upon by culture historians throughout the tenure of their paradigm (Lyman et al. 1997a). Both processes figured importantly in Ford's thinking from the beginning, but during the 1960s they came to the forefront as a result of his interest—we might even call it an obsession—in the question of why there were so many similarities in the archaeological records of such geographically remote areas as coastal Georgia and Ecuador or the lower Mississippi Valley and coastal Mexico. Was there reason to suspect that human groups had moved from one area to the other, in the process taking part or all of their material culture with them, or was the reason for the similarity something even deeper, such as a psychic unity of mankind—that nebulous glue that binds humans together into a common phylogenetic unit and which causes them to go through more or less the same thought processes and to develop the same solutions to problems? Could this phenomenon be so strong and so perfect that it caused humans to decorate their pots similarly, even though one group lived in northern Florida and another in coastal Colombia?

Frank Setzler (1933a, 1933b, 1934) had used similarities in artifacts to create a scenario in which Hopewell grew out of the northern spread of Marksville traits and perhaps the spread of people as well. In large part, his faith in diffusion/migration resided in his belief that "Independent invention of so complicated a technique of [pottery] decoration where there is such striking similarity would seem improbable" (Setzler 1933b:6). Ford and Willey (1941) adopted the same position in their summary article on eastern prehistory. Ford interpreted the evidence from Jaketown and Poverty Point to create an invasion of the lower Mississippi Valley by early Hopewellian people, who forced local Archaic peoples to build large earthen structures for them. It is clear that by the time Ford compiled the information for his monograph on design developments in the southeastern United States (Ford 1952a), he was convinced not only of migrations but also that the source of some diffused traits lay to the south, in either Mexico or perhaps South America. By the time he wrote his monograph on the Helena Mounds (Ford 1963), he was totally convinced. All that remained was for him to prove it. Keep in mind that Ford's interest in diffusion and migration in the 1950s and early 1960s was not singular. Diffusion had always been around in one guise or another (e.g., Steward 1929), and it was commonly accepted as fact that diffusion and migration not only had occurred prehistorically but also were probably responsible for many of the similarities seen in archaeological records around the world. The only question was how *much* of a role they had played.

In the mid-1960s Ford became the point person for the diffusionist-migration cause, at least for the New World, with his proposal that extensive coastal migration in the pre–Christian era had resulted in the widespread distribution of key elements in the archaeological record. He had at his disposal artifacts and information from long regional sequences over which there finally existed adequate chronological control, brought about through radiocarbon dating. It became his self-appointed duty, using advice from sympathetic colleagues, to align the chronologies and begin tracking the movement of artifacts, ideas, and people throughout the New World for the three millennia leading up to the Christian era.

To place the significance of what Ford did in historical context, we need to examine, at least briefly, the history of diffusionism during the 1950s and early 1960s, the period leading up to Ford's excursion into the American Formative. It is impossible to cover here the history of diffusion- and migration-related studies in Americanist archaeology, even for that particular fifteen-year period; instead, we focus on a few major developments during that time. Interested readers might want to look at Willey and Sabloff (1993) and Lyman et al. (1997a) for a more extended discussion.

Diffusion Studies and Chronological Sequences

One of the key statements on the topic of diffusion resulted from a series of seminars on archaeological method and theory hosted by the Society for American

Archaeology in 1955. Four seminars were held the following summer. Each one produced a report under the general editorship of one of the participants, and all four were published in a single volume the following year. One paper is of particular concern here because it captures much of the thinking at the time on the integration of the three dimensions of archaeology—time, space, and form—and how one might deal with phenomena such as diffusion.

An issue considered by one set of seminar participants was the identification and interpretation of culture-contact situations (Lathrap 1956). Participants indicated that theirs was only the second paper to deal with such events, citing Willey's (1953a) "A Pattern of Diffusion-Acculturation" as the first. Willey had described archaeological evidence for three prehistoric cases of what he considered to be culture-contact episodes. Invasion, to Willey (1953a:370, 374), was indicated by "stark" and "striking" differences between archaeological cultures superposed in the stratigraphic record. Diffusion and/or acculturation was represented by "a blend of the intrusive elements and the old local forms" (Willey 1953a:379). Such ideas can be traced as far back as Kidder's work.

Seminar participants suggested (Lathrap 1956:7) that their recognition of eight "types" of culture-contact situations rested on two dimensions of variation— "the nature of the contact and its results." The "nature-of-contact" dimension could involve intrusions at the "site-unit" level or at the "trait-unit" level; the former denoted immigration of a unique ethnic group to an area and the latter the movement of a single culture trait such as "a stylistic or technological feature or complex" (Lathrap 1956:8). The magnitude and thus type of contact was denoted by the scale of change (see Steward 1929). The "results" dimension consisted of several possibilities, depending on the level or magnitude of the contact. The trait list and traits of the receiving, or indigenous, culture could dominate the intrusive culture's trait list or traits, or those of the latter could dominate those of the former. Trait similarity might denote some contact, but as Irving Rouse (1955) noted, this was an assumption, the proof of which required various analyses and the distinction between homologous and analogous similarity.

The intent of the seminar was to provide examples and definitions of the eight types of contact situations in strict archaeological terms without recourse to "ethnographic reconstruction" (Lathrap 1956:7), though ethnographic terms and concepts were used heavily. The participants went to great lengths to present archaeological examples of each of the eight types of contact situations, but each example was represented by an *interpretation* of archaeological material and thus exemplified the type of contact situation it was meant to represent. Why a particular example characterized a particular type of contact was unclear. The closest the seminar participants came to discussing theoretical units for measuring contact is found in the statement, "Situations of culture contact are identified archaeologically by the observation of the intrusion of elements of one culture into the area of another. . . . [A]n element is intrusive in one area when we find it occurring at an earlier date in another. The probability of intrusion is strengthened if the element has immediate antecedents in the area where it occurs earlier and none in the area where it occurs later" (Lathrap 1956:7). Such a statement was little more than a verbalization of Ford's (1952a:330) earlier discussion, and, like that discussion, begged the question of how evolutionary antecedents—*primitive forms,* in paleontological terms—were to be identified.

Participants in a symposium (Thompson 1958) held three years after the 1955 seminars used basically the same archaeological criteria to identify contact events. Those criteria included such things as the degree of trait similarity, demonstrable historically antecedent forms of traits, and the like. Symposium participants, like those at the seminars, failed to explain how analogous and homologous similarities were to be distinguished.

The 1950s and 1960s were rife with speculation over contact of various sorts, some of it involving only modest movements of people from one locale to a neighboring locale and some of it movements of people over much longer distances. For the eastern United States, Albert Spaulding (1952) proposed that the Adena culture found in the Ohio River valley was a Mesoamerican import, and Edward McMichael (1964) speculated that the well-known site of Crystal River in Citrus County, Florida, was a stopover point for people from Veracruz, Mexico, carrying Hopewell culture from the Gulf Coast into the United States. For points south, there was speculation that some type of direct contact had occurred between peoples in coastal Guatemala and coastal Ecuador sometime in the first millennium B.C., based on an iridescent paint that occurred on sherds from the two regions (Coe 1960). Also, a number of Mexican and South American experts supported the notion that maize cultivation was introduced into South America from the north and that regular exchange of such things as pottery vessels went hand in hand with maize introduction (Coe 1960; Evans and Meggers 1957; Meggers 1964; Meggers and Evans 1962). Debates ensued over the legitimacy of such claims, but for the most part archaeologists tended to support them. Mexico had long been considered the center of corn domestication, and it was clear by the early 1960s that the earliest corn found in South America postdated the earliest Mexican corn. Thus it made sense that corn moved southward sometime before the birth of Christ; whether it was passed down the line from group to group or carried by Mexican emigrants was unclear, but few archaeologists flatly denied that migration could have been responsible.

Bolstered by the generally receptive mood of archaeologists in the 1950s to diffusion, a few brave souls became bolder in their proclamations. For example, Robert von Heine-Geldern (1954) argued that Peruvian metallurgy could have come only from Asia. Likewise, he argued for an Asian origin of Olmec (Mexico) and Chavín (Peru) cultures, noting that in both, as in Shang (China) art, the tiger was heavily emphasized as a motif (Heine-Geldern 1959a). That jade working occurred in China as well as on the Gulf Coast of Mexico was further support for the notion of contact. Heine-Geldern (1959b) also speculated on the influence of the Chinese in the so-called Tajín interlace design on the exteriors of some Classic-period Mexican buildings and in Honduran marble vases. Gordon Ekholm, a colleague of Ford's at the American Museum, added the fresco technique, wheeled toys, phallic sculptures, the "tree of life" motif, and several other elements to the growing complex of traits indicating Chinese influence in greater Mesoamerica (Ekholm 1953, 1955, 1964).

By 1964, with the number of articles and monographs touting diffusion and migration as explanatory devices on the rise, Berkeley archaeologist John Rowe had had enough. He wrote a short but withering critique of diffusion studies, though it did not appear until 1966. We cannot even begin to do Rowe's review full justice here, but basically, he attacked diffusionism from the ground up, commenting that most contemporary diffusionistic accounts were nothing more than off-the-wall speculation:

> There are times when one cannot help sympathizing with [A. R.] Radcliffe-Brown, whose disgust with doctrinaire diffusionists was so profound that he organized a new anthropological sect ("social anthropology") in order to disassociate himself from them. . . .
>
> Doctrinaire diffusionism is a hardy weed, however, and no sooner had it been poisoned in ethnological pastures than it crossed the fence and began to infest archaeology. We are now being subjected in archaeological meetings to ever more strident claims that Mesoamerican culture was derived from China or southeast Asia, early Ecuadorian culture from Japan, Woodland culture from Siberia, Peruvian culture from Mesoamerica, and so forth. In the science-fiction world of the diffusionists, a dozen similarities of detail prove cultural contact, and time, distance, and the difficulties of navigation are assumed to be irrelevant. (Rowe 1966:334)

Rowe made an interesting distinction between the diffusionists of the early twentieth century, who had gotten under Radcliffe-Brown's skin, and contemporary diffusionists, who took a different course than their predecessors:

> Unlike the diffusionists of 50 years ago, who knew what they were doing and said so, those of today avoid stating their principles in general terms. They are aware that the principles on which arguments for long-distance diffusion rest have been subject to severe criticism, and perhaps they hope to avoid being reminded of the criticism by concerning themselves only with one limited "problem" at a time, such as transpacific contacts or diffusion between Mesoamerica and the central Andes. This evasion of the general theoretical issues has some interesting correlates and consequences.
>
> In the first place, it means that only those cultural similarities which are directly related to the "problem" under discussion are considered. Any isolated similarity between Mexican and Chinese art is emphasized because it is considered to be pertinent to the "problem" of transpacific contacts, but parallels between Greek

vase-painting of the sixth century B.C. and Moche vase-painting on the north coast of Peru of about the fourth century A.D. are studiously ignored.

In the second place, no attempt is made to determine and consider the complete distribution of the features compared. Many of the features which enter into arguments for transpacific contacts have extensive Old World distributions in western Asia, Africa, and Europe, as well as in eastern Asia, but only the occurrences on the shores of the Pacific are cited. (Rowe 1966:334)

As an example of what he meant by the highly selective nature of modern diffusionism, Rowe compiled a list of sixty specific cultural traits of limited distribution but that were shared by ancient cultures of the Andes and the Mediterranean prior to the Middle Ages. These included such things as trumpets with mouthpieces, cubical dice, adobe bricks, rulers to whom divine honors were paid, and hunchback dwarfs used as court attendants. Of course, many if not all of these traits occurred elsewhere in the world at the same time, but Rowe simply noted that he was playing by the same rules as the diffusionists. Then he asked, "Will the proponents of transpacific diffusion please explain why cultural similarities between the Andean area and the Mediterranean are not significant, while similarities on opposite shores of the Pacific indicate ancient contacts?"

Strong objections to Rowe's critique were made by Stephen C. Jett and George F. Carter, who wrote a joint response to it (Jett and Carter 1966) in which they suggested Rowe had overlooked studies that examined diffusion of traits from the Mediterranean region to the Americas. They also wondered if the only evidence of transpacific contacts that archaeologists like Rowe would consider were sherds stamped "Made in Japan." Carter had long been a proponent not only of transpacific contact (e.g., Carter 1963) but of the occupation of the Americas by Lower Paleolithic peoples several hundred thousand years ago (e.g., Carter 1952, 1954a, 1954b).

Rowe was general enough in his comments that the uninitiated wouldn't have known to whom he was referring in his biting essay—he cited no specific works— but it was clear enough to those he lampooned. Certainly the most celebrated case for migration, and one that Rowe made frequent reference to, began life in the late 1950s when an Ecuadorian archaeologist, Emilio Estrada, and two American colleagues working in Ecuador, Betty Meggers and Clifford Evans, raised the possibility of transoceanic contact between Japan and coastal Ecuador sometime around 3000 B.C. Soon, the possibility became firm belief (Estrada 1961; Estrada and Evans 1963; Estrada and Meggers 1961; Estrada et al. 1962; Evans et al. 1959; Meggers et al. 1965). The basis for their claim lay in similarities between some of the pottery they were excavating on the coast of Ecuador, part of what Estrada and his colleagues called the Valdivia phase, and Middle Jomon pottery they had seen in the collections of amateurs and local museums on Kyushu, the southernmost island in the Japanese chain. Bolstering their claim was the apparent contemporaneity of the Japanese and Ecuadorian pottery as determined through radiocarbon dating. If the pottery on the Ecuadorian coast *was* derived from Japan, how did it get there? The investigators had an answer for this: Japanese fishermen were blown off course, and Pacific currents carried them to the Ecuadorian coast. There they taught local fishermen the art of pottery making:

> If a boatload of Early Middle Jomon fisherm[e]n left the sheltering bays of Kyushu and went out into the sea off the southeastern coast in October or November, they would have entered a zone with some of the strongest currents in the northern Pacific. A canoe caught too far from shore by [a typhoon] might easily be swept . . . far out to sea before control was regained. Even if the occupants retained possession of their paddles, they might have been unable to turn back. . . .
>
> The currents would have carried a canoe southward as it neared the Pacific coast of the Americas. . . . An estimate of the number of months necessary to make a trip of some . . . 8230 nautical miles . . . involves so many incalculables . . . as to be of little value. It can only be said with certainty that the trip must have taken many months, and that one or more members of the original crew must have survived, probably well tanned!
>
> Arriving on the Ecuadorian shore, the travelers were met or soon found by the local residents, who presumably were living much the same kind of life as had been left behind on Kyushu—fishing, shellfish gathering, a little hunting and gathering of plants for food and fiber. The results make it apparent that the newcomers were welcomed and incorporated into the community. In the process, they introduced the art of pottery making, and very probably new religious practices that are reflected in the stone figurines. Other new ideas may also have been incorporated, but no tangible evidence has been recognized. (Meggers et al. 1965:167–68).

Rowe (1966:336), in his critique of diffusion studies, stated that "No sound basis has ever been established for the romantic theory that occasional castaways will be listened to, like the Connecticut Yankee at King Arthur's court, rather than knocked on the head or put to work cleaning fish."

According to Meggers et al., once the local Valdivians learned how to make pottery, at around 3000 B.C., the art spread up and down the South American Coast, reaching coastal Colombia at around 2800 B.C. or so and Panama several hundred years later. Radiocarbon dates for coastal Colombia (Reichel-Dolmatoff 1965) that became available after Meggers et al.'s (1965) monograph went to press suggested that the earliest pottery there might actually predate the earliest pottery on the Ecuadorian coast.

Meggers et al. followed Fordian procedure in their analysis, interdigitating excavation units from the sites to arrive at a master ordering of pottery types (Figure 6.6). They then divided the long sequence into four arbitrary periods. Meggers and her colleagues produced a wealth of information from both the Ecuadorian and Japanese sites to support their claim, including in their monograph (Meggers et al. 1965) hundreds of line drawings and photographs of Valdivia sherds and numerous plates on which they arranged sherds from both regions side by side so that they could be compared directly. To be sure, there were broad similarities, both in vessel shape and in decoration, between the pottery from Valdivia and that from Japan. The point wasn't that the sherds resembled each other but whether the similarities were a result of chance, psychic unity, or culture contact. Reaction to Meggers et al.'s proposal was mixed, with many archaeologists, including Willey (1966, 1971), adopting a middle-of-the-road, "wait-and-see" attitude (Willey and Sabloff 1993:204). Others were solidly behind the idea, and still others immediately denounced it. The monograph was reviewed in *American Antiquity* by none other than Jim Ford, who, as he noted, was not the most impartial of potential reviewers. He stated, "The intelligent reader, specifically the American archaeologist, is going to have his basic theories about human culture history rather badly shaken before he finishes the last page" (Ford 1967:258). We presume he meant the last page of Meggers et al.'s volume, not of his review.

Ford's review, short though it was, laid out in concise language exactly what his views were as he was preparing his own monograph on diffusion and migration in the Americas. Here's what he had to say about Meggers et al.'s findings:

> There are also important implications for Cultural Anthropology in general. Old World archaeologists have clearly demonstrated that Neolithic culture diffused—it was not reinvented in the Near East, China, and Africa. The last stronghold for those who argued that culture was produced by some innate capability in man and had not evolved from preceding culture was the American example. Here man crossed Bering Straits with upper Paleolithic baggage and, without outside help, created the Inca, Maya, and Aztec civilizations. Now the Meggers, Evans, Estrada evidence for early trans-Pacific contacts opens wide the door for the theories of [Heine]-Geldern and Ekholm for the coming of later traits.
>
> I think Meggers, Evans, and Estrada have demonstrated that human culture history is a single connected story. (Ford 1967:259)

Ford, when he wrote those words, was struggling mightily to bolster the claim with evidence of his own—a struggle that became a race against time when he realized in the spring of 1967 that he was dying of colon cancer. At this point we need to back up a few years and discuss a field project that Ford originally hoped would demonstrate a critical link between the coastal United States and coastal South America and an article in which Ford first set down his analysis of the American Formative.

Formative Cultures along the Veracruz Coast

At some point, probably in 1961–1962, Ford had become convinced that a key area to the diffusion/migration of ideas/people in the first two or three millennia B.C.—the period of the American Formative—was the Gulf Coast of Mexico between Tampico and Veracruz (Figure 6.7). The region was not well

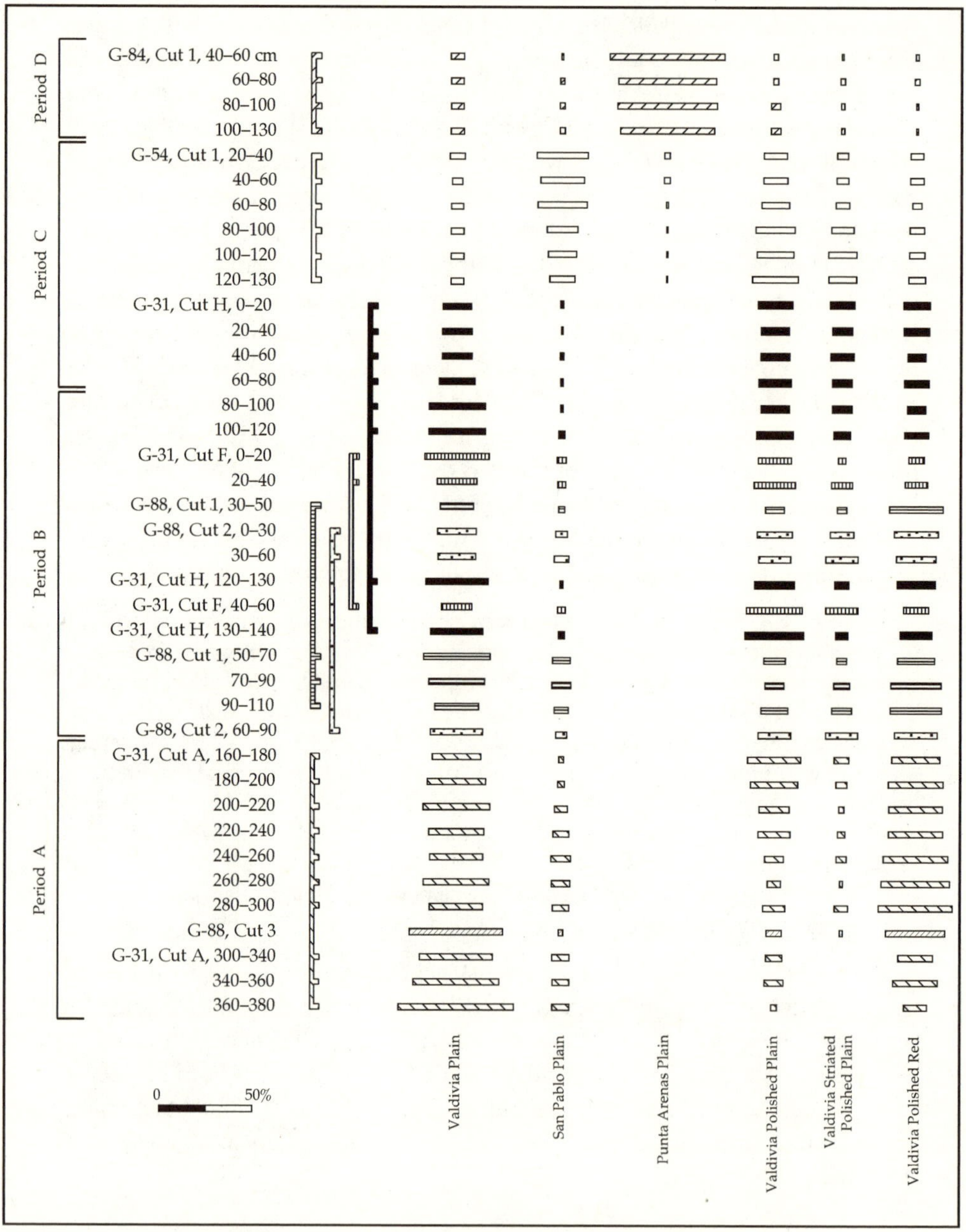

Figure 6.6. Meggers, Evans, and Estrada's summary graph for the Valdivia sites, Ecuador, showing the chronological alignment of excavated strata based on percentage occurrence of pottery types. Theirs was the same method developed by Ford in the Virú Valley and used by him to align various sequences in the Mississippi Valley (after Meggers et al. 1965).

known archaeologically in the 1960s, and for a variety of reasons it seemed to hold several keys to the Formative, not the least of which was that it lay on the northern periphery of the hot, low-lying coastal area that was the heartland of Olmec culture. Based in large part on Smithsonian-sponsored excavations at La Venta (Drucker 1947, 1952; Drucker et al. 1959) in the Mexican state of Tabasco and Tres Zapotes (Drucker 1943a; Weiant 1943) and Cerro de las Mesas in the state of Veracruz (Drucker 1943b, 1955) (Figure 6.7), it was clear that Olmec culture was older—perhaps much older—than most of the spectacular ruins in highland Mexico. In addition to the work on Olmec sites, surveys and excavations by Ekholm (1944) on the coast of northeastern Mexico and by Richard MacNeish (1947, 1954, 1958) on the northeastern coast and in the mountains of northeastern Mexico had demonstrated a relatively long prehistoric sequence, as had MacNeish's (1961, 1962) ongoing work in the highland valley of Tehuacán in the state of Puebla (Figure 6.7).

By concentrating on the Tampico-Veracruz coast, Ford would thus be filling in a gap in the prehistoric Mexican sequence. MacNeish's work in Tehuacán was pushing pottery there back to the 2300–1500 B.C. range—the boundaries of his Purrón phase—but there was a distinct possibility that an as-yet-unknown pottery might date earlier. In Ford's mind, there was every indication that such undiscovered early pottery would lie along the coast, much as it did in Ecuador and Colombia (Reichel-Dolmatoff 1961; Reichel-Dolmatoff and Reichel-Dolmatoff 1956).

In his last project undertaken under the auspices of the American Museum of Natural History, Ford, with $34,000 provided by the National Science Foundation, began his survey-and-excavation project in the fall of 1963. He didn't know the area well, and he enlisted the assistance of local archaeologist Alfonso Medellín Zenil of the Universidad Veracruzana and Matthew Wallrath of the American Museum. Over the course of the next year and a half or so, they excavated three sites—Viejón, Chalahuites, and Limoncito—just north of the city of Veracruz. Ford and his colleagues generated an enormous amount of material (Figure 6.8), but the results of the project were never reported because Ford's interests in the sites were superseded by his interest in the American Formative at large. Incidentally, the anthropology program officer at the National Science Foundation during the early 1960s was none other than Albert Spaulding, and it was he who allowed Ford to shift part of the funding over to pursue his more general interest. One might have presumed that there would have been lasting personal animosity between Ford and Spaulding from their acrimonious debates a decade earlier, but letters the two exchanged regarding the status of Ford's NSF-funded projects indicate that much more than simple civility existed between the two men.[3]

3. National Anthropological Archives.

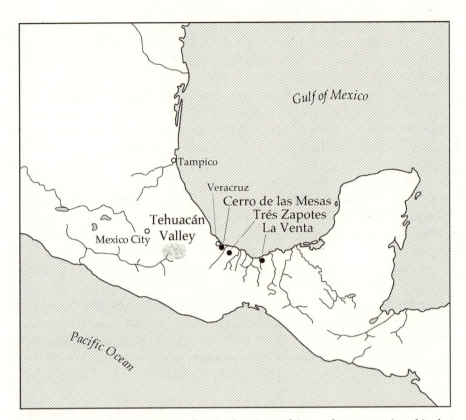

Figure 6.7. Map of eastern Mexico showing locations of sites and areas mentioned in the text.

Early Formative Cultures on the Georgia and Florida Coasts

In a historical sense, the Veracruz project was important because it brought another set of materials and information into Ford's venue and added to his growing conviction of an American Formative that linked large sections of the Caribbean, the Gulf of Mexico, and the Pacific coasts of Central and South America. Clifford Evans, in his obituary on Ford, noted, "With the appearance in late 1965 of the Estrada, Meggers, and Evans monograph that postulated the transpacific introduction of pottery to the coast of Ecuador from Japan, Jim became electrified by the fact that certain pottery complexes along the eastern Florida coast and the adjacent Georgia coast had features in common with Middle American and South American materials" (Evans 1968:1166). Ford's friendship with Evans and Meggers, together with the appearance of preliminary papers (e.g., Estrada and Meggers 1961; Estrada et al. 1962) on the subject, meant that Ford was

Figure 6.8. Photograph of Ford's field laboratory on the Veracruz, Mexico, coast, ca. 1964 (photograph courtesy W. G. Haag).

staying apprised of their fieldwork and analysis; thus he knew more or less what was in the Smithsonian monograph (Meggers et al. 1965) before it appeared. His work of a decade earlier on diffusion of design elements (Ford 1952a) indicated he was intellectually preadapted to accept their conclusions.

But it is apparent from even Ford's own words that he was not prepared for the resemblance between sherds that Meggers et al. illustrated from Ecuador and some that he himself was finding on the Mexican Gulf Coast. In the preface to his final work, "A Comparison of Formative Cultures in the Americas," Ford recounted his moment of electrification:

> I have had an interest in the American Formative culture for some years and have searched for it with limited or no success in Colombia, Peru, Mexico, and the eastern United States. However, I stumbled into the present study entirely by accident. Meggers, Evans, and Estrada's *Early Formative Period of Coastal Ecuador* was published while Matthew Wallrath, Alfonso Medellín Z., and I were finishing the classification of several hundred thousand sherds from our excavations in Pre-Classic sites on the coast of Veracruz, Mexico. Wallrath was immediately impressed by the close resemblance of engraved wares from the [Ecuadorian] Machalilla Phase to those we were working with from the site of Chalahuites. Upon careful reading of this well-illustrated tome, a

number of unexplained resemblances between ceramics and other features of early North, Central, and South American cultures began to crystallize into patterns. (Ford 1969:vii)

Ford's first major statement on diffusion and migration with respect to the American Formative appeared in 1966 and was entitled "Early Formative Cultures in Georgia and Florida" (Ford 1966). He began the article exactly as he would begin his final work on diffusion, by noting that it was in 1917 that Herbert J. Spinden presented a paper to the International Congress of the Americanists (Spinden 1917) in which he postulated a "cultural stratum" common to the high civilizations of the Andes and Middle America. Spinden, however, was trying to show that one did not need to use diffusion or migration from another continent to explain the development of agriculture and the subsequent course of cultural development in the Americas—a point he summed up in more precise terms a decade later: "The American record indicates in very complete fashion the natural history of civilizations, from the family hunting band type of association up through the farmer's and fisherman's villages to nationalities, including all the members of a language group and even to empires based on conquest and tribute" (Spinden 1927:62). Interestingly, in 1966 Ford was awarded the Spinden Medal by the Anthropological Society of Washington. Evans (1968:1166) noted the award was for "outstanding accomplishments in theory, methodology, and chronology of the archeology of the Western Hemisphere." Haag (1968:32–33) stated that the award was for "controversial concepts" and was Ford's "most cherished prize." Controversy had long surrounded Ford and his ideas, and the American Formative was no exception.

After invoking Spinden's proposition of a common cultural stratum, Ford summarized the archaeological work in the Americas that had produced the data on which he was depending for his analysis and then turned to a definition of the Formative, noting that he was moving away from that provided by Willey and Phillips (1958) because everything in their definition hinged on the presence of food production as an economic base. Such a definition, Ford stated, "is self-defeating, for it automatically excludes the coast-dwelling, seafaring people, who seem to be the prime agents of the spread of advanced cultural traits" (Ford 1966:782). Rather, he defined the Formative simply as "the 3,000 years preceding the Christian era, during which Neolithic-level cultural elements were being diffused and added to the Paleolithic-level cultures that already existed. *The term will refer to that period of time and also the cultural elements involved*" (Ford 1966:782; emphasis added).

Without question, Ford tied all of the traits he used in his analysis of the Formative back to Valdivia, noting, "That this culture was introduced by direct transpacific contact seems obvious" (Ford 1966:782). Once the Valdivian traits were in place, they began to spread, just as Meggers, Evans, and Estrada had suggested. But they had proposed a spread only as far as Colombia and Panama; Ford would show that it extended into the southeastern United States. The key elements of his proposal as to how they spread were tied to long-distance colonizing:

> The apparent facts about the American Formative Culture are liable to be somewhat strange to archaeologists who have not worked on the problem, since they involve some changes in habits of thought. The standard model of cultural diffusion has been that of a step by step geographical spread, like the expansion of the Inca Empire. Apparently major movements in Early Formative times were more similar to the long-distance colonizing ventures of the Vikings. (Ford 1966:782)

In the Poverty Point report, Ford had likened the invasion of northeastern Louisiana by a limited number of early Hopewellian people to the invasion of Britain by the Romans.

Having established both the source of the Formative traits and the mechanism involved in their transmission, Ford turned his attention to other matters:

> If the Early Formative was spread by seafaring people who established colonies on distant shores, then the transported cultural elements should have a high degree of resemblance to those of the culture from which they were derived. Since complex traits, such as pottery, were new for the regions to which they were introduced and had not passed through "cultural filters," they should be comparable almost point by point.
>
> Cultural change was slow during the early part of these three millennia, particularly in ceramics, for distinctive and competing traditions had not yet developed. Further, by some mechanism which is not clearly understood, these cultures did not spread as complete units. Groups of ceramic features and other elements tended to be transplanted, leaving behind the remainder of the features of the original cultural complex. This suggests the possibility of craft or village specialization; small groups of colonists carried with them only their own techniques and specialties.
>
> A further inference to be made from the pattern suggested here is that colonies will tend to be small. They will consist of a few villages clustered closely together in a limited geographical area like the first European settlements on the Atlantic Coast of North America. (Ford 1966:782)

As a space-time framework, Ford lined up chronologies from the Georgia and Florida coasts against those from seven other areas—the Ohio Valley, the lower Mississippi Valley, the Veracruz coast, the Tehuacán Valley, the Pacific coast of Guatemala, the northern coast of Colombia, and coastal Ecuador. These were the same chronologies that he would use in his later monograph (Ford 1969). Ford started with the earliest pottery known in the Southeast—a fiber-tempered ware found along the lower Savannah River and the northern coast of Georgia and also along the St. Johns River in northern Florida. Available radiocarbon dates suggested that this pottery might date as early as 2000 B.C. The earliest pottery was plain, but by around 1600 B.C., pottery in both localities began to be decorated.

Despite the fact that pottery from the two areas was fiber tempered and some of it was decorated, it was altogether different in terms of vessel shape and kind of decoration. We'll ignore various types that have been proposed and simply refer to the fiber-tempered Georgia pottery as Stallings Island and the fiber-tempered Florida pottery as Tick Island. Archaeologists have long recognized differences between the Tick Island incised pottery and incised pottery that occurs north of it in the large shell middens along the St. Johns and other rivers in northeastern Florida. This stratigraphically higher pottery was given the name Orange Incised (Sears and Griffin 1950); radiocarbon dates available to Ford placed it sometime between about 1000 B.C. and 1400 B.C. With respect to the two groups of incised pottery from Florida, Ford (1966:789) noted that although they were for a time coeval, "Tick Island vanished, leaving Orange to transmit its decoration techniques and motifs to the succeeding St. Johns I pottery."

Ford posed the question of how the fiber-tempered pottery got to the Southeast. Was it an independent invention, perhaps growing out of the earlier use of steatite for vessels, or did it move into the region from the north? Ford never really answered the first question, but he answered the second by noting that radiocarbon dates on northern pottery were too late by hundreds of years, thus precluding any movement from the north. The only other possibility was a more southerly origin. There was a slight problem with that possibility—no fiber-tempered pottery had ever been found in Mesoamerica—but it *had* been found on the northern coast of Colombia, with radiocarbon dates in the 3000 B.C. range (Reichel-Dolmatoff 1961, 1965). Decorations on the Colombian pottery didn't match those on Georgia or Florida pottery, though intriguingly, "the early people of the north coast of Colombia and of the Georgia coast lived in circular villages, which left doughnut-shaped middens" (Ford 1966:784).

However, by looking further back in time, Ford found the match he was looking for—similarities in vessel shape and decoration between Valdivia pottery and Stallings Island pottery from Georgia. Recall that Valdivia "culture" had been assigned an age of roughly 3000–1500 B.C. by Meggers et al. (1965), so the dates on it and those for Stallings Island pottery overlapped, just as both overlapped with the coastal-Colombian material. The only trouble with this connection was that the Valdivia pottery wasn't fiber tempered. What was going on here? Meggers et al. had already proposed that Valdivia pottery diffused to the Colombian coast at around 3000 B.C.; was there a *later* diffusion of design elements and vessel shapes from Valdivia to Georgia? Or did coastal-Colombian colonists emigrate to Georgia, carrying with them fiber tempering? Upon arriving, did they meet up with recent design-carrying colonists from Valdivia, and did the two pottery traditions fuse to create the coastal-Georgia tradition? This is more or less the way Ford handled the problem, but first he had to dispose of another problem—the distance between Colombia and the southeastern United States. Seafaring colonists might have had to stop off along the way (though Meggers et al.'s apparently hadn't), but there weren't any known sites along the Mexican coast that had the requisite pottery.

But anything is possible when diffusion and migration are added to the interpretive milieu—including the old standby, the missing site(s). Ford knew the pottery from the Veracruz coast that he, Wallrath, and Medellín Zenil were studying was too late to have been involved directly in the diffusion of ceramic traits, as it dated to only around 1000 B.C. But in his mind it was clearly related to pottery of the Ecuadorian Ayangue tradition, specifically to Ayangue Incised—an index type of the Machalilla phase, which, in Meggers et al.'s (1965) scheme, existed side by side with the Valdivia phase from about 2000 B.C. to 1500 B.C., at which point the two fused to form the Chorrera phase. (Ignore the essentialist tone of the statement; it is irrelevant to the point we are making.) Thus, Ford (1966:789) proposed it was possible that "there is in Mesoamerica a yet undiscovered culture that does date around 1500 B.C., which served to transmit these traits to Florida and was ancestral to the straight-line engraved decorations which we know in Mesoamerica." This took care of the incised pottery in the southeastern United States, but what about the earlier, undecorated material? Here, too, missing sites played a key role: "Probably in the southern part of Mesoamerica on the Caribbean Coast, sites are yet to be discovered which will date in the second and third millennia before the Christian Era, and in which fiber-tempered pottery with Valdivia-like drag-and-jab decorations will be followed by Ayangue-like decorations" (Ford 1966:796).

Putting all the information together, Ford came up with the following conclusions:

> Meggers, Evans, and Estrada (1965:166ff.) note that before 1500 B.C. the Valdivia and Ayangue [Machalilla] traditions tend to maintain their identity as they spread to other regions of South and Central America. In the Georgia and Florida complexes that have been described in the foregoing discussion, this identity is maintained to a remarkable extent. All of the ceramic features of Stalling's Island are referable either to Valdivia or to the north coast of Colombia where colonies of the Valdivia tradition were already established. In turn, nearly all of the features found in Orange compare directly with Ayangue or with early Mexican traditions that are Ayangue-related. After 1500 B.C. these traditions merge in South America, Mesoamerica, and after 500 B.C. in the Southeastern United States. In the Momil Period (post–800 B.C.) ceramics of Colombia, the Machalilla tradition motifs are expressed by dentate-stamp impressions in a striking fashion. . . . The ceramics of the Tchefuncte culture of Louisiana (Ford and Quimby 1945) clearly show the result of the combination of three early Formative traditions.

And what about the missing sites? Maybe, Ford said, in opposition to what he had claimed a page earlier, there weren't any: "The Atlantic coastal colonies in Georgia and Florida could only have been established by sea, and the Gulf stream may be the explanation as to why the earliest ceramics are on this coast rather than on the nearer shores of the Gulf of Mexico" (Ford 1966:797). Why worry about finding missing sites when one had the Gulf Stream to ride between the sites in need of connection?

The Grand Synthesis

Ford concluded his paper on the American Formative by noting, "A second paper in preparation will discuss the Middle and Late Formative features that came into the Mississippi Valley after 1700 B.C. and contributed to the rise of the Hopewellian-related cultures" (Ford 1966:797). This would have been an interesting paper, but it never appeared. Instead, Ford focused his attention on a major synthesis of the American Formative that was considerably more detailed, although it included the same areas covered in the 1966 paper. Evans (1968:1166) stated that when Ford "began the Herculean task of reviewing all the literature on the central, eastern, and southeastern United States, Mexico, Mesoamerica, and northern and Andean South America," presumably for his 1966 paper, "he soon realized the need for consultation with area specialists who commanded large amounts of unpublished materials." Ford had circulated parts of the 1966 paper to his colleagues for comments, but this time he wanted their advice up front and in person. Accordingly, in October 1966, with financial assistance provided by the Wenner-Gren Foundation for Anthropological Research, he hosted a week-long conference at his new home institution, the Florida State Museum in Gainesville.

Those who have chronicled Ford's career tend to handle the issue of Ford and Gainesville delicately, usually by simply noting that he moved there in 1964 after eighteen years with the American Museum. Such treatment is understandable, given that the chroniclers were personal friends of Ford's and had a tremendous amount of respect for him. Willey (1988:68), for example, handled the issue with his typical finesse and grace:

> In the course of [the Veracruz] project, Jim resigned from the American Museum of Natural History and took up a post at the Florida State Museum in Gainesville. He talked with me about his leaving New York, and in doing so he voiced various dissatisfactions with the American Museum. I think, though, that at heart it was his old restlessness that promoted the move. He was just not a man who could be happy for long within the confining structure of any institution. To me, that he stayed as long as he did in New York is more surprising than his leaving.

Willey might be technically correct—that Ford resigned his position at the American Museum—though it was only because the museum allowed him to resign rather than be fired. While working in Veracruz, Ford finally had had enough of what he saw as nonproductivity at the museum and on March 2, 1964, apparently after having had a few drinks (J. B. Griffin, pers. comm., 1996), fired off a nine-page appraisal both of the anthropology personnel and of the anthropology program in general, sending it to James Oliver, the museum director.[4] It was a scathing, vindictive letter in which Ford noted that "for the eighteen years I have been here, the Department of Anthropology has been slowly dying." Worse, he accused his colleagues, by name, of being stupid, incompetent, and lazy. One he openly accused of being a homosexual. This probably was the final straw, and Ford was forced to find new employment. On April 13, Harry Shapiro, chairman of the anthropology department, sent Ford a return letter saying, "It was my understanding, as well as Dr. Oliver's, that your letter . . . was in effect your resignation, and I directed that your employment at the Museum be terminated as of March 16, 1964."[5] Thus on the Veracruz shores ended a brilliant scientist's association with one of the leading scientific institutions in the United States.

The early 1960s don't seem to have been particularly good years for Ford in several respects. Various colleagues recount his moodiness and unhappiness during that period—not only with the American Museum but with things in general. For one, he couldn't have been too happy over the cool reception his technical manual from the Barranquilla seminar received from reviewers. Ford finally had had a venue in which to introduce an accounting of his views of culture, and he ended up being eviscerated. Stephen Williams (pers. comm., cited in Brown 1978:29) noted that Ford stopped attending Southeastern Archaeological Conferences at around this time, feeling that everything had been completed in the lower Mississippi Valley. Likewise, Stu Neitzel (pers. comm., cited in Brown 1978:29) recalled that prior to becoming involved with the American Formative project, Ford "was complaining all the time that he hadn't had a productive idea in so long that he was afraid he would never have another one." We've seen that the reports that he wrote during this period—the one on the Menard site in 1961 and on Helena Mounds in 1963—paled in comparison to his earlier thought-provoking monographs. Brown (1978:26) commented that it "seems as if Ford had been looking for something, a challenge perhaps, which would sustain his interest. His restlessness is indicative that these projects were not the answer." Maybe that helps explain the zeal that Ford brought to the American Formative project— he finally had latched onto something new with which to fire an innovative and productive mind. Here was another instance of his being "slightly in advance of the majority" (Ford 1952a:318). Regardless of the motivation, Ford attacked the Formative with what appears to have been his old energies.

Just as in previous times, he assembled experts who knew the specifics of local archaeological records better than he did. The question of which archaeological records to use had already been answered in the 1966 paper on Florida and Georgia, but the question of which archaeologists best knew the individual records was

4. National Anthropological Archives.
5. National Anthropological Archives.

a more involved one, and one that Ford unfortunately did not address in the preface to his monograph (Ford 1969). All of the experts he assembled certainly were natural choices—Betty Meggers and Clifford Evans (Smithsonian) to cover coastal Ecuador; Gerardo Reichel-Dolmatoff (Universidad de los Andes [Bogotá]), coastal Colombia; Michael Coe (Yale), the Gulf Coast of Mexico; Gareth Lowe (New World Archaeological Foundation [Tuxtla Gutiérrez, Chiapas, Mexico]), Pacific coastal Mexico; Richard MacNeish (R. S. Peabody Foundation [Andover, Massachusetts]) and Paul Tolstoy (Queens College of the City of New York), highland Mexico; Ramiro Matos (Universidad del Centro del Peru), Peru; and William Sears (Florida Atlantic University) and Ripley Bullen (Florida State Museum), Florida and Georgia—though others could have participated equally as well. The ten areas covered in the symposium are shown in Figure 6.9. Ford (1969) listed the participants as "collaborators," noting that all participated in the symposium with the exception of Reichel-Dolmatoff. Several others, including James Griffin, were listed as "observers." Ford's first inclination was to invite Griffin as a participant, but as Griffin (pers. comm., 1996) later recalled, when Ford sent him some material to go over in advance, he replied that some of Ford's "facts" were not accurate. As a result, "I was not invited to the meeting, but went anyway. MacNeish and I raised numerous questions which were brushed aside and ignored. We did not go the second day."

Participants were sent the agenda beforehand and expected to comment on their perceptions of Ford's chronological orderings. As he had at Southeastern Archaeological Conferences earlier in his career, Ford employed a technique that was designed to get everyone involved: he would "line his colleagues up around the blackboard, each regional specialist to his own column, and then have a community 'arguing out' of which pottery complexes matched with or equated with which others in the neighboring columns. . . . The method is simple, and has its limitations, but it is a highly effective way to engage all of the participants of a conference in the construction of a space-time framework of the basic facts" (Willey 1969:67). Ford (1969:vii) noted that discussions of the various chronologies were "spirited and lengthy."

As he prepared sections of the final manuscript for publication, he sent them to the collaborators for comment, noting in his monograph that he didn't necessarily take all of their advice into account when making revisions. Neither were all collaborators "happy with the present form of this paper" (Ford 1969:vii), mainly because Ford, in his interest in broad coverage, had to gloss over chronological details. One of these "details" was the dating of Puerto Hormiga, a series of shell mounds along the Magdalena River in northern Colombia. As we noted earlier, radiocarbon dates suggested that the earliest Puerto Hormiga pottery, with radiocarbon dates as early as roughly 3100 B.C. (Reichel-Dolmatoff 1965), might be slightly earlier than the earliest Valdivia pottery. Ford knew this but still

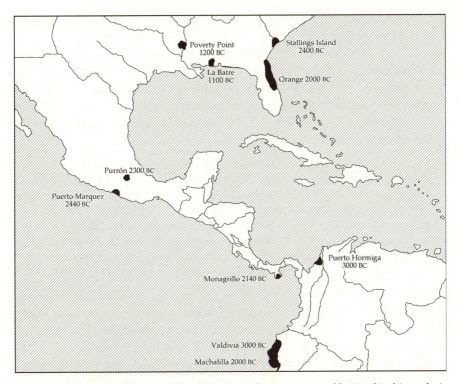

Figure 6.9. Locations of some of the chronological sequences used by Ford in his analysis of the American Formative (after Ford 1969).

placed the Puerto Hormiga pottery later, stating, "This alignment seems to agree better with the apparent cultural connections of the Colombian phases to other regions" (Ford 1969:20). It also agreed better with his story line.

The final version of the manuscript, which was published in 1969, the year after Ford's death, looks very similar to the 1966 paper on the Southeast. More or less the same areas were used for comparison, though they were subdivided differently—fifteen localities this time as opposed to the original ten. Since he was interested in the entire Formative as it applied to the eastern United States, he expanded his coverage to include Ohio, Illinois, the Georgia coast, northern Florida, Mobile Bay–northwestern coast of Florida, and Louisiana.

As he had in the 1966 paper, Ford took exception to Willey and Phillips's definition of the Formative stage (their word), tied as it was to the presence of agriculture. It was clear to Ford that the earliest pottery in the Americas had been used not by groups dependent on plant and mammal foods but by "coastal groups who subsisted principally on shellfish" (Ford 1969:5). They were the ones responsible for spreading pottery throughout the circum-Caribbean–Gulf of Mexico region, and they certainly had preceded agriculture in each region they visited: "The marriage of agriculture and ceramics seems to have taken place halfway through the 3000-year long Formative in Andean South America, about 2000 B.C. in Mesoamerica, and probably not until 1000 to 500 B.C. in the southeastern United States, where, as in Ecuador, pottery had already been made for a [millennium]" (Ford 1969:5). For these reasons, Ford argued, as in the 1966 paper, that it is preferable to define the Formative

> . . . more loosely as the 3000 years (or less in some regions) during which the elements of ceramics, ground stone tools, handmade figurines, and manioc and maize agriculture were being diffused and welded into the socioeconomic life of the people living in the region extending from Peru to the eastern United States. At the start of this span of years, all these people had an Archaic economy and technology; at its end they possessed the essential elements for achieving civilization. That civilization did not develop in the Mississippi Valley is probably due to its relative isolation from the mutual cultural stimulation that took place in Nuclear America. (Ford 1969:5)

Wasn't this bordering on the heretical, coming as it did from the man whom Phillips (1970) criticized for imposing arbitrary boundaries on periods? Maybe it wasn't exactly heresy, but by 1968, when he completed the monograph on the American Formative, Ford had moved well away from his earlier stance, one brought out perhaps most forcefully in the Greenhouse report (Ford 1951a). Look again at how he defined the Formative: "*loosely* as the 3000 years (*or less in some regions*)" during which pottery, agriculture, and other traits were being diffused. This was about as far away from simply drawing an arbitrary line at some point across the time column as one could possibly move. Although Ford consciously (we believe) waffled on exactly what the Formative was, his use of the term clearly made it less a period and more a stage—precisely as Willey and Phillips (1958) had treated it. In short, it was a stage that began with the appearance of pottery, continued through the appearance of groundstone tools, figurines, and agriculture, and ended at the threshold of civilization.

Once one's field of interest switches from pure chronology to diffusion, stages become a natural way of organizing the material record. Once this switch occurs, one has left the materialist world and entered that of the essentialist. This dichotomy underlies Robert Dunnell's (1982:8) use of the terms *space-like* and *time-like* frames to refer to the purviews of essentialism and materialism, respectively:

> In the view designated space-like, reality is assumed to be a unified, locally heterogeneous, universally homogeneous *system*. Quantity is thus a critical issue. In this framework entities are assumed to exist as bounded phenomena. . . . Time is an elapsed interval measure. Similarly, space is rendered as distance. Since a single set of entities is presumed to be phenomenological at the scale of inquiry, relations between

units are properly formulated without reference to age or location; they are timeless, universally true statements.

In actuality, as Dunnell admits, labeling essentialism "space-like" is somewhat of a misnomer, since both time *and* space are treated equally and indeed can merge when large distances are involved, but the label serves to point out that local heterogeneity need be examined in only one dimension—space. Temporal sampling can be either ignored (Dunnell 1982:8) or fiddled with, just as Ford ignored several radiocarbon dates from Puerto Hormiga. Materialism, or a time-like conception of reality, views time as a ratio measure "rendered as an age or date; space is location. Relations between observations are constrained by both time and place. Relations cannot be rendered as timeless, universally true statements among entities, because there is no constant set of entities" (Dunnell 1982:8–9).

There are epistemological similarities between a unit such as the American Formative and an archaeological stratum. Both are bounded units, both have time and space as frames of reference, and both are derived extensionally, meaning the stuff in the units is used to define them. The only difference between the two is that a stratum is localized whereas a stage encompasses (or can encompass) vast areas. In Ford's case, his unit contained the earliest pottery, regardless of temper; groundstone tools; handmade figurines; and agriculture, involving either corn (North and Central America) or manioc (South America). It could have contained other traits, but they were not widespread enough to include in the list. That other traits did *not* spread in concert with those that did was puzzling to Ford (1966, 1969).

Interestingly, even with Ford's focus on the diffusion of traits throughout the Caribbean–Gulf of Mexico region, and even with his emphasis on space-like frames, he maintained an element of materialism in his approach, swamped though it was by the essentialist elements. In Ford's mind, the Formative could be subdivided into units such as early, middle, and late, but there was no reason to think that those "divisions, however, will . . . fit the intercontinental picture" (Ford 1969:5). How could they if the appearance of pottery and other traits had to await the arrival of colonists? If pottery were diffusing from Ecuador to Colombia and then to Florida, it couldn't be expected to make the journey in only a few years. Ford presented his justification for placing internal boundaries wherever they might do the most good:

> As the writer has pointed out in regard to the establishment of pottery types or any other useful historical device, the classificatory units must be selected on the basis of a reasoned guess as to the actual sequence of events (Ford, 1962). That there is an empirical methodology for the selection of "traits," "types," or cultural phases that will reveal the historical facts when properly manipulated is a fallacy that at the moment is wasting thousands of dollars spent on computer time.

> Obviously, the division of the Formative will be a statement of the writer's guess as
> to what happened in these critical centuries. (Ford 1969:5)

This clearly is *not* what Ford had argued earlier in his career. In the lower
Mississippi Valley, his divisions were more or less arbitrary. *If* they happened to
coincide with some "event," that was OK, but it was only coincidence. But when
they didn't, as with the Troyville period, that was OK too. In the end, Ford's attempt
to maintain his air of arbitrariness in placing boundaries was bankrupted by the
very nature of the unit he was trying to subdivide. Otherwise, he could not have
made the following statement:

> An attempt will be made to break the tripartite formula [early, middle, and late]
> and use only two terms: "Colonial Formative" and "Theocratic Formative." The
> Colonial Formative will be considered to extend from about 3000 B.C. to 1200 B.C.,
> a period in which ceramics were being distributed over the Americas, apparently by
> the establishment of seaborne colonies. The beginning of the Theocratic Formative at
> 1200 B.C. is rather sharply defined by the first appearance of mound structures and
> other appurtenances of organized politico-religious control. Its ending, about 400 B.C.
> in nuclear areas, later in peripheries, is not so clear, but merges into a "Proto-Classic,"
> apparently a period of reorganization and preparation for later cultural advance.
> (Ford 1969:5)

Ford expected to spend about an equal amount of time in his monograph
discussing both substages, but he completed only three pages on the Theocratic
Formative before he died. However, he finished the discussion section—entitled
"A Historical Reconstruction"—and there we get a good summary of his views on
the later substage of the Formative. The details that bear brief mention are those
connected with the beginning of the Theocratic Formative in the United States—
an advent that Ford (1969:188) tied to the "appearance of organized religion,"
specifically among the Olmec. During that period, the monumental stone carvings
at Olmec sites such as San Lorenzo (Coe et al. 1967) were begun, and also "People
in the Mississippi Valley and Peru received the blessings of maize agriculture . . .
but in turn paid the price of being saddled with ceremonial systems that must have
absorbed just about all the spare time gained by the acquisition of a more efficient
and reliable food source" (Ford 1969:189). Not coincidentally, 1200 B.C. was the
approximate date of the earthworks at Poverty Point, which Ford (1969:191) noted
exhibited mounds oriented eight degrees west of north, just like those at the Olmec
sites of La Venta and Laguna de los Cerros.

Poverty Point wasn't the final destination of Olmec influence—or perhaps of
Olmec colonists:

> Webb and Snow (1945, pp. 310ff) bring out quite clearly the fact that the population
> of the Adena Phase of the central Ohio River Valley was brachycephalic with high skull
> vaults, and practiced occipital and fronto-occipital cranial deformation. At about 900
> B.C. the sudden appearance of this practically pure population into eastern North

America where (with the exception of the Stallings Island group) slender-bodied longheads had been the only type of man, led the authors to postulate a direct migration from Central America, a thesis that Spaulding (1952) supported. The writer considers this hypothesis to be sound, but suggests the Poverty Point Phase of the Lower Mississippi as a way-station. Unfortunately, there is, as yet, no evidence as to a Poverty Point physical type. (Ford 1969:192)

In Ford's grand scheme, Adena in the Ohio Valley finally gave way to Hopewell, which had replaced indigenous cultures in Illinois several hundred years earlier. Ford was a little light on specifics, but presumably some of the elements of Setzler's original scenario regarding the northern movement of Hopewell out of the lower Mississippi Valley came back into play. Despite the number of intervening years between the florescence of Olmec and Hopewell culture—at least 500 years and probably closer to 1,000—some traits persisted. For example, Ford (1969:193) noted similarities between Hopewellian log tombs and the "basalt-log tombs at La Venta, the log tombs at Kaminaljuyú [Guatemala], and the stone vaults in the mounds at San Agustín in Colombia."

This is how Ford summed up the apparent phyletic connection between Hopewell and Olmec-Chavín, which was a Peruvian unit contemporary with Olmec:

Hopewell thus appears to be a several centuries delayed efflorescence of the Olmec-Chavín religio-political stimulus. While the latter cultures provided the foundations in their respective regions on which the later civilizations were constructed, Hopewell was submerged by the awakened Woodland cultures about A.D. 300, and the prehistory of most of the eastern United States entered a very dreary phase until the arrival of fresh Mesoamerican influences [e.g., pyramidal mounds] at A.D. 900, this time coming overland through Texas. (Ford 1969:193)

A Matter of Opinion

After all of the pages devoted to chronologies and discussions of radiocarbon dates were prepared, after all the artifact drawings were put in place, and after Betty Meggers and Clifford Evans shepherded the manuscript through the Smithsonian's publication office, what had Ford really proved? Had he demonstrated beyond much doubt that diffusion had taken place in the Americas sometime during the three millennia before Christ? Yes, the preponderance of evidence was on his side, and only the most die-hard antidiffusionist would have argued that *some* diffusion probably hadn't taken place during that 3,000-year span. But what had diffused? The knowledge of how to make fiber-tempered pottery? The art of incising? The construction of log tombs? All of those traits? None of them but something else? Did the ideas diffuse, or did the carriers of the traits immigrate to new areas? In the end, the matter came down to personal opinion, not only of the mechanisms involved in trait transmission but, more importantly, of whether certain traits were even transmitted. Richard Diehl (1971:410), an Olmec specialist, summed up this position succinctly in his review of Ford's monograph in *American Anthropologist:* "Ford sees similarities that I do not." Again, a matter of opinion. The invocation of diffusion and migration as explanatory mechanisms is based in large part on the recognition of homologous similarity between traits or sets of traits. If we cannot even agree that two things are similar—and Diehl certainly was not the only archaeologist to have problems seeing Ford's supposed similarities (as many archaeologists had with Meggers et al.'s Jomon-Valdivia similarities)—then we're going to have a tough time invoking diffusion as a mechanism. It then becomes a matter of one person's interpretive story against another's. Ford undoubtedly would have chalked any disagreement up to the other person's lack of experience with the materials.

But even if everyone agrees that similarities exist between two assemblages, how do we know that diffusion/migration took place? Ford had an answer for this: what else *could* it be? Referring to the similarities in certain traits between Valdivia and coastal Colombia, he noted, "The reader is now faced with the classic dilemma of American archeology: either both complexes were independent inventions of ceramics, or one derived from the other. Those who choose the first conclusion should stop reading here and head for the roulette wheel and dice table. Obviously they have a superior faith in, and perhaps mastery of, the laws of probability and coincidence than does the writer" (Ford 1969:154). Shortly after writing those words, Ford died, on February 25, 1968.

7

Epilogue

As we near the twenty-first century, Americanist archaeology is at something of a standstill. There is debate, to be sure, with a few interesting flare-ups every so often, but nothing even approximating a revitalization movement has taken place within the discipline since the 1970s. There are so many *kinds* of archaeology one might do—lithic technology, zooarchaeology, geoarchaeology, archaeometry, processual archaeology, postprocessual archaeology, evolutionary archaeology, and the like, each with a plethora of possible subspecialties—that to someone just entering the discipline it must seem much like a full-service cafeteria. How is one to select among all the possibilities? What might make the greatest contribution to our understanding of the human past? We think Ford would answer these questions by making two points: an archaeologist must have solid chronological control of the archaeological record, and must study the history of culture. These two characteristics, criteria, or whatever one chooses to call them are what make archaeology different from anthropology. Archaeologists have access, at least potentially, not only to the entire time span of human existence but also to the appropriate methods for studying that existence. No other branch of anthropology, let alone another discipline, can make that claim.

We adhere strongly to the belief that we can learn much from close study of the history of archaeology, whether we examine a particular paradigm (e.g., Lyman et al. 1997a, 1997b; O'Brien 1996b), a particular event (e.g., Browman and Givens 1996; Lyman and O'Brien 1998; Lyman et al. 1998; O'Brien and Lyman 1997), a particular area (e.g., Neuman 1984; O'Brien 1996a), a particular era (e.g., Lyon 1996; Meltzer 1983), or the contributions of a particular individual (e.g., Givens 1992; Woodbury 1973). Jim Ford made such notable contributions to what came to be known as culture history that one of the hallmark books of that paradigm—Gordon Willey and Philip Phillips's (1958) *Method and Theory in American Archaeology*—was dedicated to him.

Phillips (1970:3) later made the point that although the dedication was made "with sincere respect," it also was made "in the expectation that [Ford] would disagree with everything [the book] tried to say." The published record contains no direct clues as to whether Ford disagreed or not, but it is easy to suppose, given our understanding of Ford, that he certainly *did* find much in it with which to disagree. Willey and Phillips's handling of the archaeological record, especially their method for creating spatial-temporal units, was of little use to a person to whom cultural patterns manifested themselves in percentage-stratigraphy graphs rather than the phases and foci advocated by his two friends. In like manner, he long held to the type as the basic unit of analysis and protested strongly the utility of the type-variety system brought into the Southeast by Phillips (1958), viewing it as nothing more than new terminology for old practice (Ford 1961b). Ford never changed his mind, and neither did Willey or Phillips, the latter of whom wrote, "I no longer share [Ford's] view that a sufficient majority of sites in the Lower Mississippi Valley represent single occupations of relatively short duration; nor the assumption that pottery complexes succeed one another by gradual replacement of individual types acting more or less independently of one another; nor the assumption that the life histories of individual pottery types can be represented graphically by the use of smooth unimodal 'battleship' curves" (Phillips 1970:3).

It is precisely such disagreements that make Jim Ford such an interesting subject for historical study. As we have noted throughout this book, in many ways he fell in the camp of the materialist metaphysic, whereas most of his contemporaries, including his collaborators, resided more squarely in the essentialist camp. That was the source of disagreement between Phillips and Ford, as the preceding quote makes clear. Where Ford faltered was in his inability to make this critical difference clear. He had no strong theoretical foundation—nor did most of his contemporaries—and that forced him to resort to a commonsense understanding of how cultures worked that was founded in anthropology, especially that part of anthropology which dealt with cultural evolution. Although many of his contemporaries held similar views, Ford could hardly win converts to the materialist aspects of his thinking when he used his types as if they were essentialist units while simultaneously claiming they were "arbitrary" constructs. In these respects, Ford was a product of his time, with a few, albeit significant, unique aspects.

Strong-willed and strong-minded, Ford was well aware of his stature in the field by the late 1950s. But many archaeologists, including collaborators such as Phillips and Willey, did not seem to take his views to heart—they did not perform the kinds of analyses Ford thought mandatory to doing archaeology—and perhaps this led not only to the restlessness and moodiness that friends and colleagues noted at the time but also to the production of a few seemingly self-serving autobiographical comments in one of his final publications. Given the tone of some of those comments, one gets the feeling that Ford was frustrated with his colleagues both for not following his lead methodologically and for not recognizing his contributions to Americanist archaeology.

AUTOBIOGRAPHICAL NOTES

We've said repeatedly that Ford had the annoying habit of seldom citing the relevant literature in his articles and monographs. Now, someone could claim that we've set up a straw man with this argument since what we view as relevant literature might not parallel Ford's selection. If he didn't cite a specific article or monograph, one could argue, then perhaps he didn't think it was relevant. Maybe, but after reading all of his publications and comparing his list of references on archaeological method against the literature that was available at the different times, it is clear that Ford consistently underreferenced his work. Perhaps, at times, this was because he saw the literature as superfluous to his purpose, but given the large body of methodologically oriented literature that grew out of culture history—much of which *was* germane to Ford's purposes— this attitude would have been rather cavalier. Alternatively, maybe the reason Ford didn't cite existing literature was because he didn't *know* it existed. Take, for example, his characterization in the 1962 handbook of the history of seriation and percentage stratigraphy in Americanist archaeology. Ford (1962:3) indicated, "The first stratigraphic excavations were made in Mexico in 1911 by Manuel Gamio, and in the state of New Mexico by N. C. Nelson in 1916." Not only is the date of Nelson's excavation incorrect—it took place in 1914 and was published in 1916—but so is the point that Gamio and Nelson (along with A. V. Kidder) performed the first stratigraphic excavations (Lyman and O'Brien 1998). The use of superpositioning as a way of measuring time was several decades old by the time that Gamio, Nelson, and Kidder used it. Ford also indicated that A. L. Kroeber's and Leslie Spier's seriation technique was founded on W. M. Flinders Petrie's (e.g., 1899) techniques, but we cannot fault him for this incorrect belief because it too was and is widely held by the discipline (Lyman et al. 1997a).

Ford's history of seriation is indicative of his lack of knowledge of relevant literature. Displaying a rather clever use of the technique for which he often is remembered, Ford in his Barranquilla paper provided a "graphic history of methods employed to establish archaeological chronology" (Figure 7.1) (Ford 1962:4). He admitted that "The frequency curves that pretend to show the relative popularities of each methodology are merely estimates, though the lengths of these curves are fairly accurate" (Ford 1962:4). On those curves he "superimposed . . . a *selected* number of references to books and articles that serve to illustrate the methodology" (Ford 1962:4–5; emphasis added). This graph is quite revealing, for it exemplifies some of the sloppiness in Ford's thinking, along with the fact that he was not fully cognizant of the relevant literature. To begin, Ford (1962:5) noted that

In the second decade of this century the idea became current that quantities of varieties [read *types*] of material found should be listed, and "Percentage Stratigraphy" almost became a fad. Proportions were graphed as well as tabulated, but there was as yet no idea that these frequencies might be a reflection of cultural phenomena. "Percentage Stratigraphy" was looked upon as somewhat inferior to clear-cut superposition [which consisted of] finding one culture or cultural phase superimposed over another with clear differentiation between the two.

We agree completely with the last sentence (Lyman and O'Brien 1998), for it reflects the grounding of the culture-history paradigm in the essentialist metaphysic. But we totally disagree with the second because it was none other than Kroeber (1909:5) who suggested that fluctuation in type abundances represented a "passing change of fashion" and a few years later noted that these fluctuations documented cultural periods, eras, and/or epochs in the historical development of civilizations (Kroeber 1916a, 1916b). Likewise, Clark Wissler (1917b:100) indicated that fluctuations in frequencies of types revealed "culture changes" (Wissler 1917a:275)—what he also referred to as the "story of man and his achievements." What, then, could Ford possibly have meant by his statement that "there was as yet no idea that these frequencies might be a reflection of cultural phenomena"? That no one was tracing the flow of idea streams? This was incorrect, given the efforts of Kidder (e.g., 1915, 1917, 1924), Kroeber (e.g., 1925c; Kroeber and Strong 1924a, 1924b), Erich Schmidt (1928), Spier (1917, 1918a, 1919), George Vaillant (e.g., 1930, 1931), and a host of others who used typological similarity to examine cultural influences and the like. Either Ford didn't read the relevant literature, or he was trying to rewrite the history of the discipline in an effort to establish his place in it.

Another of Ford's comments warrants mention:

In 1916, [Kroeber] published a brief paper describing how and why a chronology might be obtained by making surface collections of fragments of pottery from the abandoned villages in the vicinity of Zuñi, New Mexico (Kroeber, 1916[b]).

The following year, Leslie Spier did the suggested work and obtained a sequence. In the 1920's, students working under Kroeber's supervision developed chronologies for areas on the Peruvian coast by seriating grave-lots of pottery, which had been carefully collected by Max Uhle. The techniques used were based on those of Petrie and derived from a clear concept of the mechanics of cultural evolution. That these examples of scientific archaeology were not followed until the middle of the third decade of this century is an unfortunate illustration of cultural lag on the part of the supposed students of culture who might have known better. (Ford 1962:4)

What Ford meant in the last sentence of the quote was that the work of Spier and Kroeber was not followed until the middle of the *fourth* decade of this century, not the third. Otherwise, the sentence makes no sense. What he was saying was that after Spier (1917) had done his seriational study, and a few years later (the mid-1920s), after Kroeber and his students (Kroeber 1925a, 1925b; Gayton 1927; Gayton and Kroeber 1927; Kroeber and Strong 1924a, 1924b; Strong 1925) had

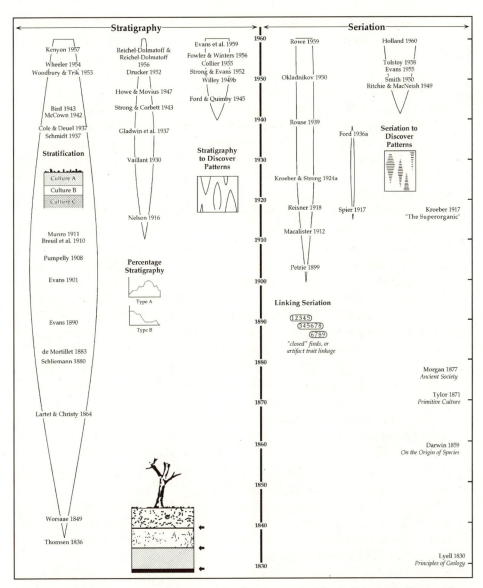

Figure 7.1. Ford's depiction in seriation style of various archaeological methods. Key articles and books and their dates of publication are listed along the right-hand margin (after Ford 1962).

completed theirs, another decade would pass before a student of culture who knew better would come along and resurrect seriation. That knowledgeable student, of course, was Jim Ford. He continued by noting that the "use of popularity curves of types, and the construction of chronologies by discovering the frequency patterns formed by types, developed in the 1930's and has become increasingly popular, particularly in the work of American archaeologists" (Ford 1962:5). Robert Ascher (1963:570) observed that this statement "distorted" the "dialectic of scholarly discourse." Of course it did, but it also served to underscore the importance in Ford's mind of what he had done in the Peck Village report (Ford 1935c) and in the surface-collection monograph (Ford 1936a), and gave them an unwarranted and near seminal character.

Our examination of much of the literature published between 1920 and 1940—not just Ford's "selected" references—suggests that there is no real gap between 1925, when Kroeber and his students published their seriational results, and 1935, the year Ford published Peck Village, in the use of artifact frequencies to determine the passage of time. Throughout the 1920s and 1930s, numerous individuals (e.g., Amsden 1931; Dutton 1938; Hawley 1934; Kluckhohn and Reiter 1939; Martin 1936, 1938, 1939; Reiter 1938; Schmidt 1928; Vaillant 1930, 1931) were tabulating the frequencies of pottery types recovered from vertical columns of sediment, and some of them (e.g., Olson 1930; Rouse 1939) were interdigitating percentage-stratigraphy data derived from multiple sites. Admittedly, seriation of *surface* collections was rare during the 1920s and 1930s; Fred Kniffen's 1938 study is the only one of which we are aware.

Maybe this is what Ford meant when he noted there was a gap—no one was seriating surface collections and deriving a chronology from such orderings—but this is only a guess. Support for our belief that Ford was rewriting history is found in Figure 7.1 in the form of the small battleship-shaped curve under the seriation side of the graph—the curve that has "Spier 1917" at its inception and "Ford 1936" at its termination, with no references in between. But Ford never seriated the surface collections reported in his 1936 monograph; he had already worked out the basic chronology using percentage stratigraphy the year before at Peck Village (Ford 1935c) and simply assigned his surface assemblages to one or more periods based on the presence of marker types. If Ford (1962) meant to imply with his graph that he reintroduced the technique of building chronologies by plotting out the popularity curves of types, he was stretching the truth considerably.

Conversely, maybe that's *not* what Ford meant. Note that the graph in Figure 7.1 contains two basic types of method—what Ford labels "stratigraphy" and what he labels "seriation." Under the first, there are three varieties listed (given his distaste for varieties, we can see Ford turning over in his grave): "stratification," "percentage stratigraphy," and "stratigraphy to discover patterns." Given the examples listed for each, we understand what he meant by each label. Following good Fordian procedure, the varieties of stratigraphic methods are extensionally defined units. Also, given post–1936 Fordian procedure, the definitions are not explicit, with only examples—type specimens—being listed. The varieties of seriation are defined in like manner, but they constitute another matter altogether in terms of the history of Americanist archaeology and Ford's place in it.

In the seriation column, Ford labeled one variety as "linking seriation," which appears to us, given that Ford's example at the bottom of the curve indicates that the linkage depends on what he called "trait linkage," to be similar to what we have termed phyletic seriation (Lyman et al. 1997a, 1998). In the figure, as opposed to in the text, Ford correctly distinguished between Spier's type of seriation and the "linking seriation" of Petrie. His placement of Kroeber and Strong (1924a) in the latter variety is appropriate. Ford also listed in the seriation column the variety he termed "seriation to discover patterns," which, based on the examples listed, involves the seriation of surface collections. Why, then, isn't Kniffen's (1938) study or Kroeber's (1916a, 1916b) work listed there? Ford (1962) cited the latter elsewhere in his text, and he certainly knew of Kniffen's work. Interestingly, nowhere did Ford list Kidder's (1915, 1917; Kidder and Kidder 1917) seminal studies in percentage stratigraphy and linking seriation. Was Ford rewriting history, or was he merely presenting what we might politely call an incomplete version of it?

Curiously, the variety of stratigraphy Ford labeled as "percentage stratigraphy" does not contain the Peck Village report (Ford 1935c). Why not? Did Ford consider what he had done at Peck Village something else? Would he have seen it as merely the first manifestation of the "seriation to discover patterns" variety, left off the figure to accommodate Ford's illustration of a bar graph? We don't know. Matters are not clarified at all because Ford listed none of his other contributions, except for the Tchefuncte report (Ford and Quimby 1945), which he placed in the variety "stratigraphy to discover patterns." We would place Ford's (1949) Virú Valley monograph and Willey's (1949b) study of the Florida Gulf Coast there as well, along with the Phillips et al. (1951) report and Ford's (1952a) design-element monograph, the latter two because percentage stratigraphy formed the basis of the chronological orderings, with vertical proveniences merely being interdigitated into a master regional chronology (Lyman et al. 1998).

Perhaps the ambiguities in Ford's graphic history are to be expected, given the context in which it was prepared. Or, perhaps, it is merely another example of Ford's failure to make explicitly clear what was in his head. He had talked about most of this before in one place or another; perhaps he believed one should be able to cobble together an understanding of his reasoning from reading what he had published. If someone *didn't* understand what he was saying, that wasn't his problem. Perhaps he simply wanted a bit more insurance concerning his place in the history of Americanist archaeology. Whatever the case, Ford did not do a very good job of presenting the aspects of the history of the discipline he chose to discuss. He thus inadvertently revealed his own misunderstanding of that history—no doubt in part due to his lack of familiarity with all of the relevant literature—while simultaneously seeming to enlarge the significance of his own role therein. In our view, he needn't have worried about the latter. His thumbs-and-paperclips illustration of how to interdigitate or seriate collections (Figure 7.2), and the method it signified, were all the insurance he needed.

FORD AND THE HISTORY OF CULTURES

In the last words Jim Ford would ever write—the concluding paragraphs to his monograph on the American Formative—he gave us perhaps the clearest insight into not only how he viewed culture but also what he thought archaeology was really all about:

> [Those] who prefer the traditional concept that American civilization arose independently of Old World developments, or that Aztec and Inca civilizations had little common foundation, should be reminded that an alternative explanation was provided a century ago by Adolf Bastian, who believed that "the psychic unity of mankind constantly impelled societies to duplicate one another's ideas" (Lowie, 1937, p. 29). If this is [true], it appears that the Middle Jomon–Valdivia ceramic comparisons and a number of other examples cited in this paper support to a remarkable degree the "psychic unity" of mankind.
>
> Archeologists have shown little interest in examining the philosophic bases of their studies. While utilizing the thesis that trait resemblances (in adjacent geographic regions) are evidence for contact, when faced with an unexplainable origin of a trait they have fallen back on independent invention theory.
>
> The origin of American civilization has a significant bearing on an important anthropological question that remains in debate after a century of development of the discipline. Did man create his culture out of innate capabilities responding to needs and desires, or is culture a superorganic phenomenon that has evolved according to its own laws, with man's role that of a more or less fortunate inheritor, depending on the time and place in which he chanced to live? (Ford 1969:194)

There never was much doubt about Ford's position on whether man created his culture or whether culture is a superorganic phenomenon that has evolved according to its own laws. In the end, he made it clear that he was as firm a believer in the superorganic as A. L. Kroeber ever was, and like Kroeber, he eschewed any pretense of studying humans and their behaviors or of finding ultimate causes of anything. The real goal should be to study culture, not the specific humans who once carried it. And to study culture properly, one had to pay close attention to history—whether it be found in written accounts or in potsherds. To Ford, the archaeological record was simply a way of tracking what it was that humans happened to inherit as they made their way through life—not necessarily in the

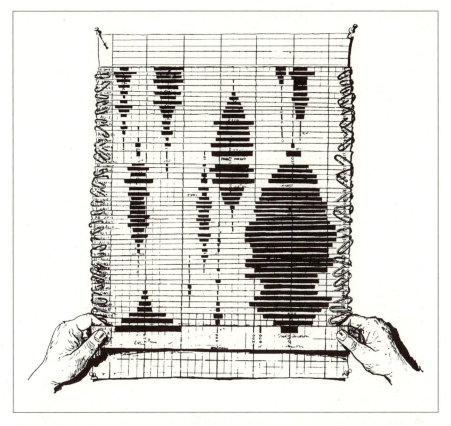

Figure 7.2. Ford's thumbs-and-paper-clips method of seriating collections. Each strip of paper represents a surface collection or excavation level; on each strip bars have been drawn to indicate the percentage of each pottery type. The strips are then moved around until the best fit is attained (from Ford 1962).

mode of automatons but certainly as organisms that had very little say either in their inheritance or in how they received it. At face value, this might seem to be a dehumanizing, sterile view of things, but whether one's perspective on human existence is sterile or not is an inappropriate question where scientific inquiry is concerned. And Ford certainly considered what he was doing to be scientific. Specifically, he was involved in developing what he saw as a "science of culture" (Ford 1952a:318)—what White (1949:116–17) called "culturology"—a science rooted deeply in chronology.

In terms of intellectual stance, would it be so difficult to believe that Ford penned the following statements?

- The aim of history is to know the relations of social facts to the whole of civilization.
- The material studied by history is not man, but his works.
- Civilization [read *culture*], though carried by men and existing through them, is an entity in itself, and of another order from life.
- The personal or individual has no historical value save as illustration.
- There are no social species or standard cultural types or stages.
- History deals with conditions sine qua non, not with causes.

Ford, of course, didn't write them—Kroeber (1915:283–87) did, in his early essay "Eighteen Professions"—but the dictums adequately sum up Ford's view of the central tenets of archaeology. Likewise, Ford just as easily could have written Kroeber's (1919:262–63) famous line about the futility of finding laws that govern human behavior—"A geologist could as usefully set himself the task of explaining the size and shape of each pebble in a gravel bed"—because at no time in his life, at least in terms of his published record, did Ford appear to have concerned himself with such things.

We assume this avoidance of laws and the role of individuals in shaping culture carried over to his personal side as well, at least based on what we can gather from the brief published statements on Ford's personality as well as from conversations we have had with some of his close associates. Clarence Webb, who spent long hours with Ford in the field and on the road, thought the contrasting views that he and Ford had on human nature important enough to include the following lines in Ford's obituary:

> Jim was a leading exponent among dirt archeologists of the theory of cultural determinism. We had many long arguments about this: Jim, the culturalist, explaining patiently how man was caught and controlled by the sweep and flow of culture, and how supposed geniuses or inventors were produced, at the right time, by the forces of culture; I, the physician and humanist, objecting to the role of man as only a culture-bearer and maintaining that unusual men could, and often did, change the course of history and alter the flow of culture. Like the chicken and egg, or the hereditary versus environment arguments, this was never settled, but it did help to pass the long, sometimes hot miles between sites in Louisiana, Mississippi, or Mexico. (Webb 1968b:143)

But were there really two sides to Ford—one that showed up in print and even in long conversations with his closest friends and another that he kept hidden from view? Gordon Willey suspected there were, and he knew Ford about as well as anyone:

> For one who was so much a master of his own destiny, who prided himself on being equal to any situation, whether it be a philosophical debate or extracting the Jeep from a mudhole, it always struck me as contradictory that Ford found the inevitability of cultural determinism so compatible. I wonder if he really believed it? He seemed

as little interested in examining the processual machinery of *in situ* culture growth and development as he was in examining the processual specifics of diffusion. . . . The closest he came to the specifics of the evolutionary process was in the uni-modal curves of his pottery-type life-history graphs; but here, again, he avoided the human dimension. The graphs, to him, were expressions of the "superorganic", the culture *geist*, and could only be understood as such. People were only the "carriers" of culture, not the causative agents of it. To attempt to look below the "culturological" level was to him reductionistic and futile. (Willey 1988:71)

Willey wondered if Ford considered it dangerous to look too deeply into the matter of force and power of personalities, perhaps because of what he might find there. Could Ford have been "satisfied by simply quantifying the flow of culture history, of measuring it as it ran passionless through predetermined channels? I cannot believe it. For James Ford was a man of strong emotions, but these were emotions, I am sure, which he felt must be held in check" (Willey 1988:71). Regardless of whether there *was* a different Ford inside, the one everyone saw was a master at measuring the passionless flow of culture as it ran through those predetermined channels. He started measuring it in a serious way in 1935 and never looked back until he had completed the job—or at least completed it to his satisfaction—in the early 1950s. Although he never used the word "materialism" in the way we employ it here, his approach to carving chunks of time out of the continuous flow of culture was clearly in the materialist camp. How could it not be, if materialism holds that things are always in the state of becoming something else? Time, then, becomes simply an elapsed-interval measurement.

Many culture historians working at or just before the beginning of Ford's career subscribed, at least implicitly, to the braided-stream model of culture change (e.g., Kidder 1936b; Nelson 1932; Vaillant 1935), including Willey (e.g., Willey 1949b; Willey and Woodbury 1942), but the source of conflict between Ford and his contemporaries no doubt resided in disagreement over how to *measure* the continuum of cultural development. Ford was using analytical units of the materialist-ideational sort at the scale of artifact that *might* correlate with particular ideas—sometimes referred to as mental templates—but not necessarily with particular sets of ideas or cultures. Most of his contemporaries, however, believed at least implicitly in such a correlation. Ford, of course, did not help his case by dividing the cultural continuum into what he argued were arbitrary periods and then turning around and discussing them as if they were real, essentialist units termed cultures.

Ironically, one of the people with whom Ford worked closely for much of his life—Philip Phillips—never understood where he was coming from on the subject of time. Phillips, remember, was still agitated as late as 1970 that Ford and Willey (1940) thirty years earlier had, in Phillips's opinion, created the Troyville period out of thin air. Phillips's position captures the essence of essentialism: periods, like cultures, phases, types, and other kinds of units, are empirical entities waiting to be discovered, and the way to discover them is by searching for boundaries—those cut-off points that signal the end of one unit and the beginning of another. Boundaries are denoted by the initiation and termination of the *essence* (read *diagnostic types*) of the periods. This is what Phillips wished Ford had done in the lower Mississippi Valley. That some of Ford's earlier periods seemed to coincide with pulses in the archaeological record was, in Ford's eyes, strictly beside the point, since he could have placed the boundaries anywhere. Archaeologists, for the most part, didn't understand this about Ford's method—it really was totally arbitrary where one drew the line between the Marksville and Coles Creek periods, just as it was entirely appropriate, once the cultural flow was known in sufficient detail, to wedge those periods apart and slip Troyville between them. We are, of course, speaking metaphorically. Ford didn't really slip Troyville between Marksville and Coles Creek. He merely redrew boundaries across the continuum and gave the chunks one new and two previously used names.

If one of his close associates had trouble understanding what Ford was saying, it should come as no surprise that others had the same problem. His difficulty in expressing himself clearly added to the confusion—one that has created a false legacy of Ford's accomplishments. Ask any dozen or so archaeologists for what Jim Ford is best remembered, and all of the answers will include the word "seriation." True, Ford used seriation to arrange archaeological assemblages—to interdigitate percentage stratigraphy data from multiple sites and relative-frequency data from surface collections—but it was much less a method for creating a chronology of artifact types than for arranging collections in a stratigraphically established chronological sequence of types. He developed some innovative visual means of presenting such data, but his major emphasis was *always* on percentage stratigraphy as a means of creating chronological order.

Some answers to the question of what Ford is most remembered for would include reference to the debate he had with Albert Spaulding over the meaning of types. Again, Ford's poor way of expressing himself not only fed into Spaulding's hands but also contributed to an inaccurate legacy. Ford's real debate with Spaulding, at least in Ford's mind, was not over whether types were real—Ford knew they weren't—but over how the archaeologist creates types. Does one use a statistical technique to identify central tendencies (the arithmetic mean) within a group of sherds, decide precisely how much variation to admit around those tendencies, and then treat them as real—emic—units, or does one simply determine what works—the historical significance test? Clearly Ford was committed to the latter approach.

Simply because Ford knew types weren't real didn't mean that he thought they were anthropologically useless. This is where history has created a red herring out of the Ford-Spaulding debates. We sometimes have the mistaken notion that Ford was so committed to materialism—measuring the continuous passage of time— that he eschewed the essentialist notion that archaeological units such as pottery types could be used to identify ethnic groups or to define ethnic boundaries. Certainly Ford took on more ethnological leanings later in his career, but from the start he was squarely in the ethnological camp, using ethnohistorical accounts and the fieldwork of Henry Collins to identify historical-period pottery (O'Brien and Lyman 1997). Clearly, one had to tie down a relative chronology somehow in order to determine which way time was going, and the use of ethnohistorical and ethnological sources didn't make Ford an essentialist any more than his use of radiocarbon dating did. But his full participation in the Phillips et al. (1951) discussion of types and ethnic boundaries *did*. This is one area where there seems to have been little or no controversy among the three archaeologists. Should it be surprising that Ford would go along with Griffin and Phillips on this particular issue? Not really; all Ford wanted to get across was that types measured time. He also was quite willing to admit the presence of a sizable spatial component in types, and if, in the course of helping to keep track of time they also informed us about ethnic groups, that was fine too. These were easy points to concede, as long as his message on time came through loud and clear. This is what Ford was trying to show, if clumsily, in his fictitious Island of Gamma diagram (Figure 5.6).

In a way, Ford was a victim of his own success. Having spent almost two decades building a chronology for the lower Mississippi Valley on the basis of changes in pottery, he essentially found himself out of a job by the mid-1950s. The house had gone up level by level in the 1930s and 1940s, and work at Jaketown and Poverty Point in the 1950s added a basement to the structure. By 1956 the house was completed, and Ford was at a loss as to what to do next. He could have stayed involved in southeastern archaeology at that point, but he didn't, except in a rather casual fashion. He became involved in several projects in eastern Arkansas, but it seems clear his heart wasn't in them. By the mid-1960s, he had flung himself into the question of an American Formative and the role of diffusion in shaping the archaeological record of much of the Americas in the three millennia prior to the Christian era.

Why, of all the things he could have chosen, did Ford finally pick *diffusion* as a topic in which to immerse himself? This seems like the last thing someone with Ford's previous interest in time would pick. Was this direction, in some sense, a natural outgrowth of his earlier work? For a long time, we didn't think so. When we started looking into Ford's work, we were mystified as to why someone whom we always considered a materialist would suddenly become so interested in diffusion, especially when it was tied to colonizing efforts on the part of seafaring potters. After a while, it slowly dawned on us that Ford's thinking hadn't changed at all, that what he proposed in his two publications on the American Formative were in line with the perspective he had *always* maintained. This underlying perspective was so strongly overwhelmed by his emphasis on chronology that it was sometimes almost impossible to detect, but it was there nonetheless.

As early as 1935, Ford acknowledged that traits moved around and that the amount of distance a trait moved could be small, or it could be considerable. The changes he detected in pottery decoration in his sample from Peck Village and in the surface collections from Louisiana and Mississippi were, he reckoned, to some degree the result of the movement of ideas and people, the latter through "gradual infiltration and conquest" (Ford 1936a:5). But for the most part, "all through the relatively *undisturbed* prehistoric period the insidious phenomenon of cultural change was in operation" (Ford 1936a:5; emphasis added). In other words, the prehistoric past was, as he put it, "in a restless everchanging flow through time" (Ford 1936a:5). Ford viewed the movements of peoples and ideas as nothing more than the way culture operated. Once in a while, those movements might show up in the archaeological record—as, for example, with the arrival of Hopewellians back into the lower Mississippi Valley during the Poverty Point period—but for the most part changes in tempo were so small that they were nothing but almost-invisible riffles in the grand flow of time. At that stage of his career, and for the next two decades or so, Ford's interests were almost entirely wrapped up in establishing chronological order, and the scale at which this was done made it difficult if not impossible to pick out the riffles. It was as if someone were tethered in a balloon high above a river, not at such an altitude as to preclude noticing which way the river flowed but certainly too high to make out deviations in tempo or mode.

Early in the 1950s, Ford began to lower the balloon, getting sufficiently close to the river to note the presence of debris that periodically reduced the flow and to see some of the major tributaries that emptied into it. He had in the 1930s and 1940s detected what he thought were disruptions, but once the chronology was worked out in sufficient detail after the Lower Mississippi Alluvial Valley Survey, typological similarities began to become clearer, and the causes of the shifts in flow came into sharper focus. For the first time, Ford saw the Southeast for what it was—not a peaceful stream but rather a major whirlpool of diffusionary influences.

In the 1960s, Ford lowered the balloon still further, this time down almost to water level. Sitting in his laboratory on the Mexican Gulf Coast, he was suddenly struck, as he put it, by the similarities in designs on sherds from Veracruz and sherds from the Machalilla phase of coastal Ecuador. The obvious question is, why was Ford so struck by the similarities? Throughout his entire career he had built chronologies around designs that had fairly widespread distributions. In his monograph on design elements in the Southeast (Ford 1952a), he even used the distributions to talk about the spread of culture over several hundred miles. And recall Collins's caution in 1935 that Ford's types, especially Coles Creek, had too large a geographic distribution to be useful. What was it, then, about those particular similarities that got him so fired up that he spent the remaining years of his life working out an elaborate scenario to explain them? One answer, we suppose, is simple enough: there was considerable distance involved between the two areas, and there were few sites in between that had produced similar pottery.

Trait diffusion throughout the southeastern United States could be accomplished primarily by short hops, with traits diffusing from one area to an adjacent area to another adjacent area, and so on. Unlike the diffusion of designs from eastern Louisiana to northern Florida, or from southern Louisiana to northeastern Arkansas, there were several thousand miles involved in the Ecuador–Gulf Coast connection. Were there intermediate way stations? Maybe a few—coastal Colombia and Panama seemed like reasonable candidates for the period of early colonization, but the later pottery from those areas was not as good a fit with the pottery from either Veracruz or Ecuador as the materials from those two areas were with each other. If pottery in Veracruz was decorated similarly to that in Ecuador as a result of down-the-line transmission, where were all the in-between sites, whose inhabitants would have received and then passed along the traits? Those sites weren't there, making it appear that the small clusters of distantly spaced sites sprang up suddenly—perhaps by seafaring, shellfish-eating colonists making landfall.

Once Ford noticed similarities in designs between sherds from the Mexican Gulf Coast and those from coastal Ecuador, he began noticing other similarities as well. For example, early pottery on the coasts of Georgia and Florida was fiber tempered, as was early pottery on the coast of Colombia, and slightly later pottery from Georgia and Florida carried designs similar to those on contemporary pottery from Ecuador. By 1966, Ford was firmly convinced that many of the traits seen in the archaeological record of the Americas had been produced by diffusion, and he expanded his geographic range to include more and more regions in his analysis. By the time the manuscript on the American Formative (Ford 1969) was submitted, much of the archaeological record of the southeastern United States had been tied to the records of Mexico and Central America. For example, Hopewell pottery, with its bird designs, was a direct result of Olmec influence, as were the earthworks at Poverty Point and perhaps Hopewellian log tombs.

It doesn't take a post facto accommodating argument to suggest this all-out, full-scale attack on the question of diffusion was a natural tack for Ford to take; all he had to do was shift his scale of analysis down to water level. On several previous occasions when we have referred to Ford's "aquatic" view of culture (to use Binford's [1965] term), we have used the term *braided* to modify "stream." The concept of a braided stream accurately characterizes Ford's view of culture, with the main channel branching, coming back together, and branching again any number of times as the water moves along. If there is still a nagging doubt that Ford's position on culture was any different than Kroeber's, a glance at Figure 7.3, which is from Kroeber's (1948) anthropology textbook, should erase it. Early on, it didn't really matter to Ford *why* the stream branched or how many branching and recombining episodes there might have been; such occurrences were a simple fact of how culture worked. If diffusion happened to cause two branches to recombine, that could easily be accommodated; if one branch split into two as a result of group fission, that was fine as well. Thus it posed no problem to have Marksville peoples move north and turn local groups into Hopewellians, just as it was no problem to have Hopewellians march south and order the local inhabitants to construct the Poverty Point earthworks. That was simply culture in operation.

We find it interesting that throughout his career, Ford had little or nothing to say on the preceramic period in the southeastern United States. The exceptions were based on his work at Jaketown and Poverty Point, both of which provided the immediate anchor for the pottery sequence in the lower Mississippi Valley. He certainly dabbled in earlier parts of the archaeological record, but it is apparent that he had little permanent interest in them. For example, he turned over the survey of Dalton-period sites in northeastern Arkansas to a junior coworker, publishing only a three-page progress report in a state archaeological society newsletter (Ford 1961a). Ford's almost complete avoidance of the prepottery portion of the record makes sense, if that's the proper way of phrasing it, when put in perspective. Nowhere in Ford's frame of reference was there any room for things such as

Figure 7.3. A. L. Kroeber's depiction of organic evolution (left) and cultural evolution (right). Note the resemblance of the reticulate tree of cultural evolution to Ford's notion of culture as a (braided) stream (after Kroeber 1948).

invention or ultimate origins because in the end they didn't matter. Prior histories of traits mattered, but only in terms of *near* pasts. It mattered, for example, where incised pottery was prior to its transport to the Georgia coast, just as it mattered when that pottery reached South America. But beyond that, Ford simply didn't care whether it arrived from Japan or from Australia. All that mattered was that it came from somewhere. Once human agents in the Americas received something via diffusion, *then* it mattered what track it took in getting around to various other parts of the continents.

This mind-set was what caused Ford to deny any role for invention. If humans were simply the recipients of what came their way—in other words, the recipients of what the superorganic gave them—then what role *could* there be for mechanisms such as invention? The answer was, none. To allow for invention was to admit that perhaps there was a psychic unity of mankind, and this was anathema to Ford. That's why we think he had no interest in anything back beyond the first appearance—always via diffusion—of pottery. History mattered to Ford, but only if it was near term and involved the Americas.

We've often wondered how Ford would have reacted to the processual revolution of the 1970s—an uprising that had started several years before his death but which was only a pup early in 1968. The full-grown dog wouldn't have the porch all to itself for several more years, but Ford must have seen what was coming. Never one to miss out on a good fight, he might have led a resistance movement of some kind, depending on what his interests were at the time. It's hard to know in which direction he might have struck off next, though Stu Neitzel (cited in Brown 1978:34) provided a clue. Neitzel recalled that the last time he saw Ford was during a visit to help him box up the plates for the American Formative monograph: "[Ford] said, 'Well . . . I've got to have something else to do now.' He didn't want to talk about dying or anything like that. He knew as well as anybody how much time he had and all that. He said, 'Now we can get down to business. It won't be quite as expansive as this thing we just finished, but you have to be my legman.' I said, 'Okay, what do you want to do?' He said, 'That's right—the Marksville report.' He died about two weeks later."

Apparently Ford never got over the fact that a final monograph on the 1933 work he and Setzler conducted at Marksville was never written. In 1961, under strained circumstances, he borrowed Setzler's notes, his incomplete manuscript on the Smithsonian-sponsored excavations, and the excavated materials from Marksville, agreeing that "For the privilege of studying the archaeological material . . . I agree to submit to you [Setzler] a copy of my final manuscript and the subsequent page proof of those sections on my monograph dealing with the Marksville excavations for your review and approval."[1] Ford, however, wrote up only the excavations Gerard Fowke had conducted in Mound 4 (Kuttruff et al. 1997).

1. Letter of March 30, 1961 (National Anthropological Archives).

Jim Ford was a lot of things to a lot of people, and his death left a void in Americanist archaeology, especially in the Southeast. Ford, like all people, had his friends as well as his detractors, but few of the latter would have argued that he hadn't left an indelible mark on the discipline. There are, as we have pointed out, numerous misperceptions of Ford's role in bringing the culture-history paradigm along during the 1940s and 1950s, some of which are no doubt a result of Ford's sometimes larger-than-life persona. A fairly quiet, at times brooding, man, but one with a large ego, Ford pushed through and executed a plan of attack regardless of the consequences. He apparently didn't much care whose toes he stepped on, especially if they belonged to someone less adept than he, whether it was at figuring out chronology or repairing a truck. Given his nature, it is no wonder he often remarked that the only literary figure he admired was Mark Twain. This, as Willey (1988:71–72) noted, is significant in understanding Ford:

> Both were peculiarly American geniuses, and both were southern Americans. They sought to escape to some purer vision of the American Dream and man's destiny—to Huck Finn and his Odyssey of the wilderness—or to archaeology and those ultimate truths of man's past, to an archaeology unfettered by petty institutional constraints. Like Twain, Ford was a romantic who scoffed bitterly at romanticism, proclaiming the practical. Like Twain, also, a courageous optimism and a dark pessimism warred in his nature. Out of these contradictions, these tensions came the singular creative drive of James Alfred Ford.

The topic of drive brings us to the way we choose to end the book—with a letter to Ethel Ford written by George Quimby a few days after the death of his longtime friend.[2] In a few lines, Quimby captured the essence of Jim Ford—at once both a scholar-teacher and a knight errant, capable of conquering anything and everything that came at him except death itself:

March 11, 1968

Dear Ethel:

I have been thinking about Jim since Walter Fairservis called me from New York to give me the sad news of Jim's death. I can only recall the great times we had together in those ancient days at the University of Michigan and in New Orleans and Baton Rouge not to mention Marksville.

I owe a great deal of my education to my early association with Jim. From him I learned seriation, a lot about scientific classifications, and many practical things about preparing illustrations and getting reports ready for publication. But most of all there was a kind of excitement, both social and intellectual about those bygone days and Jim was the King Arthur of that particular Round Table. With no one else have I ever driven at seventy miles an hour through a road-block of sugar cane stalks in a Lincoln Continental. I shall miss Jim.

2. LSU Museum of Natural Science archives.

References

Amsden, C. A. 1931. Black-on-white ware. In The pottery of Pecos (vol. 1), by A. V. Kidder. *Papers of the Southwestern Expedition, Phillips Academy* No. 5. New Haven, Conn.: Yale University Press. Pp. 17–72.

Ascher, R. 1961. Analogy in archaeological interpretation. *Southwestern Journal of Anthropology* 17:317–25.

————. 1963. Review of "A quantitative method for deriving cultural chronology," by J. A. Ford. *American Antiquity* 28:570–71.

Baker, F. C., J. B. Griffin, R. G. Morgan, G. K. Neumann, and J. L. B. Taylor. 1941. Contributions to archeology of the Illinois River valley. *Transactions of the American Philosophical Society* 32 (pt. 1).

Bayard, D. T. 1969. Science, theory, and reality in the "New Archaeology." *American Antiquity* 34:376–84.

Beals, R. L., G. W. Brainerd, and W. Smith. 1945. Archaeological studies in northeast Arizona: A report on the archaeological work of the Rainbow Bridge–Monument Valley Expedition. *University of California, Publications in American Archaeology and Ethnology* 44(1):1–236.

Beck, C. 1995. Functional attributes and the differential persistence of Great Basin dart forms. *Journal of California and Great Basin Anthropology* 17:222–43.

Behrensmeyer, A. K. 1982. Time resolution in fluvial vertebrate assemblages. *Paleobiology* 8:211–27.

Bell, R. E., and R. S. Hall. 1953. Selected projectile point types of the United States. *Oklahoma Anthropological Society Bulletin* no. 1, 1–16.

Bennett, J. W. 1943. Recent developments in the functional interpretation of archaeological data. *American Antiquity* 9:208–19.

Bennett, W. C. 1944. Archaeological regions of Colombia: A ceramic survey. *Yale University Publications in Anthropology* 30.

————. 1946. The Andean highlands: An introduction. In Handbook of South American Indians (vol. 2), The Andean civilizations. *Bureau of American Ethnology, Bulletin* 143:1–60.

Bennyhoff, J. A. 1952. The Viru Valley sequence: A critical review. *American Antiquity* 17:231–49.

Binford, L. R. 1962. Archaeology as anthropology. *American Antiquity* 28:217–25.

———. 1964. A consideration of archaeological research design. *American Antiquity* 29:425–41.

———. 1965. Archaeological systematics and the study of culture process. *American Antiquity* 31:203–10.

———. 1967. Smudge pits and hide smoking: The use of analogy in archaeological reasoning. *American Antiquity* 32:1–12.

———. 1968a. Archeological perspectives. In *New perspectives in archeology,* edited by S. R. Binford and L. R. Binford. New York: Aldine. Pp. 5–32.

———. 1968b. Some comments on historical versus processual archaeology. *Southwestern Journal of Anthropology* 24:267–75.

———. 1980. Willow smoke and dogs' tails: Hunter-gatherer settlement systems and archaeological site formation. *American Antiquity* 45:4–20.

Bird, J. B. 1943. Excavations in northern Chile. *American Museum of Natural History, Anthropological Papers* 38(4).

Boas, F. 1896. The limitations of the comparative method of anthropology. *Science* 4:901–8.

Bolton, H. E. 1925. *Arredondo's historical proof of Spain's title to Georgia: A contribution to the history of one of the Spanish borderlands.* Berkeley: University of California Press.

Braidwood, R. J. 1959. Archeology and the evolutionary theory. In *Evolution and anthropology: A centennial appraisal,* edited by B. J. Meggers. Washington, D.C.: The Anthropological Society of Washington. Pp. 76–89.

Brainerd, G. W. 1951a. The place of chronological ordering in archaeological analysis. *American Antiquity* 16:301–13.

———. 1951b. The use of mathematical formulations in archaeological analysis. In Essays on archaeological methods, edited by J. B. Griffin. *University of Michigan, Museum of Anthropology, Anthropological Papers* 8:117–27.

Brand, D. D. 1938. The Chaco Conference, August 27, 28, 29, 1938. *Clearing House for Southwestern Museums News-letter* 5:14–17. Denver: Denver Art Museum.

Brand, D. D., F. M. Hawley, and F. C. Hibben. 1937. Tseh So, a small house ruin, Chaco Canyon, New Mexico, preliminary report. *University of New Mexico Bulletin, Anthropological Series* 2(2).

Breuil, H., L. Capitan, and D. Peyrony. 1910. *La Caverne de Font-de-Gaume aux Eyzies (Dordogne).* Monaco: Chêne.

Brew, J. O. 1946. Archaeology of Alkali Ridge, southeastern Utah. *Harvard University, Peabody Museum of Archaeology and Ethnology, Papers* 21.

Brooks, R. L. 1982. Events in the archaeological context and archaeological explanation. *Current Anthropology* 23:67–75.

Browman, D. L., and D. R. Givens. 1996. Stratigraphic excavation: The first "new archaeology." *American Anthropologist* 98:80–95.

Brown, I. W. 1978. James Alfred Ford: The man and his works. *Southeastern Archaeological Conference, Special Publication* 4.

Bushnell, D. I., Jr. 1919. Native villages and village sites east of the Mississippi. *Bureau of American Ethnology, Bulletin* 69.

Caldwell, J. R. 1959. The new American archaeology. *Science* 129:303–7.

Carter, G. F. 1952. Interglacial artifacts from the San Diego area. *Southwestern Journal of Anthropology* 8:444–56.

———. 1954a. An interglacial site at San Diego, California. *The Masterkey* 28:165–74.

———. 1954b. More evidence for interglacial man in America. *New World Antiquity* 8:1–4.

———. 1963. Movement of peoples and ideas across the Pacific. In *Plants and the migration of Pacific peoples: A symposium,* edited by J. Barrau. Honolulu: Bishop Museum Press. Pp. 7–22.

Childe, V. G. 1946. *What happened in history.* New York: Pelican.

Coe, M. D. 1960. Archeological linkages with North and South America at La Victoria, Guatemala. *American Anthropologist* 62:363–93.

Coe, M. D., R. A. Diehl, and M. Stuiver. 1967. Olmec civilization, Veracruz, Mexico: Dating of the San Lorenzo phase. *Science* 155:1399–401.

Cole, F. C., and T. Deuel. 1937. *Rediscovering Illinois: Archaeological explorations in and around Fulton County.* Chicago: University of Chicago Press.

Collier, D. 1955. Cultural chronology and change as reflected in the ceramics of the Viru Valley, Peru. *Fieldiana: Anthropology* 43.

Collins, H. B., Jr. 1926. Anthropological and anthropometric work in Mississippi. *Smithsonian Miscellaneous Collections* 78(1): 89–95.

———. 1927a. Potsherds from Choctaw village sites in Mississippi. *Washington Academy of Sciences, Journal* 17: 259–63.

———. 1927b. Archaeological work in Louisiana and Mississippi. *Explorations and Field-Work of the Smithsonian Institution in 1931.* Pp. 200–207.

———. 1932a. Excavations at a prehistoric Indian village site in Mississippi. *United States National Museum, Proceedings* 79(32):1–22.

———. 1932b. Archaeology of Mississippi. In *Conference on Southern Pre-History.* Washington, D.C.: National Research Council. Pp. 37–42.

———. 1937. Archeology of St. Lawrence Island, Alaska. *Smithsonian Miscellaneous Collections* 96(1).

Colton, H. S. 1932. A survey of prehistoric sites in the region of Flagstaff, Arizona. *Bureau of American Ethnology, Bulletin* 104.

———. 1939. Prehistoric culture units and their relationships in northern Arizona. *Museum of Northern Arizona, Bulletin* 17.

————. 1965. Check list of southwestern pottery types (rev. ed.). *Museum of Northern Arizona Ceramic Series* 2.

Colton, H. S., and L. L. Hargrave. 1937. Handbook of northern Arizona pottery wares. *Museum of Northern Arizona, Bulletin* 11.

Cotter, J. L. 1951. Stratigraphic and area tests at the Emerald and Anna mound sites. *American Antiquity* 17:18–32.

————. 1952. The Gordon site in southern Mississippi. *American Antiquity* 18:110–26.

Cowgill, G. L. 1963. Review of "A quantitative method for deriving cultural chronology," by J. A. Ford. *American Anthropologist* 65:696–99.

Darwin, C. R. 1859. *On the origin of species.* London: Murray.

Davis, J. I. 1996. Phylogenetics, molecular variation, and species concepts. *BioScience* 46:502–11.

Deetz, J. 1970. Archeology as social science. In Current directions in anthropology: A special issue, edited by A. Fischer. *American Anthropological Association, Bulletin* 3:115–25.

Deetz, J., and E. Dethlefsen. 1965. The Doppler Effect and archaeology: A consideration of the spatial aspects of seriation. *Southwestern Journal of Anthropology* 21:196–206.

Dellinger, S. C., and S. D. Dickinson. 1940. Possible antecedents of the Middle Mississippian ceramic complex in northeastern Arkansas. *American Antiquity* 6:132–47.

Dickinson, S. D. 1936. Ceramic relationships of the pre-Caddo pottery from the Crenshaw site. *Texas Archeological and Paleontological Society, Bulletin* 8:56–69.

Diehl, R. A. 1971. Review of "A comparison of formative cultures in the Americas: Diffusion or the psychic unity of man," by J. A. Ford. *American Anthropologist* 73:410–11.

Dixon, R. B. 1913. Some aspects of North American archeology. *American Anthropologist* 15:549–77.

Drucker, P. 1943a. Ceramic sequences at Tres Zapotes, Veracruz, Mexico. *Bureau of American Ethnology, Bulletin* 140.

————. 1943b. Ceramic stratigraphy at Cerro de las Mesas, Veracruz, Mexico. *Bureau of American Ethnology, Bulletin* 141.

————. 1947. Some implications of the ceramic complex at La Venta. *Smithsonian Miscellaneous Collections* 107(8).

————. 1952. La Venta, Tabasco: A study of Olmec ceramics and art. *Bureau of American Ethnology, Bulletin* 153.

————. 1955. The Cerro de las Mesas offering of jade and other materials. *Bureau of American Ethnology, Bulletin* 157:25–68.

Drucker, P., R. F. Heizer, and R. J. Squier. 1959. Excavations at La Venta, Tabasco, 1955. *Bureau of American Ethnology, Bulletin* 170.

Dunnell, R. C. 1970. Seriation method and its evaluation. *American Antiquity* 35:305–19.

———. 1971. *Systematics in prehistory.* New York: Free Press.

———. 1978. Style and function: A fundamental dichotomy. *American Antiquity* 43:192–202.

———. 1980. Evolutionary theory and archaeology. In *Advances in archaeological method and theory* (vol. 3), edited by M. B. Schiffer. New York: Academic Press. Pp. 35–99.

———. 1981. Seriation, groups, and measurements. In *Manejo de datos y metodos matematicos de arqueologia,* compiled and organized by G. L. Cowgill, R. Whallon, and B. S. Ottaway. Mexico City: Union Internacional de Ciencias Prehistoricas y Protohistoricas. Pp. 67–90.

———. 1982. Science, social science and common sense: The agonizing dilemma of modern archaeology. *Journal of Anthropological Research* 38:1–25.

———. 1985a. Archaeological survey in the lower Mississippi alluvial valley, 1940–1947: A landmark study in American archaeology. *American Antiquity* 50:297–300.

———. 1985b. Methodological issues in contemporary Americanist archaeology. In *Proceedings of the 1984 biennial meeting of the Philosophy of Science Association* (vol. 2), edited by P. D. Asquith and P. Kitcher. East Lansing, Mich.: Philosophy of Science Association. Pp. 717–44.

———. 1986a. Five decades of American archaeology. In *American archaeology: Past and future,* edited by D. J. Meltzer, D. D. Fowler, and J. A. Sabloff. Washington, D.C.: Smithsonian Institution Press. Pp. 23–49.

———. 1986b. Methodological issues in Americanist artifact classification. In *Advances in archaeological method and theory* (vol. 9), edited by M. B. Schiffer. Orlando: Academic Press. Pp. 149–207.

———. 1987. Comment on "History, phylogeny, and evolution in Polynesia" by P. V. Kirch and R. C. Green. *Current Anthropology* 28:444–45.

———. 1988. Archaeology and evolutionary theory. Paper presented at the University of Missouri–Columbia.

———. 1989. Aspects of the application of evolutionary theory in archaeology. In *Archaeological thought in America,* edited by C. C. Lamberg-Karlovsky. Cambridge, England: Cambridge University Press. Pp. 35–49.

———. 1990. The role of the Southeast in American archaeology. *Southeastern Archaeology* 9(1):11–22.

———. 1995. What is it that actually evolves? In *Evolutionary archaeology: Methodological issues,* edited by P. A. Teltser. Tucson: University of Arizona Press. Pp. 33–50.

Dunnell, R. C., and J. K. Feathers. 1991. Late Woodland manifestations of the Malden Plain, southeast Missouri. In *Stability, transformation, and variation:*

The Late Woodland Southeast, edited by M. S. Nassaney and C. R. Cobb. New York: Plenum Press. Pp. 21–45.

Dunnell, R. C., and F. H. Whittaker. 1990. The Late Archaic of the Eastern Lowlands and evidence of trade. *Louisiana Archaeology* 17:13–36.

Dutton, B. P. 1938. Leyit Kin, A small house ruin, Chaco Canyon, New Mexico. *University of New Mexico Bulletin, Monograph Series* 1(6).

Ekholm, G. F. 1944. Excavations at Tampico and Panuco in the Huasteca, Mexico. *American Museum of Natural History, Anthropological Papers* 38:321–506.

———. 1953. A possible focus of Asiatic influence in the Late Classic cultures of Mesoamerica. In Asia and North America: Transpacific contacts, assembled by M. W. Smith. *Society for American Archaeology, Memoirs* 9:72–89.

———. 1955. The new orientation toward problems of Asiatic-American relationships. In *New interpretations of aboriginal American culture history.* Washington, D.C.: Anthropological Society of Washington. Pp. 55–109.

———. 1964. Transpacific contacts. In *Prehistoric man in the New World,* edited by J. D. Jennings and E. Norbeck. Chicago: University of Chicago Press. Pp. 489–510.

Estrada, E. 1961. Nuevos elementos en la cultura Valdivia: Sus posibles contactos transpacíficos. *Instituto Pan Americano de Geografía e Historia* (Quayaquil), *Sub-Comité Ecuatoriano de Antropología, Publicación.*

Estrada, E., and C. Evans. 1963. Cultural development in Ecuador. In Aboriginal cultural development in Latin America: An interpretive review, edited by B. J. Meggers and C. Evans. *Smithsonian Miscellaneous Collections* 146:77–88.

Estrada, E., and B. J. Meggers. 1961. A complex of traits of probable transpacific origin on the coast of Ecuador. *American Anthropologist* 63:913–39.

Estrada, E., B. J. Meggers, and C. Evans. 1962. Possible transpacific contact on the coast of Ecuador. *Science* 135:371–72.

Evans, A. J. 1901. The palace of Knossos: Provisional report of the excavations for the years 1900–1901. *Annual Report of the British School at Athens* 6–11.

Evans, C., Jr. 1951. Review of "Surface survey of the Viru Valley, Peru," by J. A. Ford and G. R. Willey. *American Antiquity* 16:270–72.

———. 1954. Spaulding's review of Ford. *American Anthropologist* 56:114.

———. 1968. James Alfred Ford 1911–1968. *American Anthropologist* 70:1161–67.

Evans, C., and B. J. Meggers. 1957. Formative period cultures in the Guayas Basin, coastal Ecuador. *American Antiquity* 22:235–47.

Evans, C., B. J. Meggers, and E. Estrada. 1959. Cultura Valdivia. *Museo Víctor Emilio Estrada* (Quayaquil), *Publicación* 6.

Evans, J. 1850. On the date of British coins. *The Numismatic Chronicle and Journal of the Numismatic Society* 12(4):127–37.

———. 1875. On the coinage of the ancient Britons and natural selection. *Royal Institution of Great Britain, Proceedings* 7:24–32.

———. 1890. Excavation of a barrow at Youngsbury, near Ware, Herts. *Archaeologia* 52:1–10.

Fisk, H. N. 1944. *Geological investigation of the alluvial valley of the lower Mississippi River.* Vicksburg, Miss.: U.S. Army Corps of Engineers.

Flannery, K. V. 1967. Culture history v. cultural process: A debate in American archaeology. *Scientific American* 217(2):119–22.

———. 1968. Archeological systems theory and early Mesoamerica. In *Anthropological archeology in the Americas,* edited by B. J. Meggers. Washington, D.C.: Anthropological Society of Washington. Pp. 67–87.

———. 1986. Adaptation, evolution, and archaeological phases: Some implications of Reynolds' simulation. In *Guilá Naquitz: Archaic foraging and early agriculture in Oaxaca, Mexico,* edited by K. V. Flannery. Orlando: Academic Press. Pp. 501–7.

Ford, J. A. 1934. Mound builders were pit dwellers. *El Palacio* 33:198–99.

———. 1935a. An introduction to Louisiana archaeology. *Louisiana Conservation Review* 4(5):8–11.

———. 1935b. Outline of Louisiana and Mississippi pottery horizons. *Louisiana Conservation Review* 4(6):33–38.

———. 1935c. Ceramic decoration sequence at an old Indian village site near Sicily Island, Louisiana. *Louisiana Department of Conservation, Anthropological Study* 1.

———. 1936a. Analysis of Indian village site collections from Louisiana and Mississippi. *Louisiana Department of Conservation, Anthropological Study* 2.

———. 1936b. Archaeological methods applicable to Louisiana. *Proceedings of the Louisiana Academy of Sciences* 3:102–5.

———. 1938a. An examination of some theories and methods of ceramic analysis. Master's thesis, Department of Anthropology, University of Michigan.

———. 1938b. A chronological method applicable to the Southeast. *American Antiquity* 3:260–64.

———. 1939a. Archaeological exploration in Louisiana during 1938. *Louisiana Conservation Review* 7(4):15–17.

———. 1939b. *Plan for an archaeological survey of the central Mississippi Valley.* Manuscript submitted to the National Park Service, Washington, D.C.

———. 1940. Review of "Handbook of northern Arizona pottery wares," by H. S. Colton and L. L. Hargrave. *American Antiquity* 5:263–66.

———. 1944. Excavations in the vicinity of Cali, Colombia. *Yale University Publications in Anthropology* 31.

———. 1949. Cultural dating of prehistoric sites in Virú Valley, Peru. *American Museum of Natural History, Anthropological Papers* 43(1):29–89.

———. 1951a. Greenhouse: A Troyville–Coles Creek period site in Avoyelles Parish, Louisiana. *American Museum of Natural History, Anthropological Papers* 44(1).

———. 1951b. Review of "Excavations on Upper Matecumbe Key, Florida," by J. M. Goggin and F. H. Sommer III, and of "Excavations in southeast Florida," by G. R. Willey. *American Anthropologist* 53:118–19.

———. 1952a. Measurements of some prehistoric design developments in the southeastern states. *American Museum of Natural History, Anthropological Papers* 44(3).

———. 1952b. Reply to "The Viru Valley sequence: A critical review." *American Antiquity* 17:250.

———. 1954a. Comment on A. C. Spaulding, "Statistical technique for the discovery of artifact types." *American Antiquity* 19:390–91.

———. 1954b. Spaulding's review of Ford. *American Anthropologist* 56:109–12.

———. 1954c. On the concept of types: The type concept revisited. *American Anthropologist* 56:42–57.

———. 1954d. Additional notes on the Poverty Point site in northern Louisiana. *American Antiquity* 19:282–85.

———. 1955a. Poverty Point excavations. *Science* 122:550–51.

———. 1955b. The puzzle of Poverty Point. *Natural History* 64:466–72.

———. 1957. Método cuantitativo para determinar la cronología arqueológica. *Divulgaciones Etnológicas* 6:9–22.

———. 1958. Menard site: The Quapaw village of Osotouy on the Arkansas River. *American Museum of Natural History, Anthropological Papers* 48(2).

———. 1959. Eskimo prehistory in the vicinity of Point Barrow, Alaska. *American Museum of Natural History, Anthropological Papers* 47(1).

———. 1961a. An archeological survey in the alluvial valley of the Mississippi River. *Arkansas Archeological Society, Newsletter* 2(5):12–14.

———. 1961b. In favor of simple typology. *American Antiquity* 27:113–14.

———. 1962. A quantitative method for deriving cultural chronology. *Pan American Union, Technical Manual* 1.

———. 1963. Hopewell culture burial mounds near Helena, Arkansas. *American Museum of Natural History, Anthropological Papers* 50(1).

———. 1964. A whimper from a pink granite tower. *American Anthropologist* 66:399–401.

———. 1966. Early Formative cultures in Georgia and Florida. *American Antiquity* 31:781–98.

———. 1967. Review of "Early Formative period of coastal Ecuador," by B. J. Meggers, C. Evans, and E. Estrada. *American Antiquity* 32:258–59.

———. 1969. A comparison of formative cultures in the Americas: Diffusion or the psychic unity of man? *Smithsonian Contributions to Anthropology* 11.

Ford, J. A., and J. B. Griffin. 1937. [A proposal for a] Conference on pottery nomenclature for the southeastern United States. Mimeographed. [Reprinted in *Newsletter of the Southeastern Archaeological Conference* 7(1):5–9.]

———. 1938. Report of the Conference on Southeastern Pottery Typology. Mimeographed. [Reprinted in *Newsletter of the Southeastern Archaeological Conference* 7(1):10–22.]

Ford, J. A., P. Phillips, and W. G. Haag. 1955. The Jaketown site in west-central Mississippi. *American Museum of Natural History, Anthropological Papers* 46(1).

Ford, J. A., and G. I. Quimby, Jr. 1945. The Tchefuncte culture, an early occupation of the lower Mississippi Valley. *Society for American Archaeology, Memoirs* 2.

Ford, J. A., and C. H. Webb. 1956. Poverty Point, a Late Archaic site in Louisiana. *American Museum of Natural History, Anthropological Papers* 46(1).

Ford, J. A., and G. R. Willey. 1940. Crooks site, a Marksville period burial mound in La Salle Parish, Louisiana. *Louisiana Department of Conservation, Anthropological Study* 3.

———. 1941. An interpretation of the prehistory of the eastern United States. *American Anthropologist* 43:325–63.

———. 1949. Virú Valley: Background and problems. In Surface survey of the Virú Valley, Peru, by J. A. Ford and G. R. Willey. *American Museum of Natural History, Anthropological Papers* 43(1). Pp. 11–28.

Fowke, G. 1896. Stone art. *Bureau of American Ethnology, Annual Report* 13:57–178.

———. 1922. Archeological investigations. *Bureau of American Ethnology, Bulletin* 76.

———. 1927. Archaeological work in Louisiana. *Smithsonian Miscellaneous Collections* 78(7).

———. 1928. Archaeological investigations—II. *Bureau of American Ethnology, Annual Report* 44:399–540.

Fowler, M. L., and H. Winters. 1956. Modoc rock shelter: Preliminary report. *Illinois State Museum, Reports of Investigations* 4.

Fox, G. L. 1992. A critical evaluation of the interpretive framework of the Mississippi period in southeast Missouri. Ph.D. diss., Department of Anthropology, University of Missouri–Columbia.

———. 1998. An examination of Mississippian-period phases in southeastern Missouri. In *Changing perspectives on the archaeology of the central Mississippi Valley*, edited by M. J. O'Brien and R. C. Dunnell. Tuscaloosa: University of Alabama Press. Pp. 31–58.

Fritz, J. M., and F. T. Plog. 1970. The nature of archaeological explanation. *American Antiquity* 35:405–12.

Gamio, M. 1913. Arqueologia de Atzcapotzalco, D.F., Mexico. *Eighteenth International Congress of Americanists, Proceedings*. Pp. 180–87.

————. 1924. The sequence of cultures in Mexico. *American Anthropologist* 26:307–22.

Gayton, A. H. 1927. The Uhle collections from Nievería. *University of California, Publications in American Archaeology and Ethnology* 21(8):305–29.

Gayton, A. H., and A. L. Kroeber. 1927. The Uhle pottery collections from Nazca. *University of California, Publications in American Archaeology and Ethnology* 24(1):1–46.

Ghiselin, M. T. 1966. On psychologism in the logic of taxonomic controversies. *Systematic Zoology* 15:207–15.

————. 1974. A radical solution to the species problem. *Systematic Zoology* 25:536–44.

————. 1981. Categories, life and thinking. *Behavioral and Brain Sciences* 4:269–313.

Gibson, J. L. 1974. Poverty Point: The first North American chiefdom. *Archaeology* 2:97–105.

————. 1975. Fire pits at Mount Bayou (16CT35), Catahoula Parish, Louisiana. *Louisiana Archaeology* 2:201–28.

————. 1980. Speculations on the origin and development of Poverty Point culture. *Louisiana Archaeology* 6:321–48.

————. 1982. *Archeology and ethnology on the edges of the Atchafalaya Basin, south central Louisiana.* Report submitted to the U.S. Army Corps of Engineers, New Orleans.

————. 1984. *The earthen face of civilization: Mapping and testing at Poverty Point, 1983.* Report on file, Department of Anthropology, Southwestern Louisiana State University, Lafayette.

————. 1985. Poverty Point: A culture of the lower Mississippi Valley. *Louisiana Archaeological Survey and Antiquities Commission, Anthropological Study* 7.

Gifford, J. C. 1960. The type-variety method of ceramic classification as an indicator of cultural phenomena. *American Antiquity* 25:341–47.

Givens, D. R. 1992. *Alfred Vincent Kidder and the development of Americanist archaeology.* Albuquerque: University of New Mexico Press.

Gladwin, H. S. 1936. Editorials: Methodology in the Southwest. *American Antiquity* 1:256–59.

Gladwin, W., and H. S. Gladwin. 1928. The use of potsherds in an archaeological survey of the Southwest. *Medallion Papers* 2.

————. 1930a. A method for the designation of southwestern pottery types. *Medallion Papers* 7.

————. 1930b. Some southwestern pottery types, series I. *Medallion Papers* 8.

————. 1931. Some southwestern pottery types, series II. *Medallion Papers* 10.

————. 1933. Some southwestern pottery types, series III. *Medallion Papers* 13.

————. 1934. A method for the designation of cultures and their variations. *Medallion Papers* 15.

Gladwin, H. S., E. W. Haury, E. B. Sayles, and N. Gladwin. 1937. Excavations at Snaketown: Material culture. *Medallion Papers* 25.

Goggin, J. M., and F. H. Sommer III. 1949. Excavations on Upper Matecumbe Key, Florida. *Yale University Publications in Anthropology* 41.

Goldenweiser, A. 1925. Diffusionism and historical ethnology. *American Journal of Sociology* 31:19–38.

Goodyear, A. C. 1982. The chronological position of the Dalton horizon in the southeastern United States. *American Antiquity* 47:382–95.

Gould, R. A. (editor). 1978. *Explorations in ethnoarchaeology.* Albuquerque: University of New Mexico Press.

Gould, S. J. 1986. Evolution and the triumph of homology, or why history matters. *American Scientist* 74:96–118.

Grayson, D. K. 1984. *Quantitative zooarchaeology.* New York: Academic Press.

Greengo, R. E. 1964. Issaquena: An archaeological phase in the Yazoo Basin of the lower Mississippi Valley. *Society for American Archaeology, Memoirs* 18.

Griffin, J. B. 1938. The ceramic remains from Norris Basin, Tennessee. In An archaeological survey of the Norris Basin in eastern Tennessee, edited by W. S. Webb. *Bureau of American Ethnology, Bulletin* 118:253–59.

————. 1939. Report on the ceramics of Wheeler Basin. In An archaeological survey of Wheeler Basin on the Tennessee River in northern Alabama, edited by W. S. Webb. *Bureau of American Ethnology, Bulletin* 122:127–65.

————. 1941. Additional Hopewell material from Illinois. *Indiana Historical Society, Prehistory Research Series* 2(3).

————. 1943. *The Fort Ancient aspect: Its cultural and chronological position in Mississippi Valley archaeology.* Ann Arbor: University of Michigan Press.

————. 1946. Cultural change and continuity in eastern United States archaeology. In Man in northeastern North America, edited by F. Johnson. *Robert S. Peabody Foundation for Archaeology, Papers* 3:37–95.

————. 1952a. Culture periods in eastern United States archeology. In *Archeology of eastern United States,* edited by J. B. Griffin. Chicago: University of Chicago Press. Pp. 352–64.

————. 1952b. Radiocarbon dates for the eastern United States. In *Archeology of eastern United States,* edited by J. B. Griffin. Chicago: University of Chicago Press. Pp. 365–70.

————. 1952c. Some Early and Middle Woodland pottery types in Illinois. In Hopewellian communities in Illinois, edited by T. Deuel. *Illinois State Museum, Scientific Papers* 5:93–129.

————. 1959. The pursuit of archeology in the United States. *American Anthropologist* 61:379–89.

————. 1974. Foreword to the new edition. In *The Adena people,* by W. S. Webb and C. E. Snow. Knoxville: University of Tennessee Press. Pp. v–xix.

————. 1976. A commentary on some archaeological activities in the mid-continent 1925–1975. *Midcontinental Journal of Archaeology* 1:5–38.

————. 1985. An individual's participation in American archaeology, 1928–1985. *Annual Review of Anthropology* 14:1–23.

Griffin, J. B., and A. C. Spaulding. 1952. The Central Mississippi River Valley Archaeological Survey, season 1950: A preliminary report. In *Prehistoric pottery of eastern United States,* edited by J. B. Griffin. Ann Arbor: University of Michigan Museum of Anthropology. Pp. 1–7.

Guthe, C. E. 1928. A method for ceramic description. *Michigan Academy of Science, Arts, and Letters, Papers* 8:23–29.

————. 1934. A method of ceramic description. In Standards of pottery description, by B. March. *University of Michigan, Museum of Anthropology, Occasional Contributions* 3:1–6.

Haag, W. G. 1953a. Review of "Archaeological survey in the lower Mississippi alluvial valley, 1940–1947," by P. Phillips, J. A. Ford, and J. B. Griffin. *American Antiquity* 18:275–77.

————. 1953b. Review of "Archaeological survey in the lower Mississippi alluvial valley, 1940–1947," by P. Phillips, J. A. Ford, and J. B. Griffin. *American Anthropologist* 55:118–19.

————. 1968. James Alfred Ford, 1911–1968. *The Florida Anthropologist* 21:31–33.

————. 1994. Fred B. Kniffen: As archaeologist. *Journal of Cultural Geography* 15:27–31.

Haag, W. G., and C. H. Webb. 1953. Microblades at Poverty Point sites. *American Antiquity* 18:245–48.

Hargrave, L. L. 1932. Guide to forty pottery types from Hopi country and the San Francisco Mountains, Arizona. *Museum of Northern Arizona, Bulletin* 1.

Harrington, M. R. 1924. The Ozark bluff-dwellers. *American Anthropologist* 26:1–21.

Haury, E. W. 1936. Some southwestern pottery types, series IV. *Medallion Papers* 19.

Hawkes, C. 1954. Archeological theory and method: Some suggestions from the Old World. *American Anthropologist* 56:155–68.

Hawley, F. M. 1934. The significance of the dated prehistory of Chetro Ketl. *University of New Mexico Bulletin, Monograph Series* 1(1).

Heine-Geldern, R. von. 1954. Die Asiatische Herkunft, der Südamerikanischen Metalltechnik. *Paideuma* 5:347–423.

————. 1959a. Representation of the Asiatic tiger in the art of the Chavín culture:

A proof of early contacts between China and Peru. *Actas del 33ra Congreso Internacionál de Americanistas.* Pp. 195–206.

———. 1959b. Chinese influences in Mexico and Central America: The Tajin style of Mexico and the marble vases from Honduras. *Actas del 33ra Congreso Internacionál de Americanistas.* Pp. 321–26.

Herskovits, M. 1950. *International directory of anthropologists.* Washington, D.C.: National Research Council.

Hoffman, M. 1981. The father of us all: S. C. Dellinger and the beginning of Arkansas archaeology and anthropology. Paper presented at the 38th Southeastern Archaeological Conference, Asheville, North Carolina.

Holland, C. G. 1960. Preceramic and ceramic cultural patterns in northwest Virginia. *Bureau of American Ethnology, Bulletin* 173.

Holmes, W. H. 1886a. Pottery of the ancient pueblos. *Bureau of Ethnology, Annual Report* 4:257–360.

———. 1886b. Ancient pottery of the Mississippi Valley. *Bureau of Ethnology, Annual Report* 4:361–436.

———. 1886c. Origin and development of form and ornamentation in ceramic art. *Bureau of Ethnology, Annual Report* 4:437–65.

———. 1903. Aboriginal pottery of the eastern United States. *Bureau of American Ethnology, Annual Report* 20:1–201.

Hopgood, J. F. 1969. An archaeological reconnaissance of Portage Open Bay in southeast Missouri. *Missouri Archaeological Society, Memoir* 7.

Howe, B., and H. L. Movius, Jr. 1947. A stone age cave site in Tangier: Preliminary report on the excavations at the Mugháret el ʿAliya, or High Cave, in Tangier. *Harvard University, Peabody Museum of Archaeology and Ethnology, Papers* 28.

Howe, H. V., and C. K. Moresi. 1933. The contribution of Louisiana State University to the development of Louisiana geology. *Louisiana Conservation Review* 3:23–33.

Hull, D. 1965. The effect of essentialism on taxonomy: 2000 years of stasis. *British Journal for the Philosophy of Science* 15:314–26, 16:1–18.

Huxtable, J., M. J. Aitken, and J. C. Weber. 1972. Thermoluminescent dating of baked clay balls of the Poverty Point culture. *Archaeometry* 14:269–75.

Jackson, H. E. 1986. Sedentism and hunter-gatherer adaptations in the lower Mississippi Valley: Subsistence strategies during the Poverty Point period. Ph.D. diss., Department of Anthropology, University of Michigan.

Jennings, J. D. 1941. Chickasaw and earlier Indian cultures of northeast Mississippi. *Journal of Mississippi History* 3:155–226.

———. 1952a. Prehistory of the lower Mississippi Valley. In *Archeology of eastern United States,* edited by J. B. Griffin. Chicago: University of Chicago Press. Pp. 256–71.

———. 1952b. Review of "Greenhouse: A Troyville–Coles Creek period site in Avoyelles Parish, Louisiana," by J. A. Ford. *American Anthropologist* 54:555–56.

———. 1974. *Prehistory of North America* (2d ed.). New York: McGraw-Hill.

Jeter, M. D. (editor). 1990. *Edward Palmer's Arkansaw Mounds.* Fayetteville: University of Arkansas Press.

Jett, S. C., and G. F. Carter. 1966. A comment on Rowe's "Diffusionism and archaeology." *American Antiquity* 31:867–70.

Kenyon, K. M. 1957. *Digging up Jericho: The results of the Jericho excavations, 1952–1956.* New York: Praeger.

Kidder, A. V. 1915. Pottery of the Pajarito Plateau and of some adjacent regions in New Mexico. *American Anthropological Association, Memoir* 2:407–62.

———. 1916. Archeological explorations at Pecos, New Mexico. *National Academy of Sciences, Proceedings* 2:119–23.

———. 1917. A design-sequence from New Mexico. *National Academy of Sciences, Proceedings* 3:369–70.

———. 1924. An introduction to the study of southwestern archaeology, with a preliminary account of the excavations at Pecos. *Papers of the Southwestern Expedition, Phillips Academy* 1.

———. 1927. Southwestern Archaeological Conference. *Science* 66:489–91.

———. 1932. The artifacts of Pecos. *Papers of the Southwestern Expedition, Phillips Academy* 6.

———. 1936a. Discussion. In *The pottery of Pecos* (vol. 2), by A. V. Kidder and A. O. Shepard. New Haven, Conn.: Yale University Press. Pp. 589–628.

———. 1936b. Introduction. In *The pottery of Pecos* (vol. 2), by A. V. Kidder and A. O. Shepard. New Haven, Conn.: Yale University Press. Pp. xvii–xxxi.

Kidder, M. A., and A. V. Kidder. 1917. Notes on the pottery of Pecos. *American Anthropologist* 19:325–60.

Klippel, W. E. 1969. The Hearnes site: A multicomponent occupation site and cemetery in the Cairo Lowland region of southeast Missouri. *Missouri Archaeologist* 31.

Kluckhohn, C. 1939a. Discussion. In Preliminary report on the 1937 excavations, Bc 50–51, Chaco Canyon, New Mexico, edited by C. Kluckhohn and P. Reiter. *University of New Mexico, Bulletin* 345:151–62.

———. 1939b. The place of theory in anthropological studies. *Philosophy of Science* 6:328–44.

———. 1940. Conceptual structure in Middle American studies. In *The Maya and their neighbors,* edited by C. L. Hay, R. L. Linton, S. K. Lothrop, H. L. Shapiro, and G. C. Vaillant. New York: Appleton-Century. Pp. 41–51.

Kluckhohn, C., and P. Reiter. 1939. Preliminary report on the 1937 excavations, Bc 50–51, Chaco Canyon, New Mexico. *University of New Mexico Bulletin, Anthropological Series* 3(2).

Kniffen, F. B. 1928. Achomawi geography. *University of California, Publications in American Archaeology and Ethnology* 23(5).

———. 1935. Walapai ethnography. *American Anthropological Association, Memoir* 42.

———. 1936. A preliminary report on the Indian mounds of Plaquemines and St. Bernard parishes. In Reports on the geology of Plaquemines and St. Bernard parishes, by R. J. Russell. *Department of Conservation, Louisiana Geological Survey, Geological Bulletin* 8:407–22.

———. 1938. Indian mounds of Iberville and Ascension parishes. In Reports on the geology of Iberville and Ascension parishes, by R. J. Russell. *Department of Conservation, Louisiana Geological Survey, Geological Bulletin* 13:189–207.

———. 1939. Pomo geography. *University of California, Publications in American Archaeology and Ethnology* 36:353–400.

———. 1973. Richard Joel Russell, 1895–1971. *Association of American Geographers, Annals* 63:241–49.

Kramer, C. (editor). 1979. *Ethnoarchaeology: Implications of ethnography for archaeology.* New York: Columbia University Press.

Krieger, A. D. 1944. The typological concept. *American Antiquity* 9:271–88.

———. 1946. Culture complexes and chronology in northern Texas with extension of Puebloan datings to the Mississippi Valley. *University of Texas Publication* 4640.

———. 1947. Certain projectile points of the early American hunters. *Bulletin of the Texas Archeological and Paleontological Society* 18:7–27.

———. 1952. Review of "Greenhouse: A Troyville–Coles Creek period site in Avoyelles Parish, Louisiana, by J. A. Ford." *American Antiquity* 18:175–79.

Kroeber, A. L. 1909. The archaeology of California. In *Putnam Anniversary Volume*, edited by F. Boas. New York: Stechert. Pp. 1–42.

———. 1915. Eighteen professions. *American Anthropologist* 17:283–88.

———. 1916a. Zuñi culture sequences. *National Academy of Sciences, Proceedings* 2:42–45.

———. 1916b. Zuñi potsherds. *American Museum of Natural History, Anthropological Papers* 18(1):1–37.

———. 1916c. Cause of the belief in use inheritance. *American Naturalist* 50:367–70.

———. 1917. The superorganic. *American Anthropologist* 19:163–213.

———. 1919. On the principle of order in civilization as exemplified by changes of fashion. *American Anthropologist* 21:235–63.

———. 1925a. The Uhle pottery collections from Moche. *University of California, Publications in American Archaeology and Ethnology* 21(5):191–234.

———. 1925b. The Uhle pottery collections from Supe. *University of California, Publications in American Archaeology and Ethnology* 21(6):235–64.

————. 1925c. Archaic culture horizons in the Valley of Mexico. *University of California, Publications in American Archaeology and Ethnology* 17(7):373–408.

————. 1931a. Historical reconstruction of culture growths and organic evolution. *American Anthropologist* 33:149–56.

————. 1931b. The culture-area and age-area concepts of Clark Wissler. In *Methods in Social Science,* edited by S. A. Rice. Chicago: University of Chicago Press. Pp. 248–65.

————. 1939. Cultural and natural areas of native North America. *University of California, Publications in American Archaeology and Ethnology* 38:1–242.

————. 1943. Structure, function and pattern in biology and anthropology. *Scientific Monthly* 56:105–13.

————. 1944. Peruvian archaeology in 1942. *Viking Fund Publications in Anthropology* 4.

————. 1946. History and evolution. *Southwestern Journal of Anthropology* 2:1–15.

————. 1948. *Anthropology.* New York: Harcourt Brace.

————. 1952. *The nature of culture.* Chicago: University of Chicago Press.

Kroeber, A. L., and W. D. Strong. 1924a. The Uhle collections from Chincha. *University of California, Publications in American Archaeology and Ethnology* 21(1):1–54.

————. 1924b. The Uhle pottery collections from Ica. *University of California, Publications in American Archaeology and Ethnology* 21(2):57–94.

Kuhn, T. 1977. Second thoughts on paradigms. In *The structure of scientific theories* (2d ed.), edited by F. Suppe. Urbana: University of Illinois Press. Pp. 459–517.

Kuttruff, L. C., M. J. O'Brien, and R. L. Lyman. 1997. The 1933 excavations at the Marksville site by Frank M. Setzler and James A. Ford. Paper presented at the Southeastern Archaeological Conference, Baton Rouge.

Lartet E., and H. Christy. 1964. Caverns of Perigord. *Reveue Archéologique.* Paris.

Lathrap, D. W. (editor). 1956. An archaeological classification of culture contact situations. In Seminars in archaeology: 1955. *Society for American Archaeology, Memoirs* 11:1–30.

Lemley, H. J. 1936. Discoveries indicating a pre-Caddo culture on Red River in Arkansas. *Texas Archeological and Paleontological Society, Bulletin* 8:25–55.

Leonard, R. D., and G. T. Jones. 1987. Elements of an inclusive evolutionary model for archaeology. *Journal of Anthropological Archaeology* 6:199–219.

Leone, M. P. 1972. Issues in anthropological archaeology. In *Contemporary archaeology,* edited by M. P. Leone. Carbondale: Southern Illinois University Press. Pp. 14–27.

Lewontin, R. C. 1974a. Darwin and Mendel—the materialist revolution. In *The heritage of Copernicus: Theories pleasing to the mind,* edited by J. Neyman. Cambridge, Mass.: MIT Press. Pp. 166–83.

————. 1974b. *The genetic basis of evolutionary change*. New York: Columbia University Press.

Lipo, C., M. Madsen, R. C. Dunnell, and T. Hunt. 1997. Population structure, cultural transmission, and frequency seriation. *Journal of Anthropological Archaeology* 16:301–33.

Loud, L. L., and M. R. Harrington. 1929. Lovelock Cave. *University of California, Publications in American Archaeology and Ethnology* 25:1–183.

Lowie, R. 1937. *The history of ethnological theory*. New York: Farrar and Rinehart.

Lyell, C. 1830–1833. *Principles of geology*. London: Murray.

Lyman, R. L. 1994. Quantitative units and terminology in zooarchaeology. *American Antiquity* 59:36–71.

Lyman, R. L., and M. J. O'Brien. 1997. The concept of evolution in early twentieth-century Americanist archaeology. In *Rediscovering Darwin: Evolutionary theory and archaeological explanation,* edited by C. M. Barton and G. A. Clark. American Anthropological Association, Archeological Papers. No. 7, 21–48.

————. 1998. Americanist stratigraphic excavation and the measurement of culture change. *Journal of Archaeological Method and Theory* (in press).

Lyman, R. L., M. J. O'Brien, and R. C. Dunnell. 1997a. *The rise and fall of culture history*. New York: Plenum Press.

————(editors). 1997b. *Americanist culture history: Fundamentals of time, space, and form*. New York: Plenum Press.

Lyman, R. L., S. Wolverton, and M. J. O'Brien. 1998. Seriation, superposition and interdigitation: A history of Americanist graphic depictions of culture change. *American Antiquity* 63:239–61.

Lyon, E. A. 1996. *A new deal for southeastern archaeology*. Tuscaloosa: University of Alabama Press.

Macalister, R. A. S. 1912. *The excavation of Gezer, 1902–1905 and 1907–1909*. London: Murray.

McCown, D. E. 1942. The comparative stratigraphy of early Iran. *University of Chicago, Oriental Institute, Studies in Ancient Oriental Civilization* 23.

McIntire, W. G. 1958. Prehistoric Indian settlements of the changing Mississippi River Delta. *Louisiana State University Studies, Coastal Study Series* 5.

McIntyre, L. B. 1939. The use of negro women in W.P.A. work at Irene Mound, Savannah. *Society for Georgia Archaeology, Proceedings* 2:23–26.

McKee, J. O. 1976. Interview with Fred B. Kniffen. *The Mississippi Geographer* 4:5–6.

McKern, W. C. 1934. Certain culture classification problems in Middle Western archaeology. *National Research Council, Committee on State Archaeological Surveys*. Washington, D.C.

————. 1937. Certain culture classification problems in Middle Western archaeology. In The Indianapolis Archaeological Conference. *National Research Council, Committee on State Archaeological Surveys, Circular* 17:70–82.

——. 1939. The Midwestern Taxonomic Method as an aid to archaeological culture study. *American Antiquity* 4:301–13.

McMichael, E. V. 1964. Veracruz, the Crystal River complex and the Hopewellian climax. In Hopewellian studies, edited by J. R. Caldwell and R. L. Hall. *Illinois State Museum, Scientific Papers* 12:123–32.

MacNeish, R. S. 1947. A preliminary report on coastal Tamaulipas, Mexico. *American Antiquity* 13:1–15.

——. 1954. An early archaeological site near Panuco, Veracruz. *American Philosophical Society, Transactions* 44:539–641.

——. 1958. Preliminary archaeological investigations in the Sierra de Tamaulipas, Mexico. *American Philosophical Society, Transactions* 48(6).

——. 1961. First annual report of the Tehuacán Archaeological-Botanical Project. *Robert S. Peabody Foundation for Archaeology, Project Reports* 1.

——. 1962. Second annual report of the Tehuacán Archaeological-Botanical Project. *Robert S. Peabody Foundation for Archaeology, Project Reports* 2.

MacWhite, E. 1956. On the interpretation of archaeological evidence in historical and sociological terms. *American Anthropologist* 58:26–39.

Manners, R. A. 1973. Julian Haynes Steward, 1902–1972. *American Anthropologist* 75:886–903.

March, B. 1934. Standards of pottery description. *University of Michigan, Museum of Anthropology, Occasional Contributions* 3.

Marshall, R. A. 1965. An archaeological investigation of Interstate Route 55 through New Madrid and Pemiscot counties, Missouri. *Missouri State Highway Department, Highway Archaeology Report* 1.

Martin, P. S. 1936. Lowry Ruin in southwestern Colorado. *Fieldiana: Anthropology* 23(1).

——. 1938. Archaeological work in the Ackmen-Lowry area, southwestern Colorado, 1937. *Fieldiana: Anthropology* 23:217–304.

——. 1939. Modified Basket Maker sites, Ackmen-Lowry area, southwestern Colorado. *Fieldiana: Anthropology* 23(3).

——. 1971. The revolution in archaeology. *American Antiquity* 36:1–8.

Mason, O. T. 1896. Influence of environment upon human industries or arts. *Smithsonian Institution, Annual Report.* Pp. 639–65.

Mayr, E. 1959. Darwin and the evolutionary theory in biology. In *Evolution and anthropology: A centennial appraisal,* edited by B. J. Meggers. Washington, D.C.: The Anthropological Society of Washington. Pp. 106–24.

——. 1976. Typological versus population thinking. In *Evolution and the diversity of life,* by E. Mayr. Cambridge, Mass.: Harvard University Press. Pp. 26–29.

———. 1977. Darwin and natural selection. *American Scientist* 65: 321–37.

———. 1982. *The growth of biological thought.* Cambridge, Mass.: Harvard University Press.

———. 1987. The ontological status of species. *Biology and Philosophy* 2:145–66.

Meggers, B. J. 1960. The law of cultural evolution as a practical research tool. In *Essays in the science of culture,* edited by G. Dole and R. Carneiro. New York: Crowell. Pp. 302–16.

———. 1964. North and South American cultural connections and convergences. In *Prehistoric man in the New World,* edited by J. D. Jennings and E. Norbeck. Chicago: University of Chicago Press. Pp. 511–26.

Meggers, B. J., and C. Evans. 1962. The Machalilla culture: An Early Formative complex on the Ecuadorian coast. *American Antiquity* 28:186–92.

Meggers, B. J., C. Evans, and E. Estrada. 1965. Early Formative period of coastal Ecuador: The Valdivia and Machalilla phases. *Smithsonian Contributions to Anthropology* 1.

Meltzer, D. J. 1979. Paradigms and the nature of change in American archaeology. *American Antiquity* 44:644–57.

———. 1983. The antiquity of man and the development of American archaeology. In *Advances in archaeological method and theory* (vol. 6), edited by M. B. Schiffer. New York: Academic Press. Pp. 1–51.

———. 1985. North American archaeology and archaeologists, 1879–1934. *American Antiquity* 50:249–60.

Meltzer, D. J., and R. C. Dunnell. 1992. Introduction. In *The archaeology of William Henry Holmes,* edited by D. J. Meltzer and R. C. Dunnell. Washington, D.C.: Smithsonian Institution Press. Pp. vi–l.

Moore, C. B. 1905. Certain aboriginal remains of the Black Warrior River. *Academy of Natural Sciences of Philadelphia, Journal* 13:125–244.

———. 1908. Certain mounds of Arkansas and of Mississippi—part II: Mounds of the lower Yazoo and lower Sunflower rivers, Mississippi. *Academy of Natural Sciences of Philadelphia, Journal* 13:564–92.

———. 1909. Antiquities of the Ouachita Valley. *Academy of Natural Sciences of Philadelphia, Journal* 14:7–170.

———. 1910. Antiquities of the St. Francis, White and Black rivers, Arkansas. *Academy of Natural Sciences of Philadelphia, Journal* 14:255–364.

———. 1911. Some aboriginal sites on Mississippi River. *Academy of Natural Sciences of Philadelphia, Journal* 14:367–480.

———. 1912. Some aboriginal sites on Red River. *Academy of Natural Sciences of Philadelphia, Journal* 14:482–644.

———. 1913. Some aboriginal sites in Louisiana and Arkansas. *Academy of Natural Sciences of Philadelphia, Journal* 16:7–99.

Moorehead, W. K. 1922. The Hopewell mound group of Ohio. *Field Museum of Natural History, Anthropological Series* 16:514–77.

Moresi, C. K. 1939. The School of Geology of the Louisiana State University and Louisiana Geological Survey. *Louisiana Conservation Review* 7(2):9–10, 53–54.

Morgan, L. H. 1877. *Ancient society.* New York: Holt.

Mortillet, G. de. 1883. *Le préhistorique: Origine et antiquité de l'homme.* Paris: Bibliothèque des Sciences Contemporaines.

Munro, N. G. 1911. *Prehistoric Japan.* Yokohama.

National Research Council. 1932. *Conference on Southern Pre-History.* Washington, D.C.

Neff, H. 1992. Ceramics and evolution. In *Archaeological method and theory* (vol. 4), edited by M. B. Schiffer. Tucson: University of Arizona Press. Pp. 141–93.

———. 1993. Theory, sampling, and analytical techniques in the archaeological study of prehistoric ceramics. *American Antiquity* 58:23–44.

Neiman, F. D. 1995. Stylistic variation in evolutionary perspective: Inferences from decorative diversity and interassemblage distance in Illinois Woodland ceramic assemblages. *American Antiquity* 60:7–36.

Neitzel, R. S. 1965. Archeology of the Fatherland site: The Grand Village of the Natchez. *American Museum of Natural History, Anthropological Papers* 51(1).

———. 1991. William George Haag, life and times. *Louisiana Archaeology* 18:1–10.

Nelson, N. C. 1916. Chronology of the Tano Ruins, New Mexico. *American Anthropologist* 18:159–80.

———. 1919a. Human culture. *Natural History* 19:131–40.

———. 1919b. The Southwest problem. *El Palacio* 6(9):132–35.

———. 1920. Notes on Pueblo Bonito. *American Museum of Natural History, Anthropological Papers* 27:381–90.

———. 1932. The origin and development of material culture. *Sigma Xi Quarterly* 20:102–23.

———. 1937. Prehistoric archeology, past, present and future. *Science* 85:81–89.

Neuman, R. W. 1984. *An introduction to Louisiana archaeology.* Baton Rouge: Louisiana State University Press.

Newell, H. P., and A. D. Krieger. 1949. The George C. Davis site, Cherokee County, Texas. *Society for American Archaeology, Memoirs* 5.

O'Brien, M. J. 1995. Archaeological research in the central Mississippi Valley: Culture history gone awry. *The Review of Archaeology* 16:23–36.

———. 1996a. *Paradigms of the past: The story of Missouri archaeology.* Columbia: University of Missouri Press.

———. 1996b. *Evolutionary archaeology: Theory and application.* Salt Lake City: University of Utah Press.

———. 1996c. The historical development of an evolutionary archaeology. In

Darwinian archaeologies, edited by H. D. G. Maschner. New York: Plenum. Pp. 17–32.

———. 1998. The legacy of culture history in the southeastern United States. *Reviews in Anthropology* (in press).

O'Brien, M. J., and R. C. Dunnell. 1998. A brief introduction to the archaeology of the central Mississippi River valley. In *Changing perspectives on the archaeology of the central Mississippi Valley,* edited by M. J. O'Brien and R. C. Dunnell. Tuscaloosa: University of Alabama Press. Pp. 1–30.

O'Brien, M. J., and G. L. Fox. 1994a. Sorting artifacts in space and time. In *Cat monsters and head pots: The archaeology of Missouri's Pemiscot Bayou,* by M. J. O'Brien. Columbia: University of Missouri Press. Pp. 25–60.

———. 1994b. Assemblage similarities and differences. In *Cat monsters and head pots: The archaeology of Missouri's Pemiscot Bayou,* by M. J. O'Brien. Columbia: University of Missouri Press. Pp. 61–93.

O'Brien, M. J., and T. D. Holland. 1990. Variation, selection, and the archaeological record. In *Advances in archaeological method and theory* (vol. 2), edited by M. B. Schiffer. Tucson: University of Arizona Press. Pp. 31–79.

———. 1992. The role of adaptation in archaeological explanation. *American Antiquity* 57:36–59.

———. 1995a. The nature and premise of a selection-based archaeology. In *Evolutionary archaeology: Methodological issues,* edited by P. A. Teltser. Tucson: University of Arizona Press. Pp. 175–200.

———. 1995b. Behavioral archaeology and the extended phenotype. In *Expanding archaeology,* edited by J. M. Skibo, W. H. Walker, and A. E. Nielsen. Salt Lake City: University of Utah Press. Pp. 143–61.

O'Brien, M. J., T. D. Holland, R. J. Hoard, and G. L. Fox. 1994. Evolutionary implications of design and performance characteristics of prehistoric pottery. *Journal of Archaeological Method and Theory* 1:259–304.

O'Brien, M. J., and R. L. Lyman. 1997. The Bureau of American Archaeology and its legacy to southeastern archaeology. Paper presented at the 62d Annual Meeting of the Society for American Archaeology, Nashville.

O'Brien, M. J., and R. W. Wood. 1998. *The prehistory of Missouri.* Columbia: University of Missouri Press.

Okladnikov, A. P. 1950. Neolii i Bronzovyy vek Pribaikaliya. *Materialy i Issledovaniia po Arkheologii SSSR* 18.

Olson, R. L. 1930. Chumash prehistory. *University of California, Publications in American Archaeology and Ethnology* 28(1):1–21.

Opler, M. E. 1961. Cultural evolution, southern Athapaskans, and chronology in theory. *Southwestern Journal of Anthropology* 17:1–20.

———. 1963. Cultural anthropology: An addendum to a "working paper." *American Anthropologist* 65:897–902.

————. 1964a. Reflections on the downgrading of man and the grading of cultures: A reply. *American Anthropologist* 66:401–5.

————. 1964b. The human being in culture theory. *American Anthropologist* 66:507–28.

Orton, C. R. 1975. Quantitative pottery studies: Some progress, problems and prospects. *Science and Archaeology* 16:30–35.

Osgood, C. 1951. Culture: Its empirical and nonempirical character. *Southwestern Journal of Anthropology* 7:202–14.

Peabody, C. O. 1904. Explorations of mounds, Coahoma County, Mississippi. *Harvard University, Peabody Museum of Archaeology and Ethnology, Papers* 3(2).

Peterson, C. H. 1977. The paleoecological significance of undetected short-term variability. *Journal of Paleontology* 51:976–81.

Petrie, W. M. F. 1899. Sequences in prehistoric remains. *Journal of the Royal Anthropological Institute of Great Britain and Ireland* 29:295–301.

Phillips, P. 1939. Introduction to the archaeology of the Mississippi Valley. Ph.D. diss., Department of Anthropology, Harvard University.

————. 1940. Middle American influences on the archaeology of the southeastern United States. In *The Maya and their neighbors*. New York: Appleton, Century. Pp. 349–67.

————. 1942. Review of "An archaeological survey of Pickwick Basin in the adjacent portions of the states of Alabama, Mississippi, and Tennessee," by W. S. Webb and D. L. DeJarnette. *American Antiquity* 8:197–201.

————. 1951. Review of "Archeology of the Florida Gulf Coast," by G. R. Willey, and of "The Florida Indian and his neighbors," edited by J. W. Griffin. *American Anthropologist* 53:108–12.

————. 1955. American archaeology and general anthropological theory. *Southwestern Journal of Anthropology* 11:246–50.

————. 1958. Application of the Wheat-Gifford-Wasley taxonomy to eastern ceramics. *American Antiquity* 24:117–25.

————. 1970. Archaeological survey in the lower Yazoo Basin, 1949–1955. *Harvard University, Peabody Museum of Archaeology and Ethnology, Papers* 60.

Phillips, P., J. A. Ford, and J. B. Griffin. 1951. Archaeological survey in the lower Mississippi alluvial valley, 1940–1947. *Harvard University, Peabody Museum of Archaeology and Ethnology, Papers* 25.

Phillips, P., and G. R. Willey. 1953. Method and theory in American archaeology: An operational basis for culture-historical integration. *American Anthropologist* 55:615–33.

Pierce, C. 1998. Theory, measurement, and explanation: Variable shapes in Poverty Point objects. In *Unit issues in archaeology: Measuring time, space and material*, edited by A. F. Ramenofsky and A. Steffen. Salt Lake City: University of Utah Press. Pp. 163–89.

Pumpelly, R. (editor). 1908. *Explorations in Turkestan: Expedition of 1904*. Washington, D.C.: Carnegie Institution of Washington.

Quimby, G. I., Jr. 1951. The Medora site, West Baton Rouge Parish, Louisiana. *Field Museum of Natural History, Anthropological Series* 24(2):81–135.

———. 1957. The Bayou Goula site, Iberville Parish, Louisiana. *Fieldiana: Anthropology* (47)2:89–170.

———. 1979. A brief history of WPA archaeology. In The uses of anthropology, edited by W. Goldschmidt. *American Anthropological Association, Special Publication* 11:110–23.

Quimby, G. I., Jr., and C. E. Cleland. 1976. James Bennett Griffin: Appreciation and reminiscences. In *Cultural change and continuity: Essays in honor of James Bennett Griffin*, edited by C. E. Cleland. New York: Academic Press. Pp. xxi–xxxvii.

Rambo, A. T. 1991. The study of cultural evolution. In Profiles in cultural evolution, edited by A. T. Rambo and K. Gillogly. *University of Michigan, Museum of Anthropology, Anthropological Papers* 85:23–109.

Rands, R. L. 1961. Elaboration and invention in ceramic traditions. *American Antiquity* 26:331–40.

Rands, R. L., and C. L. Riley. 1958. Diffusion and discontinuous distribution. *American Anthropologist* 60:274–97.

Rau, C. 1876. The archaeological collections of the United States National Museum in charge of the Smithsonian. *Smithsonian Contributions to Knowledge* 22(4).

Redfield, A. 1971. Dalton Project notes, vol. 1. *University of Missouri, Museum of Anthropology, Museum Brief* 20.

Redfield, A., and J. H. Moselage. 1970. The Lace place: A Dalton project site in the Western Lowland in eastern Arkansas. *Arkansas Archeologist* 11:21–44.

Reichel-Dolmatoff, G. 1961. Puerto Hormiga: Un complejo prehistórico marginal de Colombia. *Revista Colombiana de Antropología* 10:347–54.

———. 1965. Excavaciones arqueológicas en Puerto Hormiga. *Ediciones de la Universidad de los Andes, Antropología* 2.

Reichel-Dolmatoff, G., and A. Reichel-Dolmatoff. 1956. Momíl: Excavaciones en el Sinú. *Revista Colombiana de Antropología* 5:109–333.

Reisner, G. A. 1918. Preliminary report on the Harvard–Boston excavations at Nuri: The kings of Ethiopia after Tirhaqa. *Harvard African Studies* 2.

Reiss, W., and A. Stübel. 1880–1887. *The Necropolis of Ancón in Peru* (3 vols.). Berlin.

Reiter, P. 1938. Review of "Handbook of northern Arizona pottery wares," by H. S. Colton and L. L. Hargrave. *American Anthropologist* 40:489–91.

Richardson, J., and A. L. Kroeber. 1940. Three centuries of women's dress fashions: A quantitative analysis. *University of California, Anthropological Records* 5(2):111–54.

Richardson, M. B. 1994. Fred B. Kniffen: A special kind of anthropologist. *Journal of Cultural Geography* 15:19–26.

Ritchie, W. A., and R. S. MacNeish. 1949. Pre-Iroquoian pottery of New York state. *American Antiquity* 15:97–124.

Roberts, F. H. H., Jr. 1929. Shabik'eshchee Village, a Late Basketmaker site in the Chaco Canyon, New Mexico. *Bureau of American Ethnology, Bulletin* 92.

Robinson, W. S. 1951. A method for chronologically ordering archaeological deposits. *American Antiquity* 16:293–301.

Rouse, I. B. 1939. Prehistory in Haiti: A study in method. *Yale University Publications in Anthropology* 21.

———. 1954. Review of "Measurements of some prehistoric design developments in the southeastern states," by J. A. Ford. *American Antiquity* 19:296–97.

———. 1955. On the correlation of phases of culture. *American Anthropologist* 57:713–22.

———. 1967. Seriation in archaeology. In *American historical anthropology: Essays in honor of Leslie Spier,* edited by C. L. Riley and W. W. Taylor. Carbondale: Southern Illinois University Press. Pp. 153–95.

Rowe, J. H. 1959. Archaeological dating and cultural process. *Southwestern Journal of Anthropology* 15:317–24.

———. 1961. Stratigraphy and seriation. *American Antiquity* 26:324–30.

———. 1962. Alfred Louis Kroeber: 1896–1960. *American Antiquity* 27:395–415.

———. 1966. Diffusionism and archaeology. *American Antiquity* 31:334–37.

Russell, R. J. 1936. Reports on the geology of Plaquemines and St. Bernard parishes. *Department of Conservation, Louisiana Geological Survey, Geological Bulletin* 8.

———. 1938. Reports on the geology of Iberville and Ascension parishes. *Department of Conservation, Louisiana Geological Survey, Geological Bulletin* 13.

Saucier, R. T. 1963. Recent geomorphic history of the Pontchartrain Basin. *Louisiana State University Studies, Coastal Studies Series* 9.

———. 1968. A new chronology for braided stream surface formation in the lower Mississippi Valley. *Southeastern Geology* 9:65–76.

Sayles, E. B. 1937. Stone: Implements and bowls. In Excavations at Snaketown: Material culture, by H. S. Gladwin, E. W. Haury, E. B. Sayles, and N. Gladwin. *Medallion Papers* 25:101–20.

Schapiro, M. 1953. Style. In *Anthropology today,* edited by A. L. Kroeber. Chicago: University of Chicago Press. Pp. 287–312.

Schiffer, M. B. 1976. *Behavioral archeology.* New York: Academic Press.

Schindel, D. E. 1980. Microstratigraphic sampling and the limits of paleontologic resolution. *Paleobiology* 6:408–26.

Schliemann, H. 1880. *Ilios: The city and country of the Trojans: The results of researches and discoveries on the site of Troy and throughout the Troad in the years 1871–72–73–78–79.* London: Murray.

Schmidt, E. F. 1928. Time-relations of prehistoric pottery types in southern Arizona. *American Museum of Natural History, Anthropological Papers* 30(5): 247–302.

———. 1937. *Excavations at Tepe Hissar, Damghan.* Philadelphia: University of Pennsylvania Press.

Schuyler, R. L. 1971. The history of American archaeology: An examination of procedure. *American Antiquity* 36:383–409.

Scully, E. G. 1951. *Some central Mississippi Valley projectile point types.* Ann Arbor: University of Michigan, Museum of Anthropology.

Sears, W. H., and J. B. Griffin. 1950. Fiber-tempered pottery of the Southeast. In *Prehistoric pottery of the eastern United States,* edited by J. B. Griffin. Ann Arbor: University of Michigan, Museum of Anthropology.

Senter, D. 1937. Tree rings, valley floor deposits, and erosion in Chaco Canyon, New Mexico. *American Antiquity* 3:68–75.

Setzler, F. M. 1933a. Hopewell type pottery from Louisiana. *Washington Academy of Sciences, Journal* 23:149–53.

———. 1933b. Pottery of the Hopewell type from Louisiana. *United States National Museum, Proceedings* 82(22):1–21.

———. 1934. A phase of Hopewell mound builders in Louisiana. *Explorations and field-work of the Smithsonian Institution in 1933.* Washington, D.C.: Smithsonian Institution. Pp. 38–40.

———. 1935. Review of "Outline of Louisiana and Mississippi pottery horizons," by J. A. Ford. *American Antiquity* 1:74–76.

———. 1940. Archaeological perspectives in the northern Mississippi Valley. In Essays in historical anthropology of North America: Publications in honor of J. R. Swanton. *Smithsonian Miscellaneous Collections* 100:253–90.

———. 1943. Archaeological explorations in the United States, 1930–1942. *Acta Americana* 1:206–20.

Shetrone, H. C. 1927. Explorations of the Hopewell group of prehistoric earthworks. *Ohio Archaeological and Historical Publications* 35.

Simpson, G. G. 1944. *Tempo and mode in evolution.* New York: Columbia University Press.

Smith, A. B. 1994. *Systematics and the fossil record: Documenting evolutionary patterns.* Oxford: Blackwell.

Smith, C. S. 1950. The archaeology of coastal New York. *American Museum of Natural History, Anthropological Papers* 43(2).

Sober, E. 1980. Evolution, population thinking, and essentialism. *Philosophy of Science* 47:350–83.

———. 1984. *The nature of selection: Evolutionary theory in philosophical focus.* Cambridge, Mass.: MIT Press.

Solecki, R., and C. Wagley. 1963. William Duncan Strong, 1899–1962. *American Anthropologist* 65:1102–11.

Spaulding, A. C. 1948a. Committee on nomenclature. *Plains Archaeological Conference Newsletter* 1(3):37–41.

———. 1948b. Committee on nomenclature: Pottery (continued). *Plains Archaeological Conference Newsletter* 1(4):73–78.

———. 1949. Cultural and chronological classification in the Plains area. *Plains Archaeological Conference Newsletter* 2(2):3–5.

———. 1951. Recent advances in surveying techniques and their application to archaeology. In Essays on archaeological methods, edited by J. B. Griffin. *University of Michigan, Museum of Anthropology, Anthropological Papers* 8:2–16.

———. 1952. The origin of the Adena culture of the Ohio Valley. *Southwestern Journal of Anthropology* 8:260–68.

———. 1953a. Review of "Measurements of some prehistoric design developments in the southeastern states," by J. A. Ford. *American Anthropologist* 55:588–91.

———. 1953b. Statistical techniques for the discovery of artifact types. *American Antiquity* 18:305–13.

———. 1954a. Reply (to Ford). *American Anthropologist* 56:112–14.

———. 1954b. Reply to Ford. *American Antiquity* 19:391–93.

———. 1955. Prehistoric cultural development in the eastern United States. In *New interpretations of aboriginal American culture history,* edited by B. J. Meggers and C. Evans. Washington, D.C.: Anthropological Society of Washington. Pp. 12–27.

———. 1957. Review of "Method and theory in American archeology: An operational basis for cultural-historical integration," by P. Phillips and G. R. Willey, and "Method and theory in American archeology II: Historical-developmental interpretation," by G. R. Willey and P. Phillips. *American Antiquity* 23:85–87.

———. 1960. The dimensions of archaeology. In *Essays in the science of culture in honor of Leslie A. White,* edited by G. E. Dole and R. L. Carneiro. New York: Crowell. Pp. 437–56.

Spier, L. 1916. New data on the Trenton Argillite culture. *American Anthropologist* 18:181–89.

———. 1917. An outline for a chronology of Zuñi Ruins. *American Museum of Natural History, Anthropological Papers* 18(3):207–331.

———. 1918a. Notes on some Little Colorado ruins. *American Museum of Natural History, Anthropological Papers* 18(4):333–62.

———. 1918b. The Trenton Argillite Culture. *American Museum of Natural History, Anthropological Papers* 22(4):167–226.

————. 1919. Ruins in the White Mountains, Arizona. *American Museum of Natural History, Anthropological Papers* 18(5):363–88.

————. 1931. N. C. Nelson's stratigraphic technique in the reconstruction of prehistoric sequences in southwestern America. In *Methods in social science,* edited by S. A. Rice. Chicago: University of Chicago Press. Pp. 275–83.

Spinden, H. J. 1917. The origin and distribution of agriculture in America. *Proceedings of the 19th International Congress of Americanists.* Pp. 269–76.

————. 1927. The prosaic vs. the romantic school in anthropology. In *Culture: The diffusion controversy,* edited by E. Smith. New York: Norton. Pp. 47–98.

Steen, C. R. 1953. Review of "Archaeological survey in the lower Mississippi alluvial valley, 1940–1947," by P. Phillips, J. A. Ford, and J. B. Griffin. *American Journal of Archaeology* 57:55–57.

Steward, J. H. 1929. Diffusion and independent invention: A critique of logic. *American Anthropologist* 31:491–95.

————. 1941. Review of "Prehistoric culture units and their relationships in northern Arizona," by H. S. Colton. *American Antiquity* 6:366–67.

————. 1944. Re: archaeological tools and jobs. *American Antiquity* 10:99–100.

————. 1954. Types of types. *American Anthropologist* 56:54–57.

————. 1962. Alfred Louis Kroeber. *Biographical Memoirs* 36:192–253.

Steward, J. H., and F. M. Setzler. 1938. Function and configuration in archaeology. *American Antiquity* 4:4–10.

Stirling, M. W. 1932. The pre-historic southern Indians. In *Conference on Southern Pre-History.* National Research Council, Washington, D.C. Pp. 20–31.

Strong, W. D. 1925. The Uhle pottery collections from Ancon. *University of California, Publications in American Archaeology and Ethnology* 21(4):135–90.

————. 1935. An introduction to Nebraska archeology. *Smithsonian Miscellaneous Collections* 93(10).

————. 1936. Anthropological theory and archaeological fact. In *Essays in anthropology: Presented to A. L. Kroeber in celebration of his sixtieth birthday, June 11, 1936,* edited by R. H. Lowie. Berkeley: University of California Press. Pp. 359–68.

————. 1948. Cultural epochs and refuse stratigraphy in Peruvian archaeology. In A reappraisal of Peruvian archaeology, edited by W. C. Bennett. *Society for American Archaeology, Memoirs* 4. Pp. 93–102.

————. 1953. Historical approach in anthropology. In *Anthropology today,* edited by A. L. Kroeber. Chicago: University of Chicago Press. Pp. 386–97.

Strong, W. D., and J. M. Corbett. 1943. A ceramic sequence at Pachacamac. In Archaeological studies in Peru, 1941–1942, by W. D. Strong, G. R. Willey, and J. M. Corbett. *Columbia Studies in Archeology and Ethnology* 1.

Strong, W. D., and C. Evans, Jr. 1952. Cultural stratigraphy in the Virú Valley, northern Peru. *Columbia Studies in Archaeology and Ethnology* 4.

Suhm, D. A., and E. B. Jelks. 1962. Handbook of Texas archeology: Type descriptions. *Texas Archeological Society, Bulletin* 25.

Suhm, D. A., A. D. Krieger, and E. B. Jelks. 1954. An introductory handbook of Texas archeology. *Texas Archeological Society, Bulletin* 25.

Taylor, W. W. 1948. A study of archeology. *American Anthropological Association, Memoir* 69.

Teltser, P. A. 1995a. Editor. *Evolutionary archaeology: Methodological issues.* Tucson: University of Arizona Press.

———. 1995b. Culture history, evolutionary theory, and frequency seriation. In *Evolutionary archaeology: Methodological issues,* edited by P. A. Teltser. Tucson: University of Arizona Press. Pp. 51–68.

Thomas, C. 1884. Who were the mound builders? *The American Antiquarian* 6:90–99.

———. 1894. Report on the mound explorations of the Bureau of Ethnology. *Bureau of Ethnology, Annual Report* 12:3–742.

Thompson, R. H. Editor. 1958. Migrations in New World culture history. *University of Arizona, Social Science Bulletin* 27.

———. 1972. Interpretive trends and linear models in American archaeology. In *Contemporary archaeology,* edited by M. P. Leone. Carbondale: Southern Illinois University Press. Pp. 34–38.

Thomsen, C. J. 1836. *Ledetraad til Nordisk Oldkyndighed.* Copenhagen.

Tolstoy, P. 1958. Surface survey of the northern Valley of Mexico: The Classic and Post-Classic periods. *American Philosophical Society, Transactions,* 48 (pt. 5).

Toth, E. A. 1974. Archaeology and ceramics of the Marksville site. *University of Michigan, Museum of Anthropology, Anthropological Papers* 56.

Trigger, B. G. 1989. *A history of archaeological thought.* Cambridge: Cambridge University Press.

Tylor, E. B. 1871. *Primitive culture.* Murray, London.

Uhle, (F.) M. 1907. The Emeryville shellmound. *University of California, Publications in American Archaeology and Ethnology* 7:1–107.

———. 1913. Die Muschelhügel von Ancón, Peru. *Eighteenth International Congress of Americanists,* 22–45.

Vaillant, G. C. 1930. Excavations at Zacatenco. *American Museum of Natural History, Anthropological Papers* 32(1):1–198.

———. 1931. Excavations at Ticoman. *American Museum of Natural History, Anthropological Papers* 32(2):199–432.

———. 1935. Early cultures of the Valley of Mexico: Results of the stratigraphical project of the American Museum of Natural History in the Valley of Mexico, 1928–1933. *American Museum of Natural History, Anthropological Papers* 35(3):281–328.

Vescelius, G. S. 1957. Mound 2 at Marksville. *American Antiquity* 22:416–20.

Walker, H. J., and M. E. Richardson. 1994. Fred Bowerman Kniffen, 1900–1993. *Association of American Geographers, Annals* 84:732–43.

Walker, W. M. 1932. A reconnaissance of northern Louisiana mounds. *Explorations and field-work of the Smithsonian Institution in 1931.* Washington, D.C.: Smithsonian Institution. Pp. 169–74.

———. 1934. A variety of Caddo pottery from Louisiana. *Washington Academy of Sciences, Journal* 24:99–104.

———. 1936. The Troyville mounds, Catahoula Parish, La. *Bureau of American Ethnology, Bulletin* 113.

Wallis, W. D. 1925. Diffusion as a criterion of age. *American Anthropologist* 27:91–99.

———. 1945. Inference of relative age of culture traits from magnitude of distribution. *Southwestern Journal of Anthropology* 1:142–59.

Webb, C. H. 1944. Stone vessels from a northeast Louisiana site. *American Antiquity* 9:386–94.

———. 1948. Evidence of pre-pottery cultures in Louisiana. *American Antiquity* 13:227–32.

———. 1959. The Belcher Mound: A stratified Caddoan site in Caddo Parish, Louisiana. *Society for American Archaeology, Memoirs* 16.

———. 1968a. The extent and content of Poverty Point culture. *American Antiquity* 33:297–321.

———. 1968b. James A. Ford, 1911–1968. *Texas Archeological Society, Bulletin* 38:135–46.

———. 1977. The Poverty Point culture. *Geosciences and Man* 17.

Webb, W. S., and D. L. DeJarnette. 1942. An archaeological survey of Pickwick Basin in the adjacent portions of the states of Alabama, Mississippi, and Tennessee. *Bureau of American Ethnology, Bulletin* 129.

Webb, W. S., and C. E Snow. 1945. The Adena people. *University of Kentucky, Reports in Archaeology and Anthropology* 6.

Wedel, W. R. 1938. Hopewellian remains near Kansas City, Missouri. *U.S. National Museum, Proceedings* 86:99–106.

Weiant, C. W. 1943. An introduction to the ceramics of Tres Zapotes, Veracruz, Mexico. *Bureau of American Ethnology, Bulletin* 139.

Wheat, J. B., J. C. Gifford, and W. W. Wasley. 1958. Ceramic variety, type cluster, and ceramic system in southwestern pottery analysis. *American Antiquity* 24:34–47.

Wheeler, R. E. M. 1954. *Archaeology from the Earth.* Oxford: Clarendon Press.

White, L. 1943. Energy and the evolution of culture. *American Anthropologist* 45:335–56.

———. 1945. History, evolutionism, and functionalism. *Southwestern Journal of Anthropology* 1:221–48.

———. 1948. Man's control over civilization: An anthropocentric illusion. *Scientific Monthly* 66:235–47.

———. 1949. *The science of culture: A study of man and civilization.* New York: Farrar, Straus and Giroux.

———. 1959a. The concept of evolution in anthropology. In *Evolution and anthropology: A centennial appraisal,* edited by B. J. Meggers. Washington, D.C.: The Anthropological Society of Washington. Pp. 106–24.

———. 1959b. *The evolution of culture.* New York: McGraw-Hill.

Whittaker, F. 1993. Lowland adaptation during the Late Archaic in the central Mississippi River valley. Paper presented at the 58th Annual Meeting of the Society for American Archaeology, St. Louis.

Willey, G. R. 1937. Notes on central Georgia dendrochronology. *University of Arizona, Tree Ring Bulletin* 4(2).

———. 1938. Time studies: Pottery and trees in Georgia. *Society for Georgia Archaeology, Proceedings* 1:15–22.

———. 1939. Ceramic stratigraphy in a Georgia village site. *American Antiquity* 5:140–47.

———. 1945. Horizon styles and pottery traditions in Peruvian archaeology. *American Antiquity* 10:49–56.

———. 1949a. Excavations in southeast Florida. *Yale University Publications in Anthropology* 42.

———. 1949b. Archeology of the Florida Gulf Coast. *Smithsonian Miscellaneous Collections* 113.

———. 1953a. A pattern of diffusion-acculturation. *Southwestern Journal of Anthropology* 9:369–84.

———. 1953b. Prehistoric settlement patterns in the Virú Valley, Peru. *Bureau of American Ethnology, Bulletin* 155.

———. 1957. Review of "Poverty Point: A Late Archaic site in Louisiana," by J. A. Ford and C. H. Webb. *American Antiquity* 23:198–99.

———. 1966. *An introduction to American archaeology* (vol. 1), *North and Middle America.* New York: Prentice-Hall.

———. 1968. One hundred years of American archaeology. In *One hundred years of anthropology,* edited by J. O. Brew. Cambridge, Mass.: Harvard University Press. Pp. 26–53.

———. 1969. James Alfred Ford, 1911–1968. *American Antiquity* 34:62–71.

———. 1971. *An introduction to American archaeology* (vol. 2), *South America.* New York: Prentice-Hall.

———. 1988. *Portraits in American archaeology: Remembrances of some distinguished Americanists.* Albuquerque: University of New Mexico Press.

———. 1996. Philip Phillips: 1900–1994. *American Antiquity* 61:39–43.

Willey, G. R., and P. Phillips. 1944. Negative-painted pottery from Crystal River, Florida. *American Antiquity* 10:173–85.

———. 1955. Method and theory in American archaeology, II: Historical-developmental interpretation. *American Anthropologist* 57:723–819.

———. 1958. *Method and theory in American archaeology.* Chicago: University of Chicago Press.

Willey, G. R., and J. A. Sabloff. 1974. *A history of American archaeology.* San Francisco: Freeman.

———. 1993. *A history of American archaeology* (3d ed.). New York: Freeman.

Willey, G. R., and R. B. Woodbury. 1942. A chronological outline for the northwest Florida coast. *American Antiquity* 7:232–54.

Williams, S. 1957. The Island 35 mastodon. *American Antiquity* 22:359–72.

———. 1960. A brief history of the Southeastern Archaeological Conference. *Southeastern Archaeological Conference, Newsletter* 7(1):2–4.

Wilson, T. 1899. Arrowheads, spearheads, and knives of prehistoric times. *U.S. National Museum, Annual Report* (1897), pt. 1. Pp. 811–988.

Wissler, C. 1916a. The application of statistical methods to the data on the Trenton Argillite culture. *American Anthropologist* 18:190–97.

———. 1916b. Correlations between archeological and culture areas in the American continents. In *Holmes anniversary volume: Anthropological essays.* Pp. 481–90.

———. 1917a. *The American Indian.* New York: McMurtrie.

———. 1917b. The new archaeology. *American Museum Journal* 17:100–101.

Woodbury, R. B. 1973. *Alfred V. Kidder.* New York: Columbia University Press.

———. 1993. *60 years of southwestern archaeology: A history of the Pecos Conference.* Albuquerque: University of New Mexico Press.

Woodbury, R. B., and A. S. Trik. 1953. *The ruins of Zaculeu, Guatemala.* New York: United Fruit Company.

Worsaae, J. J. A. 1849. *The primeval antiquities of Denmark.* London: Parker.

Index

Addis Plain, 250
Adena, 144, 145, 262, 265, 295, 314, 315
Agriculture, 144, 267, 311, 312. *See also* Horticulture; Maize agriculture
Albany Landing site (Louisiana), 258
Albrecht, Andrew C., 129
Alexander complex, 268
Alto focus, 230, 231
American Anthropological Association, 53, 148
American Anthropologist, 140, 316
American Antiquity, 122, 137, 162, 268, 299
American Formative, 276, 280, 281, 283, 293, 299, 301, 301, 302, 303, 304, 305, 308, 309, 311, 312, 313, 314, 324, 329, 331, 333
American Indian Exposition, 61
American Museum of Natural History, 8, 10, 157, 161, 233, 254, 273, 296, 301, 308, 309
Americanist archaeology, xv, xvi, xvii, 1, 2, 6, 11, 16, 17, 19, 24, 30, 38, 83, 96, 124, 159, 177, 184, 211, 231, 257, 276, 317, 318, 334
Amsden, Charles A., 111
Analogous similarity, 24, 25, 26, 27, 180, 225, 282, 294, 295
Analytical-formula system, 85, 86, 106
Ancestral-descendant relationships, 30, 34, 35, 188, 225, 228, 274
Ancón cemetery (Peru), 155, 166
Andes, 159
Anna site (Mississippi), 244
Anthropological Society of Washington, 53, 304

Archaeological Survey in the Lower Mississippi Alluvial Valley, 1940–1947, 184, 200, 204
Archaic period, 255, 262, 267, 268
Arkansas Post, 276. *See also* Osotouy settlement
Arkansas River, 49, 276
Ascher, Robert, 287, 288, 289, 322
Asian immigrants, 264
Atchafalaya River, 42
Avoyelles Parish (Louisiana), 128, 132, 204
Ayangue incised, 307
Ayangue tradition, 307

Bastian, Adolf, 324
Battleship-shaped curves, 198, 228, 233, 318
Bayou Bartholomew, 42
Bayou Cutler complex, 99, 100, 104, 105. *See also* Bayou Cutler period
Bayou Cutler period, 102, 106
Bayou Cutler pottery, 106
Bayou Cutler–Marksville period, 102, 105, 106
Bayou Goula site (Louisiana), 134, 146
Bayou Maçon, 42
Bayou Petre complex, 99, 100
Baytown period, 142, 144, 145, 199, 202, 244, 245, 248, 250, 251, 253, 278
Baytown Plain, 248, 249, 250, 251, 276
Baytown pottery, 203
Benedict, Ruth, 151
Bennett, John W., 21
Bennett, Wendel C., 157; Virú Valley Project 159, 160, 161

Tchefuncte period, 105, 134, 135, 138, 140, 146, 147, 164, 173, 205, 207, 210, 260, 268, 307
Tchefuncte Plain, 250
Tchefuncte site (Louisiana), 134, 258
Tchefuncte sites, 164
Tchefuncte Stamped, 245, 248, 280
Tchefuncte-Tchula cultural stage, 268
Tchefuncte-Tchula pottery, 262
Tchula period, 245, 247, 251, 269
Tehuacán Valley, 301, 305
Temper, 170, 191; clay, 188, 245, 255; fiber, 255, 305, 306, 307, 315; sand, 203; shell, 144, 188, 203, 245
Tempo, 92, 106, 226, 269, 330
Tennessee River, 265, 268
Tennessee Valley Authority, 110, 114, 127, 187, 258
Tensas River, 42
Texas Technological College, 96
Thomas, Cyrus, 40, 41, 42, 276
Tick Island, 306
Time: and cultural change, xv; importance of measurement, 25, 78; study of, 19; problems with units of measurement, 22, 27; views of, 4, 5
Time averaging, 177
Time lag, 225
Tolstoy, Paul, 310
Tonti, Henri de, 276
Tozzer, Alfred M., 187
Trade, 88, 91, 94
Traits, 100
Tres Zapotes site (Mexico), 301
Troyville period, 105, 134, 135, 142, 204, 205, 207, 208, 210, 255, 265, 314, 327, 328
Troyville Plain, 209, 250, 250
Troyville site (Louisiana), 42, 135, 147, 204, 205
Tunica complex, 69, 94
Tunica Indians, 46, 50, 65, 77, 87
Tunica pottery, 50, 105
Tunica sites, 49
Tylor, Edward B., 13, 26
Type-variety system, 80, 85, 318
Types, 29, 30, 32, 36, 37, 47, 81, 85, 87, 91, 101, 140, 178, 188, 193, 197, 218, 231, 234, 238, 241, 242, 243, 285, 288, 318,

328; as anthropological constructs, 191; as archaeological constructs, 188, 189, 190, 191; as cultural norms, 171, 216, 217, 230, 231, 234, 238; definition and description of, 121, 123, 131; historical, 173, 176, 194; transitional, 237, 290. *See also* Pottery types
Typological connection, 76
Typological creep, 131, 193, 225, 241, 285, 290
Typological thinking, 70, 169, 200
Typology, 8, 17–19, 23, 33, 38, 249, 285

Uhle, F. Max, 12, 97, 153, 154, 155, 179, 320. *See also* Ancón cemetery
U.S. National Museum. *See* Smithsonian Institution
U.S. State Department, 157
Units, 30, 145, 234, 328. *See also* Empirical units; Ideational units
Universidad de los Andes, 310
Universidad del Atlantico, 283
Universidad del Centro del Peru, 310
Universidad Veracruzana, 301
University of Arkansas Museum, 182
University of Arizona, 107, 113
University of California, Berkeley, 96, 97, 129, 150, 153, 179, 296
University of California Publications in American Archaeology and Ethnology, 97
University of Chicago, 110, 128, 261
University of Illinois, 115
University of Kentucky, 114
University of Michigan, xvi, xvii, 26, 96, 107, 110, 118, 119, 128, 150, 183, 236, 261, 334
University of Mississippi, 244
University of Nebraska, 128
University of New Mexico, 107, 129
University of Utah, 128, 129
University of Vienna, 129

Vaillant, George C., 74, 157, 162, 320
Valdivia phase, 297, 299, 304, 306, 310, 316, 324
Vermillion Parish (Louisiana), 134
Viejón site (Mexico), 301
Viking Fund, 236